Naval Blockades and Seapower

D0143949

This new collection of up-to-date essays by well-known scholars covers the most significant naval blockades of the nineteenth and twentieth centuries, including Napoleon's Continental Blockade of England, and the American Civil War, as well as blockades in more recent conflicts such as World War II, the Korean War, the Cuban Missile Crisis, the Persian Gulf interdiction program, and the Chinese "missile" blockade of Taiwan in 1996.

Each chapter addresses the causes of the blockade in question, its long- and short-term repercussions, and the course of the blockade itself, and takes advantage of new research and methodologies to provide the most complete information to both the specialist and non-specialist reader. This volume presents fresh insights into issues such as what a naval blockade is, why countries might choose them, which navies can and cannot make use of them, what responses lead to satisfactory or unsatisfactory conclusions, and how far-reaching their consequences tend to be.

This book will be of great interest to all students and scholars of strategic studies, military history, and maritime studies.

Contributors: Ken-ichi Arakawa, Jeffrey G. Barlow, Roger W. Barnett, Wade G. Dudley, Bruce A. Elleman, James Goldrick, Paul G. Halpern, John B. Hattendorf, Mark L. Hayes, Wolff Heintschel von Heinegg, Charles W. Koburger Jr., Andrew D. Lambert, Silvia Marzagalli, Richard A. Mobley, Malcolm Muir Jr., S.C.M. Paine, Chris Rahman, David M. Stevens, David G. Surdam, Geoffrey Till, Spencer C. Tucker.

Bruce A. Elleman is an Associate Professor in the Maritime History Department at the US Naval War College, and most recently is author of *Modern Chinese Warfare, 1795–1989* (Routledge, 2001) and co-editor with Christopher Bell of *Naval Mutinies of the Twentieth Century: An International Perspective* (Frank Cass, 2003).

S.C.M. Paine is an Associate Professor in the Strategy & Policy Department at the U.S. Naval War College and author of *Imperial Rivals: China, Russia and Their Disputed Frontiers* (M.E. Sharpe, 1996) and *The Sino-Japanese War of 1894–1895: Perceptions, Power and Primacy* (CUP, 2003).

CASS SERIES: NAVAL POLICY AND HISTORY
Series Editor: Geoffrey Till
ISSN 1366–9478

This series consists primarily of original manuscripts by research scholars in the general area of naval policy and history, without national or chronological limitations. It will from time to time also include collections of important articles as well as reprints of classic works.

Naval Blockades and Seapower

Strategies and Counter-Strategies, 1805–2005

Edited by Bruce A. Elleman and S.C.M. Paine

LONDON AND NEW YORK

First published 2006
by Routledge
2 Park Square, Milton Park, Abingdon, Oxon, OX14 4RN

Simultaneously published in the USA and Canada
by Routledge
270 Madison Ave, New York, NY10016

Routledge is an imprint of the Taylor & Francis Group

Transferred to Digital Printing 2007

© 2006 Bruce A. Elleman and S.C.M. Paine

Typeset in Times by
Taylor & Francis Books

All rights reserved. No part of this book may be reprinted or
reproduced or utilized in any form or by any electronic,
mechanical, or other means, now known or hereafter
invented, including photocopying and recording, or in any
information storage or retrieval system, without permission in
writing from the publishers.

British Library Cataloguing in Publication Data
A catalogue record for this book is available from the British Library

Library of Congress Cataloging-in-Publication Data
A catalog record for this book has been requested

ISBN10: 0-415-35466-8 (hbk)
ISBN10: 0-415-43871-3 (pbk)

ISBN13: 978-0-415-35466-0 (hbk)
ISBN13: 978-0-415-43871-1 (pbk)

Printed and bound by CPI Antony Rowe, Eastbourne

Taylor & Francis Group is the Academic Division of T&F Informa plc.

To George W. Baer, for his dedication to the Naval War College's use of maritime history to teach officers and the general public about the U.S. Navy's role in national and international affairs.

Contents

Illustrations

Contributors

Ken-ichi Arakawa is an Associate Professor in the School of Defense Science at the National Defense Academy in Yokosuka, Japan. In 2003, he retired at the rank of colonel from the Japanese Ground Self Defense Force (JGSDF) and is currently a PhD candidate in economics at Hitotsubashi University. His many articles include 'The Maritime Transport War: Emphasizing a strategy to interrupt the enemy sea lines of communication (SLOCs)', *NIDS Security Reports*, no. 3 (March 2002).

Jeffrey G. Barlow is a professional historian with the Naval Historical Center's Contemporary History Branch and author of *Revolt of the Admirals: The Fight for Naval Aviation, 1945–1950* (Washington, D.C.: Naval Historical Center, 1994). Awarded the 1995 John Lyman Prize for U.S. naval history, this book was republished by Brassey's in 1998. He recently completed the manuscript for the first of a multi-volume history of the U.S. Navy and National Security Affairs during the Cold War.

Roger W. Barnett, USN (ret.), has been Professor Emeritus, U.S. Naval War College, since 2001. He completed an MA and PhD in International Relations at the University of Southern California. He is the author, with Colin Gray, of *Seapower and Strategy* (Naval Institute Press, 1989), and of 'Information Operations, Deterrence, and the Use of Force', *Naval War College Review* (1998), 'What Deters? Strength, Not Weakness', *Naval War College Review* (2001), 'Naval Power for a New American Century', *Naval War College Review* (2002), and *Asymmetrical Warfare* (Brassey's, 2002).

Wade G. Dudley is an Assistant Professor at East Carolina University in Greenville, NC, and author of the 2002 John Lyman Prize-winning *Splintering the Wooden Wall: The British Blockade of the United States, 1812–1815* (Naval Institute Press, 2002), and *Drake: For God, Queen, and Plunder* (Brassey's, 2003). In addition to numerous fictional naval stories published by Greenhill Books, he is completing a monograph on historical methodology.

Bruce A. Elleman is an Associate Professor in the Maritime History Department at the Center for Naval Warfare Studies of the U.S. Naval War College, and most recently author of *Modern Chinese Warfare, 1795–1989* (Routledge, 2001), *Wilson and China: A Revised History of the Shandong Question* (M.E. Sharpe, 2002), and co-editor with Chris Bell of *Naval Mutinies of the Twentieth Century: An International Perspective* (Frank Cass, 2003).

James Goldrick is a Commodore in the Royal Australian Navy, and currently Commandant of the Australian Defence Force Academy. He commanded the Australian task group deployed to the Persian Gulf and also served as Commander of the multinational Maritime Interception Force enforcing UN sanctions on Iraq from February until June 2002. In addition to his BA from the University of New South Wales, he holds an MLitt degree from the University of New England, Armidale. His numerous published works include *The King's Ships Were at Sea: The War in the North Sea August 1914–February 1915, With the Battle Cruisers* (edited), and most recently 'The Role of the Royal Australian Navy in the Persian Gulf', *Journal of the Royal United Services Institute of Australia* (2002).

Paul G. Halpern has recently retired as Professor of History at Florida State University and is the author of numerous books, including *A Naval History of World War I* (Naval Institute Press, 1994), *Anton Haus: Österreich-Ungarns Grossadmiral* (Verlag Styria, 1998), and *The Battle of the Otranto Straits: Controlling the Gateway to the Adriatic in World War I* (Indiana University Press, 2004). He has edited four volumes for the Navy Records Society and is currently working on a study of the Mediterranean naval situation in the inter-war period.

John B. Hattendorf is Ernest J. King Professor of Maritime History and Chairman of the Maritime History Department in the Center for Naval Warfare Studies at the U.S. Naval War College. He is the author, co-author, editor, or co-editor of more than thirty volumes on maritime history and has been awarded an honorary doctorate and the National Maritime Museum's Caird Medal. Among his most recent works are *Naval History and Maritime Strategy: Collected Essays* (Krieger Publishing, 2000), and Naval *Strategy and Policy in the Mediterranean: Past, Present, and Future* (Frank Cass, 2000). He is currently editor-in-chief of the *Oxford Encyclopedia of Maritime History*.

Mark L. Hayes is a professional historian in the Early History Branch of the Naval Historical Center, Washington, D.C, and co-author of *The Spanish–American War: Historical Overview and Select Bibliography* (Naval Historical Center, 1998).

Wolff Heintschel von Heinegg is Professor of Public International Law and Dean of the Faculty of Law, Europa-Universität, Frankfurt (Oder), academic and comparative examination of eighteen selected case studies from maritime history used to illuminate a range of concepts and uses of naval blockade, an important type of naval operation rarely analysed but recently used by a number of countries and navies around the world.

This volume's contributors and editors have jointly worked to deepen and widen modern understanding of naval blockades. Their work provides the basis for the conclusions that Elleman and Paine have reached, which significantly expand the theoretical understanding that Sir Julian Corbett expressed nearly a century ago. They provide here a basis for a more thorough understanding of the uses and limitations of naval blockade in the context of new maritime technologies and within a wider range of modern national policy goals. Above all, this collection provides a sound basis for comparative analysis of varying historical experiences that can stimulate new and original thinking about a basic type of naval operation that is often overlooked.

John B. Hattendorf,
Ernest J. King Professor of Maritime History, and
Chairman, Maritime History Department, U.S. Naval War College*

Acknowledgements

We, the editors, would like to thank our contributors and the many others who shared their insights and expertise. At the Naval War College we benefited from the support of John Hattendorf, Kenneth Watman, Tom Nichols, John Maurer, Peter Dombrowski, Captain Gary Belcher, Commander Ron Oard, and Colonel Kathy Winters. We owe a considerable debt to Alice Juda, Wayne Rowe, and Bob Schnare for library assistance. For graphics, we would like to thank Gigi Davis, Art Lamoureux, and Jason Peters. Special thanks to Captain Steve Kenny, RN, for his advice and criticism from beginning to end. At Routledge, we are grateful to Andrew Humphrys, Marjorie François and Lucie Ewin. We are especially indebted to Andrew Marshall of the Office of Net Assessment for his ongoing support for this project.

On behalf of our contributors, we would like to thank Captain Norman Banks, Rear Admiral Mark Bonser, Captain Roger Boyce, Pelham Boyer, Louis Cain, Commodore Nigel Coates, Patricia Cormier, Graham A. Cosmas, Commodore Allan du Toit, Joseph Ferrie, Robert Fogel, David Galenson, Captain Ray Griggs, D. Gale Johnson, Commodore Peter Jones, Colonel Jeff Jore, Rear Admiral (ret.) Koichiro Kageyama, Nicholas Lambert, Dennis Mandsager, Captain Stephen McDowell, Commander Mark McIntosh, Ann Marsh, Captain Richard Menhinick, Simon Rofe, Mark Thornton, and Stuart Woolf.

For library and archival assistance, we would like to thank Laura M. Calkins, Assistant Archivist, Vietnam Archive, Texas Tech University, Christopher Dawkins of the American Defence Force Association library, Captain Chris Page, Kate Tilney, and Stephen Prince at the Naval Historical Branch Library, Glenn Helm at the Navy Department Library of the Naval Historical Center, and present and former members of the staff of the Naval Historical Center's Operational Archives, particularly Mike Walker and Kenneth Johnson. Thanks to the Navy Records Society for permission to reproduce the maps in Chapter 5.

PART I

Blockades and Seapower

1 Introduction

*Bruce A. Elleman and S.C.M. Paine**

Naval blockades have historically been associated with the "starvation blockade" of World War I, and more recently with the danger surrounding the Cuban Missile Crisis of October 1962. Contrary to these highly publicized blockades, many naval blockades have been conducted with little fanfare, and relatively little public awareness. This does not mean that they have been ineffective, however, and as a military tactic naval blockades have time after time shown themselves to be one of the most efficient ways to exert pressure on an opponent. While some blockades have been studied by scholars capable of placing these events in their social, political, and naval context, these authors have been the exception, not the rule. For this reason, this book hopes to fill a major gap in the academic literature.

This volume will focus on how and why naval blockades are adopted and conducted in both non-war and war-time conflicts. When re-examining some of the nineteenth and twentieth centuries' most important naval blockades, several factors become immediately apparent. First, while naval blockades have most frequently been conducted by sea powers against land powers – the most well-known examples of this, of course, were the British attempts to blockade Germany in World Wars I and II – there are times when a continental country tries to cut an island nation off from international trade, as Napoleon tried to do with Britain's trade with the rest of Europe from 1803 to 1815, or China tried to do with Taiwan in 1996.

Second, blockades can be very time-consuming affairs, especially if the country being blockaded – and this applies in particular to land powers – can turn away from its sea lines of communications (SLOCs) and instead open new land lines of communications (LOCs) to help fill the gap. As shown positively by the Crimean War and negatively by the Nationalist blockade of China during the 1950s, speed is essential, and the longer a land power has to create new communication and trade routes the less effective the blockade will be.

Third, the role of technology in naval blockades has been especially crucial, from the transition from wood to copper-hulled ships in the early nineteenth century, from coal to oil combustion in the early twentieth century, and then with the inclusion of air power and submarines to assist surface ships to keep the blockade tight; perhaps in no other sphere of military activity have changes in technology had such an immediate and obvious impact on naval tactics. Although almost all of the chapters in this volume prove this point in one way or another, good examples include the more dependable coal supplies of the U.S. Navy during the Spanish–American War, just as the modern and hi-tech ships of the 1990s gave the coalition in Iraq the leverage it needed to halt oil smuggling.

Another important factor is the relationship between International Law and blockade. As Wolff H. von Heinegg shows, confusion about the legal meaning of blockade is the norm, not the exception, when evaluating naval blockades. Because of the intricate international rules governing blockades, countries that adopt this tactic have often been hesitant to identify it as such. By never officially declaring war they can avoid many restrictions. Calling the conflict a "civil war," rather than an international conflict, allows them to ignore one group of laws, while calling blockades a "quarantine," "embargo," or "sanctions" can also affect how international law regards it.

While legal definitions of naval blockades attempt to be precise, the range of activities that have historically fit under this rubric are vast indeed. The eighteen case studies in this book reflect this wide range of activities, as well as the extraordinary diversity of experience navies have encountered while attempting to carry them out. If there is a deliberate bias in this book, it is towards naval blockades that have had major repercussions in a particular war or international conflict. The authors have focused on these cases because they provide more applicable lessons about when, how, and in what manner naval blockades have most effectively been utilized in past, and so perhaps may also be useful in future conflicts.

There is a popular image of the naval blockade as a line of ships standing off an enemy's coastline with blockade runners attempting to break their way through the wall. While sometimes true, the chapters in this volume demonstrate that naval blockades frequently take other forms. They are not always directed against a specific port or stretch of coastline, nor do they have to take place at sea at all, so long as their goal of disrupting naval trade is achieved.

In chronological order, we begin our study with one of the most famous cases of a non-naval blockade: Napoleon's "continental" blockade against Great Britain. Beginning in 1806, immediately after France's 1805 naval defeat at Trafalgar that had ceded control of the seas to England, and evolving until Napoleon's final fall in 1815, the continental blockade attempted to halt all British exports to the continent. As Silvia Marzagalli shows, however, Napoleon's blockade was undermined by greedy customs agents, desperate smugglers, and merchants who were not only willing, but eager, to purchase British goods.

Next, we turn to an example of naval blockade in the age of sail, the British blockade of American shores in the War of 1812. In his chapter,

Wade Dudley challenges the prevailing scholarly opinion that this blockade was highly effective, and instead discusses how the United States exited the war with a larger merchant marine and greater exports than before the conflict began. In particular, inadequate British interdiction gave the U.S. government the time it needed to build and outfit many new vessels. After the war, these technologically superior ships-of-the-line became the core for a new and highly modern United States Navy.

Similar to the War of 1812, the blockade during the Crimean War was a naval affair, but this time conducted in two widely distant theaters: the Baltic and the Black seas. However, as Andrew D. Lambert shows us, it remained a comparatively short war and the blockading parties had the relatively limited objectives of degrading Russia's military capabilities, weakening the state's resources, and pushing the Russian Tsar to accept peace negotiations. For the first time, steam power gave British and French warships the necessary mobility and speed to be able to enforce a tight blockade, while more powerful armaments allowed a naval fleet to attack and destroy fortified harbors. Finally, a new set of international laws, codified in the 1856 Declaration of Paris, would help regulate naval blockades during limited wars for the next 60 years.

Only a few years after the short and limited Crimean War, the much longer American Civil War revealed other uses for naval blockades. David G. Surdam shows how the Union blockade of the South reduced cotton exports, undermined the Confederacy's buying power, and inhibited the ability of the southern states to import necessary military goods, such as British iron for building railways and – most importantly – warships. Since the Civil War was not a limited war, and the goal was never to achieve a negotiated peace but total victory, the Union blockade's attrition-style methods presaged in many ways the blockades of the two World Wars.

During the late nineteenth century, Japan and China modernized their respective militaries and acquired state-of-the-art naval equipment. But Japan also Westernized its domestic political, legal, economic, and educational institutions, overturning the traditional social order, whereas China did not. S.C.M. Paine shows how these reforms bore fruit in the Sino–Japanese War of 1894–95, when Japan overturned the traditional balance of power in the Far East to supplant China as the regional hegemon. A tight naval blockade and a highly successful land campaign captured the Beiyang Fleet at anchor in Weihaiwei harbor, thus making the new maritime balance of power permanent.

In the Spanish–American War three years later, it was the American naval and land forces that surrounded, smoked out, and eventually defeated Admiral Cervera's Spanish Fleet off Santiago de Cuba. As described by Mark L. Hayes, this was really a battle of logistics, since the fleet with the most dependable energy supplies and the higher grade coal could dominate the seas. The U.S. Navy's close blockade of Cuba proved conclusively the all-important role of logistics in a new era of technological warfare.

A protracted blockade was the UN-mandated sanctions against Iraq from 1990 to 2003. As James Goldrick explains, while this effort may have been one of the longest blockades in history, it was also one of the most successful, as shown by the rapid victory obtained by coalition forces in 2003 against an Iraqi conventional military force gradually degraded by years of blockade. Smuggling oil and bringing in weapons could really only be achieved by sea, so the Iraqi government proved unable to make up for the losses due to the blockade. While it took an enormous amount of time and effort, this case shows that a selective blockade conducted by a cooperative and determined coalition can be highly effective.

While the UN-led actions in the Persian Gulf were still being carried out, the world witnessed a new kind of blockade: a so-called "missile blockade." Chris Rahman discusses this new type of blockade in his chapter on China's two missile "tests" near Taiwan in 1995 and 1996. While this missile blockade did not succeed, in large measure because of the U.S. decision to intervene with two aircraft carrier battle groups, it did create economic panic in Taiwan and put the government there under political duress. Should China decide to use this tactic again, Taiwan is arguably more vulnerable today than it was before, in particular because its economic exposure to the Chinese market is larger and its strategic oil reserves are smaller.

Our final case study focuses on Australia's recent attempt to impose a naval barrier, or "reverse blockade," aimed at keeping unauthorized immigrants away from its shores. David M. Stevens investigates the Australian government's efforts beginning in August 2001 to prevent SIEVs (suspected illegal entry vessels) and SUNCs (suspected unauthorized non-citizens) from entering Australian waters. Just as the Chinese "missile blockade" may reveal how military blockades could be enacted in the future, the Australian case shows how countries have reacted to the very real threat of being overwhelmed by an ever-increasing wave of illegal immigrants. Navies of the future must face many missions outside traditional warfighting, and be equally well trained to deal with tasks across the spectrum of maritime operations.

We round out this collection of case studies with a discussion of the importance of technology to naval blockades. As Roger W. Barnett discusses, a post-9/11 world (referring to the terrorist attacks on New York's World Trade Center and Washington D.C.'s Pentagon on 11 September 2001) that includes "Weapons of Mass Destruction" (WMD) may change forever how naval blockades are conducted, in particular by putting a new and much-needed focus on ports of embarkation rather than simply on ports of debarkation. The creation of the Container Security Initiative (CSI) in 2002 and the Proliferation Security Initiative (PSI) in 2003, for example, will allow many cargoes heading for the U.S. to be prescreened before they are loaded on board a container ship. Rapid changes in ship propulsion, reconnaissance and surveillance, weapons, and inspection and detection equipment will impact upon how well the components of WMD can be kept from potential perpetrators and how well the actual WMD can be detected, isolated, and detained. Since the effects of WMD are so cataclysmic, the success of these efforts must be 100 percent.

This volume concludes with an analysis of naval blockades during the past two centuries that discusses the time, space, and force factors that have had most impact upon blockades in the past, and which will most likely continue to have an impact in the future. In opposition to simple bean-counting, with clerks calculating how many imports were denied their opponent, naval blockades can also be viewed in terms of what they prevent from happening. In this regard, evaluating the success or failure of a naval blockade in wartime requires looking at what happened as well as at what *did not happen* as a result of the naval interceptions; the inability of the Confederacy to build a strong naval force to oppose the Union navy, or Saddam's apparent failure to acquire the parts he needed to build WMDs, are just two good examples of blockades as a deterrent.

A successful naval blockade, therefore, could perhaps be defined as a naval operation that uses the minimum of friendly resources to halt or slow either the use or the development of an enemy asset within prescribed temporal and geographic limits. Devoting too many resources to the task may create a tight blockade, but at the cost of sacrificing other equally valuable objectives in another part of the theater. Meanwhile, a naval blockade that may on the surface appear porous could, in fact, be highly effective if it eliminates those items – perhaps as few as a single item – that would otherwise give the enemy a capability it did not formerly possess.

The naval blockade will continue to be a potentially highly successful means of achieving both strategic and operational objectives. Modern navies must therefore be configured and trained to conduct even more focused and specialized interdiction activities. They also must provide policymakers with the tools they need to put sufficient pressure on an enemy to obtain negotiated resolutions short of all-out unlimited war. As far as Western democratic states are concerned, naval blockades may prove to be one of the most valuable tools to motivate rogue states. As recently as 15 October 2004, the official North Korean radio service virulently denounced planned U.S.–Japanese exercises to test the Proliferation Security Initiative as an "international blockade" intended to "militarily oppress, blockade, and crush our Republic."[1]

2 Naval Blockade and International Law

Wolff Heintschel von Heinegg

According to a widely accepted definition, a blockade is "a belligerent operation to prevent vessels and/or aircraft of all nations, enemy as well as neutral, from entering or exiting specified ports, airfields, or coastal areas belonging to, occupied by, or under the control of an enemy nation."[1] The purpose of establishing a blockade is "to deny the enemy the use of enemy and neutral vessels or aircraft to transport personnel and goods to or from enemy territory."[2] If solely aimed against the enemy's economy, the legality of a blockade has to be judged in the light of the law of economic warfare and of neutrality.

However, in contrast to the practice of the nineteenth century and of the two World Wars, in modern state practice such economic blockades have been the exception. Today the establishment of a blockade is very often an integral part of a military operation that is not directed against the enemy's economy but against its armed forces. For example, a blockade may be declared and enforced in preparation for a landing operation. It may also help in surrounding enemy armed forces or in cutting off their lines of supply.

But even if an economic blockade in the strict sense were established, there would always be a strategic element: cutting off the enemy's trade links and weakening its economy will also weaken its military power of resistance.[3] No matter which purpose is pursued by the establishment of a blockade, it always involves the use of military force directed against the enemy's coastline or ports. Accordingly, a blockade is a method of naval warfare to which the general principles and rules of the law of naval warfare – the maritime *jus in bello* – also apply.[4]

While naval blockades still have to be distinguished from other, although related, concepts (e.g., operations designed to interdict contraband, unilateral embargoes, defensive measure zones, and exclusion zones),[5] there is no longer any need to deal separately with so-called "pacific blockades."[6] Since the establishment of a "pacific blockade" involves the use of military force by one state against another, there is an international armed conflict in the sense of common Article 2 of the 1949 Geneva Conventions. The (maritime) *jus in bello* applies to all belligerent measures taken in such conflicts. The existence of a state of war is not a precondition for the legality of certain methods and means of warfare anymore. If they are taken, they have to be in accordance with the applicable *jus in bello*. Hence, the same rules will apply in either case.

Whether and to what extent the *jus ad bellum* also serves as a legal yardstick for naval blockades is a highly disputed issue. Some authors take the position that the *jus in bello* and the *jus ad bellum* are distinct from one another,[7] while others argue they are the same.[8] An interesting issue that is also far from settled, but will be addressed here, is the question of whether and to what extent the rules governing naval blockades also apply to blockades established in accordance with Article 42 of the UN Charter.

Development of Blockade Law

As blockades were originally restricted to coastal fortifications, they differed only slightly from sieges in land warfare.[9] With the increasing importance of sea trade at the end of the sixteenth century, it became necessary also to cut off the enemy's sea links without taking possession of the respective part of the coastline or port.[10] Presumably, the first naval blockade was declared by the Dutch on 27 July 1584, barring Flemish ports in order to cut off the Spanish troops from supplies.[11] In fact, this blockade, as well as subsequent blockades, was declared for the sole purpose of enabling the Dutch to seize neutral merchant vessels even if they were not carrying enemy or contraband goods.[12]

In the early seventeenth century, Hugo Grotius took the view that, regardless of their contraband character, all goods destined to a blockaded location were subject to capture and seizure, provided their delivery jeopardized the success of the closure of the respective enemy port. That, according to Grotius, was the case if surrender or peace were imminent.[13] State practice at the close of the sixteenth and during the seventeenth centuries, however, fails to provide evidence for general acceptance of such a restriction. Hence, one hundred years later, Cornelius van Bynkershoek could easily establish that Grotius's opinion was not in accordance with existing treaties and edicts or even reason.[14]

Although a blockade affected all ships and goods regardless of their enemy or contraband character,[15] in those days belligerents were not obliged to maintain and enforce a blockade by a sufficient number of warships. Regularly, they were "fictitious" or, to use the more popular expression, "paper blockades" (also called "blocus de Cabinet" or "blocus per notificationem")[16] that were not enforced by capture in case of breach. Rather, as laid down in the Dutch decree of 26 June 1630,[17] or in the Anglo-Dutch Treaty of Whitehall (1689),[18] ships could be captured at far distance from the blockaded area if it was established that they clearly intended to breach the blockade ("droit de prévention").[19] Thus, the basis was laid for the doctrine of "continuous voyage," according to which ships destined to a neutral port are subject to capture if their ultimate destination is a blockaded port. According to the "droit de suite," ships were subject to capture

the 1909 London Declaration can be summarized as follows.[45] A blockade, in order to be binding, must be effective, that is to say, it must be maintained by a force sufficient to prevent access to the enemy coastline (Article 2). Whether that precondition is met is, however, a question of fact (Article 3). The delegates to the 1909 Conference were unable to agree upon a more specific rule. They expected that the determination of effectiveness was in any case reserved to the competent (international or national) prize court.[46] According to Article 4, a blockade is not regarded as raised, and thus remains effective, if the blockading force is temporarily withdrawn on account of stress of weather. It must be applied impartially to the ships of all nations (Article 5). Warships (Article 6) and merchant vessels in distress (Article 7) may be allowed to enter and leave a blockaded port or place. The declaration and notification are constitutive for a blockade's legality (Articles 8, 10, and 11).[47]

A declaration of blockade is made either by the blockading power or by the naval authorities acting in its name. It must specify (1) the date when the blockade begins, (2) the geographical limits of the coastline under blockade, and (3) the period within which neutral vessels may come out (Article 9). Additionally, both neutral powers and the local authorities must be notified (Article 11). The provisions on declaration and notification also apply to cases where the limits of a blockade are extended or where a blockade is re-established after having been raised (Article 12). Notice is similarly required upon the voluntary raising or any restriction in the limits of a blockade (Article 13).

If no declaration of blockade has been notified to the local authorities, or if no period of grace has been provided, neutral vessels must be allowed to leave the blockaded area (Article 16, paragraph 2). Vessels that in actual or presumptive knowledge of the blockade attempt to leave or enter the closed port may be captured as long as they are being pursued by a warship of the blockading force and are subject to condemnation (Articles 14, 17, 20, and 21).

The limitation of the right of capture to the area of operation of the warships detailed to render the blockade effective is the result of a compromise between the English and the continental European position. In any event, according to Articles 17, 19, and 20, neither the doctrine of continuous voyage nor the "droit de suite" that had been practiced excessively during the eighteenth century survived.[48] In case of a vessel approaching a blockaded port, without (actual or presumptive) knowledge of the blockade, notification must be made to the vessel itself (Article 16 paragraph 1). Finally, a blockade must be confined to ports and coasts belonging to or occupied by the enemy (Article 1) and may not bar access to neutral ports or coasts (Article 18).

Although the 1909 London Declaration never entered into force because of resistance by the House of Lords to ratification, its provisions on blockade were observed during the Balkan Wars and were included in a number of national prize regulations.[49] Apart from the applicability of the doctrine of continuous voyage, at the beginning of the First World War they were generally regarded as customary in character.[50]

However, in view of the rapid development of weapons technologies (long distance artillery, submarines, military aircraft) and the necessary modification of naval strategies and tactics, it soon became impossible to observe the London Declaration. The traditional close blockade was replaced by the long-distance blockade that – by a simultaneous excessive application of the doctrine of continuous voyage – in fact led to the barring of neutral ports and coasts.[51]

Neutral trade was subjected to far-reaching control measures, some even taken in their respective home ports. For instance, merchant vessels that did not possess a navicert were either diverted or captured, even if they had not approached blockaded coasts or ports. Moreover, the belligerents established huge minefields and exclusion zones ("Sperrgebiete") within which all vessels, regardless of the flag they were flying, were attacked without prior warning.[52]

During World War II that practice was repeated and led to even further restrictions of neutral trade.[53] To give but one example of the excessive use of the right of blockade, it suffices to quote the British Order-in-Council of 27 November 1939:

1   Every merchant vessel which sailed from any enemy port, including any port in territory under enemy occupation or control, after the 4th day of December, 1939, may be required to discharge in a British or Allied port any goods on board laden in such enemy port.

2   Every merchant vessel which sailed from a port other than an enemy port after the 4th day of December, 1939, having on board goods which are of enemy origin or are enemy property, may be required to discharge such goods in a British or Allied port.

3   Goods discharged in a British port under either of the preceding Articles shall be placed in the custody of the Marshal of the Prize Court, and, unless the Court orders them to be requisitioned for the use of His Majesty, shall be detained or sold under the direction of the Court. The proceeds of goods so sold shall be paid into the Court.

    On the conclusion of peace such proceeds and any goods detained but not sold shall be dealt with in such manner as the Court may in the circumstances deem just, provided that nothing herein shall prevent the payment out of Court of any such proceeds or the release of any goods at any time (a) if it be shown to the satisfaction of the Court that the goods had become neutral property before the date of this Order, or (b) with the consent of the proper officer of the Crown.

4   The law and practice in Prize shall, so far as applicable, be followed in all cases arising under this Order.

5   Nothing in this Order shall affect the liability of any vessel or goods to seizure or condemnation independently of this Order.

6   For the purposes of this Order the words "goods which are of enemy origin" shall include goods having their origin in any territory under enemy occupation or control, and the words "goods which [...] are

enemy property" shall include goods belonging to any person in any such territory.

7   Proceeding under this Order may be taken in any Prize Court having jurisdiction to which the Prize Court Rules, 1939, apply.

8   For the purposes of this Order the words "British port" mean any port within the jurisdiction of any Prize Court to which the Prize Court Rules, 1939, apply.[54]

In view of that practice, "... developments in the techniques of naval and aerial warfare have turned the establishment and maintenance of a naval blockade in the traditional sense into a virtual impossibility. It would seem, therefore, that the rules in the Declaration on blockade in time of war are now mainly of historical interest."[55]

Some consider the British practice a contribution to the progressive development of the international law on blockades.[56] Still others stress the fact that the United Kingdom had justified its practice by reference to reprisals. Hence, they maintain, the London Declaration has not been substantively derogated by that practice. They merely concede that the requirement of effectiveness today has to be interpreted in the light of the development of weapons technologies, such that the blockading forces may be deployed at some distance from enemy coasts and ports.[57]

In fact, the limitations of the traditional blockade law have, to a considerable extent, been observed in the practice of states since 1945. Of course, the principle of effectiveness as well as the requirement of maintaining and enforcing a blockade by solely surface warships have been modified. Moreover, it seems that today aircraft may also be subjected to blockade measures. Still, the law as laid down in the 1909 London Declaration has not become obsolete.

The customary character of the principles of the 1909 London Declaration is also widely acknowledged in the military manuals of the U.S. Navy,[58] and of the Canadian[59] and German[60] armed forces. According to those manuals, blockades must be restricted to ports or coastal areas belonging to, occupied by, or under the control of the enemy. They must not bar access to or departure from neutral ports and coasts.[61] The declaration, either by the government or by the commander of the blockading force, must include the details laid down in Article 9 of the London Declaration and must be notified to affected neutral states and to the local authorities.[62] Because knowledge of the existence of a blockade is an essential element of the offenses of breach and attempted breach of blockade, neutral vessels are always entitled to notification.[63] Moreover, according to the three manuals, a blockade, in order to be valid, must be effective. That means that it must be maintained by a force or other mechanism that is sufficient to render ingress or egress of the blockaded area dangerous.

The temporary absence of the blockading force is without prejudice to the blockade's effectiveness, if such absence is due to stress of weather or to some other reason connected with the blockade.[64] The blockade need not be restricted to vessels; it may also be applied and enforced against aircraft.[65] In any event, a blockade must be applied impartially to the vessels of all states, including merchant ships flying the flag of the blockading power.[66] However, although neutral warships and military aircraft enjoy no positive right of access to blockaded areas, the belligerent imposing the blockade may authorize their entry and exit.[67] Neutral vessels in distress should not be prevented from entering and subsequently leaving a blockaded area.[68]

According to the U.S. and the German manuals, a further exception applies to neutral vessels (and aircraft) engaged in the carriage of qualifying relief supplies for the civilian population and the sick and wounded. Those vessels should be authorized to pass through the blockade cordon (safe passage).[69] The German manual and Canadian draft manual contain provisions according to which starvation of the civilian population as a method of warfare is prohibited.[70] Neutral vessels and aircraft that know of a notified and effective blockade, breach or attempt to breach a blockade, are subject to capture.[71] If they resist an attempt to establish identity, including visit and search, they may be attacked.[72]

The Contemporary Law of Blockade

As already mentioned, some authors consider traditional blockades to have become obsolete because, in their view, developments in weapons technologies have made it impossible for belligerents to comply with the strict requirements of blockade law.[73] The short overview of modern state practice has shown, however, that states will continue to make use of this method of naval warfare at least in cases in which they possess superior naval forces and aerial reconnaissance capabilities. Blockade remains an especially efficient method for subduing the enemy in limited armed conflicts.[74]

Moreover, it is the only way by which a belligerent is entitled to prevent the enemy from not only the import but also the export of goods that would otherwise enable it to continue the armed conflict. Neutral commercial sea and air traffic can be subjected to far-reaching restrictions, even if they carry goods that do not qualify as contraband.[75] Hence, as at the beginning of the twentieth century, identifying the legal restrictions that apply if a belligerent decides to establish and enforce a naval blockade is indispensable. It may be added that, according to the position taken here, a special theoretical justification is no longer necessary because the maritime *jus in bello* is appropriately considered a legal order of necessity that prescribes the minimum standards that have to be observed by states, even if they are unwilling or unable to refrain from the use of armed force.[76]

Declaration, Notification, Impartiality and Effectiveness

In general, States are willing to accept the customary character of the principles laid down in the 1909 London Declaration. When it comes to the specification of the rights and duties, however, no general agreement exists. Of course, it is undisputed[77] that: (1) a blockade must be declared and that the declaration must contain the details laid down in Article 9 of the London Declaration; (2) it must be notified to those affected; and (3) impartial application is required. According to the prevailing position in legal literature, neutral vessels are to be granted a grace period to leave the blockaded port or roadstead.[78]

The reason for this wide agreement is that these requirements do not pose any considerable problems. The belligerent establishing a blockade will, of course, be interested in informing all those possibly affected, since it is the object and purpose of a blockade to close certain enemy areas and to cut them off. In addition, today such information will not take long to spread. Rather, it can be disseminated universally within a couple of hours.[79] Finally, any discrimination, in view of the practical problems of identification, would not be practicable.

Problems and disagreement exist, however, with regard to the principle of effectiveness. When judging the effectiveness of a blockade the development of modern weapons systems has to be taken into consideration – a stipulation that was first raised prior to World War I and which obviously is generally recognized now.[80] Accordingly, it is no longer necessary for the blockading force to be deployed in close vicinity to the coast; it may also be stationed at some distance seaward as long as ingress or egress continues to be dangerous.[81] Whether that is the case cannot be determined *in abstracto* but, as in Article 3 of the London Declaration, remains a question of fact. There exists, however, an ultimate legal limitation with regard to the area affected. A blockade must be restricted to coastal areas and ports belonging to, occupied by, or under the control of the enemy. It may not be established outside the general area of naval warfare.[82]

For the purpose of maintaining and enforcing a blockade, belligerents are not restricted to the use of surface warships. This means that they may choose a combination of legitimate methods and means of warfare provided this combination does not result in acts inconsistent with the other rules and principles of the maritime *jus in bello*.[83] In view of the overall importance of aerial reconnaissance and of the legitimate incorporation of the airspace into the regime of blockades, a blockade may be maintained by military aircraft, submarines, or even by naval mines.[84]

However, a blockade may not be maintained and enforced by naval mines alone. This prohibition does not follow from Article 2 of Hague Convention VIII of 1907, for it is nearly impossible to prove that the mines have been laid "for the sole purpose of intercepting commercial navigation."[85] Rather, it has to be observed in this context that certain categories of vessels and aircraft may not be denied ingress or egress. Hence, generally, it is necessary that manned units (or "at least one man-o-war")[86] are present in the vicinity of the blockaded area in order to make sure that such vehicles remain unharmed.[87] The mining of Haiphong is merely a single incident that fails to establish the contrary, even though only the former USSR raised protests against it.[88]

Despite the obvious perils posed by submarines and missiles to surface warships, in most cases the presence of at least one surface unit, for humanitarian reasons, remains an indispensable requirement for the legality of a naval blockade. And it makes no difference whether the blockade serves strictly military or economic purposes.[89] Only if controlled mines are laid may their sole use for maintaining and enforcing a blockade be legitimate. Of course, apart from naval mines, other obstacles, such as wrecks, can be used to close a port or a part of the enemy's coast.[90]

Consequences of Breach and Attempted Breach of Blockade

It is generally acknowledged that vessels (and aircraft) breaking or attempting to break blockade are liable to capture.[91] If, after prior warning, they clearly resist capture, they may be attacked.[92] However, it remains unclear what behavior may be characterized as attempted (inward[93]) breach of blockade.

While the German manual is silent on this issue, the U.S. manual defines attempted breach of blockade as follows:[94]

> Attempted breach of blockade occurs from the time a vessel or aircraft leaves a port or airfield with the intention of evading the blockade, and for vessels exiting the blockaded area, continues until the voyage is completed. [...] It is immaterial that the vessel or aircraft is at the time of interception bound for neutral territory, if its ultimate destination is the blockaded area. There is a presumption of attempted breach of blockade where vessels or aircraft are bound for a neutral port or airfield serving as a point of transit to the blockaded area.

This implies that the doctrine of continuous voyage may be applied to naval blockades.

As in the beginning of the twentieth century, this question is a matter of dispute in the legal literature.[95] There are good reasons to maintain that the doctrine of continuous voyage may not be applied to blockades. First, neutrals have only in rare cases been willing to tolerate interference with their merchant shipping in areas distant from blockaded coasts or ports. Second, the doctrine has not played a significant role in the practice of states since 1945. It has only been recognized in the military manuals of some Anglo-American states.

Most continental European authors have always rejected the doctrine's applicability to blockade.[96] The arguments put forward do not have to be repeated. If blockade law is perceived as part of an order of necessity that, by its nature, has to be interpreted restrictively and that merely modifies but does not abrogate the peacetime rules of international law applicable between belligerents and neutrals, an obligation of states not participating in an international armed conflict to tolerate belligerent measures can be justified only under strict conditions.

In the context of blockade, one of these conditions is the principle of effectiveness. That principle would be rendered meaningless if belligerents were entitled to enforce a blockade at a far distance from the area in question. As long as neutral merchant vessels are situated outside the range of operations of the forces maintaining the blockade, and as long as they do not carry contraband or act in a way that makes them liable to attack, the freedoms of navigation and overflight supersede the belligerents' interest in a comprehensive prohibition of imports to their respective enemies. Of course, the practical consequences of this position are of a solely secondary nature. If a neutral merchant vessel is captured outside the range of operation of the blockade forces because it – in fact or presumably – was destined to a blockaded port, that violation of the law of neutrality results in a duty to return the vessel and its cargo and compensate any damage.

Relief for the Civilian Population and the Wounded and Sick

A blockade preventing all ingress to or egress from the blockaded area by vessels and aircraft negatively affects the civilian population's supply of food and other objects essential for survival. For that reason it was – at least to a certain extent – justified to characterize the British long-distance blockades as "hunger blockades."[97] Still, that notion should not be used too easily. In World War II, the United Kingdom maintained that naval blockades did not differ from sieges in land warfare in which the responsible commander was under no duty to allow food and other goods to pass into the town.[98]

Today, according to Article 54, paragraph 1, Additional Protocol I, "starvation of civilians as a method of warfare is prohibited." Contrary to an assertion by the Australian delegation to the Geneva Diplomatic Conference,[99] as well as by some authors,[100] the position of that provision in Part IV of Additional Protocol I does not prevent its application to naval blockades. Blockade is, in the sense of Article 49, paragraph 3, Additional Protocol I, a method of "sea warfare which may affect the civilian population [...] on land." Therefore, states party to Additional Protocol I may not establish and maintain a blockade that serves the specific purpose of denying them essential foodstuffs, "whatever the motive, whether in order to starve out civilians, to cause them to move away, or for any other motive."[101] As part of customary international law, prohibitions on starving civilian populations by the establishment of a naval blockade are also binding on states not party to Additional Protocol I, since they follow from the generally accepted principles of humanity and proportionality.[102] Methods and means of naval warfare are illegal "if the damage to the civilian population is, or may be expected to be, excessive in relation to the concrete and direct military advantage anticipated."[103] In that context, it makes no difference whether the purposes served by the blockade are military or economic.

Moreover, even states not bound by Additional Protocol I recognize that belligerents are under an obligation not to prohibit relief consignments in case of a naval blockade.[104] That obligation, which is also recognized in the literature,[105] would be meaningless absent prohibition of a so-called "hunger blockade." The military and strategic interests involved are met by the fact that relief consignments must be granted free passage subject to: (1) the right to prescribe the technical arrangements, including search, under which such passage is permitted; and (2) the condition that the distribution of such supplies shall be made under the local supervision of a Protecting Power or a humanitarian organization which offers guarantees of impartiality, such as the International Committee of the Red Cross.[106]

Blockades under Chapter VII of the UN Charter

The final question that remains is whether the rules just described also apply if a blockade is ordered by the Security Council pursuant to Article 42 of the UN Charter.[107] In an annotation to paragraph 7.7.2.1, NWP1–14M, the authors hold that "it is not possible to say whether, or to what extent, a UN blockade would be governed by the traditional rules."[108]

This statement is certainly correct in so far as the Security Council, when taking action under Chapter VII, has a wide range of discretion and that it – as an organ of the UN – is not directly bound by rules of international law that are primarily designed to regulate the conduct of states in situations of armed conflict. On the other hand, a blockade ordered by the Security Council will, of course, have to be declared. The respective resolution will at least contain all the elements that are prescribed for a belligerent blockade (geographical limits, duration).

The practice of the Security Council also demonstrates that, for humanitarian reasons, certain goods essential for the survival of the civilian population may be transported to a blockaded area.[109] If feasible and if not counterproductive to the aim pursued (restoration of international peace and security), the Security Council will also ensure that access to ports and coasts of third states is not barred.

However, an important exception applies. Despite allegations to the contrary,[110] in the case of enforcement measures under Chapter VII, there is no room for neutrality. Therefore, third states may well be affected by a blockade ordered pursuant to Article 42. Affected states, according to Article 50, have the right to "consult the Security Council with regard to a solution of those [economic] problems."

A second exception concerns the applicability of the doctrine of continuous voyage. Situations are conceivable in which the Security Council is forced to order the capture of vessels (and aircraft) at great distance from the blockade area if international peace and security cannot otherwise be restored.

Finally, in view of the binding force of the decisions taken under Chapter VII and of the ultimate goal of maintaining international peace and security, a blockade pursuant to Article 42 will not have to comply fully with the principle of effectiveness.[111]

It must, however, be realized that, in view of the lack of UN armed forces proper, a blockade ordered by the Security Council will always be maintained and enforced by the members of the United Nations and their (national) armed forces. Those forces are bound by the rules and principles of the maritime *jus in bello* that, according to the position taken here, has to be considered an "order of necessity." That legal order has to be conceived of as primarily formulating duties which, as a minimum, have to be observed if states resort to the use of armed force.[112]

In other words, the restrictions contained in the rules of war are, in principle, the most that international law is ready to accept when states are unwilling or unable to refrain from the use of armed force. This means that, when ordered to maintain and enforce a blockade pursuant to Article 42, they may only deviate from the rules of blockade law described above if there is an express decision by the Security Council to that effect. Whether and to what extent the Security Council is entitled to exempt member states from the restrictions of the maritime *jus in bello* will depend on the circumstances of each case. In that regard, the Security Council's discretion is wide but – especially with regard to the elementary considerations of humanity – not unlimited.

PART II

Blockades Through World War II

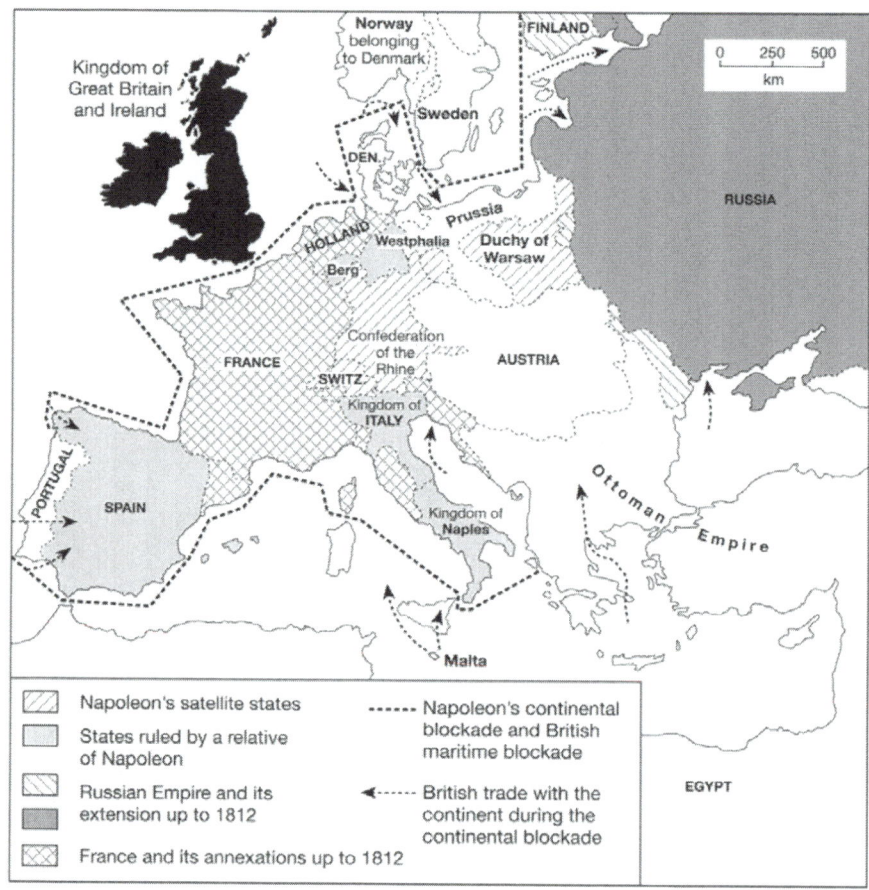

Map 3.1 Napolean's Europe and the continental blockade

3 Napoleon's Continental Blockade

An Effective Substitute to Naval Weakness?

Silvia Marzagalli

The French Wars opposing Great Britain from 1793 to 1815 are considered the ultimate episode of "the Second Hundred Years War."[1] This conflict resulted in the decline of French influence in the Atlantic, Americas, and Asia, and the rise of Great Britain as the major maritime world power. The French Wars were the longest conflict in this process, and their outcome was decisive. For more than twenty years, belligerents fought worldwide on both land and sea. Besides military and naval aspects, these wars also adopted economic warfare and privateering against enemy trade.

The continental blockade decree, issued on 21 November 1806, aimed to shut the continent to British manufactured goods and British trade. Napoleon hoped to weaken Great Britain and to force it to accept peace. The year before, Nelson at Trafalgar had put an end to Napoleon's ambition to exert control over maritime routes and trades. The continental blockade was designed as a counter-offensive to British naval superiority. Historians have questioned the validity of this plan, arguing that the British economy depended more upon extra-European markets than on European ones. However, François Crouzet convincingly demonstrated that the plan could have succeeded, if only Napoleon had been able to implement his policy for some years over a large portion of the continent.[2]

This chapter focuses on those factors that led to the failure of this policy. While Napoleon believed he could prevent British goods from entering Europe, his blockade attempt led to harsher and more repressive legislation, and later annexed increasing parts of Europe's coastline into the Empire. When allies and vassals proved unreliable, Napoleon believed his administration might execute his policy more effectively alone. The failure of the blockade proved that Napoleon was wrong.

The Continental Blockade: the Law of Necessity

The war between France and Great Britain started in 1793. From the beginning, the sea played a strategic role both militarily and economically. British naval supremacy prevented France and her allies from defending their colonies, which became independent, like Haiti, or progressively fell under

British control. The British Navy and privateers could prevent the adversary from importing strategic goods – including food for the starving French population in 1793 – and limit profits, thus affecting the nation's wealth. Neutral trade was tolerated, although impediments increased over time.

The French attitude towards international trade was largely determined by circumstances. Naval blockades of enemy ports were traditional weapons of early modern warfare, but the situation of the French Navy after the Revolution made it impossible to implement an effective maritime blockade of enemy ports. France turned rapidly towards other means. In 1793, the importation of British-manufactured products was prohibited, to the great satisfaction of French industrialists. By 1796, this interdiction extended to goods that were usually traded by the British – such as Indian cotton, nankeens, etc. – thus adding a commercial dimension to industrial protectionism.

As long as such prohibitions applied to France only, they had limited effects upon the enemy's economy. French politicians began to consider military conquest of European coastal countries and the creation of allied, or "satellite," states as an effective means of defeating a fragile British economy that largely rested upon credit. If France could affect credit and interest rates in Britain by stopping its foreign trade, then the enemy might be forced to accept peace.

The idea of shutting Europe to British commerce was first advanced by Antoine-Bernard Caillard, French plenipotentiary minister in Ratisbonne in 1795. In 1798, both Emmanuel-Joseph Sieyès and Napoleon Bonaparte suggested that France should control the North Sea coasts and prevent German ports from trading with Great Britain.[3] In 1798, France authorized the capture of any vessel transporting British products, but with no other effect than coming close to war with the United States; in 1800, France repealed this legislation against neutral carriers, but maintained the interdiction of British products.[4]

After the short Amiens' Peace in 1802–1803, on 20 June 1803 Napoleon forbade the importation, not only of British manufactured products, but also of any goods from Great Britain or her colonies. From 1803 to 1805, when the French Army occupied Hanover, Napoleon tried to shut the rivers Elbe, Weser, and Ems to British trade. Success was limited, since the Hanseatic merchants rapidly diverted their trade routes to minor Prussian and Danish ports that were not under French control, such as Emden and Tonning. Prussia's defeat at Jena in October 1806, however, made it possible for Napoleon to close the North Sea coasts and the Baltic more effectively to British trade.

By 20 November 1806, French troops occupied the three Hanseatic ports of Hamburg, Bremen, and Lubeck. The next day, the French Emperor issued in Berlin the decree declaring the British Isles to be under a so-called continental blockade. The preamble of the decree claimed it to be a reply to the "barbarian" British Order in Council of May 1806 which had established a blockade of the coast between Brest and the river Elbe. The French denied that a blockade could be applied to such a large portion of a continent, calling it a "paper" blockade. Napoleon recognized the right of the enemy to shut a port effectively, by preventing merchant ships to enter or to clear, but not to stop any kind of trade over an unlimited period of time without systematically enforcing the measure. He also contested the transformation of naval blockades, which were admitted internationally as a military step to prevent the provisioning and the activity of military ports, into an instrument of commercial war.

In fact, the Berlin decree was much more than simple retaliation for the May Order in Council. Napoleon was conscious that France lacked an efficient navy, particularly after Trafalgar. The continental blockade was a substitute for naval weakness; instead of preventing the enemy using its own ports, it shut European ports to the enemy's trade. As such, it could not be as effective as a real blockade, because the enemy could still trade with America and Asia without being seriously affected by French privateering. However, European markets were important enough to Great Britain, and essential for some imports and exports, and hence Napoleon's plan was not completely unrealistic.

Judging from Napoleon's attempts to justify the blockade's legitimacy and goals, he was conscious of the enormity of the project. The preamble of the Berlin decree was actually longer than the decree itself. All trade and correspondence with the British Isles was forbidden. Goods of British origin, or belonging to British subjects, were to be seized in Europe. Vessels having once touched Great Britain and arriving in French ports should depart without discharging. Both the ship and the cargo should be seized if the captain tried to conceal such a call.

The decree did not change everyday life for French merchants. The real novelty was Napoleon's desire to make the Berlin decree a law enforced in all European coastal states.[5] The 9th article of the decree ordered the French Minister of Foreign Affairs to send a copy of the act to Spain, Holland, Tuscany, and the Kingdom of Naples. In a letter to Minister of Foreign Affairs Charles-Maurice de Talleyrand, Napoleon ordered him to insist that Hamburg also adopt the same measures.[6] The French Emperor had clearly understood that his only chance to weaken the enemy was to close the entire continent to British trade.

From this moment onwards, Napoleon's politics were deeply affected by this goal. European ports fell under his control one after another. Military campaigns and political pressure forced most European countries to adopt the Berlin decree. By the end of 1807, this was the case not only of the satellite states that Napoleon controlled indirectly, but also of former enemies such as Russia, Prussia, and Austria. British bombing of Copenhagen in September 1807 certainly destroyed a large part of the Danish Navy, but also pushed the King of Denmark to adopt some Napoleonic views on halting British trade. French troops firmly occupied Hanseatic and Swedish Pomeranian ports. Portugal, which dared to refuse to implement the blockade, was invaded in November 1807. Napoleon controlled the western Mediterranean as well:

October 1811 their wages from February to July. Under such circumstances, they were susceptible to bribes: "How can you prevent a custom officer earning 40 francs a month [...] from refusing an offer of 200 or 300 francs just to pretend to be sleeping for half an hour, when he is alone at his post?" wondered the chief of police in Leghorn.[18]

Bribery was widespread, affecting a majority of customs officers. It was hardly punished, as it was extremely difficult to prove complicity. In some instances, police, customs officers, and soldiers were arrested smuggling British goods across the border, hoping their uniform and rank would protect them. Not all customs officers, of course, could be bribed. Some simply closed their eyes in order to survive. Smugglers acted in groups, were armed, and generally had superior numbers. They did not hesitate to defend themselves if someone dared to try to arrest them.

Those customs officers who stopped smuggling obtained one-sixth of all goods they seized. This was a welcome source of income for badly paid civil servants. But, as the chief of police in Leghorn put it, "on the one side in order to benefit from smugglers [through bribes], on the other side to obtain a part of the goods of those who do not find an agreement with them, customs officers are and must be from the very nature of things the greatest partisans of fraud."[19]

Existing legislation also allowed those arrested to avoid a trial by paying a fine to the Customs bureau. Merchants organizing smuggling were, therefore, able to rescue their agents before the court enquired closely into their organization. Despite the adoption of strong repressive measures, most of the smugglers were neither tried nor sentenced. Because of the small quantities of goods they tried to introduce, and the evident poverty of the porters, customs officers often let them go after seizing their goods.

In port cities close to the border, smuggling was a popular activity. Contemporary estimates suggest that one-tenth to one-sixth of Hamburg and Leghorn inhabitants participated actively in smuggling. Because the continental blockade paralysed maritime activities, this illegal source of revenue was essential to hundreds of families, and local authorities hesitated to arrest smugglers for fear of rebellion.[20] These fears were not irrational. Local populations repeatedly defended smugglers and universally hated customs officers. In Lubeck, a mob forcibly liberated a man accused of the murder of two customs officers.[21] In Leghorn, an anonymous leaflet urged people not to provide accommodation and food to customs officers in order to get rid of them.

Repression encountered other obstacles. In the annexed European territories, French authorities experienced difficulty in finding competent, reliable, and bilingual judges for their new courts. Persistent rumors in Leghorn accused a judge and the public prosecutor of investing in local merchant houses.[22] Similar problems existed in France. Nicolas Buhan, son of a Higher Court public prosecutor responsible for repressing smuggling and nephew of a Bordeaux Custom Court judge, was also married to the daughter of a local wholesale merchant.[23] The zeal of officers who were related to merchant houses in stopping smuggling is questionable.

As a matter of fact, merchants were rarely questioned about smuggling. Some bought immunity by offering Napoleon's senior civil servants an interest in their profits. In 1811, for instance, Bordeaux authorities discovered that a senior civil servant participated in a plan to discharge British manufactured goods on the coast of south-western France.[24] More generally, however, merchants owed their impunity to the very essence of Napoleon's regime. The regime rested on the support of the *notables*, those wealthy landowners who exerted authority in the cities. It was from among these *notables* that the regime chose its municipal and departmental representatives. Tax lists served as a basis of identifying local *notables*: in maritime cities, merchants represented between 50 and 90 percent of this group.

Finally, Napoleon needed the support of bankers, and the latter were linked to merchant houses. To keep his own credit flowing, Napoleon allowed merchants to divert trade routes and avoid a total paralysis of commerce. By doing so, Napoleon weakened the impact of the Continental Blockade against Great Britain.

Merchants' Networks and International Trade

Merchants in the eighteenth century were used to warfare and knew how wars hampered maritime transactions. Merchant networks were particularly effective at carrying on maritime trade with relative success and moderate risk, despite a belligerent navy and privateering.[25] By intensifying police control over the land, however, and provoking a general paralysis of maritime activities in 1808–9, the continental blockade proved to be a particularly difficult challenge.

Belligerents traditionally forbade the provisioning of enemy ports with war contraband, consisting of weapons and naval stores. They also seized enemy property at sea. Since 1756, Great Britain had not recognized that neutral ships had the right to carry goods belonging to enemy merchants. She also denied that neutral vessels could service any maritime itineraries they were not entitled to carry on in peacetime, such as between a colonial port and the mother-country, or between two enemy ports.

These obstacles were not insurmountable, however, since merchants could stop in a neutral port and make their cargo appear to be the property of a neutral merchant. During most of the French Wars, for example, U.S. ships could transport colonial wares from French Guadeloupe to Bordeaux simply by stopping in New York in order to obtain a new clearance.[26] Neutral shipping, therefore, increased enormously. According to their capacity for maintaining their neutral status, the United States, Denmark, the Hanseatic ports, several German towns and principalities (Kniphausen, Oldenburg, Papenburg), or Ragusa (Dubrovnik) in the Mediterranean, played at some moments a vital role in maintaining active shipping.[27] In many cases, these neutrals also conducted business on the belligerents' account.

Neutral shipping allowed French merchants to carry on indirectly their former trade with French colonies, but neutrals also threatened Napoleon's plan to ban British goods from the Empire. He therefore required that all imported goods be accompanied by a certificate of origin signed by the French consul in the port of embarkation. Had this measure been effective, no British wares could arrive in France even after calling at a neutral port. Luckily enough for merchants, however, consuls and French authorities generally accepted bribes to sign fraudulent certificates. Louis-Antoine Fauvelet de Bourrienne, for instance, former private secretary of Napoleon and French minister plenipotentiary in Hamburg from 1806 to 1810, received about a million francs (200,000 U.S. dollars) by demanding merchants pay a slight commission on all certificates he counter-signed.[28] After occupying Lisbon in 1807, General Andoche Junot authorized shipping to Great Britain in exchange for substantial bribes.

Merchants were also successful in finding new trade routes. As soon as authorities strengthened their control over an area of coastline, trade and shipping moved elsewhere. When Great Britain blockaded the Weser and the Elbe rivers in 1803 as a response to Napoleon's invasion of Hanover, trade from Bremen and Hamburg continued through Prussian Emden and Danish Tonning instead. The latter – a fishing port of no more than 2,000 inhabitants – was again very active in 1809–10, when dozens of American ships unloaded huge quantities of colonial wares which were subsequently smuggled through Hamburg. The island of Heligoland in the North Sea, Malta in the Mediterranean, and Gothenburg in Sweden all served as huge British warehouses, whence small craft smuggled goods to the Empire.

Thus, bribes and smuggling contributed to making the continental blockade ineffective. British exports to Europe had dropped severely by 1808, parallel to the reinforcement of Napoleon's control of Europe, British manufactureres lost 40 percent of their European markets from 1802 to 1808, and 60 percent of British colonial re-exports. However, the British economy did not collapse, because it was able to find compensatory markets outside Europe. Total British exports fell by only 16 percent during 1802–1808; America and Asia decisively contributed to maintaining the British economy.[29] In fact, much of the British import and export trade with neutral countries such as the United States was ultimately intended for European markets.

The downward trend of British trade to Europe – which, as a matter of fact, began long before the issue of the Berlin decree – did not last after 1808. Through the Balkans, the Baltic, the North Sea coast, Portugal, and Gibraltar, British products continued to reach European consumers. Napoleon largely underestimated the ability of merchants to divert and reorganize trade routes. The reduction of maritime and international trade affected an important part of the European population, who were only too eager to find new sources of legal or illegal revenue. The number of people involved in fraud and smuggling activities was consistently larger than the number of officials who could stop them.

If merchants were effective in reorganizing trade and in rapidly reacting to changes in international shipping, this was largely due to their flexibility. Most trade was carried out by individual merchant firms, generally composed of between one and four partners. These firms corresponded with a large number of foreign houses, who informed them constantly of changes in legislation and business opportunities. Such trade connections spanned political frontiers, and merchants ignored political obstacles. Despite the war, French merchants could still call upon their British correspondents for remittances and insurance. Whenever new opportunities arose, merchants sent an agent to foreign cities, travelled, or emigrated in order to establish new links. Many Bordeaux merchants, for instance, settled in Philadelphia, New York, Baltimore, and Charleston during the French Wars, in order to reorganize colonial trade to France through American neutral ports. Neutral merchants profited too. Out of a dozen firms monopolizing about half of the consignments of some 2,400 American ships arriving in Bordeaux from 1795 to 1815, two-thirds of them were run by U.S. merchants who had settled in the French city.

Geographic mobility and the willingness of neutral merchants to cover belligerents' property for a modest commission – varying from 2.5 to 5 percent of the value of the cargo – allowed firms to reorganize maritime trade despite all attempts to limit their trading activities. After all, Napoleon was not completely wrong when he claimed that merchants knew "neither faith nor country."[30]

Conclusion

Napoleon's plan to cut the continent of Europe off from British trade was an ambitious project that he had inherited from French Revolutionary policy-makers and that he constantly adapted according to circumstances. As years passed, he realized that the plan could achieve its goal only if he was able to extend the prohibition to all British products coming to Europe. The Berlin decree was a major step in this process, but the system he conceived did not cease to evolve until his final fall.

Although the continental blockade created difficulties for the British economy, it was ultimately unable to crack Britain's credit and financial structure. Whereas a powerful navy can effectively prevent trade to and from enemy ports, the blockade of a continent requires exerting control over thousands of miles of coastline and forcing an unwilling population to comply. Napoleon could not fully achieve either of these goals.

Historians generally credit Napoleon for his rational administration and institutions, and the rapid progress in increasing efficiency, but his inability to apply the continental blockade is a concrete demonstration of the limits of his power. Napoleon could not rely on an efficient and devoted customs service. His means were also insufficient to defeat powerful mercantile interests and thousands of hungry subjects who could only earn their living through smuggling. Ultimately, just as with any other kind of protracted blockade, the successful implementation of the continental blockade depended on its conformity to the economic needs and goals of ordinary people, and had little to do with the plans of policy-makers, even one as famous as Napoleon.

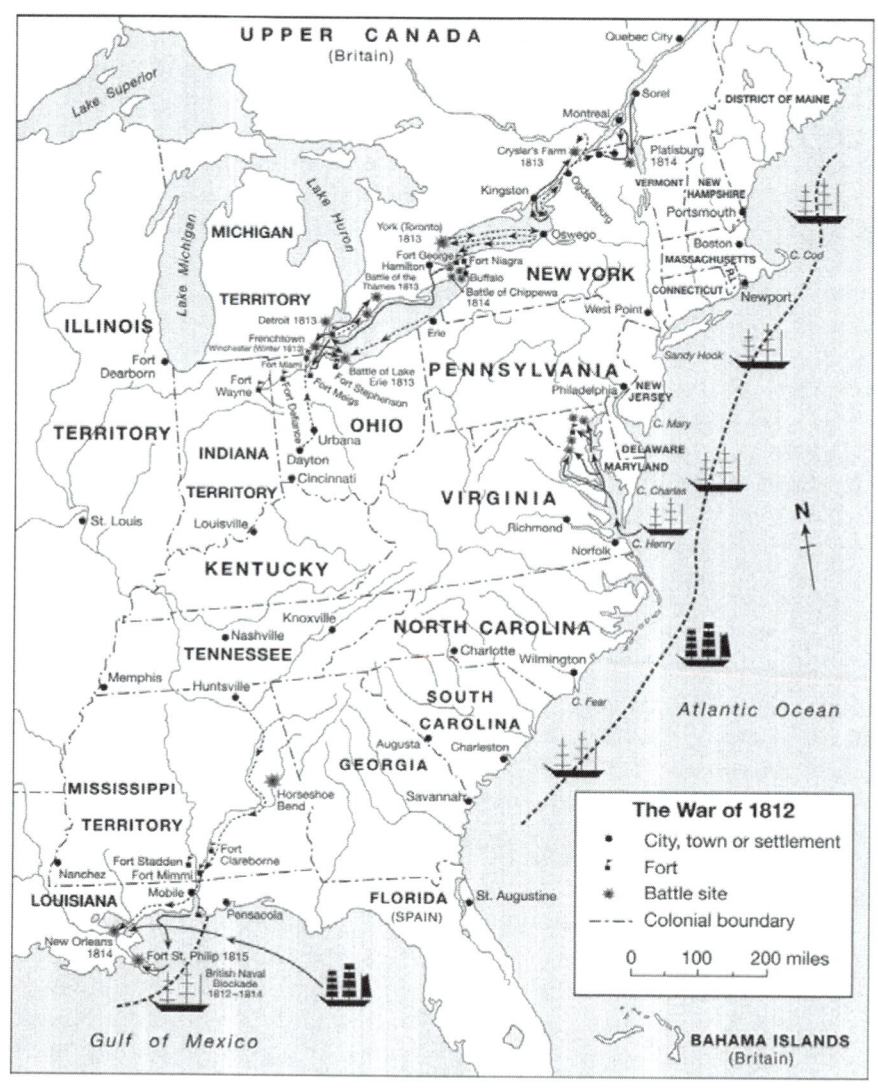

Map 4.1 The War of 1812, American theatre of operations

4 The Flawed British Blockade, 1812–15

Wade G. Dudley

Scholarly debates on the underlying causes of the War of 1812 have been contentious, but historians tend to agree that the British naval blockade of the United States proved extremely effective. One even stated that "the overwhelming naval pressure the British were able to exert along the whole length of the American Atlantic coast wiped out American seaborne traffic and communications and gradually inclined the government in Washington to become more disposed to peace."[1]

However, the Royal Navy faced setbacks at Baltimore, and British forces were crushed on Lake Champlain. On 24 December 1814, Parliament ordered the Treaty of Ghent to return the belligerents to a *status quo ante-bellum*. The editor of the London *Times* lamented: "We have retired from the combat with the stripes yet bleeding on our backs ... with the bravest seamen and the most powerful navy in the world, we retire from the contest when the balance of defeat is so heavy against us."[2]

Popular voices echoed that sentiment across the breadth of the British Empire, and Americans were soon celebrating Andrew Jackson's victory at New Orleans and the end of the war, often confusing the two until victory in the first often equated to winning the second. Meanwhile, U.S. merchantmen, long penned in by British blockade, burst forth upon the world's trade lanes.

These issues raise serious questions about the British blockade's effectiveness. In fact, the U.S. Navy was stronger, and there were more American merchantmen, at the war's end than at its beginning. Therefore, this chapter will discuss the failings of the British naval blockade, and in particular strategic failures made by British commanders of the blockading forces.

Background

The warships of 1812, ranging in size from gigantic three-decked ships-of-the-line to smaller ketches and cutters, constituted the most complex and expensive machines of their day. Fleets of warships protected a nation's merchant marine and prevented enemy incursions onto home soil. Trapping enemy squadrons within their own ports prevented sallies against trade lanes and homelands. Nor could a trapped fleet protect its merchantmen or defend distant colonies.

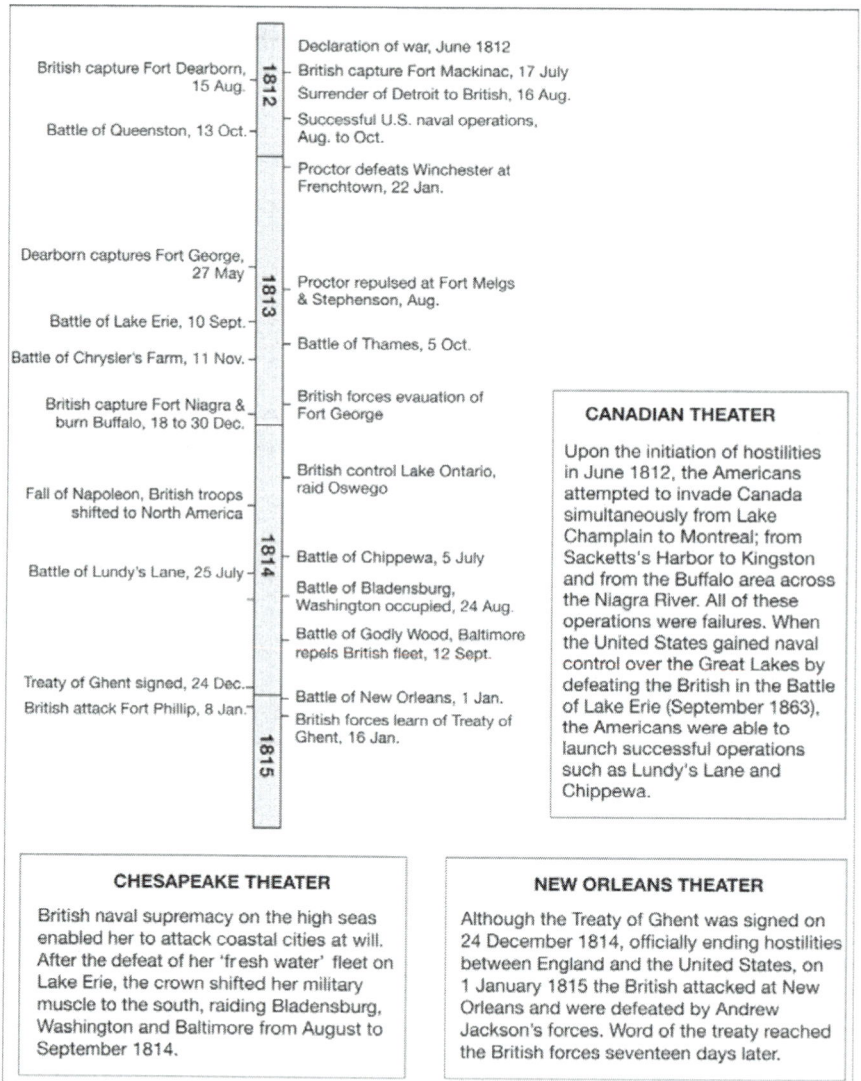

Figure 4.1 Time line of the war of 1812

The capability of maintaining long-term naval blockades appeared late in the age of sail. The coppering of ship bottoms, mandated for the Royal Navy only near the end of the American Revolution, dramatically extended time between ship refits. The British Admiralty adopted the lightweight carronade in 1779, which reduced tonnage, crewing needs, and cost. This allowed the fielding of smaller warships by 1812, about half of the active Navy List of 653 ships. Finally, by the late 1700s naval medicine had conquered scurvy, a vitamin C deficiency. Coupled with dramatic improvements in shipboard hygiene and medical personnel, sailors could spend months and sometimes years at sea. Thus, only by the last decade of the 1700s could a naval blockade be effectively maintained for more than a very few months.

France declared war on Great Britain on 1 February 1793. On the high seas, French naval squadrons and individual raiders tried to destroy Britain's merchant marine, the largest in the world. Unless contained or destroyed, these squadrons could seize Britain's rich West Indian sugar colonies, or eliminate its influence in Asia. Worse, should France gain support from the Spanish fleet and unite that fleet with its own scattered squadrons in the English Channel, the British Isles could be threatened. Until the spring of 1814, the Royal Navy fixated on these fears, and so conducted a near-continuous naval blockade against France.

For most of the war against republican France (1793–1802), Britain relied on a distant blockade. But the blockade formed only the first line of defense. Squadrons of lighter vessels, usually supported by one or more ships-of-the-line, aggressively cruised from distant stations such as Halifax, Nova Scotia, or Port Royal in search of French warships and privateers sailing under a *Letter of Marque and Reprisal* granting them temporary men-of-war status. Should enemy raiders escape both the first and second lines, they still faced a well-organized convoy system. British law required that merchantmen bound for foreign ports sail together or sail without maritime insurance. These convoys, frequently numbering in the hundreds, were escorted by Royal Navy warships, hired auxiliaries, or both. Although entire convoys could fall prey to a large enemy fleet, unless scattered by the weather they formed fearsome targets for raiders.

After Britain's 1805 victory at the Battle of Trafalgar, French raiders declined and had virtually disappeared from the high seas by 1812. A close blockade in Europe prevented the French Navy from succoring their colonial possessions as the Royal Navy concentrated its forces and overwhelmed them one by one. The loss of foreign bases limited French raiding to the Channel, the Baltic, and the Mediterranean. So many French sailors languished in British prison hulks that few privateers could be effectively manned. Although Napoleon maintained a large fleet and continued an aggressive naval building program, the manpower needs of his armies sapped crews from his battle fleet.

In 1811, the Eleventh U.S. Congress appropriated money to expand the American army while failing to build up the navy. This implies that President James Madison had formulated military plans against Canada months before the declaration of war. The two Royal Naval incursions into Copenhagen, the Battle of Trafalgar, and the ever-increasing size of the British fleet had perhaps convinced Madison that victory must be won ashore. More importantly, the inevitability of blockade dictated the necessity for the rapid seizure of Canada for use as a diplomatic lever against Britain.

As for the small U.S. Navy, to use it would be to lose it. Even in port, as the British exploits at Copenhagen had illustrated, vessels could be taken or destroyed. Besides, the war might be short, allowing the Navy to cruise off six frigates, and six sloops. In Britain, the stinging naval losses brought an end to diplomatic efforts to end the war.

By the end of 1812, the Royal Navy had lost nine warships to enemy action and ten to natural causes, as opposed to only five small warships lost by the U.S. Navy. The British also had taken only 100 American ships as prizes and recaptured some fifty merchantmen, as opposed to over 360 captured by Americans.[8] The failure to establish a rapid blockade of major American ports, coupled with an incorrect estimate of American naval capability, cost Britain heavily during the opening months of the war.

Blockade or Concentration?

By January 1813, Warren's situation seemed well-nigh impossible. Though Admiralty numbers indicated that he commanded some 97 warships, only twenty-eight were based at Halifax or Bermuda and only six of those could be spared for actual blockade duty.[9] Because a blockade of the almost 2,000 miles of American coastline, or at the least its major ports, had not been established in June 1812, the U.S. Navy as well as dozens of privateers sailed at will. This, in turn, forced many potential British blockaders to function as convoy escorts and roving patrols. As the conflict intensified and spread, the drain of ships from the blockade of France increased. For the first time since 1805 and Nelson's victory at Trafalgar, the Admiralty found itself in the position of constantly reacting to enemy naval forces.

In a letter dated 9 January 1813, the Admiralty informed Warren that reinforcements would raise his strength to ten ships-of-the-line, thirty frigates, and fifty sloops – over 140 vessels for his combined stations, including numerous unrated vessels already in place. This would include two battalions of marines, an artillery battery, and their transports. The Admiralty also made Warren's task perfectly clear: "It is of the highest importance to the character and interests of the country that the naval force of the enemy should be quickly and completely disposed of." At that point, the bulk of Warren's warships could return to Europe and the blockade of France.[10]

The Admiralty left the methodology of how best to destroy the U.S. Navy in Warren's hands, having dictated only that the economic blockade of the Chesapeake and Delaware Bays continue. By early February, both blockades were in place, as well as weaker blockades of Boston and New York. Occasional patrols of frigates and smaller warships ineffectively covered the remainder of the American coast. Warren's first real choice lay between dispersing his reinforcements or creating a tight blockade against the U.S. Navy at the ports of Boston, New York, or in the Chesapeake Bay. Warren chose the weakly defended Chesapeake region for his summer campaign. Aside from military targets, warship-building at Baltimore, and the major naval base at the American capital, the produce and goods from several states funneled into the bay. It also served as home port to numerous successful privateers, vessels usually ignored by the Admiralty in its quest to destroy the U.S. Navy. Finally, the squadron of blockaders already assembled at the mouth of the bay could begin immediately to lay the groundwork for the campaign.

On 1 April 1813, Warren and his subordinate, Admiral Sir George Cockburn, led over fifty warships to the Chesapeake. British sailors and marines captured one small warship, several privateers, and numerous fishing boats and small coasting vessels while severely damaging the region's infrastructure. Warren dispatched Cockburn and a small force to raid the coastal waters of North Carolina, an event that frightened the populace but netted only two small privateers. Midway through the campaign, Warren received orders to abandon it and extend the commercial blockade to include the entire coast of the United States from New Orleans to Long Island if he had not yet managed to capture the frigate *Constellation*. Though that prize continued to elude him, Warren ignored the Admiralty and kept his squadron concentrated in the hopes of capturing at least one significant warship. A final repulse at Norfolk and an abandoned attempt to sail up the shallow Potomac River doomed any lingering hope of success.

Warren's concentration in the Chesapeake had left only eleven ships available to cover the blockade. Though unable to close a single port to American public or private warships, the British scored two notable successes. On 1 June, the British frigate *Shannon* captured the American frigate *Chesapeake* off Boston – the first frigate action won by the Royal Navy during the war. At the same time, the British squadron off New York managed to trap an American squadron composed of the frigates *United States* and *Macedonian*, and the brig *Hornet* in the North River above New London, Connecticut. Both frigates would remain there for the remainder of the conflict, while their guns were stripped and sent with their crews to the Great Lakes; on 6 September, an American squadron captured or destroyed the British squadron on Lake Erie, ending a British invasion into the United States.

British failures outnumbered successes as merchantmen fell to American warships or were set alight by the U.S. Navy, threatening the British economy and Britain's ability to supply the war effort against France. From the Peninsula, locked in a hard struggle with Napoleon's forces, Wellington wrote to the Admiralty: "I am certain that it will not be denied, that since Great Britain has been a naval power, a British army has never been left in such a situation."[11]

Leaving a small blockading force at the mouth of the Chesapeake on 6 September, Warren dispatched Cockburn with a small force to Bermuda to refit for the winter blockade. As Warren returned to Halifax, a late-season hurricane struck on 12 November, catching over thirty ships in the process of refitting. At the end of a long supply line, the extensive damage would not be made good until late March 1814.

By the end of 1813, the Royal Navy had lost an additional sixteen warships to wind and foe. The U.S. Navy marked only five ships from its list, while the American public and private navies had captured or burned at remained free to cover the entirety of the American coast.[16] Concentrated from the Delaware Bay northward, they could stop neither the extensive coasting trade nor the sailing of privateers, while American ports south of the Chesapeake saw virtually no interference at all from the Royal Navy.

Forcing the American gunboat flotilla defending the Chesapeake to flee up the Potomac before abandoning and burning its vessels, Cochrane landed troops on the Patuxent River on 19 August. Five days later they routed American defenders at Bladensburg, then occupied Washington and burned public buildings, including the White House, before rejoining the fleet on 26 August. Meanwhile, a small naval squadron had penetrated the Potomac River to Alexandria, looting local warehouses on the way. Finally, on 12 September, Cochrane threw his land and naval forces against a strongly defended Baltimore. The land force stalled when the British general was killed, and the naval force failed to bombard Fort McHenry into submission.

News of the failure at Baltimore did little to strengthen British political resolve. And though there had been some success in Maine, where the Royal Navy had seized part of the district bordering Canada, the war at sea showed no sign of improving. On 9 September, Liverpool merchants and shipowners publicly censured the Admiralty, claiming that 800 vessels had been lost since 1812 in that city alone. Daily, Parliament received impassioned pleas from merchants and industry to end the war. The outcry rose even higher when Lloyd's of London, on 30 September, reported that two American warships and several privateers had taken 108 prizes in September.[17] And news soon arrived that an American naval force had smashed the British fleet at Plattsburgh on Lake Champlain on 11 September, halting the British invasion from Canada. With no hope of ending the war with a military victory, the British government ordered its diplomats at Ghent to make peace with a restoration of the *status quo antebellum*. Representatives signed that treaty on 24 December 1814.

But the conflict continued until news of peace arrived. As Cochrane concentrated his forces to support the ill-fated invasion at New Orleans, blockading strength dropped to a mere twenty-one ships. Despite the capture of the American frigate *President* by a squadron of British warships, the blockade remained porous. By March 1815, the British blockaders would leave for home, but American public and private warships continued to capture and burn British shipping until June. Over the course of 1814–15, the Royal Navy lost twenty-two warships to all causes, while over 650 merchantmen fell to American raiders – a greater number than in any comparable period of the war. American losses stood at only ten warships and an estimated 250 privately owned vessels.

Conclusions

Though Great Britain had clearly mastered the art of blockade by 1812, the wooden wall that it tried to build around the United States splintered time after time under the onslaught of American warships. Those warships, once free of the blockade, operated in all the waters of the world, taking prizes estimated between 1,444 and 2,500 ships – a greater average per month, even though a smaller number overall, than France and its allies ever enjoyed against the British.[18]

Despite strong warnings since 1793 that impressment and infringement upon American sovereignty could not be tolerated forever, and despite American willingness to go to war, Great Britain refused to strengthen its squadron at Halifax. Had a squadron of ships-of-the-line or more numerous smaller vessels been present at the outbreak of war to establish a rapid blockade of the major American ports, then Britain could have stopped the bulk of privateer sailings and, with additional ships, the blockaders might have defeated the returning American naval squadron. Most importantly, instead of forcing the Royal Navy to react constantly to events on distant seas, the maritime conflict would have been largely limited to American waters, and its initial success with the blockade might have encouraged Madison to end the war sooner.

Of course, the part played by France in all war-related decisions was crucial, from the timing of the declaration of war to the unexpected collapse of Napoleon, which forced Madison to seek peace. Less evident was the logic behind the unwillingness of the Admiralty to weaken its cordon of France as the war progressed. After 1805, the ability of France to challenge the Royal Navy diminished, and by 1812 the bulk of French sailors fought as infantry in the French army. But the Admiralty refused to reinforce its North American Squadron because of Napoleon's naval building program, which was still churning out warships on the very day that he abdicated. Apparently the Admiralty feared the hypothetical threat of a French invasion of the British Isles more than they feared the actual dangers posed by the U.S. Navy and by American privateers.

Throughout the War of 1812, therefore, this British policy allowed American privateers to provide much-needed revenue even while buying time for the United States to build new warships. By 1816, both the ships-of-the-line and frigates that would form the core of a strong navy were already being outfitted; in addition, all tonnage categories within the American merchant marine had increased beyond those of 1811, while total commercial exports exceeded those of that pre-war year by 25 percent. In the end, the relatively weak British naval blockade may have actually spurred America's global trade, as well as serving as the primary rationale for the creation of a strong U.S. Navy.

5   The Crimean War Blockade: 1854–56

Andrew D. Lambert

While better known for heroic soldiers, hypothermia, and hapless generals, the Crimean War provides an important case study in the efficacy of sea powers conducting an economic blockade against a continental power. The outcome of the War of 1812 left many legal issues involving naval blockade unresolved, with the British refusing to discuss maritime rights at the Vienna settlement of 1814–15.[1] The British did recognize the need to conciliate neutral opinion in any struggle short of a total war: when Britain suppressed the Atlantic Slave Trade, America and other states interpreted this as the imposition of a maritime hegemony for commercial ends.[2] However, Britain blocked any significant change in the legal regime, using economic blockades to coerce lesser powers, such as Holland in the 1830s until it conceded Belgian independence, or Greece during 1850 until it compensated Dom Pacifico.

It is important to stress two salient features of the Crimean War, because they dominated the development and execution of allied blockade policy, and influenced the outcome of the war. The Crimean War was a maritime conflict – allied troops were never more than one day's march from the sea. It was also a relatively short, limited war – one in which the issues, for Britain and France at least, did not require the total mobilization of national resources, or the destruction of the enemy state.

By the 1850s, naval blockades were considered a prime coercive tool, deployed within a wider strategy to persuade the enemy to accept a limited, partial defeat. In the Crimean War, the Allied goal was to force Russia to abandon its ambitions in Turkey. As a gradual, cumulative strategic instrument the blockade could degrade Russian military performance, weaken the resource base of the state, and assist the move to peace. But this strategy could not secure victory unaided, and so had to be applied with considerable skill to avoid creating problems with neutral powers. In particular, the Treaty of Paris of 1856 banned *Letters of Marque* in an attempt to end the threat of privateers.

Neutrals and Allied Policy, 1853–54

When Britain went to war with Russia in the mid-1850s she quickly modified her stand on the underlying legal basis for naval blockades. Russia had limited maritime interests, while Britain's and France's overwhelming naval strength and steam-powered warships allowed an effective close blockade to be imposed. The policy of 1854 was a much more consensual interpretation of belligerent rights than had been used against Napoleon, because a limited war with Russia was not a life-and-death issue. Allied policy required blockades to be effective to be legally enforceable, while neutral flags covered enemy goods on the high seas, and the right of search was restricted to determining nationality and checking for contraband. The British urged the abandonment of privateering, clothing self-interest with humanitarian concern.[3]

In the decade before the war, British and Russian economic interests had begun to diverge sharply. Britain, pushing the agenda of free trade, and creating a world empire of economic access, found prohibitive Russian tariff barriers set up against her manufactured goods. Russian goods competed in the Middle Eastern markets. Nothing symbolized this shift so clearly as the rapid rise to prominence of Odessa as the main port for Russian grain exports, but with little demand for imports. Instead the British developed links with Ottoman Turkey, a market that exported grain, while importing British capital and manufactures. Between 1842 and 1852 the number of British ships passing the Dardanelles annually rocketed from 250 to 1,741.[4] As this market grew, the British *chargé d'affaires* considered "the safety of our vast commercial interests" far more important than issues of European policy and peace.[5] It would appear that the British blockade policy reflected such long-term considerations.

In the months immediately preceding the war, British policy-makers sought a blockade that would be effective against Russia without harming British commercial interests or antagonizing neutrals. The compromises this entailed were acceptable because this was a limited war against a largely land-locked agrarian state dependent on imports for high-technology weapons and manufacturing equipment. Their policy was to begin by blocking the export of war materiel from Britain, beginning with steam engines and warships destined for the Russian Navy. Exports of warlike stores to countries in northern and eastern Europe, close to Russia, were banned, while other European states were controlled by export licenses. This greatly reduced the amount of war materiel available to Russia, although Belgium and the United States offered alternative sources. Cargoes that were clearly contraband could be seized, and were legitimate prizes. However, British stores did reach Russia, notably saltpetre, a vital ingredient of gunpowder, from British India.

Britain unilaterally limited the right of capture at sea, and gave up the right to commission privateers, because it was inexpedient to do so. While idealists like Richard Cobden believed this action represented an advance of civilization, making private property inviolable, the Admiralty, the Foreign Office, and their legal advisers did not share such sentiments. The First Lord of the Admiralty, Sir James Graham, believed that Britain had to adopt a common policy with France to avoid stopping and searching neutral shipping on the open seas, which might antagonize key neutrals. Denmark and Sweden controlled strategic access to the Baltic, while America might supply the Tsar with privateers. Despite their different traditions on maritime legal issues, Britain and France adopted a joint policy, although Britain explicitly retained the right to revert to the older tradition in the future.

Instead of using privateers, Graham relied on the greater efficacy of a steam-powered close blockade of the limited Russian coast to stop the export of Russian produce, unless the British wished it to be exported, and to prevent any war materiel reaching the country. However, Graham was also anxious not to weaken the blockade as a strategy for a future Anglo-French war that he believed to be inevitable. Russia was a declining export market, while most of the goods that came from Russia could be obtained from other suppliers; grain exports had already been prohibited by the Tsar. Thus, the policy was based on "Free Trade" concepts.

France did not share the free trade agenda, fearing the political consequences of a grain shortage. The French were astonished when the British allowed trade with the enemy, subject only to the blockade. However, despite reservations, the French accepted British blockade policy throughout the war. It provoked little comment, and no debate in Parliament. The Queen's Advocate, J.D. Harding, a man of distinctly old-fashioned views, regularly disagreed and raised objections to anything that smacked of novelty.

Flaws in the Allied blockade policy became apparent when the anticipated tight blockade was delayed, or in the case of the Black Sea, not imposed at all. Similarly, Russian ships were widely – and all too often fraudulently – transferred to other registries, denying the Navy a reasonable return by capturing enemy merchant shipping. To add to these problems, the French showed no interest in blockading, and protested against anything that did not comply with their very strict definitions of a blockade. Such differences on blockade were just a few of many which caused the Allies problems.[6]

Anticipating that Sevastopol would fall to a quick attack in September 1854, the British began to think about a "decisive" economic warfare strategy as the only maritime method open to them once the Russian coast had been cleared. Such ideas were quickly abandoned when the amphibious Grand Raid in the Crimea turned into a prolonged campaign of attrition. Instead, in 1855, the original policy was applied with additional rigor, loopholes were closed, and extra ships were provided to ensure the blockade was tight. The consular service was heavily involved, reporting on neutral shipping and contraband cargoes, targeting individual ships for the cruisers to inspect.

The fortunes of war turned against Russia toward the end of 1855, with the fall of Sevastopol and the growing threat to St Petersburg. In addition, the Austrian ultimatum put pressure on Prussia, which had been acting as a conduit for Russian trade. Finally, on 5 January 1856, the British explicitly warned Prussia that they would use naval force if necessary to halt this trade. Within days Prussia told Russia that it could no longer guarantee remaining neutral. This was significant because Prussia had done more to help Russia limit damage caused by the naval blockade than any other power.[7]

The System in Action: the Baltic Blockade

The Crimean War was sparked by Russian demands on Turkey, but it involved fighting from the Arctic to the Pacific. Initially, the main British naval effort was in the Baltic Sea. Their goal was to counter the large Russian Baltic fleet and put pressure on the government in St Petersburg to back down.

Vice-Admiral Sir Charles Napier's largely steam-powered force entered the Baltic in March 1854. Napier had a powerful battlefleet, but relatively few cruisers. Those he had were large steam frigates and sloops. From the start Napier had reminded his political master, Graham, that for Baltic operations shallow-draft vessels were essential, but his requests were ignored.[8] Napier's orders called for a naval blockade and investigation of the Russian defenses.[9] He had useful intelligence on the main Russian bases, the fleet and the larger ports, but very little on the northern section of the Gulf of Bothnia.

When Napier considered imposing a naval blockade, he was concerned that the serried and complex Finnish coastline would be an ideal haunt for gunboats. Shortages of local pilots made matters worse.[10] First of all he imposed a strict naval blockade to prevent the enemy's fleets and warships from getting to sea; during the Crimean War the Russian Fleet displayed no interest in putting to sea, but it still had to be watched. The Admiralty was especially anxious about the possible escape of Russian warships into the Baltic, or worse still into the North Sea, which would have been monumentally embarrassing for the ministers.

After entering the Baltic, Napier quickly moved east. By mid-April he had blockaded Libau, the Gulf of Riga, and the approaches to the Gulf of Finland.[11] After inspecting the Russian positions in the Gulf of Finland, Napier sent a squadron of four steamers into the Gulf of Bothnia in early May.[12] British cruiser captains attempted to capture merchant ships before settling down to the blockade.

One such officer was Captain Astley Cooper-Key, of the screw-propeller frigate HMS *Amphion*. Even before the war, Key was resigned to blockading, since the Russians would not come out to fight and had "but little trade to care for".[13] For much of the 1854 campaign Key commanded a three-ship force along a stretch of 160 miles around Riga and Libau. On 17 May, after a careful inspection, he anchored close to Libau, landed, and demanded the ships tied up in harbor. The local authorities were unable to resist.[14]

treatment of neutrals was reduced to printed statements, leaving officers with no doubts how to act.

In 1855, Key, still commanding *Amphion,* was stationed off Helsingfors [Helsinki] closing the coastal shipping route to hostile gunboats and any merchant vessels. He took a prominent part in the attack on the fortress of Sweaborg, but saw no commercial shipping.[21] By 1855, the only vessels attempting to pass the blockade were boats, since the key trade with Russia was through Prussia and Sweden.[22] British opinion was that the impact of the blockade could only be improved by raising the level of the war from limited to total. Had the war continued into 1856, the British intended to apply a more rigorous delineation of neutral and belligerent status to close the Prussian loophole, while Sweden was about to join the allies.

The blockade of the Gulf of Bothnia was extended north as additional cruisers became available and the southern coast was blockaded by 22 June.[23] The entire Gulf was blockaded by mid-July to stop the export of Russian produce to Sweden.[24] One officer reported that the blockade in the Gulf of Bothnia had driven up the price of tar in Sweden by over 50 percent. Ships that did test the cordon were usually seized. The British remained active in the Baltic until the weather worsened and the temperature fell. Soon the blockade could be left to the sea ice. By mid-November the British cruisers had left the Gulf of Bothnia and the Gulf of Finland.[25]

The Admiralty commended the officers and men involved in the second Baltic campaign for keeping up "a most effective blockade" and for "harassing the enemy's forces on shore". The blockade had been maintained "until the last moment when the cruisers were driven away by the early severity of the weather and the ports on the Finnish coast appeared to be closed in with ice".[26] In two seasons the British had conducted a highly professional campaign, charted and mastered a complex navigation, displayed remarkable restraint, translated command of the sea into a major attack on the Russian economy, and distracted Russians forces from the land campaigns.

The Black Sea Blockade

Unlike the British fleet in the Baltic, which opened the campaign alone and had no significant military force to support, the Black Sea fleet was permanently tied to a French fleet. It also supported the army, either in Bulgaria, or after September 1854 in the Crimea, where the demands for logistics, manpower, ammunition, and other support overrode all other concerns.

Vice-Admiral Sir James Dundas was ordered to impose a blockade, but found that his French colleague, Admiral Francois-Adolphe Hamelin, had no orders on this subject.[27] Neither fleet could spare ships to impose a tight blockade of the various Russian ports, while the French were not prepared to divert their resources into economic warfare. The only blockade to be declared was that of the Danube delta, and this merely

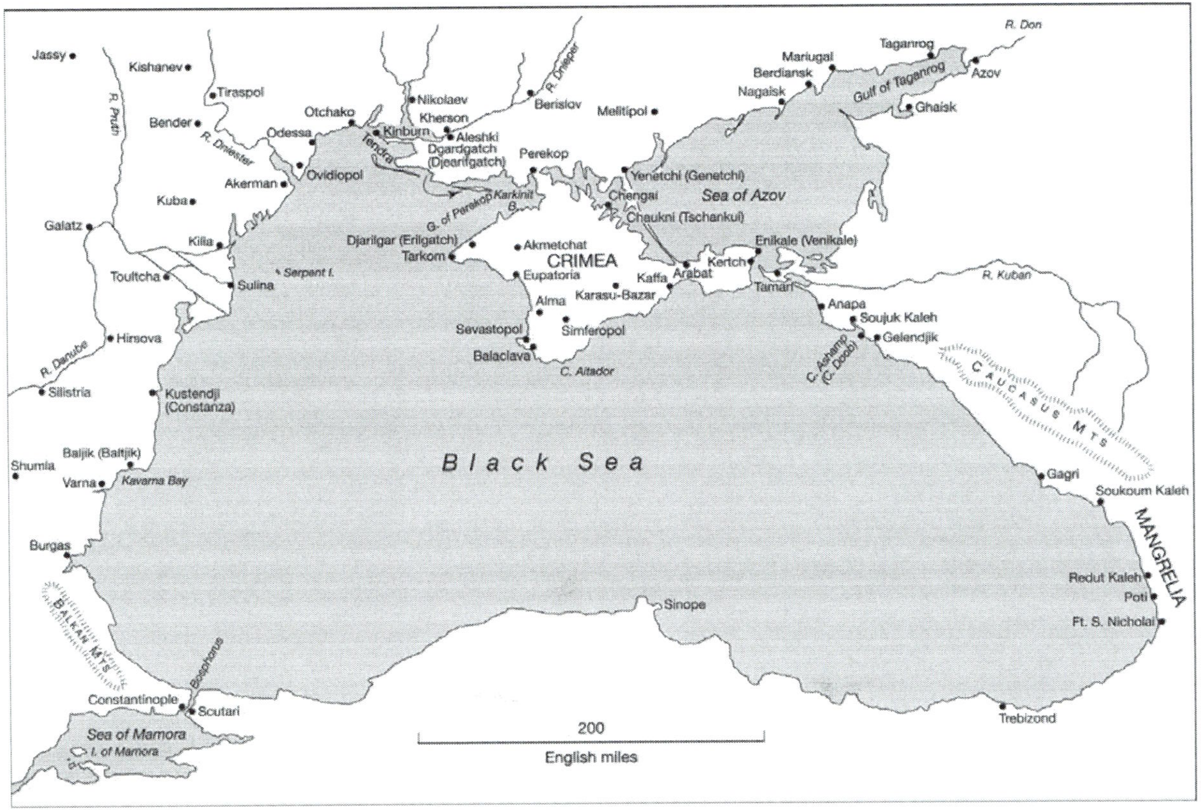

Map 5.2 The Black Sea theatre of operations

exploited the strategic necessity for cutting Russian supplies. Unable to find the ships to extend this system around the Russian coast, the two Admirals proposed to exploit the geography of the Euxine, by leaving the blockade to be imposed by Turkish ships in the Bosphorus. This was strikingly similar to the system adopted in World War I and World War II. However, it proved to be too audacious for Harding, who insisted on a formal declaration that specific locations had been placed under blockade on a particular day.[28]

In consequence, no blockade was imposed in 1854, even the strategic Danube blockade being relaxed when the armies moved to the Crimea. Dundas could only undertake to impose an effective blockade of "the whole Russian coast" after the Grand Raid on Sevastopol was over.[29] While Dundas grappled with the strategic and logistic demands of the Crimean campaign, merchants in London pressed the Admiralty for action, complaining that since no blockade had been imposed, Russian goods were undercutting supplies they had secured from alternative sources. By December the Admiralty, realizing that the French were not going to help, ordered Dundas to blockade such ports as he could on his own. Even that proved beyond his resources. Dundas and Hamelin were reduced to issuing a general notice of their intention to impose a blockade on 1 February 1855, by which time they would have handed over their commands.[30]

The Black Sea was not an important location for a blockade. Russian exports had been stopped, and any useful imports were clearly contraband, and could be seized at the Bosphorus. During the year the British captured 68 ships of a total of 2,343 tons, an average of only thirty-five tons apiece. These were small coasters, seized for carrying contraband.[31]

The Blockade's impact on Russia and Britain

The question of how far the blockade harmed Russia remains contentious. The Russian war effort was hampered throughout by the lack of modern weapons and machinery. The lack of coal was a serious problem, while industries that relied on bulky imports were crippled. However, the real weakness of Russia lay in her fiscal dependence on the regular, large exports of bulky primary produce such as timber, grain, and semi-finished iron to generate funds; by the 1850s, grain accounted for 35 percent of Russian exports, almost twice the figure of fifty years earlier.

The rapid decrease in wartime spending was linked to the collapse of import-based customs revenues. The astonishing campaign of destruction waged around the Sea of Azov against state-purchased supplies in 1855 did more damage than the blockade.[32] When imports were banned at the outbreak of war the loss of income only exacerbated a serious deficit problem. Russian state finances were already in deficit before the war, therefore interest rates were rising and the exchange rate of the ruble was falling. With state

Table 5.1 Russia: finance, revenue, and trade, 1853-57

	Expenditure (Million paper rubles)	Income (Total)	Income (Customs)	Income (Excise)	Income (Direct Tax)	Overall Trade Imp./Exp.	Grain Export (Thousand metric tons)	Trade with Britain Imp./Exp.	Trade with Germany Imp./Exp.
1853	313	220	28	82	48	2,556	102–148	28–66	22–16
1854	384	213	20	77	46	637	70.4–65.3	9–12	24–20
1855	526	209	18	81	47	145	72.7–39.5	1–0	43–18
1856	619	232	30	91	51	1,713	123–160	22–64	41–23
1857	348	241	36	92	55	1,770	152–170	39–72	38–22

Source: Brian R. Mitchell, *European Historical Statistics*. 2nd revised edn (London: Macmillan, 1980) 360, 511, 580, 610, 750, 735.

revenue meeting only one quarter of wartime expenditure, inflation was soon eroding the value of the paper ruble, ending the dream of convertibility and forcing the Russian government to print ever more paper.[33] This led to rampant inflation, which reached 38 percent.

When Tsar Alexander met his Crown Council in early 1856 to discuss the Austrian Ultimatum he was left in no doubt that, if the allies were joined by Austria, Sweden, and possibly Prussia, the blockade would become far more effective, inflicting long-term damage on the Russian state that would leave it weakened for decades.[34]

The war led to an 800-million ruble deficit. Heavy cuts in defense spending were essential to bolster the state's credit rating after 1856.[35] The banking system collapsed, and the exchange rate never recovered. As late as 1873, the Finance Minster argued: "the destruction of the monetary system, the insolvency and consequent liquidation of the banks, economic enfeeblement and the disarray of the finances were the consequences of the Crimean War ... our finances even now have not entirely recovered."[36]

It would be absurd to claim that a limited blockade of less than two years' duration against a continental empire with vast resources was "decisive". Russia was forced to concede defeat in the Crimean War by the failure of her armies, the increasing threat posed by the allied coalition – with Sweden and potentially Austria joining the belligerents in 1856 – the specific threat posed to St Petersburg by the Royal Navy, and the inability of the Russian state to wage modern war. Yet the impact of the blockade was steadily growing, gnawing away at the vital organs of the state, and in a longer war would have proved catastrophic. Russia could not obtain or manufacture adequate supplies of modern weapons, steam machinery, coal, and other vital stores. State revenues had collapsed, and food riots and related civil disorder were a growing distraction for the army. Because the allied demands did not pose a fundamental threat to the existence of the Russian state, the decision to accept peace was relatively easy.

By contrast the British escaped the worst effects of economic warfare, because they had access to global markets and undisputed command of the sea. Although war interrupted the supply of grain from Odessa, and poor harvests in 1854 and 1855 kept the price of wheat high, supplies from Turkey, Egypt, and Spain filled the gap. Interest rates remained low, because of the steady receipt of gold from Australia, which explains the Admiralty's concern to protect this traffic from privateering. Australian gold sustained the convertibility of paper money, and secured the British fiscal system throughout the war.[37] Alternative sources and smuggled goods kept the core trade open. As British trade with Russia was already in decline, the war merely accelerated the process.

Once the Russians agreed to begin peace negotiations, divergent views among the allies on the utility of the blockade quickly surfaced. By the end of March 1856 the French and Sardinians were anxious to secure Russian grain. Palmerston was prepared to sacrifice the commercial blockade, but wanted the naval blockade maintained until peace was signed.[38]

The Declaration of Paris

While the representatives of the powers were assembled at Paris, the issue of war at sea came under review, specifically the two most controversial areas of blockade and privateering. Initially the delegates intended to sign a resolution against privateering, but extended their discussions to cover blockades.[39] Having played a major role in forming British maritime warfare policy, British Foreign Secretary Earl Clarendon decided Britain could earn much international goodwill by renouncing the old arbitrary system. His action was prompted by an American circular to the maritime powers urging them to accept that a neutral flag should cover goods carried. This was clearly anti-British. Convinced the Americans would not renounce privateering, Clarendon outmaneuvered them. Prime Minister Lord Palmerston was pleased, stressing that if America did not sign Britain would be free to use the old rules against her in the event of war, stating: "of course such engagements would be binding only as between countries which might be parties to them".[40] He also ensured that the Declaration would be sent to all nations, inviting their adherence.[41]

Palmerston's deft approach left the United States almost entirely isolated, a major advantage of the new legal regime for Britain.[42] First Lord of the Admiralty Sir Charles Wood was cautious, but considered the bargain a good one.[43] Britain, France, Prussia, Sardinia, and Turkey signed the Declaration of Paris on 16 April 1856. As expected, the United States refused to sign any declaration against privateering.

The terms of the document were a codification of allied practice during the war, both an admission of its value in preserving good relations with neutrals, and a reflection of the efficiency of the steam blockade. The four clauses of the Declaration are often cited: "Privateering is, and remains abolished; The neutral flag covers enemy's goods, with the exception of contraband of war; Neutral goods, with the exception of contraband of war, are not liable to capture under enemy's flag; Blockades, in order to be binding, must be effective, that is to say, maintained by a force sufficient really to prevent access to the coast of the enemy." However, the text went on to say: "The present Declaration is not and shall not be binding, except between those powers who have acceded to it, or shall accede to it."[44] This was clearly intended to stop the Americans exploiting the Declaration in an Anglo-French war. Furthermore, as Clarendon stressed, the impact of the Declaration depended on the definition of contraband, which he ensured remained unsettled, so it could be drawn very widely in wartime.[45]

Opinion in Britain, both contemporary and historical, was predominantly hostile. Most considered that the Declaration removed the most formidable element of seapower from Britain's arsenal. This was wrong; in the French wars privateers made the greatest number of merchant ship captures and with steam they would become even more effective, as *Alabama* demonstrated ten years later. The essential point was that under

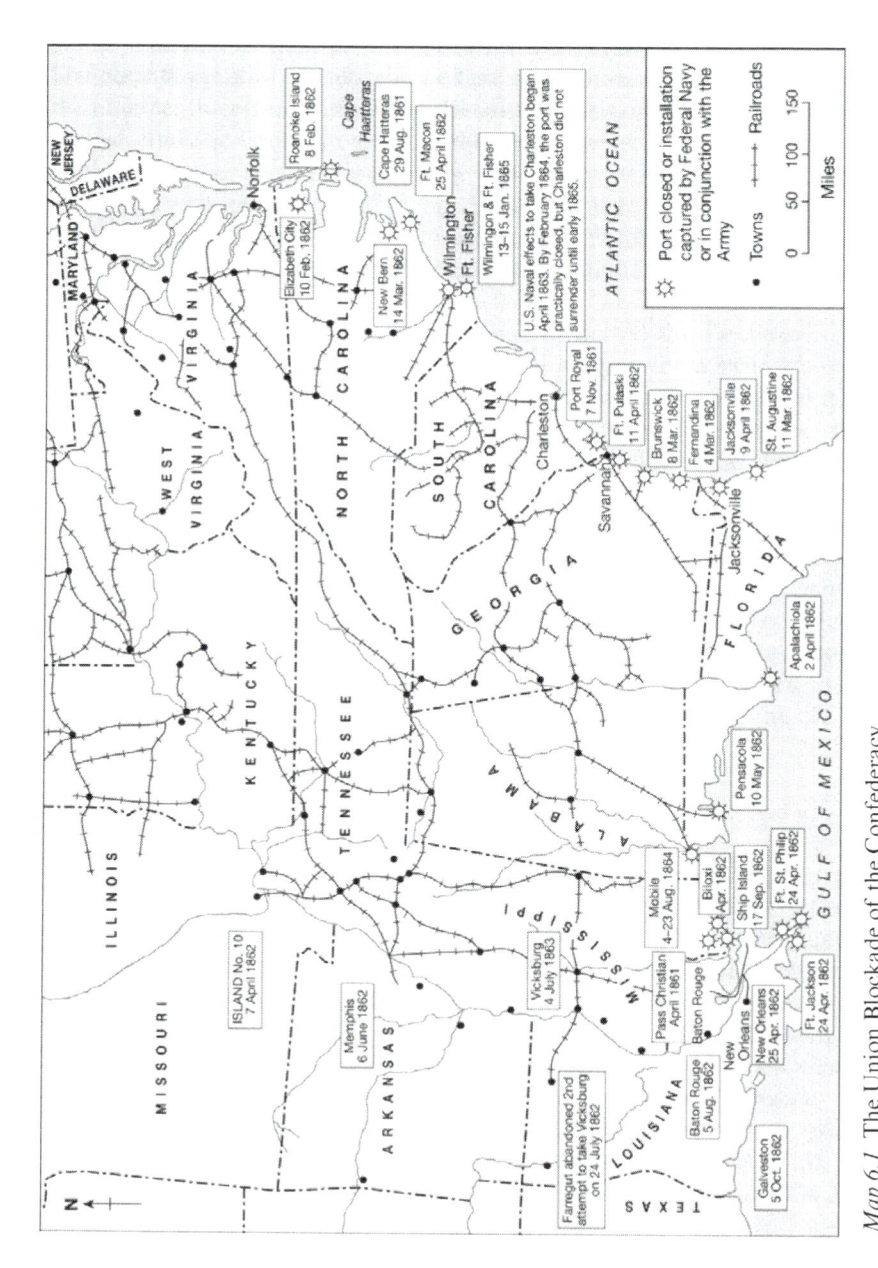

Map 6.1 The Union Blockade of the Confederacy

Roanoke Island
8 Feb. 1862

Cape
Hatteras

Cape Hatteras
29 Aug. 1861

Ft. Macon
25 April 1862

Elizabeth City
10 Feb. 1862

New Bern
14 Mar. 1862

Wilmington &
Ft. Fisher

Wilmington & Ft. Fisher
13–15 Jan. 1865

U.S. Naval efforts to take Charleston began
April 1863. By February 1864, the port was
practically closed, but Charleston did not
surrender until early 1865.

Port Royal
7 Nov. 1861

Ft. Pulaski
11 April 1862

Brunswick
8 Mar. 1862

Fernandina
4 Mar. 1862

Jacksonville
9 April 1862

St. Augustine
11 Mar. 1862

Apalachicola
2 April 1862

Pensacola
10 May 1862

Mobile
4–23 Aug. 1864

Biloxi
Apr. 1862

Ship Island
17 Sep. 1862

Ft. St. Philip
24 Apr. 1862

Pass Christian
April 1861

Baton Rouge
5 Aug. 1862

New
Orleans

New Orleans
25 Apr. 1862

Ft. Jackson
24 Apr. 1862

Galveston
5 Oct. 1862

ISLAND No. 10
7 April 1862

Memphis
6 June 1862

Vicksburg
4 July 1863

Farragut abandoned 2nd
attempt to take Vicksburg
on 24 July 1862

☆ Port closed or installation
    captured by Federal Navy
    or in conjunction with the
    Army

• Towns   +++ Railroads

0   50   100   150
        Miles

ATLANTIC OCEAN

GULF OF MEXICO

NEW JERSEY
DELAWARE
MARYLAND
WEST VIRGINIA
VIRGINIA
NORTH CAROLINA
SOUTH CAROLINA
GEORGIA
FLORIDA
ALABAMA
MISSISSIPPI
TENNESSEE
KENTUCKY
ILLINOIS
MISSOURI
ARKANSAS
LOUISIANA
TEXAS

Norfolk
Charleston
Savannah
Jacksonville
Baton Rouge

N

6 The Union Navy's Blockade Reconsidered

*David G. Surdam**

The Union Navy's blockade during the American Civil War (1861–65) possesses a blemished reputation, as it did not completely deprive the Confederacy of imports of food, arms, and munitions. According to Wise: "In terms of basic military necessities, the South imported at least 400,000 rifles, or more than 60% of the nation's modern arms. About 3 million pounds of lead came through the blockade, which by [General Josiah] Gorgas's estimate amounted to one-third of the Army's requirements. Besides these items, over 2,250,000 pounds of saltpeter, or two-thirds of this vital ingredient for powder, came from overseas. Without blockade running the [Confederate] nation's military would have been without proper supplies of arms, bullets, and powder."[1] Many other prominent scholars agree.[2]

However, the blockade's economic contributions to the war effort have been largely underestimated. Some of this arises from the focus on imports rather than exports, overlooking the fact that the antebellum South was the nation's primary export region, especially of cotton. The blockade severely reduced exports of staple products and thereby curtailed Southern purchasing power, as witnessed by the growing difference in price between raw cotton in the South and in England. William Seward, U.S. Secretary of State during the war, noted the three- and even four-fold price increases in Europe while prices stagnated, if not fell, in the South, leading him to conclude: "Judged by this test of results, I am satisfied that there was never a more effective blockade."[3]

The Union's naval blockade depended on attrition to exhaust gradually the Confederacy's ability to sustain its military. The blockade also dislocated the intraregional movement of goods, particularly fodder and meat. Finally, although arms and munitions were smuggled through the blockade, the inability to import bulky rail iron and iron plating contributed to the deterioration of Southern railroads and to delays in constructing Confederate ironclads. While not a "sufficient condition" for victory, therefore, the Union blockade may have been a "necessary" one.

The Movement of Goods in the Antebellum Economy

In the years before the war, Southern ports were leading exporters of U.S. domestic produce. Although New York was the largest, New Orleans,

Table 6.1 Value of domestic exports from leading Southern ports (year ending 30 June 1860)

Port	Total Value ($)	Raw Cotton Total Value ($)
New Orleans	107,812,580	96,166,118
Mobile	38,670,183	38,533,042
Charleston	21,179,350	19,633,295
Savannah	18,351,554	17,809,127
Texas	5,772,158	5,744,981
Richmond	5,098,720	41,483
Wilmington	650,092	–
Key West	580,165	401,919
Norfolk	479,885	14,783

Source: U.S. Department of the Treasury, 1860, pp. 317 and 350.

Mobile, Charleston, and Savannah ranked second through fifth, respectively. New Orleans handled about 90 percent of the value of New York's domestic exports, while the other three Southern ports easily outranked Boston (the sixth-largest exporter). Richmond and Texas ports were also significant export centers, rivaling Philadelphia in terms of value.[4]

New Orleans was the great Southern trade center, dwarfing all the remaining Southern ports; indeed, the value of its domestic exports was more than those of the remaining Southern ports combined. The antebellum South exported primarily staple products, with New Orleans exporting almost half of the South's raw cotton (see Table 6.1).

Direct Southern imports of foreign goods were relatively small. The region's imports ($30 million) were only one-seventh the value of its exports. However, this ratio understates the Southern importation of foreign goods, many of which initially arrived in Northern ports. Still, an examination of direct Southern imports is illuminating. In terms of value of foreign imports, New Orleans took in over five-sixths of the Southern ports' total value; what wartime officials would later characterize as luxuries constituted a significant share of the imports. Southerners imported large quantities of manufactured iron and steel, the bulk of it railroad iron (almost $2,000,000). Tin imports were valued at $460,000. Southern ports imported no saltpeter prior to the war, and only a handful of guns.[5]

In most manufacturing categories, the Southern states produced less than 10 percent of the value of the total U.S. production (see Table 6.2). The South's production of woollen goods, men's clothing, boots, and shoes were each less than 5 % of total national output; the region's production of cotton goods and leather was only slightly more than 5 %. The Southern states built 84 of the nation's 1,071 vessels, including forty-five of the 264 steamers, with Virginia, North Carolina, and Louisiana building the most. Southern output of railroad iron (12,180 tons) was about 5 % of the national figure. All of the railroad car wheels were produced by Northern firms, as were all but nineteen of 470 loco-

Table 6.2 Value of U.S. manufacturing production

	Confederate	*Total U.S.*
Agricultural implements	$1,018,913	$17,597,960
Scythes	$0	$ 552,753
Shovels, spades, forks, hoes	$0	$1,638,876
Boots, shoes	$3,973,313	$91,889,298
Cotton goods	$8,072,067	$107,337,783
Firearms	$72,652	$2,362,681
Flour and meal	$37,996,470	$248,580,365
Bar, sheet, railroad iron	$2,449,569	$31,888,705
Bar (tons)	14,072	227,682
Rail (tons)	12,180	235,107
Boiler plate (tons)	–	30,895
Car wheels (railroad)	$0	$2,083,350
Locomotive engines	$133,000	$4,866,900
Engines (number)	19	470
Machinery, steam engines	$5,750,650	$46,757,486
Pig iron	$953,903	$20,870,120
(tons)	36,790	987,559
Men's clothing	$2,573,045	$80,830,555
Provisions	$145,000	$31,986,433
Salt	$451,484	$2,289,504
Ship and boatbuilding	$772,870	$11,667,661
Wagons	$1,381,887	$8,703,937
Woollen goods	$1,995,324	$61,895,217

Source: U.S. Bureau of the Census, *Eighth Census of the United States–Manufacturing*, 1865, clxxvii–clxxxvi, 715–18, and 733–42 (data from 1860).

motive engines. The South produced less than 4 % of the pig iron (36,790 tons). The region also lagged in producing machinery, steam engines, and guns.[6]

Thus, the South needed to import boots and shoes, clothing, heavy manufactures, arms, munitions, and railroad supplies. A railroad official estimated that almost 50,000 tons of rails were needed annually just to *maintain* the Southern railroads and that existing iron mills in the South were capable of supplying less than half of this. Indeed, during the antebellum era Southern railroads had imported the bulk of their railroad iron from Europe; in some years, these imports amounted to 65,000 tons.[7]

However, the South was not entirely bereft of the heavy industry needed to supply its railroads and new navy. The Tredegar Iron Works, near Richmond, Virginia, was a major iron producer. The company had experience in producing naval ordnance, but the Confederate states were destined to be short of iron for armor plating and rails.[8] The Confederate secretary of the navy, Stephen Mallory, sent a naval officer to Tennessee and Georgia to see whether rolling mills there could produce the requisite iron plating, but this officer reported in late May 1861 that the mills south of Kentucky were unable to roll iron of the desired thickness.[9] In addition, the seceding states could not manufacture the large engines and boilers necessary for ironclad warships. The Confederacy's inability to roll iron plating of sufficient thickness or to produce propulsion machinery would not have been severe drawbacks had the Confederate navy enjoyed easy access to British production, which the Union blockade precluded.

The antebellum South also required considerable intra- and interregional movement of foodstuffs. Large quantities of Northern packed meat were shipped down the Mississippi River to New Orleans for consumption there or for reshipment to river towns and Gulf ports. In addition, New Orleans received over 50,000 head of cattle per annum from "Western" and Texas sources; antebellum trans-Gulf shipments of Texas cattle represented a potential solution to the South's meat supply problem.[10] In addition, in the absence of an effective blockade, foreign and even Northern producers could have alleviated any potential shortages of meat.

As for grain, most of the grain shipped along the Atlantic seaboard went by sailing vessels. In addition, much of the wheat received internally at Richmond arrived via river and canal; railroads typically were not the main carriers of foodstuffs. A similar situation occurred in the Mississippi valley. Loss of water transportation, whether through blockade or nonintercourse, would force an overreliance upon rail and wagon transportation, which were simply inadequate to do the job.

Supplying cavalry, artillery, and transport animals with adequate fodder was potentially a greater problem than supplying humans with food. When an army was on the march its animals might find adequate grazing along the way; however, a stationary force would rapidly deplete available forage. The Confederate states were not large producers of hay, so the region imported it; New Orleans imported 25,000 tons in 1859–1860. Virginia produced the most hay in the Confederacy, but that state itself imported hay from other states, with Richmond receiving over 12,500 tons of hay from coastwise shipments in the three years prior to the Civil War. Without coastal trade, the difficulty of collecting adequate amounts of fodder and transporting it by rail proved insurmountable during the Civil War.

The Blockade's Effects upon the Confederate War Effort

Southern revenues from exporting raw cotton, tobacco, rice, and other staple products dropped precipitously during the war. Table 6.3 shows trade decreases at New Orleans: even with the resumption of trade at that port in mid-1862 the port's exports plunged. Mobile and Savannah suffered even greater relative declines in export revenue, as very few blockade runners left those ports during the war. Charleston and Galveston probably had decreased export revenues too. Of the remaining ports, Wilmington, North Carolina, and the Rio Grande towns had greater export revenues during the war, but these fell far short of offsetting the decline in export revenues of other Southern ports.

Table 6.3 Volume and value of receipts received at New Orleans from the interior

Year	Cotton	Sugar	Molasses	Tobacco	Value ($)
1856–57	1,573,247	43,463	84,169	58,928	158,061,000
1857–58	1,678,616	202,783	339,343	90,147	167,156,000
1858–59	1,774,298	257,225	353,715	85,133	172,953,000
1859–60	2,255,448	195,185	313,840	95,499	185,211,000
1860–61	1,849,312	174,637	313,260	43,756	155,864,000
1861–62	38,880	225,356	401,404	7,429	51,511,000
1862–63	22,078	85,531	202,616	4,774	29,766,000
1863–64	131,044	75,173	143,460	15,547	79,234,000
1864–65	271,015	9,345	18,725	16,346	111,013,000

Source: *New Orleans Price Current*, "Annual Reports".

Notes:

Year: 1 September through 31 August

Cotton: in bales

Sugar: in hogsheads

Molasses: in barrels

Tobacco: in hogsheads and bales

Value: value of all receipts received from interior

New Orleans surrendered to Farragut's forces in May 1862; the capture of Vicksburg opened the entire Mississippi River to Union commerce in July 1863.

Although the informal Confederate-imposed embargo on raw cotton exports initially reduced export revenues, the Union blockade was the main problem. Southern planters produced some 6 million bales of cotton during the war. Large amounts of raw cotton were stored in Alabama until near the war's end. Shipping the cotton to blockade-running ports and then through the blockade was so difficult that neither the Confederate government nor the planters were able to market much of their cotton.[11] During the war the South exported perhaps 1.5–1.9 million bales of raw cotton, much of which was traded across the lines with Yankees. This volume of exports was roughly one-ninth the antebellum volume.

The Southerners would have had to receive nine times the antebellum price per bale of raw cotton for export revenues not to have been adversely affected during the war. Unfortunately for the Southerners, real prices of raw cotton only trebled or quadrupled, so total export revenues tumbled. A conservative estimate of the revenue shortfall is $500 million during the four years of the war; if, as has been estimated, the real cost of the war to Southerners was $1.1 billion, the revenue shortfall from the Union's efforts to block exports of raw cotton was significant, perhaps equaling half of the South's war costs.[12]

Furthermore, the nonintercourse acts and the Northern blockade of the mouth of the Mississippi River and of Mobile wrecked the regional economy.

Cotton growers in Mississippi, Louisiana, Arkansas, and western Alabama faced unattractive alternatives: they could try to ship cotton by wagon and rail to eastern ports, by river and wagon to Texas ports or even to the Rio Grande, or store the cotton on the plantation, subject to deterioration, burning, confiscation, and theft. In 1861, sending raw cotton from Memphis to Norfolk and on to Liverpool would cost roughly $12 per 500-pound bale, while sending it from Memphis to Liverpool via New Orleans cost only $8.25 per bale[13] The Union blockade of Galveston, Texas, caused desperate growers to resort to a 200-mile wagon haul to the Rio Grande, where their cotton faced Mexican duties and dilatory loading aboard cargo ships.

Revenue shortfalls contributed to the Confederacy's chronic lack of purchasing power. Purchases of foreign-produced arms, munitions, food, iron plating for warships, machinery, and other war materiel were delayed while the Confederate and state governments scraped together funds. Of course, such purchasing-power deficiencies were part of a larger failure by the Confederate government adequately to finance the war; government purchases of domestic produce were also often delayed for lack of funds.

The rising cost of importing goods also contributed to the Confederate government's problem. Although it imported enough war materiel to keep the troops fighting, the blockade raised the cost of such supplies through higher shipping costs and actual losses and captures of vessels conveying the Confederate purchases. The Confederate secretary of the treasury, George Trenholm, described the expense of importing goods via private blockade runners:

> The Collie contract [between a British firm and the Confederate government] alone will furnish supplies to the extent of £200,000, and this amount and all others of like character should be deducted from the estimates. Two steamers under this contract have already arrived. By the terms of this agreement 50 per cent. is to be added to the value of the goods, so that the sum to be allowed for these supplies in reduction of the estimates is in fact £300,000. And as payment is to be made in cotton at 6 pence, it will require 30,000 bales of cotton for this single contract. As 5,000 bales at present prices in England would have yielded £200,000, this unfortunate arrangement entails a positive loss of 25,000 bales of cotton, and places in a conspicuous point of view the necessity that existed for abandoning this mode of obtaining supplies.[14]

Chief of Ordnance Brigadier-General Josiah Gorgas, equally frustrated, lamented that "a large proportion of [his purchasing agent's] purchases have fallen into the hands of the enemy."[15]

Despite these disadvantages, imports were the main source of small arms for the Confederacy, as the Southerners were able to manufacture only modest numbers of these weapons. It is estimated that the South imported the majority of its total arsenal of shoulder-fired arms. The Confederacy also needed to import nitre, as it had been unable to stockpile enough from British India before the Union blockade tightened. Although some nitre seeped through the blockade, the Confederacy was forced to establish a Nitre Bureau in early 1862; the bureau succeeded in providing the South with minimal levels of the chemical, but the cost was very high, perhaps five times as high as the market price in Britain.[16] Iron was also imported in bundles, plates, and sheets, especially after 1863. Cartridges and ammunition were imported until 1863, but the traffic fell off in 1864.[17]

Since blockade running was so expensive, some Confederate leaders urged Jefferson Davis to promote interbelligerent trading – that is, with the North. Davis never reconciled himself to the necessity of such trade, unlike some of his secretaries of war. One of them, George Randolph, advised Davis that the Confederate government could legally trade with Northerners; indeed, he argued, such trade was necessary to sustain the Confederate army.[18]

Transportation Problems

The antebellum Southern transportation system was designed to drain goods toward such ports as New Orleans, Richmond, Norfolk, Charleston, Savannah, and Wilmington. It was not meant to ship them across the South. Indeed, the provincial nature of the system was quite marked. Therefore, the antebellum Southern railroads were a fragile foundation upon which to rest the Confederate logistical needs. Many of the Southern railroads were primarily intended to ship cotton to navigable rivers and seaports, or to protect local commercial interests. The system suffered from differing gauges, incomplete linkages between lines in major cities, critical gaps in the east–west rail lines, and dependence upon Northern and foreign suppliers. Even if these deficiencies had been remedied, the Southern railroads' ability to meet a significant increase in demand would have been dubious: almost all were single-tracked, as the antebellum volume of traffic had not warranted the expense of double trackage. One official reckoned that a double-tracked line could handle up to five times the volume of a single-track railroad.[19]

The Southern railroads' deficiencies were unlikely to improve during wartime. An effective blockade coupled with the nonintercourse acts forced Southern railroads to rely upon domestically produced railroad supplies. Collectively, the Union blockade, the nonintercourse acts, and the necessary rearrangement of intraregional movements of goods to supply new concentrations of men and animals in armies and in Richmond were to increase the demands on rail services dramatically. Clearly, the Southern railroads were inadequate conduits for the mass of war materiel and foodstuffs required to sustain the Confederate armies and the burgeoning population of Richmond as well as other urban centers. The Confederate government attempted to improve the railroad system by filling in some of the gaps between lines; the Piedmont Railroad was the most important upgrade. These improvements, however, were delayed by shortages of rail iron and other supplies.

The Southern railroads were hard pressed just to maintain themselves, since domestic resources were woefully insufficient for improving the existing lines. However, in the absence of an effective blockade, Southern railroads might have easily purchased and shipped the requisite material from Europe and perhaps even from the North. Southern railroads attempted to import railroad iron and supplies through the blockade, but with limited success. With the growing stringency of the Union blockade, blockade runners naturally preferred to bring in small-volume, high-value commodities, not bulky iron rails and railroad equipment. The railroads decided in January 1862 to press the Confederate government for help in importing supplies, but it refused. Eventually the Confederate War Department assisted some Virginia railroads in obtaining supplies from England, but such instances were rare. Some companies used cotton exports as a basis for purchasing supplies to be smuggled through the blockade. However, such efforts netted trivial amounts. As a sop to the railroads, the Confederate government rescinded its duty upon railroad iron and other supplies.[20]

In addition to their physical shortages of equipment, many Southern railroads faced financial difficulties. The initial uncertainty triggered by secession, the imposition of an informal embargo on exports of raw cotton, and eventually the Union naval blockade, combined to disrupt the normal flow of raw cotton to the ports, so receipts from shipping private freight plummeted. Thus, many railroads found themselves in financial trouble early in the war, impeding their ability to maintain themselves. The government's policy of paying below-market freight rates exacerbated the railroads' situation.

Water transportation also loomed large in the Southern economy. For moving bulky goods any considerable distance, water transportation was more efficient: "Although the railroads ... were primitive by modern standards, they enabled armies far from water transport to supply themselves. Yet the slow, short trains, which carried 10 to 15 tons of cargo per car, were less efficient than large river steamers, which could carry 500 tons of cargo. A river could easily carry more steamers than a rail line could trains, a factor counterbalancing the higher speed of locomotives. Sabotage or destruction by raiders could disable railroad tracks far more easily than it could harm steamers in a river."[21] The Mississippi River was certainly the most important artery in the Southern transportation system, while other rivers and canals conveyed upland produce to ports. Coastwise movement of goods was also important, from Texas cattle shipped across the Gulf to bulky grainstuffs moved along the Atlantic coast. The Union blockade interfered with much of this coastal trade.

As the war continued, the Southern railroads' carrying capacity dwindled significantly. Assistant Adjutant-General [of Railroads] William Wadley issued a gloomy report on the condition of Southern railroads in April 1863, estimating freight capacity for thirty-four of the key lines. Fourteen were able to run only one train in each direction per day, or fewer, and none of the lines was able to send more than three trains in each direction per day. The daily tonnage capacity was equally distressing.[22] Unfortunately for the Confederacy, the dwindling carrying capacity of Southern railroads coincided with growing burdens on rail shipment due to wartime and blockade-induced changes in shipping patterns. The loss of Gulf and Atlantic coastal shipping and the interruption of inland traffic on the Mississippi River and Chesapeake Bay merely compounded the demand for rail service.

Conclusions

The Union Navy's control of the American waters had three main economic effects: denying the Confederacy the badly needed purchasing power that exporting its staple products would have generated; raising the costs and reducing the volume of imported goods; and dislocating intraregional trade. While it would be too much to claim that the Union naval superiority alone tilted the scale against the Confederacy, these factors suggest that without its superior naval power the North would have faced much greater and perhaps insuperable difficulties in subduing the South.

A final strategic effect of the Union blockade on the Confederate war effort was that, in the process of enforcing it, the Union navy helped stunt the embryonic Confederate navy. By blockading the mouth of the Mississippi River, the Union forced the New Orleans shipbuilders to bring iron and machinery they needed from Virginia and the eastern Confederacy by rail. The rickety Southern railroads were inadequate to transport these vital materials. Completion of the CSS *Mississippi* was delayed while a Richmond firm shipped the propeller shaft (recovered from a vessel that had been burned) across the Confederacy to New Orleans, and while railroad iron was collected for the ship's armor. As a result, this vessel was not completed in time to contest Farragut's attack on New Orleans and was later destroyed to prevent its capture.[23]

Since Southern manufacturers lacked sufficient raw material, skilled labor, and in some cases the ability to produce machinery and armor for warships, the strategic necessity for a rapid build-up of ironclad vessels entailed imports from England and France. Indeed, a Confederate naval officer, James Bulloch, advised the secretary of the navy, Stephen Mallory, that instead of concentrating on buying European-built warships and risking violation of neutrality laws, the Confederacy should import the iron plates, rivets, bolts, and other supplies needed to construct the warships in Southern ports.[24] Clearly, the Union blockade thwarted any such possibility, since blockade runners were hesitant to ship those bulky and relatively low-value items.

Finally, the Union Navy's capture of New Orleans and Memphis, as well as the reoccupation of Norfolk, eliminated key Confederate shipbuilding centers. Therefore, when viewed as a deterrent, the Union blockade proved crucial in protecting the Northern navy against a Southern fleet. If the Union had never adopted the blockade, or if it had proved to be a weak blockade, this would have significantly eased the Confederacy's difficulties in constructing or obtaining a naval force to sweep away the blockaders and to attack the North.

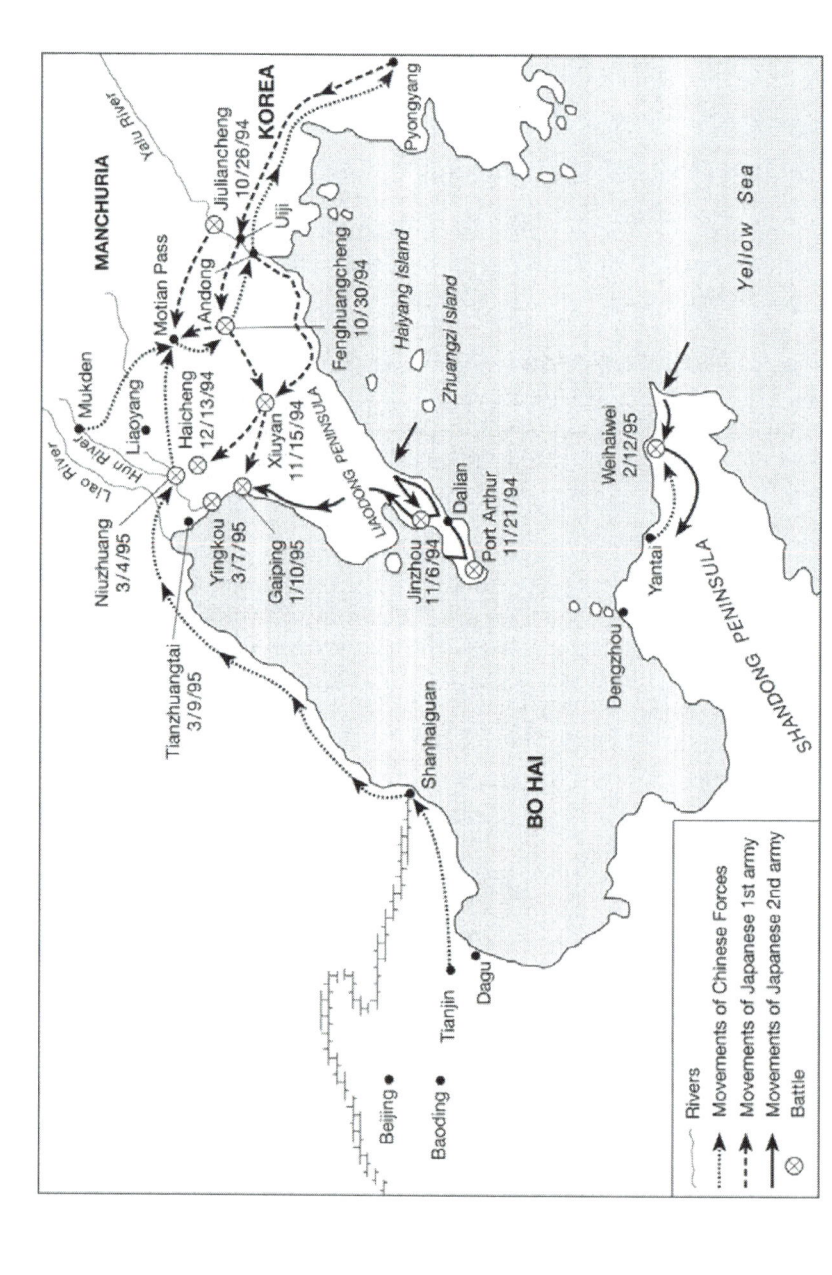

MANCHURIA

KOREA

Yalu River

Pyongyang

Jiulancheng
10/26/94

Uiji

Andong

Motian Pass

Fenghuangcheng
10/30/94

Haiyang Island

Zhuangzi Island

Mukden

Liaoyang

Haicheng
12/13/94

Xiuyan
11/15/94

LIAODONG PENINSULA

Liao River

Hun River

Niuzhuang
3/4/95

Yingkou
3/7/95

Gaiping
1/10/95

Jinzhou
11/6/94

Dalian

Port Arthur
11/21/94

Tianzhuangtai
3/9/95

Shanhaiguan

Weihaiwei
2/12/95

Yantai

Dengzhou

SHANDONG PENINSULA

Yellow Sea

BO HAI

Beijing

Baoding

Tianjin

Dagu

Rivers

Movements of Chinese Forces

Movements of Japanese 1st army

Movements of Japanese 2nd army

⊗ Battle

Map 7.1 The Sino-Japanese war, 1894–5

7 The First Sino-Japanese War

Japanese Destruction of the Beiyang Fleet, 1894–95

*S. C. M. Paine**

The Japanese blockade of Weihaiwei and the destruction of the Beiyang Fleet anchored inside was the final major battle of the first Sino-Japanese War. Japan and China had both responded to increasing political instability in Korea by intervening militarily. China came at the invitation of the Korean king with the intent to retain its traditional suzerain-tributary relationship, while Japan came bent on war with the intent to prevent Russian annexation of the Korean Peninsula, foreshadowed by the construction of the Trans-Siberian Railway, announced in 1891. This war began a half century of Sino-Japanese rivalry for empire in north-east Asia.

In mid-September 1894 the Japanese seized and retained the initiative at sea with the Battle of the Yalu, and also rapidly took control of the entire Korean Peninsula with the Battle of Pyongyang. Afterward, the Beiyang Fleet, the modern part of China's navy, made avoiding the loss of ships its top priority.[1] Throughout the war the orders to Admiral Ding Ruchang, the commander of the fleet, remained to defend the coast of the Bo Hai from Weihaiwei to the Yalu River – in other words, to protect Beijing and the Manchu government ensconced there. This strategy wasted the Beiyang Fleet on convoy duty instead of interrupting the transport of Japanese troops to the theater.[2]

The second pair of key battles occurred over the winter of 1894–95. In November the state-of-the-art naval refitting facilities and fortress of Port Arthur (Lüshun) fell to the Japanese army with little fighting. This gave Japan the northern approaches to Beijing, while control of Weihaiwei would give it the southern approaches, allowing a pincer movement on the capital. After taking Port Arthur, the First Army would continue the land campaign in Manchuria to clear the way to Beijing, while the Second Army attacked the home base of the Beiyang Fleet at Weihaiwei. If successful, the Japanese forces would obliterate the Chinese navy and have Beijing at their mercy.

Background

Right after the war, the U.S. secretary of the navy, Hilary A. Herbert, provided his analysis: given the well-known and endemic weaknesses of the

Chinese army, "China had in this war a chance, and only one chance to win, and that lay in her fleet."[3] Although the Beiyang Fleet had arrived at Port Arthur early in November 1894, it soon received orders to return to Weihaiwei. As a result, it did not participate in the defense of China's only facilities capable of refitting severely damaged ships. Worse yet, on the return to Weihaiwei, the *Zhenyuan*, one of China's two large German-made battleships for which Japan had no counterpart, was damaged while navigating the entrance to Weihaiwei harbor. In the absence of docking facilities – those at Port Arthur were under imminent attack – the ship had to be beached, rendering it useless for the remainder of the war.

Before the Battle of Port Arthur, Colonel J.F. Maurice, commander of the British Royal Artillery at Colchester, argued that "a comparatively small Chinese naval force could make it very difficult for the Japanese to transport large quantities of troops to the Asian mainland."[4] Yet Admiral Ding did nothing to impede the Japanese troop build-up in preparation for the assault on Port Arthur. The editors of *The Japan Weekly Mail* were dumbfounded: "... Port Arthur alone is not invested. The Japanese are holding the entrance to Pechili [Bo Hai] Gulf ... Yet despite its easy accessibility for purposes of relief, and despite the crippling consequences involved in its capture, the Chinese seem resolved to leave it to its fate."[5]

It was incomprehensible to foreigners how China could possess a modern fleet but not use it to prevent Japan from supplying its forces. The sea lanes were the lifeline for the Japanese military, yet "ordinary unarmed merchantmen, have been regularly plying to and fro without any escort, and they could have been waylaid and sent to the bottom time after time had China but risen to the occasion," wrote a reporter for *The North-China Herald*.[6] "The movements of the Chinese fleet have throughout the war been ... utterly and incomprehensibly imbecile ... [T]he Chinese fleet has not attempted to meet the Japanese fleet in the open sea, or weighed a single anchor to hinder and debar the unprotected transports of Japan passing to and fro with their freight of eager invaders."[7]

With the best of the Chinese army destroyed in Korea, the Chinese navy offered an essential means to defend Beijing.[8] But it could do so only if it engaged the enemy. To seize this chance required aggressive use of its warships. Instead, China transported troops to Korea, the battlefield Japan had chosen, even though Japan had shorter sea lines and three times the transports that China did. This resulted in China's defeat at Pyongyang and the loss of Port Arthur.

The Blockade of Weihaiwei

The primary Japanese objective after the fall of Port Arthur was the great naval base at Weihaiwei. In January 1895, as the march through Manchuria, the northern part of the pincer toward Beijing, slowly progressed, the Japanese divided the Second Army. In the third week of January the entire

Second Division and most of the Sixth Division, both under the command of Marshal Iwao Ōyama, would be redeployed across the Yellow Sea to Shandong Province in preparation for the attack on Weihaiwei.[9] Because the Japanese were deciphering China's telegram traffic, they were well aware that little attempt had been made to defend the Shandong coastline, but only the city of Weihaiwei.[10]

Whereas at Port Arthur the goal had been the capture and retention of the naval facilities, at Weihaiwei the goal would be the destruction of the fleet. This would leave China hobbled after the war so that the Japanese navy could dominate the Far East.[11] Japanese military successes had demonstrated the importance of seapower. Without command of the sea, Japan could not have deployed its troops at will. A key objective became the long-term neutralization of Chinese seapower.

The move on Weihaiwei began with a diversionary bombardment of the town of Dengzhou on 18–19 January 1895. Dengzhou was located to the west of Yantai (Chefoo), which in turn was located to the west of Weihaiwei. The Japanese planned to divert Chinese attention westward while the actual landing point for Japanese troops was thirty miles to the east of Weihaiwei, at the easternmost tip of the Shandong Peninsula at Rongcheng. Japanese troops left Dalian between 19 and 22 January, landing unopposed between 20 and 23 January. On 26 January, the army divided into two parts and headed westward toward Weihaiwei, one part by the coastal road and the other by a parallel road about four miles inland. The Japanese ushered in the Chinese lunar New Year, traditionally a day of celebrations and sacrifices to ensure luck in the following year, with an attack on Weihaiwei.[12]

Weihaiwei had three categories of defense: those on the two harbour islands, those on the mainland overlooking the north-western entrance to the harbour, and those overlooking the south-eastern entrance. The fortifications were equipped with the best artillery available and should have been extremely difficult to take. The Chinese had closed the harbour to unwelcome visitors, while the Japanese had laid contact torpedoes and maintained a naval patrol outside to prevent any exits. This left the Beiyang Fleet bottled up inside in the midst of a bitterly cold blizzard.[13]

The Japanese launched a three-pronged joint attack on 30 January 1895, and soon took the main forts to the south and east of Weihaiwei. The next day they attacked the forts in the immediate vicinity of the city. The Beiyang Fleet had responded by training its guns on the invaders. The morale of the Chinese troops shattered. When the Japanese entered the town of Weihaiwei on 2 February, they found the remaining garrisons abandoned. Admiral Ding had succeeded in having only a few of the forts surrounding the harbor destroyed before they fell on 2 February; because the army had fled, this left the navy alone to defend Weihaiwei. The Japanese soon trained the repairable guns on the remaining Chinese positions and on the fleet stuck in the harbor.

On the night of 4 February, the Japanese successfully removed the booms blocking the entrances to the harbor. Two squadrons of torpedo-boats entered

With the advantage of twenty-twenty hindsight, it seems obvious over a century after the war that, with the fall of Port Arthur, China was already finished and should have agreed to peace negotiations. Yet many high-ranking members of the Chinese government did not believe such a turn of events to be possible. The despised Japanese could not bring China to her knees. It was a logical and physical impossibility. It violated such fundamental beliefs about the natural order that these persons, who were by no means few in number, continued to be convinced that China would crush Japan in the end. Over a century later, such thinking seems delusional. But these people believed that they had 5,000 years of uninterrupted Chinese history in support of their views. Surely this world was immutable. How could it be overturned in the space of a few months?

On the eve of the attack on Weihaiwei, Wu Dacheng, president of the Board of War and governor of Hunan, had made an official proclamation to the Japanese. He had grandly offered them a chance to surrender, noting that he was "of a charitable state of mind" and so could not bear to see Japanese troops "going to destruction before my fresh battalions in this severe cold."[32] Wu was an outstanding scholar who was famous among educated Chinese for his views that China could bring Japan to her knees.

One can only speculate that such a proclamation must have confirmed Japanese intentions to humble China once and for all. At about the same time, Reuters News Agency reported that the Japanese "Diet unanimously passed a resolution that they consider the objects of the war yet unattained, and are prepared to grant whatever amounts are necessary for military expenses to establish the country's prestige, and adopted this resolution with the express intention of making the country's sentiments generally known."[33] Wu was given enough rope to hang himself when, after Weihaiwei, he was put in command of the Hunan and Hubei Armies, which were promptly trounced in their first engagement under his brief command.

Although the Li Hongzhang faction remained in power if not always in official capacity, its position was being steadily eroded by the relentless assault of those still living in the past. They blamed their country's greatest modernizer for betraying China, citing her uninterrupted string of military defeats as proof. They believed that China's vast superiority in population should deliver victory. True, if the population had been united. But China's population divided along the lines of provincial loyalties, Han–Manchu ethnicity, and civil–military divisions. While the age of nationalism had arrived in Japan, it would not flower in China for another half century. People remained wedded to their village, considering the war a problem of North China and the Qing or Manchu dynasty. Manchu or Japanese rule were both foreign from the point of view of the Han who constituted the vast majority of both the population and the military conscripts. The Han denigrated military service and often did not even deign to pay their soldiers. Under these circumstances, why fight? The Manchus could not afford a protracted war lest the Han coalesce around overthrowing the dynasty whose incompetence defied concealment.

Westerners also could not understand the Chinese naval strategy. They wondered why Admiral Ding had refused to vacate Weihaiwei before the Japanese had cut off his retreat. If the Chinese had been unable to flee the harbor, the boats should have been sunk "rather than allowed to fall bodily into the enemy's hands."[34] This is what happened. China's loss became a direct contribution to Japanese naval expansion. The Japanese netted four warships and six gunboats.

Unknown to the outside world, Admiral Ding had tried to scuttle his boats at the very end, but by that time his crews had mutinied and refused to carry out the order.[35] He had also ordered that the mainland forts be dismantled, but was overruled by a Chinese general who "declined the responsibility, declaring it might cost him his head."[36] The general's decision simply reflected a reward system that prevented officers from altering plans to meet changed circumstances and a punishment system that sought individual scapegoats to blame for systemic problems. The Qing legal code mandated decapitation for the destruction of twenty firearms or more.[37] One can only speculate on the punishment for scuttling an expensive imported battleship or for dynamiting a gun emplacement housing an imported artillery piece. Ding did succeed in having the engine room of his remaining great battleship dynamited, so that the best remaining ship in his fleet did not fall into Japanese hands in a repairable condition.[38]

The failure of Chinese land forces to coordinate with, let alone make sacrifices for, their naval counterparts was endemic. Most of the land forces fled or surrendered before seriously engaging the Japanese. They left the navy to defend coastal cities unassisted. This lack of jointness proved fatal for China.

After the Battle of Weihaiwei, Prince Gong, the uncle of the emperor, ordered the closing of the Admiralty since China no longer had a navy. Five million taels were missing. Allegedly these had been diverted to the Empress Dowager for an extensive refurbishment of the Summer Palace in anticipation of her 65th birthday celebrations.[39]

Captain William M. Lang, an Englishman formerly charged with training Chinese naval forces, had stated in the fall of 1894: "In my opinion Weihaiwei is impregnable, and no Japanese fleet dare approach it."[40] Four days after its capture, the Japanese allowed British officers to tour the fallen citadel. "After their examination of the fortress they pronounced it to be impregnable if any real attempt had been made to defend it by the Chinese."[41] "When the Japanese came to examine the forts, they were found to be practically undamaged. The splendid construction of the forts excited general admiration, and it was pretty evident that but for incipient mutiny and scarcity of provisions they could have held out indefinitely."[42]

During the subsequent occupation, the Japanese made sure to destroy these forts in which the Chinese had invested so much money. *Le Temps* later provided a telling accounting for the Chinese navy: during the war, twenty-two of its warships had been destroyed and twelve had surrendered to become additions to the Japanese navy. By contrast, Japan had lost two vessels, making a net gain of ten ships.[43] This was the end of a world-class Chinese navy for the next hundred years. At the opening of the first Sino-Japanese War, the Chinese navy ranked among the top eight in the world.[44] The blockade of Weihaiwei and the destruction of the Chinese fleet trapped inside marked the end of an era.

Conclusions

With the fall of Weihaiwei there was general recognition in Europe that the Far Eastern balance of power had changed. China was no longer the dominant regional power; rather, Japan was. Japanese military achievements received recognition throughout the European press, which credited the Japanese army for mastering the Chinese despite the difficult terrain in Korea and Manchuria.[45] During the siege at Weihaiwei, the editors of *Le Siècle* stated: "... the Chinese soldier is so badly commanded, its leaders so slovenly and so incapable, that even behind the most solid walls its resistance cannot last more than a few hours." They concluded: "The facility and fullness with which the Empire of the Rising Sun has assimilated the military institutions and the diplomatic customs of our ancient Europe are truly marvellous."[46]

According to the official newspaper of the Russian Foreign Ministry, "Since the beginning of this war, the Chinese have provided a lamentable spectacle. No one suspected such weakness.... Japan vanquisher of China!... It is remarkable – and this alone is sufficient to prove the complete absence of any Chinese resistance – that this war ... has only caused the Japanese armies insignificant losses ... China has no military organization whatsoever...The Japanese, in contrast, have resolutely begun a war European style."[47]

A front-page story in *The New York Times* noted: "You know how it has been the fashion to speak of China with bated breath as a sleeping leviathan, which it was dangerous to stir ... The time has come now when it should be realized that the continued existence of China, under present methods, is a standing menace to the peace of the world. China is an anachronism." The author believed that the world owed Japan "a debt of gratitude" for puncturing the overly positive international image of China.[48] In the United States, some went so far as to call the Japanese the "Yankees of the Orient."[49]

An article in *The Japan Weekly Mail* summed up the strategic situation after the fall of Weihaiwei: "In the present war between the two Eastern Powers, China has been defeated in every battle.... China has lost defences on which she had exhausted the contents of her treasury for more than twenty years.... By the fall of Port Arthur and Weihaiwei, the gateway to the capital of China has been thrown open, and no power in China can stay Japanese entry into Pekin [Beijing]."[50] At this juncture, the Manchus had no choice but to negotiate. Utter military incapacity meant that a continued

Japanese drive to Beijing would result in their overthrow by the Japanese if not sooner by some enterprising Han Chinese. The Manchus correctly concluded that their only hope for survival rested with diplomacy.

The Chinese debacle at Weihaiwei demonstrated that the best equipment in the world is useless in the wrong hands. It also demonstrated the foolhardiness of never risking the fleet, particularly for a land power. Ironically, this decision guaranteed the navy's annihilation, since barricading it at Weihaiwei depended on strong land defenses, but China's land forces rapidly fled the field. Since they did not even bother to destroy the abandoned fortifications, the Japanese soon trained China's own guns on the Beiyang Fleet trapped below in the harbor. China's defeat demonstrated the high costs exacted by a lack of jointness: the Japanese defeated Chinese land and sea forces in detail at times and places of their own choosing.

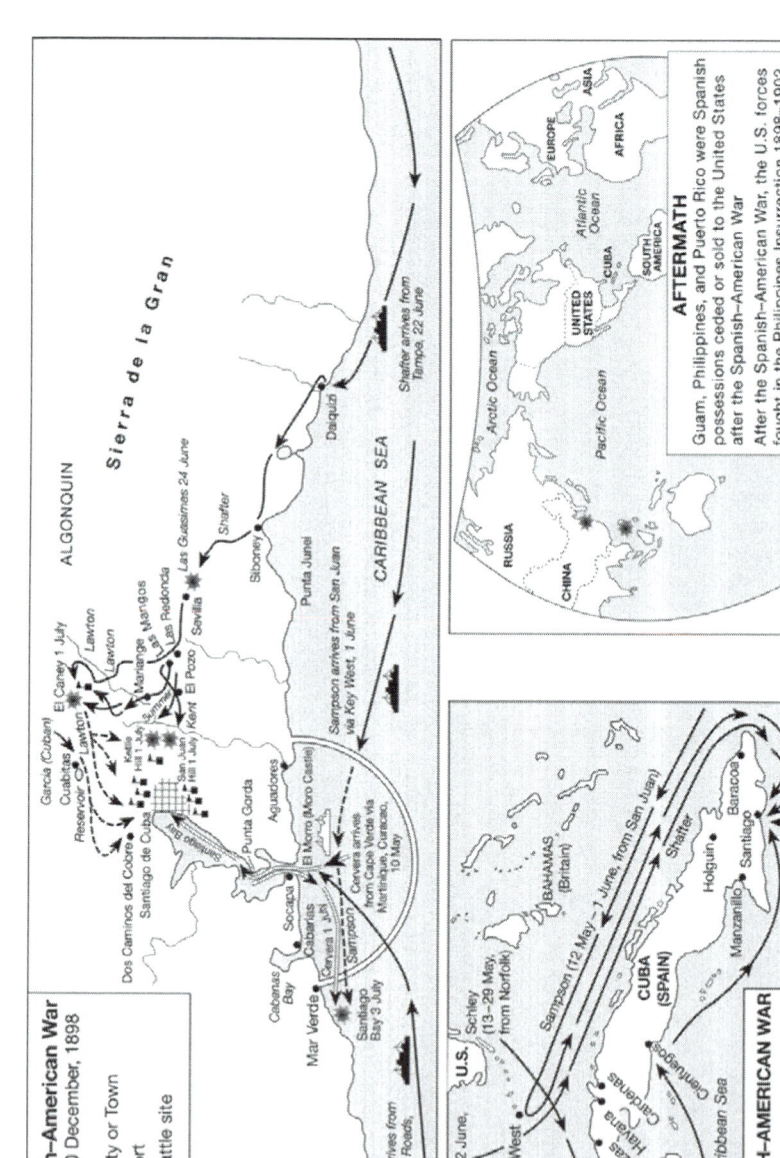

The Spanish–American War
25 April to 10 December, 1898

● City or Town
⌐ Fort
✳ Battle site

Sierra de la Gran

ALGONQUIN

Garcia (Cotan)
Cuabitas
Dos Caminos del Cobre
Santiago de Cuba
Reservoir
Lawton
El Caney 1 July
Lawton
Mariange Mangos
Las Redondas
Las Guasimes 24 June
Lawton
Shafter
Siboney
Sevilla
Kent
El Pozo
San Juan Hill 1 July
San Juan Hill 1 July
Kettle Hill 1 July
Punta Junei
Daiquiri
2nd offensive
Aguadores
Punta Gorda
El Morro (Moro Castle)
Sampson arrives from San Juan via Key West, 1 June
Cervera arrives from Cape Verde via Martinique, Curacao, 10 May
CARIBBEAN SEA
Shafter arrives from Tampa, 22 June
Cabanas Bay
Socapa
Cabanas
Sampson
Cervera 1 July
Mar Verde
Santiago Bay 3 July
Schley arrives from Hampton Roads, 29 May

AFTERMATH

Guam, Philippines, and Puerto Rico were Spanish possessions ceded or sold to the United States after the Spanish–American War

After the Spanish–American War, the U.S. forces fought in the Philippines insurrection 1898–1902 and in the Boxer Rebellion in 1900.

RUSSIA
EUROPE
ASIA
AFRICA
CHINA
UNITED STATES
Arctic Ocean
Atlantic Ocean
Pacific Ocean
CUBA
SOUTH AMERICA

THE SPANISH–AMERICAN WAR

Cervera (29 May to 29 April, from Cape Verde)

U.S.
Schley (14–22 June, from Tampa)
Schley (13–29 May, from Norfolk)
Sampson (12 May–1 June, from San Juan)
Shafter
Key West
Gulf of Mexico
BAHAMAS (Britain)
Matanzas
Havana
Cardenas
Cienfuegos
Caribbean Sea
Schley
CUBA (SPAIN)
Holguin
Manzanillo
Santiago
Baracoa
Shafter

Map 8.1 The Spanish–American War, 1898

8   The Naval Blockade of Cuba during the Spanish–American War

Mark L. Hayes*

On 22 April 1898, Rear-Admiral William Sampson, acting on orders received the previous day from Secretary of the Navy John Long, directed the ships of the North Atlantic Squadron to begin the blockade of Cuba, thereby initiating the Spanish–American War. International law required that a blockade be effective to be legal, and with the absence of colliers, and with a portion of the Atlantic fleet forming the Flying Squadron at Hampton Roads, Virginia, the American effort was initially limited to the north coast of Cuba between Cardenas and Bahia Honda, and Cienfuegos on the south coast. By 23 April, the advance ships of the blockading fleet were patrolling off their assigned ports, and additional vessels reinforced them over the next several days.[1]

Secretary Long instructed Sampson to maintain a tight blockade, but not risk his armored ships unnecessarily against land fortifications. The secretary expected Spain to send a squadron of cruisers to the Caribbean, and he wanted to ensure that an American naval force was prepared to meet the threat. The Navy Department considered occupying the port of Matanzas, garrisoning it, and then opening communications with the insurgents, but Long wanted Sampson to keep his strongest ships ready to escort transports should President William McKinley order an early army landing in Cuba.[2]

The strategic purpose of the blockade, and the primary U.S. war aim, was to force Spain to relinquish control of the island. The blockade would also serve to deny the Spanish Navy the use of friendly bases to support its operations. While the government could send a strong armored squadron to the Caribbean, there were few places where the ships could receive the coal necessary to operate effectively. Efforts to prevent Spanish warships from entering one of these ports would dominate U.S. Navy operations in mid-to-late May. Furthermore, a close blockade was necessary to prevent many smaller Spanish armed vessels, already in Cuba from the start of hostilities, from interfering with U.S. naval operations.

Beginning Preparations for a Naval Blockade

War between the United States and Spain appeared unavoidable following the destruction of USS *Maine* in Havana harbor on 15 February 1898, and

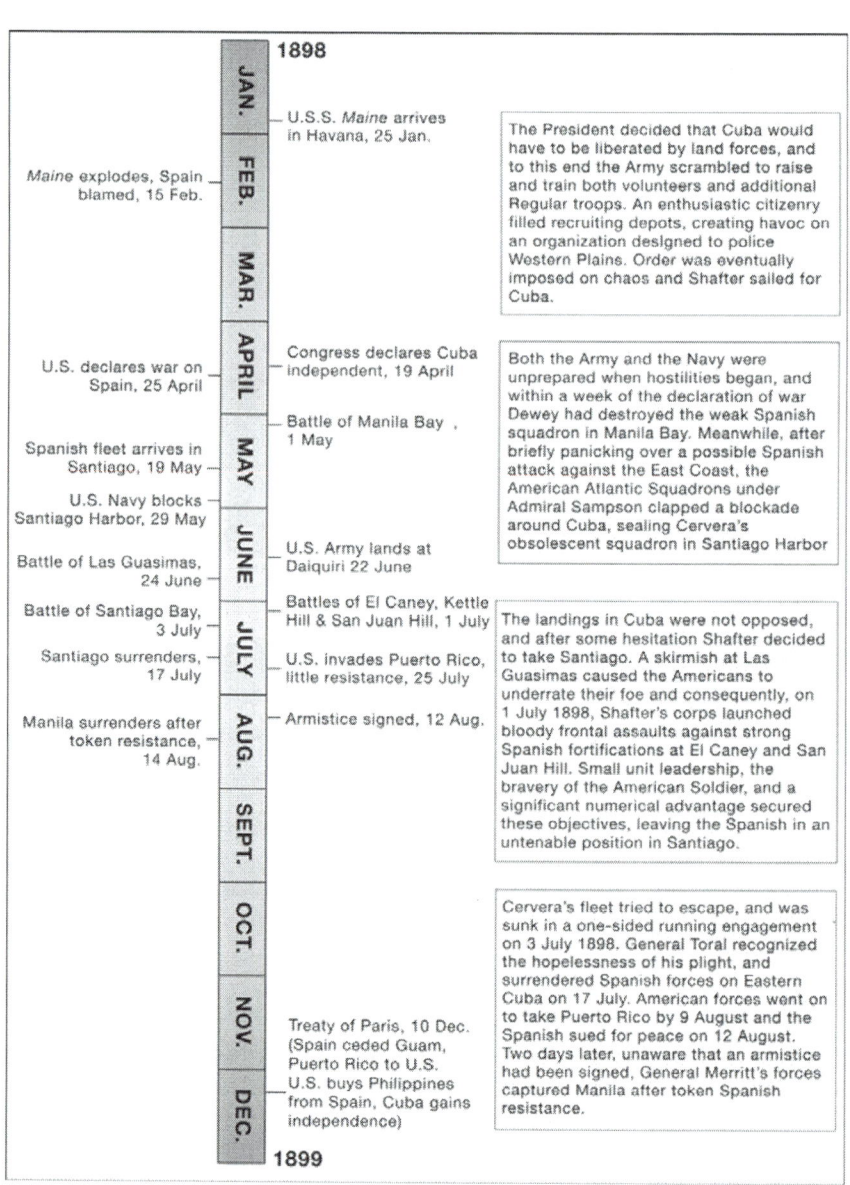

1898

JAN.

U.S.S. *Maine* arrives in Havana, 25 Jan.

Maine explodes, Spain blamed, 15 Feb.

FEB.

The President decided that Cuba would have to be liberated by land forces, and to this end the Army scrambled to raise and train both volunteers and additional Regular troops. An enthusiastic citizenry filled recruiting depots, creating havoc on an organization designed to police Western Plains. Order was eventually imposed on chaos and Shafter sailed for Cuba.

MAR.

U.S. declares war on Spain, 25 April

APRIL

Congress declares Cuba independent, 19 April

Both the Army and the Navy were unprepared when hostilities began, and within a week of the declaration of war Dewey had destroyed the weak Spanish squadron in Manila Bay. Meanwhile, after briefly panicking over a possible Spanish attack against the East Coast, the American Atlantic Squadrons under Admiral Sampson clapped a blockade around Cuba, sealing Cervera's obsolescent squadron in Santiago Harbor

Battle of Manila Bay, 1 May

Spanish fleet arrives in Santiago, 19 May

MAY

U.S. Navy blocks Santiago Harbor, 29 May

JUNE

U.S. Army lands at Daiquiri 22 June

Battle of Las Guasimas, 24 June

Battle of Santiago Bay, 3 July

Battles of El Caney, Kettle Hill & San Juan Hill, 1 July

JULY

The landings in Cuba were not opposed, and after some hesitation Shafter decided to take Santiago. A skirmish at Las Guasimas caused the Americans to underrate their foe and consequently, on 1 July 1898, Shafter's corps launched bloody frontal assaults against strong Spanish fortifications at El Caney and San Juan Hill. Small unit leadership, the bravery of the American Soldier, and a significant numerical advantage secured these objectives, leaving the Spanish in an untenable position in Santiago.

Santiago surrenders, 17 July

U.S. invades Puerto Rico, little resistance, 25 July

Manila surrenders after token resistance, 14 Aug.

AUG.

Armistice signed, 12 Aug.

SEPT.

OCT.

Cervera's fleet tried to escape, and was sunk in a one-sided running engagement on 3 July 1898. General Toral recognized the hopelessness of his plight, and surrendered Spanish forces on Eastern Cuba on 17 July. American forces went on to take Puerto Rico by 9 August and the Spanish sued for peace on 12 August. Two days later, unaware that an armistice had been signed, General Merritt's forces captured Manila after token Spanish resistance.

NOV.

Treaty of Paris, 10 Dec. (Spain ceded Guam, Puerto Rico to U.S. U.S. buys Philippines from Spain, Cuba gains independence)

DEC.

1899

Figure 8.1 Timeline for the Spanish–American War

the Navy Department had a solid body of plans prepared over four years by its leading officers. Although the realities of war would force several modifications, many of the concepts discussed in these plans were implemented: a strong blockade of Cuba; support for the insurgents; operations against Spanish forces in the Philippines and Puerto Rico; and the formation of a squadron to operate in Spanish waters. Most importantly, nearly every plan called for merchant vessels to serve as auxiliary cruisers, colliers, and transports.

By contrast, the Spanish were ill prepared to defend their overseas possessions. Most of the forty vessels stationed in Cuba were obsolete and primarily intended to help the colonial government put down insurrection. A relieving squadron from Spain would be severely handicapped by the lack of properly positioned colliers, inadequate coal stockpiles, and poor coaling facilities at Cuban and Puerto Rican ports. Spain possessed only one battleship, a recently modernized vessel. This ship and an armored cruiser were not ready for action until after the war began, while the four cruisers that steamed across the Atlantic were not truly ready for combat.

Nevertheless, six torpedo gunboats stationed in Cuba were of particular concern to U.S. naval planners. A single torpedo could disable or even sink an American warship, reducing U.S. naval superiority in any confrontation. The Navy Department recommended that Sampson counter this threat by establishing three lines of blockade off Havana; in the Age of Sail, sudden storms made a close blockade dangerous. In the Age of Steam, however, enemy torpedo boats were the greatest threat.

At the beginning of 1898 the U.S. fleet consisted of six battleships, two armored cruisers, thirteen protected cruisers, six steel monitors, eight old iron monitors, thirty-three unprotected cruisers and gunboats, six torpedo boats, and twelve tugs.[3] Noticeably absent were colliers, supply vessels, transports, hospital ships, repair ships, and the many small vessels necessary for maintaining an effective blockade of Cuba's numerous ports. As the Navy Department's war plans clearly indicated, the government would need to purchase or contract for scores of ships in the event of war. Assistant Secretary of the Navy Theodore Roosevelt organized a Board of Auxiliary Vessels that prepared a list of suitable private craft. On 9 March Congress passed a $50 million emergency defense appropriation bill, and the Navy Department began to acquire vessels. By the end of the war, the navy had purchased or leased 103 warships and auxiliaries. After the war such auxiliary vessels as colliers, refrigerator ships, and distilling ships became a permanent part of the fleet.[4]

Coal availability was the single most important factor determining naval operations in 1898. A lack of coal severely limited Admiral Pascual Cervera's options upon arriving in the Caribbean with his Spanish squadron in the middle of May, while American concerns over coaling nearly allowed him to escape from Santiago de Cuba near the end of the month. There were three sources of fuel: (1) friendly bases; (2) neutral ports; and (3) other ships (usually colliers). Key West served as the base for U.S. naval operations in the Caribbean. International law permitted, but did not require, neutrals to provide belligerent ships just enough coal to allow them to reach the nearest friendly port. Colliers were the most common source of fuel for vessels blockading Cuba. Six were available at the start of the war, and an additional eleven were purchased by August.[5]

Ship endurance depended on factors such as bunker capacity, coal storage on deck, coal quality, the number of boilers, and the ship's speed while under way. Most major U.S. warships had an operational range of around 4,000 nautical miles, or just over two weeks of continuous steaming at ten knots.[6] Naturally, commanding officers were reluctant to allow their bunkers to get anywhere near empty.

Refueling warships was a time-consuming operation. Coaling from open lighters in port was the quickest and most efficient means. Winches set up on the warships hauled the coal on deck in bags, where carts carried them to chutes leading down to the bunkers. Coaling from colliers was safest in an anchorage sheltered from rough seas. Coaling in the open sea with a ship alongside was always considered dangerous, and was not attempted when swells were sufficient to cause either ship to roll more than three or four degrees or rise more than one or two feet. Thus, coaling at sea was often problematic, if not impossible. The time required for coaling varied widely, and depended upon the weather. One ship took on coal at a rate of eighteen tons per hour one day, but nearly 57 tons per hour a week later. The weather rarely cooperated long enough for more than a few hundred tons to be loaded before rising seas halted the operation.[7]

As the Navy Department worked with the president and the War Department in developing strategy, Long began repositioning naval units in preparation for opening hostilities. Since January, much of the North Atlantic Squadron had been concentrated for winter exercises at Key West. The first colliers did not reach the fleet until 3 May, nearly two weeks after the blockade began. The formation of a Flying Squadron under Commodore Winfield Scott Schley, consisting of two battleships, an armored cruiser, and two protect cruisers, was intended to protect the U.S. coast from any Spanish attack.[8]

Anticipating a showdown with the Spanish fleet in the Atlantic theater, Long ordered the battleship USS *Oregon* to depart from its home port at Bremerton, Washington, for San Francisco, California, on 7 March, to begin the first leg of a 14,700-nautical-mile journey to Key West. *Oregon* steamed into the American base at Key West on 26 May and was made ready for operations against the Spanish fleet.[9]

The U.S. Blockade of Cuba

Although President McKinley continued to press for a diplomatic settlement, he accelerated military preparations begun in January. McKinley asked Congress on 11 April for permission to intervene in Cuba. On 21 April, he ordered the Navy to begin the blockade, and Spain followed with a declaration of war on 23 April. Congress responded with a formal declaration of war on 25 April, made retroactive to the start of the blockade.

The U.S. Navy struggled during the first weeks of the war to assemble the logistical apparatus necessary to support the blockade. Ships had to keep steam up in their boilers to pursue unknown vessels as they came into sight. Until colliers were fitted out and sent south, most of the blockading ships had to return to Key West to coal. Fresh water and food were also in short supply during the early days of the war.

Spanish commanders in Cuba attempted to loosen the blockade by constructing new batteries and engaging the smaller U.S. vessels with their own gunboats. Although the Navy Department prohibited Sampson's vessels from engaging heavy batteries, like those near Havana, it allowed the bombardment of smaller field works. On 27 April, U.S. ships shelled Point Gorda at Matanzas to prevent the completion of new batteries. Two days later, Commander Bowman H. McCalla led an unsuccessful attempt to intercept two Spanish steamers arriving from Martinique. The American force did capture a mail steamer and damaged the defending Spanish torpedo gunboat.

The Spanish tried to take advantage of the aggressive posture of the smaller vessels on the blockade by initiating engagements and trying to lure them within effective range of shore batteries. Few actions were as intense as the one at Cardenas on 11 May when Spanish gunboats drew the U.S. Navy gunboat *Wilmington*, the torpedo boat *Winslow*, and the Revenue Cutter *Hudson* deep into the harbor. Hidden Spanish batteries ambushed *Winslow*, severely damaging her, killing ten and wounding twenty-one of her crew. While under heavy fire *Hudson* towed the torpedo boat out of the harbor as *Wilmington* covered the withdrawal with rapid fire against the Spanish guns.[10]

The U.S. blockading forces also undertook operations to cut telegraphic communications to Madrid via Cienfuegos, Santiago, and Guantánamo. The most celebrated action of this type occurred on 11 May off Cienfuegos, when McCalla planned an operation to cut the underwater cables leaving the city. Marine sharpshooters and machine guns in steam cutters poured a continuous fire into Spanish positions on shore, along with gunfire support from *Marblehead* and the gunboat *Nashville*, while sailors in launches dragged the sea floor with grappling hooks for the cables. The launch and cutter crews endured heavy Spanish fire for three hours and cut the two main telegraph cables (leaving a third, local line), and dragged the ends out to sea. Every member of this expedition was awarded the Medal of Honor.[11]

The Actions of the Spanish Fleet

Admiral Cervera had repeatedly warned the Spanish Ministry of Marine that his squadron would face certain destruction if sent to the Caribbean.

Nevertheless, he departed the Cape Verde Islands under orders on 29 April with his squadron of four armored cruisers, and towing three torpedo-boat destroyers, intending to steam for Puerto Rico. To look for the Spanish squadron, the U.S. Navy Department had three fast former mail steamers establish a patrol line stretching from Puerto Rico and along the Leeward and Windward Islands. As long as Cervera's location remained uncertain, the strength of the U.S. fleet would be divided between Sampson's North Atlantic Fleet based in Key West and Schley's Flying Squadron based in Hampton Roads. The former would maintain the blockade of Cuba, while the latter would guard the U.S. east coast from a sudden descent by the Spanish cruisers.[12]

Sampson correctly deduced that Cervera intended to make for San Juan, Puerto Rico. Leaving his smaller ships to maintain the blockade of Cuba's northern ports, Sampson embarked on an eight-day journey, plagued by the slow speed and mechanical unreliability of his two monitors. His force arrived off San Juan early on 12 May. After a nearly four-hour bombardment of the Spanish works, he broke off the engagement and returned to Key West, satisfied that Cervera's ships were not in San Juan.[13]

Cervera's crossing of the Atlantic was slowed because of his fragile destroyers. As he approached the West Indies, he dispatched two of them to the French island of Martinique to gain information on American movements and the availability of coal. On 12 May, Cervera learned that Sampson was at San Juan. He also discovered that the French would not sell him any coal. Driven by the need to refuel and the desire to avoid combat with a superior American squadron, he steamed for the Dutch harbor of Curaçao. He arrived there on 14 May, only to be further disappointed when the expected Spanish collier failed to arrive, and the Dutch governor authorized the purchase of only 600 tons of coal. After considering his options, Cervera chose to take his fleet to Santiago de Cuba where he arrived on the morning of 19 May.[14]

With Sampson out of touch for long periods during his return from Puerto Rico, the Navy Department on 13 May at first ordered Schley's Flying Squadron to Charleston and then to Key West. The Navy Department believed that Cervera's most likely objective was Cienfuegos because of its rail connection to Havana. Therefore, on 18 May, Schley received orders to take his squadron, reinforced by the battleship *Iowa* and several small vessels, and proceed to Cienfuegos. On 19 May, the White House learned that Cervera had run into Santiago de Cuba. The source of this information was Domingo Villaverde, an agent working as a telegraph operator in the governor-general's palace in Havana. This connection was a closely guarded secret, so when the information reached the Navy Department as an unconfirmed report, Long's telegram to Sampson sounded less than certain.[15]

Sampson forwarded Long's notice to Schley along with his own decision to maintain the Flying Squadron off Cienfuegos, believing that even if

Cervera had put into Santiago, he would have to bring his squadron west to deliver the munitions thought to be an essential part of his mission. As additional information arrived at the Navy Department confirming Cervera's presence at Santiago, Long and Sampson dispatched several messages encouraging Schley to proceed to that port and prevent the Spanish squadron from escaping.[16] On 24 May, Schley learned through Cuban insurgents that Cervera's ships were not in port, and that evening the American squadron headed east.

Schley's message informing Sampson of his departure also conveyed concerns about potentially insufficient coal supplies. The one collier then with the squadron was insufficient to coal enough ships even when the weather afforded an opportunity. Schley informed Sampson that these concerns and his desire to coal his ships at a protected anchorage led him to choose Môle St Nicolas, Haiti, as his next destination.[17]

The Flying Squadron arrived off Santiago on 26 May, and Schley communicated with the American cruisers watching the port. Engine problems on the collier caused the squadron to average only seven knots in its journey from Cienfuegos. The weather was also too rough to allow coaling at sea, so several of his smaller vessels were running low. Rather than remaining on station with his larger ships and trusting Sampson to supply him, Schley ordered his squadron to head west for Key West to refuel. Sampson, who had since returned to Key West, and Long were shocked when they learned of Schley's intentions. Making it clear that the Flying Squadron was expected to remain on station, Sampson assembled his squadron and departed for Santiago. On 27 May, the weather off the south coast of Cuba improved, and Schley reversed course once again, finally establishing a blockade at Santiago de Cuba on 29 May.[18]

Schley's coaling problems impressed on Sampson and the Navy Department the need to seize a sheltered anchorage on the south coast of Cuba. Guantánamo Bay had already been considered. Shortly after Schley established the blockade of Santiago, Sampson ordered the First Marine Battalion at Key West to embark on its transports and prepare to land in Cuba. He also sent McCalla to reconnoiter Guantánamo Bay's anchorage. McCalla's report was favorable. On 10 June, the Marine battalion under Lieutenant-Colonel Robert Huntington landed, establishing a position on the east side of the outer harbor that served to protect the fleet during its coaling operations throughout the campaign.[19]

Having a reliable location to refuel so close to Santiago proved invaluable to the blockading fleet. It allowed American captains to keep steam up and be ready to pursue Cervera's squadron when it attempted to break out. On the morning of 3 July, the battleship *Oregon* had all four boilers lit, giving her the speed necessary to catch the *Cristobal Colon* in the running fight during the Battle of Santiago de Cuba. This high rate of coal consumption could only be maintained because *Oregon* was able to refuel four times from 1 June to 3 July, once at sea and three times at Guantánamo Bay.[20]

Joint Land–Sea Operations

McKinley and his advisers had intended to wait until the end of the rainy season to send a major land expedition to Cuba. However, they believed that the bottling-up of the Spanish squadron at Santiago afforded an opportunity to strike a blow against Spain's military capability in the Caribbean. On 1 June, Sampson received a report from Secretary Long that 25,000 men under Major-General William Shafter were preparing to embark for Cuba from Tampa, Florida. The North Atlantic Fleet should convoy the troops and assist their landing near Santiago. While waiting for the troops, Sampson tightened the blockade.

Taking advantage of the obsolete shore batteries, Sampson had his armored ships maintain a tight blockade of Santiago de Cuba, coaling in open water when the seas were calm and from colliers at Guantánamo Bay when the weather required it. Major-General Shafter's troop transports, carrying 17,000 men, departed from Tampa on 14 June, making rendezvous with their navy escorts the following day. The expedition arrived off Santiago on 20 June, and began to disembark east of the city at Daiquiri two days later. In addition to providing escort for the convoy, Sampson's ships furnished 52 steam launches, sailing launches, whaleboats, lifeboats, and cutters to help the army and its equipment ashore.[21] Shafter immediately began his march westward, intent on capturing Santiago de Cuba by land. His victories at San Juan Hill and El Caney on 1 July left the Americans in control of the heights overlooking the town. The Spanish position became desperate. On the evening of 2 July, Cervera revealed to his officers that authorities at Havana had ordered his squadron to break out as soon as possible, before the town and control of the harbor fell to U.S. troops.

Cervera's ships were in no condition to challenge the most powerful elements of the U.S. Fleet. He had been forced to leave Spain before the two ten-inch guns had been installed on the armored cruiser *Cristobal Colon*. Two of the 5.5-inch guns on *Vizcaya* and one on *Almirante Oquendo* were useless. To make matters worse, the Spanish sailors found that only one in every seven of the 300 shells available for these guns actually fit into the gun breech. Many of Cervera's crewmen were new to the navy and few had ever fired a practice shot.[22]

Spanish hopes depended on their ability to outrun the U.S. warships. Although their ships were designed to make twenty knots, two months in Caribbean waters had left their bottoms so foul that one officer described one vessel as "nothing more than a buoy". Cervera's ships suffered further from availability of only low-grade coal at the antiquated port facilities in Santiago. The best speed that any of the Spanish cruisers could make on 3 July was fourteen knots.[23]

Sampson ordered his ships to remain close inshore and their crewmen to keep a constant watch on the narrow entrance to the harbor. Quartermaster Anderson began his watch on 3 July on the forward bridge of the armored cruiser USS *Brooklyn*, guarding the entrance to Santiago de Cuba along with the battleships *Texas, Oregon, Iowa,* and *Indiana,* and the armed yachts *Vixen* and *Gloucester.* Anderson had been studying the smoke rising above the hill that blocked the view to the Spanish ships in the harbor. Just before 0930 he spotted the column of smoke moving toward the entrance, and reported the change to the ship's navigator Lieutenant Hodgson. After confirming the quartermaster's statement, Hodgson grabbed a megaphone, and called for signal "250" (meaning "Enemy coming out – action") to be hoisted. Three minutes later, the American cruiser was underway with guns ready to shoot, ammunition on hand, fire hoses laid out, and watertight hatches shut. *Brooklyn* steamed toward the enemy, opening the fight by firing its eight-inch guns, and the other U.S. warships quickly followed.

Most of the battle was a running fight as the blockading vessels attempted to get up enough steam to stay with their quarry. Ranges between the combatants were often in excess of 4,000 yards, greater than the American crews had trained for and longer than their new rangefinders could handle. In addition, radical turns in the early stages of the battle complicated the American gunnery problem. Smoke from the weapons' brown powder and frequent mechanical failures further reduced the effectiveness of their gunfire. The battleships and *Brooklyn* generally registered hits when they were able to maintain a parallel or near-parallel course with the Spanish cruisers. Although only 1.29 percent of American shots hit their targets, the volume of fire proved sufficient to destroy or run aground all of Cervera's vessels. The U.S. fleet suffered one man killed and ten wounded, while the Spanish lost 350 killed or drowned and 160 wounded. Nearly 1,700 Spanish officers and men became prisoners.[24]

The destruction of the Spanish cruiser squadron at Santiago de Cuba freed McKinley and the Navy Department to pursue other strategic options. Washington activated the Eastern Squadron on 7 July, under the command of Commodore John C. Watson, to meet a second squadron under Rear-Admiral Manuel de la Cámara y Libermoore, centered on the battleship *Pelayo* and the armored cruiser *Emperator Carlos V.* Spain ordered it to the Philippines to attack the small American squadron under Rear-Admiral George Dewey. Now the Navy Department widely circulated news of the Eastern Squadron's formation, including the battleships *Oregon* and *Massachusetts,* and its intended target: the Philippines. Spain responded by recalling the Reserve Squadron to Cadiz, validating the American success in the Pacific.

Conclusions

The victory off Santiago de Cuba and the effectiveness of the blockade against the remaining Spanish armed vessels in Cuban waters permitted the U.S. Navy to support the invasion of Puerto Rico during the final week of July. These

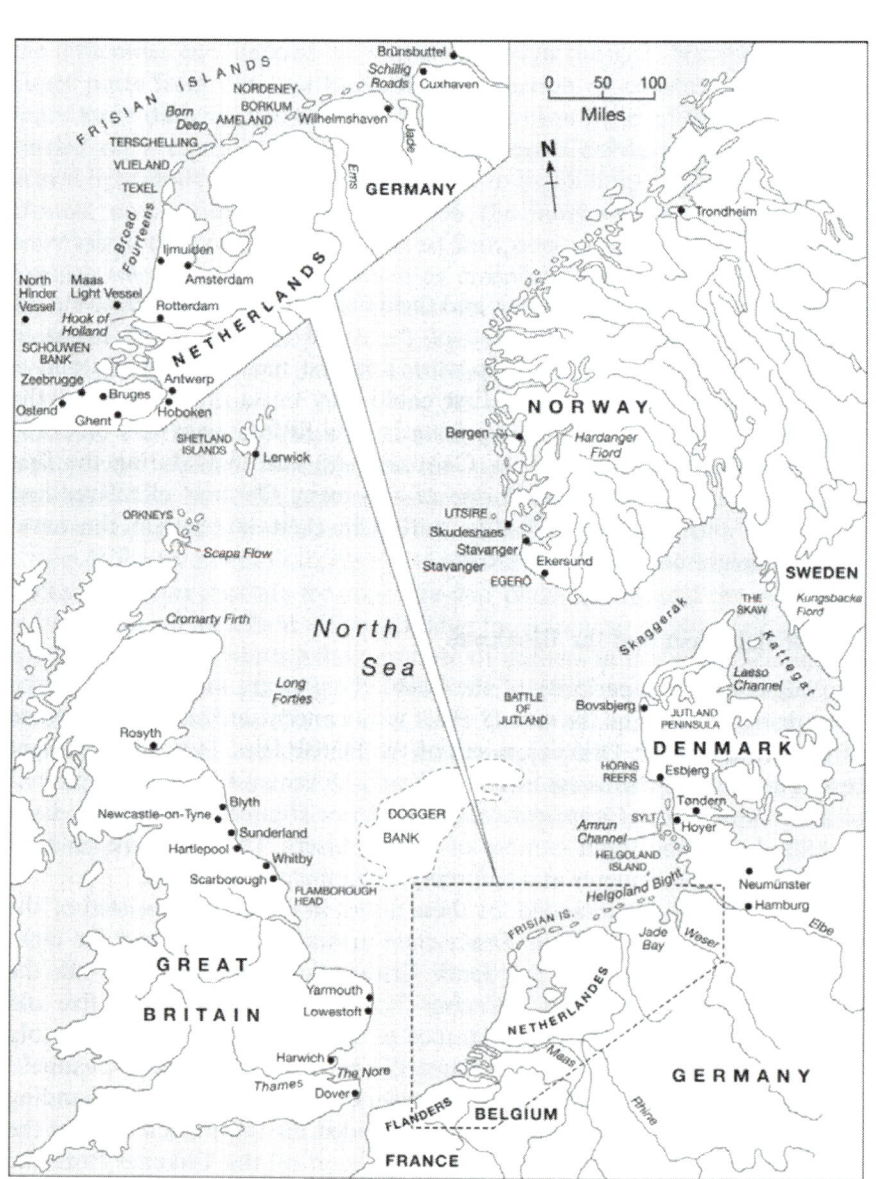

Map 9.1 The North Sea

In the north, given the extensive line to be covered, the number of cruisers available was none-too-large, especially since all ships could not be expected to be at sea all the time. The brunt of the work fell on Rear-Admiral Dudley De Chair and his Tenth Cruiser Squadron, later to be known as "The Northern Patrol," deployed on a line from the Shetlands to the coast of Norway in the north and from the Shetlands to the Scottish coast in the south. In addition, the cruiser squadrons of the Grand Fleet operating out of Cromarty and Rosyth, although primarily concerned with screening the battle fleet, might also be considered as forming a second blockade line further to the south.[3] Sea conditions in these northern waters were arduous. With the onset of autumn and winter storms, the old *Edgar*-class cruisers proved unequal to the task. During the winter of 1914–1915 they were replaced by armed merchant cruisers.

The British merchant marine, the world's largest, proved an invaluable asset by providing suitable ships. De Chair flew his flag in the former Allan liner *Alsatian* (18,000 tons), large enough to withstand the sea conditions and when packed with coal able to keep to the seas – thirty days in the case of *Alsatian* – far longer than the old cruisers. The squadron was, in theory, by April 1915 composed of twenty-four very diverse ships. These included, for example, a number of former banana boats. De Chair estimated six ships would always be in harbor coaling and refitting at the same time.[4] The ships were initially given 4.7-inch guns drawn from obsolete cruisers, but were soon re-armed with 6-inch guns to counter the threat of potential German raiders. The number of ships in the squadron grew, and armed trawlers subsequently joined the larger armed merchant cruisers. Vice-Admiral Reginald Tupper, who succeeded de Chair in March 1916, had twenty-two armed merchant cruisers and six armed trawlers under his command in September 1916.[5] Nevertheless, there were hundreds of square miles to be covered, often with restricted visibility in poor weather. In the absence of the now common electronic devices, they were still dependent – as ships were in the days of Nelson – on what could be seen from the mast head.

The development of the submarine also created new possibilities for a close blockade of the German coast. Fisher, when chairman of the committee to investigate fuel oil supplies for the Royal Navy, warned that submarines might sink unarmed British merchant ships without warning and the only thing for the British to do would be to make reprisals. Fisher's famous words, "The essence of war is violence and moderation in war is imbecility," caused general consternation.[6] Nevertheless, First Lord Winston Churchill at the end of 1913 seemed ready for a major shift in naval building. He now believed that patrol submarines were necessary for a tactical blockade of German ports. The naval estimates of 1914–1915 would have seen twenty submarines substituted for two of the planned capital ships. The war intervened before this became public knowledge.

distinct effect in Constantinople, although the situation was eased for the Turks by the opening of direct links with Germany at the beginning of 1916.

The Mechanics of Implementing the Blockade

In the eyes of the Foreign Office, "the fleet would be little but constables and controllers of neutral traffic," and the central authorities in Whitehall determined what rights of interception could be legally exercised.[13] Technically the British never declared a formal blockade and control was exerted through Orders-in-Council.[14]

The maritime Order-in-Council of 20 August 1914 adhered to the Declaration of London, except that if there was enough evidence on hand that a cargo of conditional contraband was destined for the enemy, regardless of what was stated in the ship's papers, that cargo was liable to seizure. Furthermore, conditional contraband destined for enemy use was liable to capture whatever port the cargo ship was bound for or in whatever port the cargo was destined to be discharged.

A second Order-in-Council, of 29 October 1914, deviated still further from the Declaration of London on the immunity of conditional contraband bound for a neutral port. Henceforth, if a ship's course deviated from the port of discharge listed on the ship's papers, and no adequate explanation could be given, capture was possible regardless of what the ship's papers indicated. Furthermore, if British authorities determined the enemy was drawing supplies through a neutral country, ships carrying conditional contraband would not be immune from capture if destined for that country.

Probably the most famous of the Orders-in-Council was that of 11 March 1915, the so-called "reprisal" order issued after the German proclamation of waters around the British Isles as a war zone with ships liable to submarine attack, without regard to their cargo or the safety of passengers and crew. Henceforth, no ship proceeding to or sailing from a German port would be allowed to continue, nor would any ship having sailed from or proceeding to a neutral port with goods intended for the enemy, or of enemy origin or ownership, be allowed through. Furthermore, any ship that entered a German port after clearing for a neutral or allied port would be liable to condemnation if encountered on a subsequent voyage.[15]

The mechanism for implementing these orders grew as the war progressed. In November 1914, a "Contraband Committee" led by Sire Eyre Crowe was established at the Foreign Office including representatives from the Admiralty. It was, in effect, the real executive of the naval blockade. Meanwhile, at the Admiralty, the Restriction of Enemy Supplies Committee was formed with representatives from the Committee of Imperial Defence, the Board of Trade and the Foreign Office. This was an advisory committee to make recommendations for hindering or if possible stopping supplies of food and raw materials to Germany and Austria

The latter committee was eventually superseded after the formation of the Ministry of Blockade by the War Trade Advisory Committee under Lord Crewe. As part of the newly formed ministry, it was charged with coordinating measures taken by other departments and advising the Cabinet on questions of policy. Goods exported from Germany and Austria were supervised by an Enemy Exports Committee, authorized to order suspect cargoes held up until certificates of neutral origin were produced.[16] For both the Contraband Committee and the Enemy Exports Committee delay was a deliberate part of a coercive procedure, that is, neutrals – even if their ships or goods were not condemned by a prize court – were to be made to feel the inconvenience of carrying German goods and, consequently, the advantage of not doing so.[17]

On 23 February 1916, in an effort to coordinate the activities of different government departments, and at least partly in response to vociferous criticism in some quarters about the progress and effectiveness of the measures against Germany, the Ministry of Blockade was created. Lord Robert Cecil, under-secretary at the Foreign Office, served as minister. The Contraband Department under Sir Eyre Crowe, who had been a strong advocate of the creation of the ministry, functioned as a central executive, assisted by War Trade Statistical and War Trade Intelligence Departments. The ministry also included a Foreign Trade Department, responsible for the black-lists of firms known to be or suspected of trading with the enemy, a Financial Transactions Department, the Enemy Exports Committee, and the War Trade Advisory Committee mentioned above.

The first French body to deal with the blockade was formed in November 1914. The *Comité de protection contre les approvisionnements de l'ennemi* was expanded in March 1915, and evolved into the *Comité de restriction,* with representatives from the ministries of Foreign Affairs, War, Marine, Public Works, Agriculture, Commerce, and Colonies. An admiral would preside, while the secretary-general was nominated by the Ministry of Foreign Affairs. The committee was a consultative body and reviewed all proposals for inter-allied agreements or conventions with neutrals, as well as centralizing intelligence on enemy and neutral commerce. In the course of 1915 the French also created the *Commission internationale de contingents* to negotiate with the Swiss the quota of imports they would be permitted to receive. This organization paralleled similar ones established by the British to deal with the Netherlands or Scandinavian countries.[18]

On 23 March 1916, Denys Cochin, a minister of state with undefined responsibilities, was named to preside over the *Comité de restriction,* commonly known as "*Comité R.*" This was far less comprehensive than the British Ministry of Blockade, but Cochin's powers were enhanced somewhat in August 1916 when he was charged with reporting to the cabinet on matters concerning the blockade; the different departments were to consult him before reaching decisions, and he would also serve as arbiter in case of disagreement between the departments. By December 1916, Cochin had been named Under-Secretary of State of Blockade, attached to the Ministry of Foreign

Affairs, a victory for the latter in the ongoing dispute between the navy and the foreign office as to who had primary responsibility for the blockade.

Finally, on 20 February 1917, the *Comité français du blocus* was formally constituted to serve as a weekly meeting place for representatives of all government departments concerned with the blockade. Cochin subsequently received authorization to take immediate executive actions, but left office in August 1917. It was not until the formation of the Clemenceau cabinet in November 1917 that the position was raised to ministerial rank and Albert Lebrun became *Ministre des blocus et des régions libérées.*[19]

The Impact of the Blockade on Neutrals

The geographical realities of the situation contributed toward making the blockade as much if not more a diplomatic action than one that was purely naval. The British fleet could not pass through the Sound – the narrow strait between Denmark and Sweden – and operate in the Baltic. This made it impossible for the British to impose a complete blockade of the German coast; meanwhile, the Russian fleet in the Baltic was not strong enough to enforce a blockade.

Because of their relative security from British warships, the Germans left for the most part obsolescent vessels in the Baltic. Although they concentrated their best ships in the North Sea, the Kiel Canal permitted them to rapidly shift forces to counter any potential Russian threat. Furthermore, as the war progressed and German armies pushed ever eastwards, the situation became even more disadvantageous for the Russians, whose navy was primarily concerned with the defense of the Gulf of Finland. The British managed to pass a few submarines into the Baltic in the autumn of 1914 and, although primarily directed against warships, in 1915 they along with Russian submarines also operated against German shipping. They achieved only limited success, especially because the Germans took advantage of Swedish territorial waters. The Swedish navy patrolled those waters to enforce Sweden's neutrality and even formed convoys to safeguard shipping in Swedish territorial waters.[20]

Sweden probably ranked second only to the United States as the most difficult neutral for the British to manage. The Swedes also had leverage of their own to apply since, aside from the danger of their joining the struggle on the side of Germany, the route through Sweden was important for the transfer of supplies to Russia. This was particularly true before the completion of the railway running south from the Murman peninsula in North Russia, the sole region not blocked by ice in the winter. Sweden was also an important source of ball bearings for British industry.

The delicate act of balancing coercion and diplomacy continued throughout much of the war. There was a sharp conflict between the British ambassador in Sweden, Sir Esmé Howard, and the British naval attaché in Scandinavia, Rear-Admiral Consett, over how hard the neutrals should be pushed. This conflict led to Consett's recall in April 1917, an event symbolic of the real direction of blockade policy in London.[21] An agreement was concluded in May 1918 allowing a certain amount of Swedish exports to Germany, and a designated amount of commodities through the Allied blockade to Sweden, as well as providing for the chartering of Swedish tonnage to the Allies.[22]

As the war continued, the lists of contraband grew and items considered conditional contraband were moved to the list of absolute contraband. The fact that the imports of the neutrals bordering Germany rose sharply above their normal peacetime total during the first few months of the war seemed to indicate that goods went to Germany. Consequently, this led to a system of rationing the neutrals, a subject of negotiation throughout the war. It was always a delicate balance between throwing the neutrals into the arms of Germany or, as in the case of the Netherlands and Denmark, provoking a German occupation that the Dutch and the Danes would have little chance of resisting.

The Dutch had been particularly hard hit, for Rotterdam had been an important port for the importation of goods transshipped to Germany. Furthermore, the Netherlands had normally obtained its coal from Germany and Belgium, but its grain from beyond Europe. The Dutch also had to maintain links with overseas territories, notably the Dutch East Indies. In December 1914, the Dutch sought to appease the British by forming the Netherlands Overseas Trust Company, a semi-private organization of the leading shipping and trading firms that would handle all imports so as to guarantee that they would not be re-exported to Germany. The relationship was often difficult, but the Netherlands Overseas Trust (NOT) helped keep the Netherlands out of the war.[23]

There were similar agreements with Danish, Norwegian, Swedish, and other neutral governments or trade groups. In Switzerland, for example, the *S.S.S. (Société suisse de surveillance économique)* was created in October 1915 to act as a receiving trust with a monopoly on imports into Switzerland. They also had responsibility for insuring that their distribution via export licenses remained within restricted limits, and so did not violate the Allied blockade. The workings of these agreements were complex, and negotiations continued throughout the war. However, they were an important component of the economic pressure exerted on Germany and its allies.[24]

British measures led to constant friction with the leading neutral, the United States. In an effort to reduce that friction, the system of "navicerts" was instituted in March 1916. Exporters had to apply to British authorities for permission regarding specific cargoes, and if approved after investigation, received a navigational certificate assuring the cargo would not be disturbed in passage. It was an effort to make the system more efficient and was due, at least partly, to suggestions made by the American Consul-General in London, R.P. Skinner. It eventually turned into an excellent and powerful means of coercion. For example, during 1916 it gave neutral shippers an inducement to ship cargoes that had been rationed by agreement and so would receive preferential treatment.[25]

Bunker control was another effective instrument of coercion, given the importance of Great Britain as a source of coal for transatlantic shipping. The system went into effect in October 1915 and stipulated that no coal would be given to any ship that traded with a German port or carried goods destined for the enemy or of enemy origin. Moreover, coal would not be provided to ships chartered by an enemy subject or a firm on the black-list. Ships receiving British coal had voluntarily to call at British ports, where their cargoes could be approved.[26]

German Reaction to the Blockade

The German navy never really found a satisfactory solution to the problem of the distant blockade, even though it was apparent even before the war that the British would pursue this strategy. They had expected to wear down British forces engaged in a close blockade through mines and submarines, until the balance of strength permitted the German battle fleet to risk an encounter under favorable circumstances. The Germans would also send out minelayers and submarines that could operate along the British coast. But, beyond this, they were frustrated should the British not present themselves as targets in the Heligoland Bight. This predicament is reflected in a famous unanswered question by Admiral Alfred von Tirpitz, the State Secretary of the Reichsmarineamt, to the commander of the High Sea Fleet in May 1914: "What will you do if they do not come?"[27]

The Germans also do not appear to have made any serious effort to attack the ships enforcing the blockade. Certainly the armed merchant cruisers would have been relatively easy targets for a real warship. Rear-Admiral Franz von Hipper, commanding the German battle-cruiser squadron, did elaborate in November 1914 on a proposal submitted by one of his captains to sortie with the four newest battle-cruisers to attack trade and overwhelm any cruisers protecting that trade. But this plan was directed at sending the ships either to the West Indies or to the South Atlantic to operate on the trade routes, not attacking the blockaders. It was never implemented, largely because of insoluble logistical difficulties.

Those surface raiders that did break out disguised as merchantmen would have been intent on avoiding the blockading squadrons, not always success-fully, in order to attack softer targets far from European waters. German submarines were responsible for sinking some of the ships belonging to the Northern Patrol, but this seemed to be more the result of fortuitous encoun-ters rather than any organized campaign. Once the submarine campaign began in earnest, the German objective would have been destroying tonnage, not targeting warships.[28]

British successes in the actions of the Heligoland Bight and the Dogger Bank reinforced German reluctance to risk the High Sea Fleet, but some spectacular sinkings by German submarines in the autumn of 1914 eventu-ally indicated a possible way to counter the blockade. Even Tirpitz, the man who had played such a large role in building the High Sea Fleet – centered on battleships as a challenge to Britain at sea – proposed a submarine blockade, as well as minelaying in the Thames, and sending cruisers out into the Atlantic to attack British trade.

The result was the German declaration of 4 February 1915 (referred to on p. 96) that, effective from 18 February, the waters around Great Britain and Ireland, including the entire English Channel, constituted a military area in which every enemy merchant ship might be destroyed even if it was not possible to provide for the safety of passengers and crew. Even neutral vessels might be attacked, because of the alleged misuse by the British of neutral flags, or because of accidents of naval war.[29] This marked the start of the German submarine campaign as a counter-blockade around Britain and France. This campaign had serious consequences for neutral shipping.

The most troublesome neutral for the Germans was the United States. Prosecution of the submarine campaign shifted during the war, especially after major incidents such as the sinking of the *Lusitania* in 1915. The Germans ultimately made the fateful decision at the end of January 1917 to launch unrestricted submarine warfare, even at the risk of bringing the United States into the war. They calculated that shipping losses would bring the British to their knees, notably by interrupting the supply of grain, before American assistance could be effective.

The German assumptions were faulty and, interestingly enough, grain reserves in Britain actually increased, despite the losses, because cargoes of grain were given priority.[30] By a number of methods, including the introduction of the convoy system, submarine losses were reduced to manageable proportions, though they were never eliminated completely. In addition, increasingly centralized control of shipping made better use of what tonnage was available.

Perhaps most important of all, by bringing the United States into the war the German unrestricted submarine campaign resulted in an even tighter blockade by eliminating the United States as a source of even indirect trade through neutral ports. American power and diplomacy was added to that of the Allies in enforcing the blockade. The country that had formerly championed the rights of neutrals now adopted an embargo and methods such as navicerts, black lists, and bunker control, as well as the control of neutral shipping. In addition, a permanent Allied Blockade Committee met in London in March 1918 to coordinate blockade policy.[31] The German counter-blockade through unlimited submarine warfare ultimately proved counterproductive.

The Blockade's Effectiveness

In evaluating the effect of the Allied blockade, one must conclude that at first the blockade did not work well at all. After a year of war Admiral John Jellicoe, on examining the statistics of neutral trade, complained that exports of cotton had increased "to a still more remarkable degree during 1915," and that most of the cotton in excess of normal consumption was going to Germany.

He also complained that, of ships sent in to Kirkwall and Lerwick in recent weeks, only 13 percent were sent south for further examination and probably many of the latter were eventually allowed to proceed unhindered. Jellicoe concluded that, taking everything into consideration, "it is doubtful whether the work of the Tenth Cruiser Squadron, and the heavy cost of its upkeep, is producing any effect other than slight inconvenience in Germany."[32]

In 1916, the number of neutral ships intercepted or examined was far from negligible. In the period 23 March–30 June 1916 the number of eastbound ships in Dutch or Scandinavian ports from overseas ports, and westbound ships sailing from those neutral harbors heading for the open seas, was a combined total of 926. Of this number 275 passed through the Downs, 287 were intercepted by the patrols, 330 called voluntarily at Kirkwall, Stornoway, Lerwick, or other British ports, and thirty-four were known to have evaded the patrols. For the longer period 1 July–31 December 1916 – the half year before unrestricted submarine warfare and the entry of the United States into the war radically changed the situation – the combined total of eastbound and westbound ships was 2,422. Of this total, 886 passed through the Downs, 633 were intercepted by the patrols, 840 called voluntarily at British ports, and 63 were not intercepted by the patrols.[33]

The idea that the blockade was not being effectively enforced was held by many naval officers. Rear-Admiral Consett argued that British trade with Scandinavia had continued unchecked for two years, and agreements that this trade would not benefit Germany had been openly and continuously violated. All analyses and statements that proved trade was passing to Germany had been disregarded.[34]

In June 1916 the Admiralty sent Jellicoe a letter explaining the true nature of the blockade:

> ... for geographical and other reasons, no blockade of Germany in the strict and technical sense of the term has been declared, and that consequently under existing circumstances there can be no question of vessels breaking the blockade. The measures which have been adopted aim at achieving a result similar to that intended by regular blockade by restricting as far as possible the importation of commodities into Germany through the conclusion of agreements and the development of the rationing system in the adjacent neutral countries, and as regards direct maritime pressure, through the provisions of the Order-in-Council of the 11th March 1915 and the extension of belligerent rights of visit and search and the principles relating to contraband.

Consequently, under these conditions "it would be impossible and undesirable" to detain every vessel bound for a neutral port as though a strict blockade were in force. Instead, neutrals were granted certain facilities for imports necessary for their own consumption in return for their agreement to measures restricting exports to Germany.[35]

Given these limitations, the blockade took a long time to be fully effective. Until 1916, German industry does not seem to have been seriously affected. It was evident that, during the period of the so-called restricted blockade, that is, up to the Orders-in-Council of March 1915, there remained a considerable transit trade through the neutrals to Germany. Nevertheless, the German government was still obligated in January 1915 to issue food cards for bread and flour, the prelude to a general system of rationing in 1916. At the same time, the government ordered potato flour to be added to wheat to produce the infamous *k-brot*, another indicator of a growing decline in the quality as well as quantity of German food. If one could generalize about a complicated subject, it would be to say that German demand was rapidly exceeding production.[36]

Certainly German armies in 1916 brought some respite by the conquest and overrunning of most of Rumania, thereby permitting the Germans and Austrians to exploit its grain and oil, and opening the Danube to traffic that could not be touched by Allied sea power. The Germans even used military engineers to improve the flow of traffic through the rapids of the Iron Gates. The tonnage that moved upstream and downstream in 1916–1917 was more than twice that of the highest year before the war.[37] But this was a poor substitute for full access to the world's produce. The winter of 1916–1917, with its poor potato harvest, was long remembered as the "turnip winter."

Conclusions

By the end of World War I there is no question that the German and Austrian populations were suffering as a result of the blockade. After the collapse of Russia, even the economic booty extracted from the Ukraine proved to be only a fraction of what had been anticipated.[38] Therefore, German propagandists found it easy to blame civilian suffering on the so-called "hunger blockade," but it is difficult to pin this down, and there is a lively historical debate about the effectiveness of the blockade.

Economics in highly industrialized societies are indeed a complex subject, and one historian has argued for the "desperate need for a competent 'Economic General Staff,'" especially in a situation where economic statistics themselves can be a weapon of war.[39] Other factors were at work as well, such as the exhaustion of German credit for financing imports from neutrals, excessive demands on labor, an inadequate transportation system, black marketeers siphoning-off food to make exorbitant profits, waste and mismanagement by the authorities, and, in the case of the Habsburg Monarchy, the withholding of grain supplies by the Hungarian government from the Austrian half of the monarchy.[40]

What can be said with some authority is that, in spite of the fact that it did not save Serbia, Rumania and, ultimately, Russia, the blockade had its effect, regardless of the debate over the extent of that effect. However, it must also be emphasized that an enterprise of this size and complexity took a long time to have that effect, and in the meantime the military operations on land were unfolding.

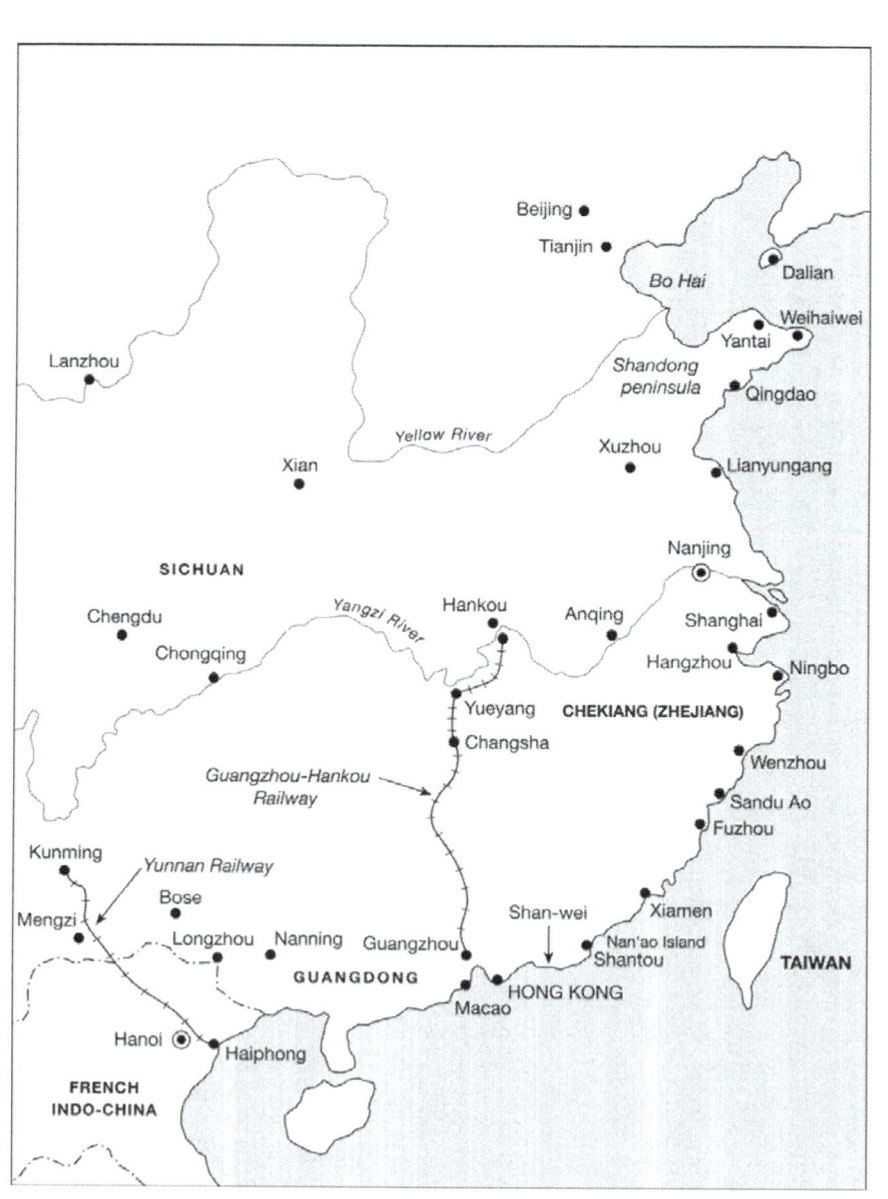

Map 10.1 The Chinese theatre of operations

10 Japanese Naval Blockade of China in the Second Sino-Japanese War, 1937–41

*Ken-ichi Arakawa**

Japan's blockade of China during 1937–1945 resulted from unimaginative thinking by the Japanese military. Although the Imperial Japanese Army had detailed war plans for the USSR, and the Imperial Japanese Navy had war plans against the U.S., both underestimated the importance of clear and coherent war plans for China. In fact, the Army and Navy wanted to avoid an all-out war and, if it happened, to limit the battlefield to northern and central China. Chiang Kai-shek, however, retreated and drew the Japanese forces ever deeper into the interior, thus prolonging the war. It was over-extension, rather than defeat on the battlefield, that led to attrition and the commensurate loss of power of the Japanese forces.[1]

The naval blockade of China prior to U.S. entry into the war had three main characteristics: it was a pacific blockade, meaning it did not affect neutral ships; its goal was to support ground operations along the coast by eliminating Chinese resistance; and enforcement of the blockade was a joint mission – the army became heavily involved in cutting alternate land lines of communication.

Despite the enormous effort expended, the blockade was imperfect. Japan lacked the forces to occupy the entire Chinese coast; rather, its forces were concentrated in coastal cities, various inland cities, and along the main transportation arteries linking them, creating a deployment pattern of dots and lines. Neutral ships not carrying weapons or soldiers were exempt from the blockade; after passing inspection, third-party shipping still often conveyed vital commodities through the Japanese occupation zone. Finally, geography became a major impediment to the blockade because of the numerous alternative land routes. Severing these routes required the cooperation of the Soviet Union in the north, Burma in the west, and French Indochina to the south. Otherwise large air and ground deployments were needed to accomplish the task. This, however, risked conflicts with third countries.

Naval Blockade and Japan's War Objectives

The Imperial Japanese Navy's basic war plans focused on the U.S. and Great Britain, not China. In fact, a campaign against China was never seriously

Statistics compiled by the Japanese Fifth Fleet document the efficiency of the blockade. From January to March 1938, the Fifth Fleet inspected forty-four ships, all of them neutral; nineteen ships – by far the largest number – were British registered; followed by eleven Portuguese; three apiece for France, Norway, and Greece; two apiece for the Netherlands and Panama; and one Italian ship.[12] Five out of the forty-four that were seized were recently reflagged former Chinese ships. These records estimated pre-war third-country shipping for the main ports of southern China – including Canton, Hong Kong, Shantou, and Xiamen – to total 1,255 vessels per month, with Britain accounting for 78 percent. Only one month into the conflict, this number shrank by almost half to only 698 vessels. Yet the ratio of British ships remained virtually unchanged.

The Imposition of the Blockade (1938–39)

When the first stage of the blockade had been fully implemented on 25 August 1937, it had stopped 700 government and private ships, the approximate number of vessels owned by China at outbreak of war on 7 July 1937. Because of the dramatic reduction in foreign war materiel, the Nationalist army retreated.[13] During 1938–39, Japanese naval operations took the major cities on the Shandong peninsula, including Qingdao, Yantai (Chefoo), and Weihaiwei. Meanwhile, the Hankou and Canton campaigns secured Japan's position along China's coast and along the Yangzi River, just as the Hainan and Nanning campaigns extended this control further south.

Following the success of the Shandong campaign, operations moved further south and focused on capturing the enemy's supply depots and obtaining bases. However, before the Japanese could move inland into South China, they had to establish control over the Yangzi River, which meant taking control of Hankou, a commercial and naval port hundreds of miles up the river.[14] The Hankou Campaign began in March 1938 with naval units sweeping away mines, blocking-ships, and obstacles along the Yangzi River. By December 1937, the navy had opened the water route to Nanjing, which also opened the river approaches to Hankou, which fell to a joint army–navy attack on 26 October 1938.[15]

This put the Japanese Navy in control of the Yangzi River area from Shanghai to Hankou, permitting the extension of the pacific blockade up the river. This interrupted virtually all exchange of goods between China's coastal area and the hinterland. Meanwhile, similar Japanese army operations attempted to cut the all-important railway connecting Canton and Hankou, which accounted for almost 80 percent of the total supplies being smuggled to Chiang Kai-shek's forces.[16]

In the ensuing Canton Campaign, the army dispatched a large number of "strategic troops" (greater than a division) to block Chiang Kai-shek's supply route, but the city had many foreign companies. In particular, capturing Canton meant undermining British influence. Air raids by naval paratroopers on the railways connecting the city with Hong Kong and Hankou were necessary to take the city. Yet the air raids directly infringed British and French interests because they had financed the railways. As a result of the campaign, trade dropped precipitously, particularly through the southern ports of Longzhou, Shantou, and Mengzi. Exports from this area dropped from 37 percent of all Chinese exports in 1938 to 21 percent in 1939, while imports dropped even more, from 31 percent in 1938 to only 12 percent in 1939.[17]

Although the Canton Campaign was a huge operational success, Chiang Kai-shek still did not surrender. In fact, his supply route from French Indochina quickly expanded to compensate for the loss of Canton. The Chongqing government, based at Chiang's new capital in Sichuan province, rerouted supplies via Hanoi and even opened a new route via Burma to help compensate for the loss of the Hong Kong–Canton and Canton–Hankou railroads. A large number of supplies were also brought from the Zhejiang coastal area, especially from Wenzhou and Ningbo, by taking advantage of gaps in the blockade.[18]

In November 1938, after the victorious Hankou and Canton campaigns, Prime Minister Fumimaro Konoe made his Declaration of a New Order of East Asia.[19] His objectives were to defend what Japan had already taken and to build an economic cooperation zone to provide both self-sufficiency and self-defense in case of U.S. or British economic sanctions. The U.S. considered this as a challenge to its Open Door Policy and began considering economic sanctions that would go beyond a moral trade embargo.[20] In December 1938, it granted China a U.S.$25 million credit to open the Burma Road to supply China via Burma. This was the first active intervention by the U.S. in the Sino-Japanese War.

During February 1939, the campaign to capture Hainan Island dramatically changed the blockade. Hainan had an important strategic significance as a "trigger." It signaled the navy's "Southward Advance" strategy that went far beyond the scope of the pacific blockade, eventually entailing operations into Burma to cut the Burma Road. This required the construction of new bases and further air attacks.[21] In the eyes of many third parties, capturing Hainan signaled Japan's intent to expand the war beyond China.[22] In March 1939, Great Britain provided China with a £5.5 million credit to help support its currency.[23]

In early 1939, Chiang Kai-shek opened a Hanoi supply route and the Burma Road, transporting even more war materiel via Yunnan and Sichuan provinces. By autumn 1939, these two routes provided between 4,000 and 6,000 tons of supplies per month.[24] France and Britain rejected Japan's requests to cease aiding Chiang Kai-shek. On 15 November 1939, the Japanese Army began the Nanning Campaign to sever the Hanoi route. China responded to the Japanese victory by opening the Paise route, rendering the Nanning Campaign strategically ineffective.[25]

Negotiations remained deadlocked. On 30 December, the navy began air raids on the Yunnan railway bridges. On 1 February 1940, however, the bombing of a train claimed over 100 victims, including French women and children.[26] Diplomatic talks with France resumed but made no progress, and air raids were resumed in late April.

Attempts to cut the Yunnan railway backfired, since it was run by the French and the raids infringed French interests. Instead of leading to victory, these air raids actually made the blockade even more difficult to enforce. Japan's South China campaigns revealed the extraordinary difficulty of blockading a land power like China. As land routes were severed, new routes took their place. U.S. attempts to interdict the Ho Chi Minh trail twenty years later during the Vietnam War would run into many of the same problems.

The Expansion of the Blockade (1940–41)

The blockade advanced to a new stage in 1940 when it expanded to include neutral ships. Although it did not apply to neutral ships carrying goods unrelated to war, the navy closed several ports to shipping. The international environment had changed. With the establishment of the Wang Jingwei government in China, Japan defined the hostilities as a civil war, declaring its support for the Wang government. Japan argued that this gave it the right to blockade neutral shipping. With Germany's invasion of France during the spring of 1940, Japan gambled that Britain and the U.S. would focus their attention on Europe, not Asia.

Vice-Admiral Shigetaro Shimada, who was appointed Admiral of the China Theater Fleet in July 1940, ordered the blockade ships stationed near Hangzhou Bay to intercept Chinese ships, as well as all neutral ships. He also ordered attacks on Chinese military bases and along the southern coast. There were quick results: 60 junks were burned in a surprise attack on Sandu Bay, Fujian, on 21 July, with almost another 100 junks destroyed on 27 July in the Shanwei, Guangdong, operation.

Blockades of neutral ships were implemented from July 1940 to 1941 in an area running from Hangzhou (four ports in and near Wenzhou, Fuzhou, and Sanduao) through Guangdong province. This meant that the blockade covered almost the entire area from central to south China.[27] Eventually, implementation was extended to fourteen districts. The blockade required that all of the 100 ships of the China Theater Fleet be dispatched to this one area.

Meanwhile, the Japanese Army advanced into French Indochina on 22 September 1940 following negotiations with the new, and dramatically more cooperative, Vichy government of France. Great Britain and the U.S. concluded that Japan's ambitions including obtaining unrivaled supremacy in Asia. The Tripartite Pact between Japan, Italy, and Germany on 27 September merely confirmed these suspicions.

Japan also increased pressure upon Britain to close the Burma Road. On 12 July, the British ambassador to Japan agreed to cut war materiel shipments through the Burma Road for three months.[28] The Japanese advance into French Indochina and the Tripartite Pact made this agreement null and void. Britain notified Japan that it would reopen the Burma Road on 8 October 1940. Japan responded with bombing raids beginning on 25 October, but bridges were soon reconstructed while raids over narrow mountain valleys could not be conducted with pinpoint accuracy.[29] To close the Burma Road required ground troops, but this could lead to war against Britain. The Japanese Navy and diplomatic staff searched for alternatives.[30]

In response to Japan's more aggressive policies, the U.S. started to implement an embargo or an economic blockade. Previously Washington had taken relatively mild measures, such as abolishing the U.S. and Japan Trade and Commerce Agreement. On 25 September 1940, it announced that it would grant US$25 million credit to the Chongqing government. The next day, it prohibited scrap metal exports to any foreign country except Great Britain.[31] The Japanese blockade of China tightened just as the U.S. decided to embargo Japan. The Question and Answer Session on "War Plans for the Sino-Japanese War," held jointly by the Imperial General Headquarters of the Navy and Army in November 1940, shows that the Imperial Headquarters considered its economic strategy to be key to success in China.[32]

To further this strategy, the Japanese Navy began to blockade all neutral shipping at specific ports. Yet supplies were still reaching Chiang from ports in central and southern China.[33] The navy and army jointly designed new tactics to cut these supplies, called "Operation C," and issued these plans on 26 February 1941. The army dispatched seven divisions. Two were assigned to the blockade. The navy declared Hong Kong and Macao within the blockade zone, while the army strengthened the "regulations cracking down on transportation," to extend the blockade line between captured areas and enemy districts, and to restrict supplies to the Chinese hinterland.[34]

Nevertheless the overall impact of the blockade on the war remained questionable. After World War II, Lieutenant-General Jun Atomiya, former Commander of the Army of Southern China, concluded that the significance of the blockade strategy had been of little importance to the South China Campaign.[35]

The Overall Effectiveness of Japan's Naval Blockade Strategy

The naval blockade had a devastating impact on China's foreign trade. Customs office statistics from 1936 to 1940, compiled in Table 10.1, show that the total tonnage of ships visiting China decreased from 145 million gross tons in 1936 to 41 million gross tons in 1940. In 1936, there were 59 Japanese ships, totaling 141,000 gross tons, in service on and around the Yangzi River. In 1938, their number had fallen by two-thirds, mainly because so many ships had been requisitioned by the military. Even with

Table 10.1 Changes in the percentage and gross tonnage of shipping to and from China

Year	Japan	Britain	China	Others	Total
1936	17	39	27	17	100
	24,913	57,345	39,355	23,426	145,019
1937	14	40	24	22	100
	12,815	36,105	21,593	19,524	90,037
1938	14	48	9	29	100
	8,743	28,563	5,623	16,208	59,137
1939	30	37	5	28	100
	15,755	19,233	2,696	14,242	51,926
1940	45	26	5	24	100
	18,738	10,843	2,224	9,581	41,391

Source: The Northern China Merchant Service Association, "Northern China Merchant Service Pandect" (1942), 42.

Notes
Units: upper = percentage
       lower = thousands of metric tons.

these sharp decreases in ships, Japanese shipping in China expanded from only 17 percent of the total tonnage to account for 45 percent in 1940, surpassing even Great Britain.

China maintained 312 ships, totaling about 456,000 gross tons before the implementation of the blockade. Almost all of them, except for ships on the inland rivers and on lakes, were rendered useless by the blockade. Chinese tonnage declined by a total of 270,000 gross tons, including 31,000 gross tons from ships captured or impounded and 14,000 gross tons for ships reflagged to other countries. In just three years China's percentage of the trade dropped from 27 percent to only 5 percent.

Great Britain had dominated the merchant service for coastal China since 1900. Britain initially took advantage of the Japanese blockade to raise freight charges. With the expansion of the blockade, and especially after the Hankou Campaign, which blocked British ships from the Yangzi River and cut this main transportation artery, the positions of Great Britain and Japan were reversed. British influence in the area, especially around Hong Kong, was threatened by the expansion of the Sino-Japanese War, resulting from Japan's capture of Chinese ports and its advance into French Indochina.

Consequently, Britain developed new routes through the unoccupied areas from the Zhejiang–Guangzhou district to Chongqing. As a result, British shipping increased between Shanghai and the ports of Sanduao, Fuzhou, and especially Ningbo and Wenzhou.[36] But the Nationalists closed the Chongqing ports by the Ordinance of Embargo of Shanghai, which prohibited transport benefiting the enemy. This, combined with the Japanese blockade of southern Chinese ports, meant that the transport blockade was tight. However, Britain, by re-flagging third-party ships, essentially retained

Table 10.2 China's trade figures after the Marco Polo Bridge incident.

Year	Exports	Imports	Total
1936	42,271 (100)	56,404 (100)	98,675 (100)
1937	49,990 (118)	56,787 (101)	106,777 (108)
1938	32,770 (78)	53,568 (95)	86,338 (87)
1939	25,949 (61)	81,390 (144)	107,338 (109)
1940	32,302 (76)	89,756 (159)	122,058 (124)

Source: Toa Institute, "Economic Development of Occupied Areas in China" (1944), 367.

Notes
Units: thousands of pounds (percentage change, 1936=10)

the same rights as before to conduct marine transport in the Far East. It did so, even though it was forced to narrow its activities around China and lost a large number of merchant ships in Europe.[37]

Other neutral shipping was affected more by the European situation than by the Japanese blockade. In particular, Germany and Italy tried to advance into the Far Eastern transportation business after December 1937. After the outbreak of war in Europe, however, both Germany and Italy retrenched for fear of internment by the British Navy. Meanwhile, France, Denmark, Norway, the Netherlands, and Greece were safer in the Far East than in Europe because of Germany's weak naval presence. Their merchant ships in China remained under the protection of Great Britain.

In November 1940, the Japanese government reported that: "Almost the entire Chinese coast has been blockaded since this spring [of 1940] when Japan strengthened the blockade. China is now smuggling small quantities of goods with small craft calling at Hong Kong and Shanghai as intermediate ports. The route from French Indochina was blocked by our troops in charge of inspections and by the troops stationed there. And the Burma Road was also crushed by our air force. It will take quite a while for the enemy to repair the Burma Road." The Imperial Headquarters judged the blockade to be a success whose positive effects would continue to grow.[38] This assessment was not exaggerated: on the coastline; the blockade was effective.[39]

But, it is important to consider Soviet aid and the Soviet supply route. During the first half of the Sino-Japanese War (1937–40), the Soviet Union was the primary foreign benefactor of the Nationalist government. Prior to 1940, there were over three times more Soviet than Western credits.[40] During this period, Japan underestimated Soviet intervention. According to Imperial Japanese Naval public papers published in May 1939, army attacks and navy air bombing had destroyed the railways necessary for the Soviet route,[41] while research conducted by the Manchurian Railway Company in

Unlike Japan's pacific blockade of China, which was not imposed under wartime conditions, the U.S. blockade strategy against Japan was a total blockade. Japanese trade and communications from overseas, including even land routes inside China, were blockaded by U.S. forces. Starvation soon loomed large in Japan's future. The Pacific War that ravaged much of East Asia and the Pacific had begun with a Japanese pacific blockade of China. Ultimately, it ended in the Allies' more complete and more devastating total blockade of Japan.

11 Naval Blockade and Economic Warfare in the European War, 1939–45

*Geoffrey Till**

As was the case in World War I, a major portion of the British naval strategy against Germany between 1939 and 1945 was to enforce a naval blockade. Anglo-American relations were particularly strained, at least until Pearl Harbor and the U.S. decision to enter the European conflict on the side of the Allies. Interestingly, the extent to which the ambiguities in the interpretation and implementation of blockade were susceptible to national circumstances were most startlingly revealed by the United States itself, after it became a blockading power. As Alan Milward justly observes, "The power which had most sustained the international law of neutrality now became its most virulent enemy."[1]

Pre-war British and German Expectations

Both the British and the Germans had exaggerated ideas of the potential effectiveness of a naval blockade, derived in large measure from their experience in World War I. The British, and indeed the Americans, took the whole concept of economic warfare much more seriously than did their Axis adversaries. Conditioned perhaps by their maritime nature, they fully appreciated that the approaching war would not be over by the first Christmas. Indeed, the Prime Minister announced in the House of Commons, on 11 September 1939, that the country should prepare for a war of at least three years. The British were under no illusion that they had any means of achieving a quick victory over Germany, and they knew that a great war would absorb all the resources of a modern state in a brutal contest of attrition.

The British were, none the less, confident that in the end they would prevail, because, with the French, their combined war economy could produce more military striking power than Germany.[2] Their confidence was buttressed by an exaggerated view of the past achievements of the naval blockade of World War I and of the potential effectiveness of bombing. They were impressed by the intelligence that seemed to show how critically the new Germany, say of 1938 – which could be seen as appreciably weaker than the old Germany of 1914 – depended on overseas supplies of strategic materials like oil, rubber, iron-ore, manganese, edible fats, metal alloys, and

Map 11.1 The North Atlantic theatre of operations

so forth. To some extent, they were prey to wishful thinking that "... blockade, sanctions or economic warfare ... could be employed as a substitute for military force".[3]

Paradoxically, the British regarded the preparations that they knew the Germans were taking to guard against the threat of blockade as evidence that such expectations were on the right track. The extent of these precautions, however, did reinforce the conclusion that the economic blockade of Germany would not be a quick and easy process. In the end, though, it was expected to make a significant contribution to victory.

With these aspirations, the British in the interwar period set about gathering economic intelligence and setting up an administrative system to coordinate this form of warfare. A Ministry of Blockade was created in 1929 and extensive studies were carried out, particularly in the late 1930s, of Germany's perceived economic vulnerabilities and how a campaign to exploit them would best be achieved.[4]

The Germans took the apparent lesson of World War I equally to heart, for they expected an effective British blockade from the start.[5] In the 1920s, General Groener began a major shift in German strategic thinking away from the purely operational approach of Moltke and Schlieffen towards conceptions of war for the industrial age. Hitler's view of the modern economy was, if anything, even more mercantilist. He saw it as an instrument of power, "the material springboard for military conquest",[6] and the central element in the war capability of a modern state.

Accordingly, from the time he seized power, Hitler set about preparing his country to withstand this kind of pressure from outside. The Four Year Plan promoted the technical improvement of agriculture; there was large scale rationalization of the labor market; as early as 1933 firms were encouraged to develop synthetic alternatives to natural raw materials that could not be found within the borders of the Reich. Relations were developed with neighboring or potentially sympathetic countries that could provide a reliable source of such materials. Indeed, with the re/acquisition of the Ruhr, Austria, and the Sudetenland, Hitler's aspiration for economic autarchy became more of an objective of his foreign policy than a means.

In their preparations for the coming conflict, and indeed in their terminology, both protagonists demonstrated the way in which economic warfare was steadily becoming a much broader matter than merely operating, or evading, a naval blockade. To the British, economic warfare came to incorporate blockade, counter-production, and attack behind the enemy's fighting front. Blockade itself was taken to incorporate all those "... operations by which supplies of raw materials or finished goods were prevented from reaching Germany or her allies from neutral sources in or outside Europe".[7]

Naval blockade was certainly a part of the process, but how important it would be remained to be seen. None the less, the specifically *naval* blockade, an image redolent with the portentous memories of World War I, dominated thinking and expectations in the final days before the war. Both sides remained acutely aware of the potential vulnerability of their own shipping to hostile action. According to Speer, Hitler often devoted his spare time to devising a transcontinental railway system that would keep his empire together. Apparently he felt that sea travel was never safe enough even in peacetime, and was certainly unreliable in wartime. Moreover, a single train could transport as much as a freighter.[8]

The Royal Navy remained as committed to the defense of its sea lines of communication as ever, and despite the advent of sonar, was not as relaxed about the ease with which the future submarine threat could be contained as is sometimes claimed.[9] Indeed, this was one reason why the British ensured that the future of the submarine was the subject of so much international debate during the interwar period. For their part, elements within the German Navy were determined to justify such concerns, by developing its capacity to attack British shipping by submarine and surface raider.

Trade attack of this sort was certainly a very significant dimension of economic warfare. However, it was not, technically, an aspect of blockade, since it was by no means limited to the interception of neutral goods and shipping, although both were certainly amongst its main victims. Nor was its extent as absolute and predictable as blockades are legally supposed to be. None the less, the division between the two sorts of activity was sufficiently fuzzy for the two to be closely related in the debate about the moral and political acceptability of economic warfare before and during the war.

The Gradual Abandonment of Restraint

Despite high expectations, the British were circumspect in their introduction of naval blockade as a part of economic warfare. In effect, this action was initially limited to the modest and limited "contraband control" system introduced in 1914, under which neutral ships were searched for contraband; if found, the latter was impounded. They did not initiate early pre-emptive purchasing of neutral supplies, strategic bombing, or any other form of attack on the adversary's war economy.

This was partly in deference to neutrals, since even the constrained system of "contraband control" attracted a hostile response from them. In October 1939, the Russians declared that British control measures "... violate the elementary principles of free navigation by merchant shipping"; moreover, regarding foodstuffs such as bread, meat, and butter as contraband indirectly hurt women, children, and the old, and so broke the accepted laws of war. The British response to such criticisms became increasingly robust. First, there was nothing new about any of this. The British *were* conforming to current interpretations of the relevant law and customary practice. Second, Article 24 of the International Declaration on the Law of Warfare of 26 February 1909 specified that food could be regarded as conditional contraband, when it was "susceptible of use in war".[10]

As Sir William Beveridge, Master of University College, Oxford, showed in *The Times*, foodstuffs could indeed be used for military purposes. Fats were necessary for making propellants. The starch in grain can be converted into alcohol, and thence into fuel for tanks and lorries. Since Germany was self-sufficient in grain, though not in meat and fats, the government could easily make up for any blockade shortfalls in the latter by producing more of the former, directly or indirectly, for civilian consumption. For the Germans it *was* therefore a question of guns or butter. Since, the belligerent government controlled the allocation of food, especially in totalitarian states, any responsibility for civilian distress was theirs and not the blockader's.[11]

The Americans were also a factor since their goodwill was likely to be important. In the United States, there was a strong, almost ideological, commitment to the freedom of navigation, and in some circles there were dark suspicions that the British might use the blockade as a means of improving their relative commercial position. This caused acrimony and what Lord Lothian (Philip Kerr), the British ambassador, called "a minor crisis in British–American relations". On the other hand, the administration was clear that a German victory would not be in U.S. interests, and so trod a delicate line in supporting a policy of helping Britain, but very much on American terms. "No help to Germany, but no dominion status for ourselves" was the catchphrase of the time.[12]

This desire not to get drawn into the European war led to the Neutrality Act of November 1939, which forbad U.S. ships and citizens from entering clearly defined war zones. But this was a cause of friction too. The American *Mormacsum*, on passage to Bergen and outside any such zone, was taken by the Royal Navy to Kirkwall, which was inside one, for examination. The United States protested, and so Churchill ordered that no more American ships be stopped under such circumstances. But American objections to British attempts to control trade remained a problem, especially in the Caribbean.[13]

To an extent, these American reactions and the original assertions of British rights were a reflection both of the moral and legal ambiguities of the naval blockade, and of sensitivity to the way in which they might be viewed in neutral countries. For their part, the Germans made the most of it, both for domestic opinion and in the propaganda battle for foreign support. Incidents such as the interception of the *Altmark* in Norwegian waters were used by Germany to demonstrate Britain's willingness to trample on neutral rights and its ruthless determination to interpret and implement its own.[14]

There were some hard economic reasons for restraint, too. The operations of the war market drove up prices for both raw materials and manufactured goods. This increased business incentives in neutral countries to trade as much as possible with both sides. Sweden provides an excellent example of this. Its world-class S.K.F. ball bearing works lost much of its physical access to the Western allies through the exigencies of war after the spring of 1940; it naturally sought to compensate for this by exploiting increasing opportunities in Germany. The Swedish government had to make some difficult calculations about its present and future interests, calculations influenced by its sense of which side was likely to win and so determine the shape of the post-war world in which Sweden would have to operate. The British Foreign Office was well aware of this, and of the dangers of antagonizing Swedish opinion. It consequently counseled against too cavalier an interpretation of British rights with respect to Sweden's trade.

None the less, despite such early counsels of caution, the rigor of the naval blockade increased step by step, and at faster rates than in World War I. There was widespread support for the notion that the maritime British had to make the very most of their opportunities, especially in their parlous position after the fall of France:

> We are ourselves a great sea and air Power. We are fighting for our national existence against a great land Power, disposing also of great strength in the air. We cannot afford to be too solicitous of the interests of third parties in our mortal peril. We must make use of all the weapons of our armoury without over-much regard for the safety of those who have stood aside from the conflict.[15]

In effect, Britain needed to be as ruthless as Germany: "Nothing less that totalitarian methods will suffice when we are engaged in a totalitarian war."[16] There must not be a repeat of World War I, when a real blockade was only imposed in the last eighteen months of conflict.[17]

Britain's willingness to engage in the progressive escalation was reinforced by perceptions of German behaviour. The British Order-in-Council of 27 November 1939, which required every merchant vessel to discharge enemy goods intended for export in a British or allied port, was represented as fair and legal retaliation for the German sinking of merchant ships in violation of the Submarine Protocol of 1936, and indiscriminate mining in violation of the Hague Convention, No. VIII of 1907.[18] Any infringement of neutral rights this implied was held to be of small consequence when compared to the manner in which the enemy had already violated them by its attitude to international law generally. The British were merely doing something to restore the balance.[19] The same kind of tit-for-tat interaction between the two sides was equally evident in the progressive extension of declared war zones in European waters.

The result of such pressure was, first, an increasing rigor in the implementation of the naval blockade. When the Northern Patrol was established on 6 September 1939, the remit was to stop enemy imports; later, in November, this was extended to enemy exports as well. Second, and much more important, the naval blockade was incorporated in an intensifying and widening economic campaign that eventually included an ambitious program in the strategic preemption of key raw materials and finished goods, relentless pressure on neutrals, a ferocious air assault on German cities and industry, and the wholesale mobilization of Allied industrial potential. The paradoxical consequence of these policies was that the more rigorous the naval blockade became, the less important it was as a means of putting pressure on Germany, in comparison with other aspects of the economic campaign.

The Operation of the British Naval Blockade

The naval blockade had two immediate objectives: contraband control, and the interception of German ships. Initially the British Home Fleet, under Admiral Sir Charles Forbes, was responsible for both in local waters. Forbes set up the Northern Patrol on 6 September 1939; in August 1940 this was supplemented by a Western Patrol operating out of Gibraltar. The Northern Patrol, commanded by Vice-Admiral Sir Max Horton, initially comprised Reserve Fleet cruisers of the 7th and 12th Cruiser Squadrons, manned in the main by reservists and pensioners. With limited endurance, these old cruisers were hardly appropriate either in terms of number or of quality, but they served the purpose.

In December 1939, they were successively replaced by armed merchant cruisers (AMCs) which were much better in many respects except in that, being slow and weakly armed, they would be vulnerable to German warships and submarines. Fifty-six AMCs were produced in due course, and this number allowed several ships to patrol in each of the Shetlands–Faeroes, Faeroes–Iceland, and Iceland–Greenland gaps. In due course, their efforts were supplemented by smaller Armed Boarding Vessels (ABVs) and Ocean Boarding Vessels (OBVs), intended for merchant-ship interceptions in narrow waters and on the open ocean respectively. The Northern Patrol was also reinforced by Coastal Command aircraft, and could call on the support of the rest of the Home Fleet when necessary. The Northern Patrol was eventually wound up as a separate command on 10 June 1941.[20]

The contraband control system became complex and sophisticated. As many incoming or outgoing ships as possible were intercepted on the high seas. German ships were either captured or they scuttled themselves. Neutral ships were checked for contraband, which the Ministry of Economic Warfare defined very widely as all kinds of arms, plus materials for their manufacture, fuel, all forms of communication equipment, currency and bullion, food and clothing, and metal materials of all kinds. In effect almost anything bound for Germany was regarded as contraband. "It was even suggested that a shipload of Bibles could be contraband, as the scriptures could be pulped down and turned into packing for ammunition."[21] Since searching at sea was impractical, merchantmen were diverted to search ports, particularly Kirkwall in the Orkneys. If they proved not to be carrying contraband, they were issued with the appropriate documentation and allowed to proceed, wearing a special flag against further examination. Contraband, on the other hand, was seized.

In the seven months before Scandinavia was engulfed by war, the Northern Patrol stopped 1,053 neutral ships, of which 361 were diverted for examination; another 93 went to Kirkwall of their own volition. During one week early in the war, 131 ships were examined at one center; 114 were allowed to proceed, while one entire cargo and elements of another twenty shiploads were seized.[22] From the beginning, masters could obtain a "Cargo Navicert" or a "Ship Navicert" from British officials abroad; this documentation advised examination officers that the cargo or even the whole ship had already been cleared. This saved everyone much time. In July 1940, the British made Navicerts compulsory, but by this time the only surviving European neutrals all had easy access to the Reich's land borders, so the work of the Contraband Control Service in Home Waters effectively ended.[23]

During the same period, twenty-seven German ships caught outside home waters by the outbreak of war tried to get home by running the blockade. Of these, twelve were taken as prizes by the British (including the 13,615 ton *Cap Norte*, a major capture, and the *Poseidon* which sank afterwards, and the *Borkum* which was torpedoed by a U-boat), the French took the *Rostock*, twelve were scuttled by their crews when intercepted, two were lost at sea or wrecked, and only one, the *Wangoni*, made it to Germany. The latter featured in the special Home Fleet operation W.R. in February 1940 to intercept a group of six German ships in Vigo, the other five of which were all caught. During this operation the Northern Patrol was reinforced by eight Home Fleet destroyers and the 10th A/S Striking Force. However, in the period up to 5 April 1940, while Germany lost 58 merchant ships totaling some 300,000 tons, a further 82 amounting to 480,000 tons got through.[24]

The French participated in the naval blockade as well, operating their own examination centers, with the *Ministère de Blocus* working closely with London's Contraband Committee and the Ministry of Economic Warfare. Indeed, one of their submarines achieved a notable first in September 1939 by taking as prize the 5,522-ton *Chemnitz*, the first ship in history to be captured by such means.[25] *Chemnitz* had an interesting cargo of cotton, lead ingots, copper, flour – and parrots. Whether the latter would have constituted contraband is a moot point.

As satisfactory as this overall outcome might seem, there were costs as well as benefits for the British. Reactivating the reserve cruisers and equipping the AMCs represented quite an investment. The work of interception, and especially boarding, was hard in such difficult weather. Three-quarters of the crew of one AMC were reported as never having been at sea before, and even trawlermen were badly affected by the weather; "they will become inured to the hardships in course of time" was the Vice-Admiral's somewhat heartless response.[26] And indeed they did. There was always the additional danger of the ships of the Northern Patrol running up against German warships or disguised commerce raiders. On 23 November 1939, the AMC HMS *Rawalpindi* came across the German battlecruisers *Scharnhorst* and *Gneisenau* and was lost in the most gallant circumstances imaginable. Three more AMCs were torpedoed by U-boats in June 1940, and the ABV *Northern Rover* was lost in November 1940.

By the early summer of 1940, with most of Northern Europe in German hands, normal sea traffic practically ceased in northern waters and attention switched to traffic to and from the Iberian Peninsula. The British were also well aware that German occupation of Western France made it much easier for blockade-runners to reach the Reich. In the north, the number of ship interceptions declined dramatically; the bulk of interceptions, 1,281 out the total of 1,428, were conducted by the AMCs and trawlers of the Western Patrol operating out of Gibraltar. By this time, the Navicert system was well developed and very few neutral ships had to be diverted for examination.

In parallel with this, there was continuing interest in the UK in the possibility of interfering with Germany's iron ore trade with Sweden. By November, the Swedish port of Lulea in the Gulf of Bothnia was ice-bound and iron ore had to be taken by train to Narvik and then shipped to Germany through the Indreleia, the inner leads. Since these were Norwegian territorial waters, the British could not legally get at such shipping. One solution might be to mine the leads, if the Norwegians could not be persuaded to do it themselves, in order to force the ships out onto the high seas. The Foreign Office refused to sanction this gross violation of Norway's neutral rights, much to the frustration of Churchill, then First Lord of the Admiralty. At one stage, his frustration found vent in the suggestion that a couple of British merchant ships, fitted with rams, could "carry merchandise and travel up and down the Leads looking for German ore ships or any other German merchant vessels, and then ram them by accident".[27]

Through the exceptionally hard winter of 1939–40, the German iron ore trade proceeded through Norway with impunity, and this was one of the factors that led to the eventual British change of heart and a chain of events that ended with the ill-fated Norway Campaign of 1940. Germany's subsequent control of Norway and Denmark considerably reduced the effectiveness of the British blockade. To the extent that such expectations encouraged the Germans to invade, it might even be said that British economic pressure proved to be counter-productive.

The Blockade through June 1941

It is hard to come to a conclusion about the cost-effectiveness of the British naval blockade up to the summer of 1941. German war material totaling 558,857 tons had been seized from neutrals. These were substantial achievements but, compared to the overall costs of the war, this seems a useful rather than a decisive contribution to the outcome. But to the ships and cargoes actually captured must be added the benefit the Germans might otherwise have derived from uninhibited sea-based trade. According to one estimate, the Navicert system had perhaps denied the Germans a further 3,600,000 tons of material, although these results are notoriously difficult to quantify.[28] The Northern Patrol clearly had a considerable deterrent effect. Concentrations of German ships remained in neutral ports such as New York, Rio de Janeiro, and in the River Plate, rather than risk running the blockade. Altogether there were some 246 German merchantmen lurking around the world in April 1940.[29] Moreover, the efforts of the Northern Patrol helped the British negotiate satisfactory War Trade Agreements with Sweden, Norway, and Denmark.

Germany's strategic reaction to the likelihood of such pressure undermined even these achievements, however, since Berlin had taken precautions before the war against the possible effects of a British blockade. In 1931, for instance, Germany set up the secret naval Etappe organization in order to gather information on all ports and movements of shipping and cargo in neutral countries and to establish what support might be available in the event of armed conflict.

There was a growing realization through the 1930s by the German Navy that the conduct of naval warfare had to be thought about holistically, and that this would need to include measures to deal with a British blockade. In 1937, the German Navy drew up a Memorandum on Economic Warfare that was accepted by the Armed Forces Economics Staff as a provisional manual in 1939. It emphasized the need for detailed statistical and scientific intelligence about the economic needs of both sides because: "Economic warfare is a decisive weapon in able hands. It is capable of winning bloodless political victories. It creates an indispensable basis for success in an armed conflict, and it supports actual warfare in a decisive manner."[30]

In fact, no such centralized intelligence body was set up, and it is not clear how much influence this naval report had. In the period to 1939, however, the Nazi regime none the less devoted much energy to the task of mobilizing for war. Perhaps two-thirds of all industrial investment went into war-related sectors of the economy. Large stockpiles of strategic materials were built up, and wherever possible industries were tasked to find substitutes for strategic materials that would always be hard to come by. The firm I.G. Farben, for example, devoted much effort to the development of "Buna", a successful synthetic rubber made from butadience and natrium. By 1939, I.G. Farben was producing 25,000 tons of Buna per year. The Germans were also capable of making three million tons of oil annually from brown coal and shale.[31]

Once the war began, Germany tightened up its own organization to beat the blockade. A naval conference in February 1941 concluded that "the breaking of the blockade will be organized on the basis of private business and with the assistance of the state" in the provision of information, communications, contact men, false papers, and so forth coordinated under the office of the Deputy for the Four Year plan. "A list of urgent imports is to be compiled including for instance rubber, oil and fats, nickel, copper, tin, molybedenum, beryl, concentrates of wolframite, wool, cotton, furs, leather, tanning acid, meat extracts, grain and legumes." Surprisingly, the emphasis was very much on private enterprise, even with the most unlikely of partners:

> The blockade breaking will be carried out on the basis of private business. All risk is to be borne by the individual who is granted a proportionate share of the profits. Cooperation with Jewish and other undesirable companies is permissible. Price ceiling limitations will not be enforced.[32]

Far more important than this, however, was the fact that the Germans were able to obtain much of what they needed from the Russians in two deals of 11 February 1940 and 10 January 1941. In October 1939, for instance, the German naval staff reported that Russian economic assistance was crucial to counter a British economic blockade. The amounts anticipated were substantial, including 872,000 tons of mineral oil products per year, 500,000 tons of iron ore, 934,500 tons of fodder and legumes, 91,500 tons of cotton, etc. These supplies came to Germany by train and their extent dwarfed those carried to Germany by sea, whether intercepted or not.[33] Moreover, Russia was also a conduit for economic relations with the Japanese empire.

Finally, the conquest and exploitation of much of Northern and Western Europe provided the Reich with substantial new sources of raw materials: iron ore from France, Luxemburg, and Norway, molybedenum from Norway, access to the huge oil stocks of France, dairy products from Denmark and the Netherlands, wool from Belgium, fish of all sorts from Norway, lead and fodder from Poland, antimony from Czechoslovakia, and so on. By 1942, the overall contribution of the conquered territories to the German war economy was to more than double the 1940 rate.[34] Moreover, neutral states became more cooperative, especially those that now found themselves to be neighbors of the Reich. Rumania, Bulgaria, Hungary, Yugoslavia, Spain, and Portugal provided foodstuffs, copper, nickel, chrome, wolframite, and bauxite.

According to many historians, in fact, the economic position of the Reich during this period was sufficiently comfortable for Hitler not to have to impose the rigors of total war on his own people. This position has more recently come under attack from those who believe that Germany mobilized and that civilian consumption was cut back more in the period from 1939 to 1941 than has often been realized.[35] Even so, the overall result seemed to demonstrate the validity of the view that the Mackinderite heartland had the resources with which to withstand the economic pressure brought by the maritime powers.

With the German invasion of Russia in June 1941, an important part of this highly beneficial arrangement came to an abrupt end. From now on, connections with Japan and the Far East could only be maritime. Worse still, the demands of an additional and major war in the East put huge new strains on the German war economy. For the Germans, this was uncharted territory. Coincidentally, the British wound up the Northern and Western patrols in the same month, and their work came to be subsumed in the general activity of the fleet around the world.

German Blockade-Running, June 1941–May 1945

Even if the problem of contraband from neutral sources had largely been controlled through a combination of patroling and the Navicert system, there still remained the issue of German blockade-runners bringing strategic materials to Germany from non-European sources. There were three main periods of German blockade-running: April 1941–May 1942, when allied distraction resulted in quite high levels of German success; the winter of 1942–43; and the winter of 1943–44. Allied success in the latter period resulted in the practical cessation of blockade-running, although it was hoped that the new Type XX transport U-boats would allow another season to start in autumn 1945.

Blockade runners were technically owned by the original shippers, but were operated for the German Navy by the Merchant Shipping Federation. It was estimated by the British that the Germans had available something like 1,560 ships of 2,500 tons or more (including Swedish vessels owned by German firms). Such ships flew the *Reichshandelsflagge*, the equivalent to the British Red Ensign. The crews of successful runners were awarded a special badge, the *Blockadebrecherabzeichen*, and a handsome financial reward.[36] Typically, such operations began from, and ended in, Atlantic ports in occupied France; the round trip to Japan and the Far East would often take nine months or so. These voyages not infrequently also involved support for German surface raiders and submarines operating in distant waters, through the transport of supplies, torpedoes, and so on, and the ability to collect prisoners taken from prizes.

The passage and cargo of the celebrated 2,729-ton blockade-runner *Alsterufer*, sunk on 27 December 1943, was fairly typical, although she flew the Blue Ensign of the *Reichsdienst* since she took out torpedoes and other equipment for the German U-boat base at Penang. She carried a large amount of crude rubber, 200 tons of tin ingots, and 300 tons of tungsten concentrates. Her crew comprised ten Merchant Navy officers, twenty-eight Merchant Navy seamen, and thirty-eight naval ratings under a Chief Petty Officer. She left France in February 1943, took on cargo at Bangkok and at Singapore, and went on to Japan before returning to Europe. She was sunk in the Bay of Biscay on 27 December 1943.[37]

Other goods of interest to Germany were animal fats and vegetable oils, fish preserves, quinine bark, manganese ores, hides, and to a far lesser extent luxury items like tea, cocoa, and peppers. These goods were often especially targeted when stocks ran low. The need for imports of natural rubber and animal fats and vegetable oils was a constant refrain. Both of these were very short by late 1941, but something like 33,000 tons were brought in during the successful season up to the early summer of 1942.[38]

This success soon proved to be temporary, and both types of material were in short supply by the beginning of 1943, when it was decided to concentrate on restoring the rubber situation. The Ministry of Economic Warfare calculated that another 16,000 tons of rubber were brought in during the twelve months to June 1943, at a time when it was thought that the 4,500 tons of rubber sunk on the *Regensburg* in May 1943 would equip and maintain three armoured divisions for one year.[39]

There is no doubt that, however difficult it might be to quantify the exact strategic importance of getting such "bottleneck" materials through the blockade, the Germans devoted considerable effort to the task.[40] Blockade-running was the subject of many Führer Naval Conferences.[41] Thought was given to the conversion of the *Deutschland* class of pocket battleships, and even the incomplete aircraft carrier *Graf Zeppelin*, to the blockade-running role; operational U-boats were diverted to the purpose and a new class of transport submarines was planned for 1945. The fact that the cargo-carrying capacity of U-boats was no more that 120–130 tons[42] shows how desperate the Germans had become to receive these supplies by the end of the war. Evidently just one or two cargo-loads could make a real difference.

Allied success in catching such blockade-runners needs to be assessed against this background. In 1941–42, when allied naval resources were under particular strain, a high percentage suceeded. According to one estimate, possibly eighteen out of thirty-one runners from non-European ports got through in 1941. Another source says twelve out of fifteen runners succeeded between April 1941 and May 1942.[43] Through 1943–44, this rate dropped rapidly. Of the five runners from Japan in the winter of 1943–44, only one made it home.

Another way of measuring the blockade's success was to assess the percentage of enemy cargoes intercepted. In 1943, the Ministry estimated that they intercepted 29,000 tons of rubber (64 percent of the amount sent), 20,000 tons of vegetable oils (66 percent of the total), 6,500 tons of tin (86 percent), 250 tons of tea (14 percent), and so on.[44] These are significant losses, especially when set against Dönitz's 1944 estimate that Germany's requirements in tin from non-European sources were only 2,440 tons per year.[45]

Allied success was attributable to a general improvement in the level of sea control, particularly in the Atlantic, the relative decline of the U-boat threat, the increased availability of submarines and maritime patrol aircraft, and improving intelligence from photo-reconnaissance and ULTRA sources. The latter gave blockading forces a significant advantage over their predecessors. Unlike them, the modern blockader did not need to spend months at sea waiting for a chance encounter with a blockade-runner.[46]

Conclusions

The real question concerning the World War II blockade, however, is not just the extent of contraband prevented from reaching Germany or the percentage of runners intercepted, but the more strategic question of assessing the degree to which the British naval blockade made a difference to the outcome of the war. Set against Allied losses in the Battle of the Atlantic, the achievement of the British blockade may seem to fade into insignificance, certainly when measured by ships intercepted or sunk and cargoes lost. Moreover, the strategic effect of the blockade in the war up to June 1941 was offset by the extent to which Germany had been able to build up stockpiles, develop substitutes for difficult materials like oil and rubber, and rely on the resources of a considerably expanded Reich. By March 1942, Lord William Waldegrave Palmer Selborne, the new Minister of Economic Warfare, had concluded that Germany had made itself self-sufficient in all but rubber, wolfram, and tin, and that substitution meant that only relatively small quantities of these materials would be needed – perhaps a dozen good ship-loads a year.[47]

Fortunately for the Allies, these advantages were gradually lost as the war went on, since Germany's adversaries multiplied in number and strength and the military and industrial demands of containing them increased. The fear of the long-term effects of blockade was one reason for this situation, since, as Admiral Raeder pointed out, "It is urgently necessary to defeat Russia and thus create a *Lebensraum* which is blockade-proof and easy to defend. Thus we could continue to fight for years."[48] The extent to which such fears were partly responsible for Germany embarking on an adventurist grand strategy, which it was unlikely to win, was indeed one of the most important, if frequently unremarked, benefits of the blockade.

Map 12.1 The Nationalists blockade of the PRC as of July 1949

12   The Nationalists' Blockade of the PRC, 1949–58

*Bruce A. Elleman**

During the Nationalist retreat from the mainland in 1949, the Republic of China (ROC) on Taiwan instituted a naval blockade of the People's Republic of China (PRC). Although the Nationalist Navy was comparatively large, its forces were retained mainly for defense of the island's coastal perimeter. To conduct the blockade, the Nationalists worked with a number of guerrilla movements located on offshore islands not far from China's coast. Later, the U.S. Navy helped defend Taiwan even while providing military assistance – especially aircraft – that made air patrols of the blockade possible. The Nationalist blockade lasted from 1949 through 1958.

The blockade had mixed results. While it generally succeeded in interdicting China's coastal and international trade, Nationalist cooperation with a number of guerrilla groups – really little different than pirate organizations – aggravated foreign shippers, especially those flying the British flag based in Hong Kong. Over time, elaborate systems for paying off the guerrillas were created, and international trade was resumed, albeit at a reduced level. In the meantime, China had to make up the losses by redirecting its trade over land via the Soviet Union, which helped exacerbate Sino-Soviet tensions.

The blockade was made possible only because the Nationalists and their guerrilla allies established bases on a large number of islands right off China's south-eastern coastline. Control of these islands was fiercely contested throughout the 1950s, including the two Taiwan Strait crises of 1954–55 and 1958. Ever since, these islands have played an important role in contemporary cross-strait relations. In particular, any future PRC attempt to "blockade" Taiwan would have to take them into account.

Adopting a Blockade Strategy

In 1947, in order to halt Soviet shipments to its Communist allies in Manchuria via Port Arthur and Dalian, the Nationalists adopted a naval blockade, albeit on paper. On 20 August 1947 they ordered these ports closed to "all foreign shipping." Two days later, however, the Nationalists' Executive

Yuan clarified this was not a blockade *per se*; rather, it was an official closure order to allow the Chinese government to interdict Soviet ships coming from Manchuria to Chinese ports under Nationalist control. Because Manchuria's ports were already closed to most foreign shippers, the blockade of Port Arthur and Dalian had elicited "no complaint" from the foreign powers.[1]

Low morale throughout the Nationalist Navy decreased the impact of this interdiction program. During 1947–49 there were several important mutinies, including the *Chongqing*, which then defected to the Communists on 25 February 1949. The mutiny of the Nationalist flagship proved to be a huge loss of face for Chiang Kai-shek, since it suggested that he and his Nationalist followers were losing their "mandate of heaven."[2] During the spring of 1949, many other Nationalist ships and crews switched to the Communist side, in particular thirty ships from the Second Squadron, on patrol between Nanjing and Wuhan.[3]

These losses left the Yangzi River undefended, and allowed the Communists to cross into southern China during May 1949. However, the remaining battleships in the Nationalist Navy played a crucial role in transporting Chiang Kai-shek's government-in-exile to Taiwan and in fortifying and protecting a large number of offshore islands from Communist attack. From this position, the "Nationalist navy of some 80 seagoing vessels is believed capable of maintaining under present conditions a reasonably effective blockade of the ports of China from Shanghai to Fujian [province]."[4]

Prior to the Nationalist withdrawal from the mainland, the navy reportedly mined various ports. On 9 June 1949 there were even reports that Nationalist ships were engaged in mining operations in the narrowest part of the Yangzi estuary. Although the Nationalists denied such reports, several ships – including the American *China Victory* and the British *Shengking* – cancelled their scheduled departures until after the area had been swept for mines.

In mid-June the Nationalist government announced that all Chinese ports not under their control would be closed to trade as of 18 June. Beginning at midnight on 25 June all of China's territorial waters would be closed to foreign vessels from a point just north of the Min River (119 degrees 40 minutes East, 26 degrees 15 minutes North) all the way to the mouth of the Liao River (122 degrees 20 minutes East, 40 degrees 30 minutes North). In practical terms, this included virtually all of China's coastline from northern Taiwan to Beijing. If foreign ships ignored the prohibition, then the Nationalist government would "accept no responsibility for the consequences." Major ports to be closed included Qinhuangdao, Tianjin, Shanghai, Ningbo, and Wenzhou.[5]

International Reaction to the Blockade

On 1 July 1949 the British government protested to the Nationalists that their action was not "a valid proclamation of blockade in International

Law, and, on the information at present available to them, [the government] are not prepared to respect it." War had never been officially declared, and so the British government had received "no indication from the Chinese Nationalist Government that they recognize, or are about to recognize, the Chinese Communists as having belligerent status." Furthermore, because the Nationalist Navy was not actively enforcing the blockade, "a mere decree of a lawful Government purporting to close ports occupied by insurgents, without the maintenance of a real and effective blockade, cannot be regarded as valid ... and such a decree cannot be recognized as resulting in a blockade in the sense of International Law."[6]

According to one British analysis of the Nationalist blockade, submitted on 4 July 1949, the 1947 blockade had been simply a closure order allowing the Chinese government to interdict Soviet ships trading between Manchuria and other Chinese ports under Nationalist control, so: "There was therefore no reason why any Government except the Soviet should object to the closing of the port, and as far as is known here none did so." However, in 1949 the Nationalists were attempting to impose a real – as opposed to "paper" – blockade to close Chinese ports to foreign trade, including "even those ports which they do *not* control."[7]

A 9 July 1949 report by the Admiralty's Intelligence Division was more optimistic about the Nationalist blockade. By comparing the number of major Communist warships (30) to the Nationalists' (32), analysing the problem of refueling and rearmament, and evaluating which offshore island bases a blockading force would need for logistical support, this study concluded that retaining the Miao Islands in the north would allow the Nationalists to blockade most of the ports on the Bo Hai and provide them with a "50% cover" of Qingdao. From their naval base at Dinghai, they could mount an "effective" blockade of the Yangzi River in league with troops on the Miao Islands, but only a "restricted" blockade if forced to act on their own. Finally, if the Nationalist forces lost the Miao Islands and the entire Zhoushan area including Dinghai, the blockade would have no effect north of the Yangzi River, only a "limited and sporadic" effect on trade entering and leaving the Yangzi River, and "could only be effective south of Fuzhou."[8]

The British response to the Nationalist blockade was mixed, therefore, with the government publicly advocating continuing trade with China since British shipping from Hong Kong was most affected by the blockade, while groups within the government were secretly supportive. Although the British government initially considered using its naval forces in the Far East to break the blockade, the Commander-in-Chief Far Eastern Squadron Afloat argued on 18 July 1949 that "the fact remains that the blockade is effective and is delaying Communists," and that, when joined with the massive political problems in China, it "may hold up

Communist advance and bring about accommodation between last elements in the country. This presumably accords with our aim." Therefore, he recommended: "I am strongly averse in present circumstances to breaking the blockade which Nationalists appear to be operating very reasonably."[9]

The U.S. government was less ambivalent, perhaps because U.S. trade with China was not as important. While condemning the blockade as illegal and warning that "the U.S. government would take a serious view of any Nationalist attack upon American merchant ships running the blockade which, the U.S. government wished to reiterate, it did not recognize as legal,"[10] on 24 December 1949 Washington warned American shipowners that their license could be revoked if they attempted to run the Shanghai blockade.[11] In sharp contrast to the official British view that the blockade was illegal, *The American Journal of International Law* concluded in 1950 that "within the limits of territorial waters unrecognized belligerents enjoy the right to prevent access of supplies to their domestic enemies."[12]

During July 1949, the U.S. Minister to China told the British Consul-General in Guangzhou (Canton) that the British and American investments in China were "patently lost anyhow," and that the best possible policy would be to allow the Soviet Union to "demonstrate, if they could, that they were able to give a communist China the assistance she will need." Once Beijing realized that Russia could not possibily finance China's development alone, then "China would have to turn to us again and we might then be able to come back on terms which would suit us."[13] Beginning in the summer of 1949 and intensifying through early 1950, the U.S. adopted a policy of allowing the "Communists to stew in their own juices" by supporting "an intensification of the effort to seal the Communists into their continental territory, possibly by an encouragement of the present blockade measures."[14]

With tacit support from the United States, therefore, the Nationalist forces tightened the blockade through the summer of 1949, especially at Shanghai. On 8 October 1949 the *China Weekly Review* reported: "The blockade, meanwhile, was forcing Shanghai's business – long dependent on trade with foreign countries – almost to a standstill."[15] U.S. West Coast trade was particularly hurt, with Portland, Oregon, experiencing a drop of over 90 percent in its trade with China.[16]

The Offshore Island Bases

During the summer and fall of 1949, Nationalist forces fiercely defended their hold over numerous offshore islands. The importance of retaining control over the most strategic of China's 5,000 or more offshore islands was first demonstrated by the seventeenth-century Ming loyalist, Zheng Chenggong, who used the Penghu Islands (Pescadores) in 1661 to "command landing operations to expel the Dutch colonizers and recover Taiwan."[17] The Nationalists initially kept one regiment of marines on the Miao Islands north of Shandong Peninsula to blockade Bo Hai and the northern ports, while they fortified Zhoushan and the Saddle Islands to blockade the Yangzi River. Meanwhile, the Lema and Wan Shan Islands near Guangzhou, the Penghu Islands halfway between the mainland and Taiwan, and Hainan Island, fifteen miles off China's southern coast, blockaded southern China.

In total, the Nationalists' control over various offshore islands allowed them to blockade two-thirds, or approximately 12,000 kilometers, of China's coastline. One early British report to the Admiralty was positive about their chances of making the blockade effective: "Nationalists considered capable at least in initial stages of maintaining ... effective closure of major ports though could not ... easily control junk traffic."[18]

This situation began to change during the fall of 1949. While an early Communist attack on the Nationalist-held base on Jinmen Island (Quemoy) failed during October 1949, the southern city of Guangzhou soon fell, and the loss of a number of strategic islands effectively narrowed the Nationalist blockade to central and southern China. As early as October 1949, Admiral Sa Cheng-ping, the former commander of the Chinese Navy during the Qing dynasty, warned of the probable impact of losing these islands on the conduct of the Nationalist naval blockade: "Judging from the liberation of Changshan Island in Bo Hai Bay and Pingtan island off the Fujian coast, the blockade will not last long."[19] Communist forces, in spite of naval and air inferiority, succeeded in overwhelming the Nationalist base on Hainan Island during February–April 1950, the Zhoushan Archipelago during May 1950, and Tatan Island as late as July 1950.

By the summer of 1950, therefore, the Nationalists had lost their crucial island bases in the Bo Hai, off the mouth of the Yangzi River, and on Hainan Island. Although the Communist victories diminished the blockade area by half, the Nationalists used their remaining offshore bases to continue their blockade of the ports of Shantou, Xiamen, Fuzhou, and Wenzhou, which were critical to deter the Communists from launching an invasion of Taiwan.

It was widely believed that the Communists' "riverine tactics" used to take Hainan would not be of much use against Taiwan.[20] However, there was ample evidence that the Communist forces were preparing to mount an amphibious invasion of Taiwan, as the PRC began concentrating thousands of motorized junks in the port cities along the Taiwan Strait in preparation for a massive amphibious invasion.[21] According to one U.S. Navy estimate, the Communists could assemble "7,000 merchant steamers and other large vessels" to transport 200,000 troops across the Strait.[22]

before.[32] During 1954–55, and again in 1958, China tried to break the blockade.

Beginning in November 1949, the U.S. had imposed an embargo on strategic materials to the PRC, eventually led by the Coordinating Committee for Multilateral Export Controls (COCOM). In 1951, Congress adopted the "Battle Act" to cut economic and military aid to allies and neutral countries that refused to conform. China Committee (CHINCOM) controls were soon instituted that were even tighter, embargoing industrial machinery, steel mill products, and metal of all types. Meanwhile, the U.S. "embargo was also broadened through the inclusion of more countries in COCOM and CHINCOM – Japan at the time of the Korean War, Greece and Turkey in 1953 – and strengthened by pledges of cooperation from important neutral countries, notably Sweden and Switzerland."[33]

In early 1954, the Nationalist blockade entered a new phase as it shifted to a more intensive use of air power with the addition of American-made jet bombers. Nationalist bombers damaged or sunk many British-owned ships. As one blockade-running captain complained: "I can handle any two Nationalist warships. I don't mind their guns or their old planes. But I hate these jets! They come screaming out of nowhere, blast you and then they're gone. You don't have a chance."[34] As a result, the British "were especially troubled by U.S. support of the Nationalist blockade of China and American actions that they feared would spread war throughout Asia."[35]

Stopping these Nationalist air patrols also became one of the PRC's highest objectives. In 1954, there was a total of thirty-two incidents in which Nationalist forces attacked British shipping. During this period, "Warship incidents have been steadily decreasing and in recent times aircraft incidents have been predominant."[36] In November 1954, PRC leaders explained to the visiting Indian Prime Minister, Jawaharlal Nehru, that the Nationalists from their offshore bases were conducting "nuisance raids and interference with shipping." Nehru warned the British high commissioner in India that China was "determined not to tolerate this situation any longer."[37] With the outbreak of the first ROC–PRC crisis later that month, the Communist Army took Dachen Island, the northernmost offshore island used in the blockade.

During December 1954, Taiwan and the U.S. signed a bilateral mutual-security pact reaffirming that the U.S. would defend Taiwan and the Penghus. However, it was less clear about protecting offshore islands: "The pact will be deliberately vague about how the U.S. might react if the Reds were to invade any of the other Nationalist-held islands off the China coast. The U.S. doesn't want the Reds to know which it will defend, and which it will simply write off. It prefers to keep them guessing."[38] In January 1955, Congress passed the "Formosa Resolution" stating that the

U.S. President would judge whether a PRC attack on the offshore islands was part of an invasion of Taiwan.[39]

During early 1955, Washington, fearful that the developing crisis in the Taiwan strait could lead to a general war, even asked Taipei to consider giving up its bases on Jinmen and Mazu. In return, President Eisenhower promised to create a joint U.S.–Taiwan "defense zone" from Shantou to Wenzhou "in which the movement of all seaborne traffic of a contraband or war-making character would be interdicted." In particular, the U.S. Navy would be responsible for setting minefields that "would force coastwise junk traffic to come out where it also could be intercepted and controlled." Chiang Kai-shek refused, arguing that, once he gave up Jinmen and Mazu, the U.S. would quickly halt any "effective shipping interdiction scheme in the face of strong and inevitable opposition by the British and others."[40]

With the Taiwanese–PRC naval balance shifting in favor of the latter, the Nationalists held the remaining offshore islands only by default. The Communist army and naval forces were considered capable of taking the offshore islands with massive force, of by-passing the offshore islands entirely and striking for Taiwan, or continuing their "hit-and-run campaign against individual islands, without apparent plan." By the mid-1950s, the new air phase of the blockade was beginning to lose steam, the number of attacks declined, while the overall impact of the blockade was described by one source as strategically "puny."[41] However, as late as June 1957 the Nationalist government was still warning foreign shipping entering Communist ports that they did so at "their own risk."[42]

When the second cross-strait crisis broke out in August 1958, however, Prince Norodom Sihanouk, the president of the Council of Ministers of Cambodia, visited China to mediate by talking with Mao Zedong and Zhou Enlai. In mid-September, Prince Sihanouk explained to Walter S. Robertson, assistant secretary to the U.S. Mission to the UN, that the PRC leaders were "concerned by the fact that the offshore islands are being used to mount Commando attacks on the mainland and to impose a blockade." U.S. negotiators argued that "shipping has been moving freely out of Chinese ports for the last two years," and they denied that the islands were "used for aggressive purposes," but the Communist accusations against the pro-Nationalist guerrillas were essentially accurate.[43]

Washington's support for the Nationalists' continued hold over the offshore islands was not a blank check. In October 1958, Secretary-of-State John Foster Dulles tried to persuade Taiwan to reduce the number of Nationalist forces on the islands, even while halting "commando raids and blockades."[44] In an attempt to ease tensions, Dulles flew to Taiwan and convinced Chiang Kai-shek "to renounce the use of force in an attempt to reunify China."[45] This decision effectively ended the Nationalists' decade-long naval blockade of China, which had already lasted longer than any other modern naval blockade up until this time.

Conclusions

During July 1949, one British official based in Hong Kong was highly complimentary of the Nationalist blockade of China, concluding that "the blockade is probably the only really effective piece of warmaking the Nationalists have carried out in the last couple of years."[46] From their naval bases on Taiwan and on dozens of offshore islands, the Nationalists blockaded China's coast from Shanghai through south-eastern China; between 1950 and 1952 the Nationalists halted and searched some 90 ships heading for Communist ports, two-thirds of them British-flagged ships registered in Hong Kong.[47] During 1954–55, Nationalist bombers damaged or sunk an estimated 54 blockade runners, many of them flying British flags.[48]

Economically, the blockade initially halted a significant percentage of all of China's international trade. By the mid-1950s its scope shrank to south-east China, where it helped deter a Communist invasion of Taiwan. Over time, however, Beijing's investment in its own naval forces put serious constraints on the Nationalist Navy, even while Communist successes in reclaiming crucial offshore islands and the Communist army's intermittent bombardment of Jinmen – the Nationalists' only remaining blockade base of any size – eventually convinced Taiwan of the blockade's futility.

Taiwan's attempts to enforce the blockade using pro-Nationalist guerrilla forces meant that the blockade was porous; the guerrillas based on the offshore islands were clearly more interested in their own financial gains – either by taking bribes or confiscating foreign shipments – than they were in exerting economic pressure on the Communists. Meanwhile, many foreign ship captains paid bribes to the guerrillas in order to pass unharmed into port.

For all of these operational failings, however, the Nationalist blockade may have had an important strategic impact. Beijing's decision to intervene in the Korean War resulted in further diplomatic isolation, even while China's military needs grew. The PRC largely made up its trade losses by turning to the Soviet Union. Before World War II, only 1 percent of China's foreign trade was with the USSR, while by 1957 this figure had increased to 50 percent.[49] This overwhelming reliance on Moscow restricted Beijing's diplomatic leverage, so that it could not negotiate equitable relations. This, in turn, may have exacerbated border demarcation, return of Manchurian ports and railways to Chinese sovereignty, and sharing control of the international Communist movement. Perhaps it was not a total coincidence that the Nationalist naval blockade ended during 1958, right at the time the first signs of what would soon be called the Sino-Soviet "split" began to appear.

Finally, the blockade had profound geopolitical consequences. Since 1949, the offshore islands have acted as one of the most reliable barometers of China–Taiwan relations. When the PRC and ROC were actively considering invading each other during the 1950s, these islands were hotly contested. Should the PRC ever invade Taiwan, reducing the offshore islands would almost certainly be part of any successful military strategy.[50]

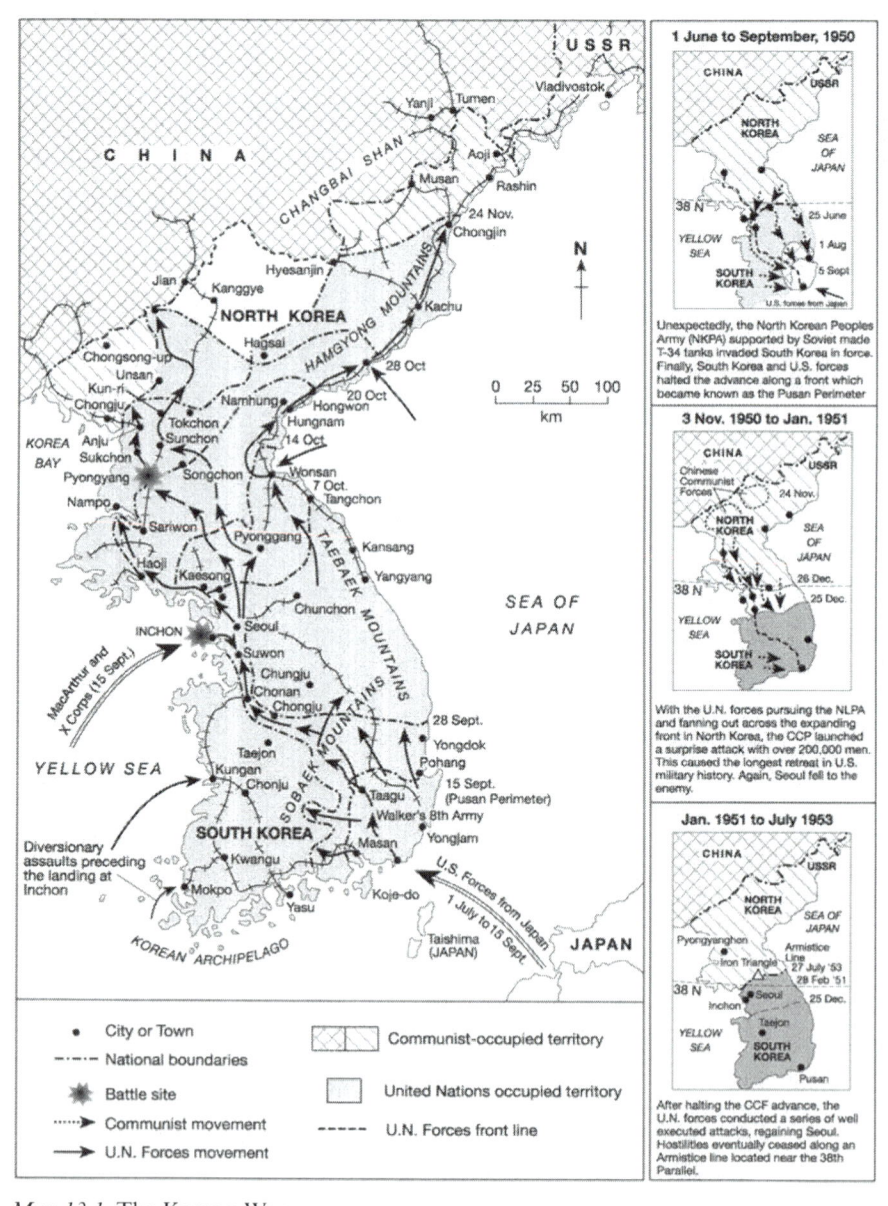

Map 13.1 The Korean War

13 A Failed Blockade

Air and Sea Power in Korea, 1950–53

Malcolm Muir Jr.

To many air power advocates, the Korean War offered a perfect test case for the efficacy of blockade. With the United Nations controlling both the surface of the sea and, after the opening days, the air over the theater as well, UN air and sea power seemed poised to cut the enemy's supply lines and to reduce his ground forces to impotence. Yet the subsequent operational trial rendered a verdict that could only charitably be described as mixed, with the Korean War illustrating the limitations of superior aerial and naval arms when matched against a determined foe possessing vast manpower. That this Allied effort ended in frustration – if not failure, at least by some measures – should have served as an object lesson for planners contemplating war in South-east Asia in the early 1960s.

Background to the Blockade

Following the North Korean surprise offensive of 25 June 1950, President Harry S. Truman took a number of actions designed to leverage maximum use from the limited resources at his disposal. He quickly and successfully appealed to the United Nations for support. Shortly thereafter, on 30 June, the president formally declared a naval blockade of North Korea to be enforced by UN surface and aerial forces. His newly named theater commander, General of the Army Douglas MacArthur, ordered the U.S. Air Force to attack Communist supply lines, an effort quickly joined by aircraft from American and British carriers. Gunfire supplied by Allied warships soon augmented this aerial interdiction effort by striking at enemy railroad and road traffic near the coasts.

Given the meager military assets available to MacArthur, the UN attempts to maintain a coastal blockade and to cut land traffic by aerial bombardment were initially frustrated. Although playing a significant supporting role, air efforts paled in importance to the determined stand of U.S. Army troops at the Pusan perimeter and the joint Army–Navy–Marine riposte at Inchon. With the North Koreans thrown completely off balance, the Allied counteroffensive swept into North Korea itself in the fall of 1950. At this point, the People's Republic of China (PRC) joined the fray. The Red forces. Beginning on 16 February 1951, UN troops occupied some of the small islands in the harbor; from these, observers could monitor – and call fire upon – Communist rail and road traffic coming down the main routes on the eastern side of the peninsula. U.S. naval aviation and surface warships thus brought their armaments to bear under very favorable conditions. Active Communist countermeasures consisted of gunfire from shore artillery and, more lethal, of mines planted at night in the harbor. Passive resistance consisted of repairing breaks in the roads and railroad tracks. At the latter, in particular, the Communists excelled.

The U.S. Navy soon stationed a force, generally numbering four or five minesweepers backed by two or three destroyers, in the harbor. Officially called the Wonsan Defense and Blockade Unit (Task Unit 95.2.1), its commander enjoyed the jocular title of the "Mayor of Wonsan." By constant effort, the minesweepers kept clear channels for destroyers, light and heavy cruisers, and even battleships to bring their artillery to bear. From the 55lb shell fired by the destroyers to the 1,900lb 16-inch bombardment projectiles of the Iowa-class battleships, the weight of shellfire hurled at the enemy city, marshalling yards, and truck traffic was remarkable. Within the first six months of the "siege," the warships fired more than 50,000 rounds of 5-inch and larger ammunition at enemy targets.[6] Aircraft augmented this with bombing runs. An early Navy assessment of the effort concluded that the Allied pressure caused "considerable interference with through rail traffic and required extensive diversion of truck traffic to routes further inland …"[7] However, it also conceded that "trains and trucks still pass through Wonsan nearly every night and troops and supplies are still housed in the city."[8]

Throughout 1952, naval units kept the pressure on, and in February 1953 the siege entered its third year, with the only respite for Communist forces being Typhoon Karen, during August 1952, which drove the bombarding warships offshore. Under the constant deluge of U.S. gunfire, Wonsan was reduced, in the words of one observer, to "a cluttered mass of ruins."[9] Still, given the importance of the transportation hub that passed through it, the Communist forces dedicated large work parties to keeping the railroads and highways open for logistical movement, especially at night. In this, the repair crews were aided by the stout nature of the transportation infrastructure. For example, Communist laborers repeatedly restored timber bridges resting on concrete foundations to working order within hours after they had suffered damage. Where bridges were knocked down, the enemy often built bypass roads.[10]

This war of attrition at Wonsan paid certain dividends for the UN forces. Besides drawing large Communist manpower reserves to the area, the siege also focused the enemy's artillery resources. By 1952, the U.S. Navy calculated that the Communists had amassed 1,003 guns in the Wonsan area, or over one-half of all the tubes available to the North Korean army.[11] Such a concentration made life hazardous for the blockaders; the enemy gunners were not reluctant to fire on U.S. cruisers or, even on occasion, the battleships. Although no big ship was badly damaged, U.S. officers concluded that it was only a matter of time before the enemy scored a crippling hit on a smaller, unarmored warship such as a destroyer.[12] Such a warship, steaming out of control in the narrow confines of Wonsan harbor, was almost certain to run upon a minefield.

Because of this hazard, much of the navy's gunfire was directed, not at cutting Communist supply lines, but at neutralizing the enemy's artillery. Although destroyer batteries could disperse repair parties and harass enemy command posts, the lighter guns generally proved ineffective against the dug-in Communist artillery emplacements; thus, battleships and cruisers repeatedly counterpunched at enemy batteries.[13] In fact, by 1953, the larger warships were concentrating almost exclusively on such targets; one skeptical cruiser commander noted: "It appears that the only worthwhile benefits accrued to the enemy: we provided a juicy target for his artillerymen to practice on and gave him an incentive (which he accepted) to drastically improve his fire control methods against ships."[14]

Over the long term, U.S. Navy evaluators became increasingly dubious about the effectiveness of the Wonsan siege. Part of their problem lay in the lack of reliable intelligence; much of the time, the attackers felt that they were firing blind, or "for effect," with no way of measuring that effect.[15] Doubts as to the entire effort filtered down to sailors at their gunnery stations – so much so that morale suffered.[16]

The 861-day siege concluded only with the truce that ended hostilities; in fact, the last shells were fired by the destroyer *Wiltsie* a few moments before the 2200 cease fire deadline on 27 July 1953 took effect.[17] In some ways, Wonsan exemplified in miniature the entire Korean War, in that the siege dragged on interminably with UN gunners keeping the enemy under heavy bombardment, while the Communists maintained their transportation lines by unremitting effort.

Operation *Strangle* and the Aerial Blockade

Wonsan, important in its own right, was only part of the larger effort aimed at starving enemy frontline forces of "beans and bullets." Certainly the North Korean topography seemed ideally suited for such a campaign. The rugged mountains channeled trains and trucks onto a relatively few highways and railroads. The lack of natural cover in most places meant that enemy logistical movements during daylight would be naked to aerial attack and, in certain places, to coastal bombardment. Of course, the United Nations enjoyed absolute control of the sea along with air supremacy almost all the way to the Yalu.

Consequently, in May 1951, the Far East Air Force (FEAF) command of the U.S. Air Force concocted a joint aerial campaign with the Navy dubbed Operation *Strangle*, to paralyse the North Korean rail and road network. The choice of the term "Strangle" was hardly propitious, given that a campaign in

1944 with the identical name and objective had aimed to cut the supply lines of German troops in Italy. That effort, carried out over terrain quite similar to that of North Korea, had failed to deliver decisive results.

History in this instance proved prescient. The Korean version of Operation *Strangle* quickly ran into difficulties. The U.S. Air Force calculated that the front-line enemy forces required 2,400 tons of supply daily, which required for its transportation 6,000 trucks or 120 boxcars. The Soviet Union met these requirements easily by dipping into its vast reserves of trucks, locomotives, and railroad rolling stock, much of it provided by U.S. lend-lease during World War II. The enemy also transported much material on foot, south from the Yalu on the A-frames of porters, also available in essentially unlimited numbers from mainland China.

Within months, Operation *Strangle* was successful in pushing the Communist forces into moving mainly under the cover of darkness; the Air Force responded with night attacks. In the month of September 1951 alone, the U.S. Air Force claimed 5,318 vehicles destroyed. So effective were its operations, alleged the Far East Air Force, that U.S. prisoners of war were forcibly substituted for North Korean drivers who had deserted their vehicles. Such claims convinced some air planners that Communist ground forces would soon abandon their front-line trenches.

Unfortunately, claims, even by the most conscientious airmen, did not always match reality, especially when made in the uncertain environment of night combat operations. For example, late in the war, a B-26 bomber manned by experienced airmen mistakenly struck five times an illuminated South Korean motor pool. Returning to base, the U.S. crew claimed six trucks destroyed, whereas the actual toll was four ROK soldiers killed and two jeeps lightly damaged by bomb fragments. Heightened skepticism within the Air Force over the validity of claims led to a test in August 1952 whereby B-26s bombed derelict trucks at night. Despite the rigged conditions, the bombers damaged slightly fewer than two trucks for every 100 bombs dropped – a far cry from the average of .97 enemy vehicles per sortie that the airmen advanced in their after-action reports.[18]

Dragooned into *Strangle* were the fast carriers of the U.S. Navy's Task Force 77. Two U.S. Navy historians sketched the enormity of the task confronting naval aviators: "How could they, operating an average of 150 naval aircraft in the northeast area of Korea three days out of four, hinder (and if possible prevent) the movement of enemy supplies through an area the size of the state of Minnesota, opposed by an energetic and ingenious enemy operating some 6,000 to 8,000 trucks and hundreds of trains, dispersing and camouflaging his supplies, working only at night and opposing our air attacks with the ever-increasing antiaircraft fire?"[19]

Given these challenges, the commanding officer of Task Force 77, Vice-Admiral Arthur D. Struble, preferred to use his planes for the close air support of UN troops on the frontline. Overruled, Struble was assigned responsibility for the enemy supply routes in the north-eastern part of the peninsula, while the Air Force carried the burden against the western side of the peninsula – a parceling of targets remarkably similar to the Route Package plan for targeting North Vietnam during Operation *Rolling Thunder* over a decade later. In North Korea, the roads were little more than gravel trails; the railroads were mostly single track lines that snaked over bridges and through tunnels. Although the last seemed logical chokepoints, tunnels actually proved remarkably resistant to damage, so much so that naval forces offshore frequently resorted to sending in at night small landing parties to sabotage the tracks. Battleships occasionally collapsed sections of tunnels with 16-inch shellfire, but Communist repair parties demonstrated their expertise by clearing the rubble in surprisingly short order.

Bridges, another apparent weak link in the enemy's transportation network, showed themselves to be tough targets too. The bridge component most vulnerable to damage – the flooring – could be quickly replaced, while more vital elements, such as the girders and abutments, offered smaller targets and were, by their very nature, extremely resistant to damage. U.S. Navy analysts concluded that the destruction of a bridge normally took twelve to sixteen sorties by AD Skyraiders dropping between thirty-six and forty-eight one-ton bombs. Alternatively, battleships expended an average of 60 rounds of 16-inch main battery fire in collapsing a bridge. With each battleship projectile weighing almost one ton, the aircraft delivered a slightly more effective attack measured from the standpoint of ordnance costs alone. However, the battleships, with their heavy armor and crushing counterbattery capabilities, generally drew no opposing fire, while the aircraft ran into frequent opposition. In fact, airmen found bridges, flanked by strong anti-aircraft batteries, to be "flak traps."

At the request of FEAF commander Lieutenant-General George Stratemeyer, Task Force 77 took on the mission of cutting six major Yalu River bridges connecting North Korea to Manchuria. The naval aviators, like their Air Force compatriots, found most frustrating the politically imposed limits which restricted them to bombing only the bridge spans on the North Korean side of the river and prevented the airmen from entering Communist Chinese airspace. These two mandates made the bridges even more difficult targets than usual because the airmen were forced to approach the structures at right angles. And during the wintertime, the Communist forces simply drove trucks across the Yalu on the ice.

Another *cause celebre*, at least in naval aviation circles, was the campaign against the bridges near Kilchu, better known as the battle of Carlson's Canyon and made famous by James Michener's novel *The Bridges at Toko-ri*. In the spring of 1951, naval aviators, in concert with B-29s, attacked the two railroad bridges in the North Korean canyon. After an entire month of effort, the spans were finally knocked down, but the enemy simply constructed a four-mile bypass of the area. Eighth Army commander General James Van Fleet gave a clear-headed appraisal: "We won the battle to knock out the bridge[s], but we lost the objective, which was to knock out the traffic."

Overall, the campaign against bridges in North Korea proved disappointing, in large part due to the "highly effective" enemy repair efforts.[20]

And if downing bridges brought only momentary advantage, even less productive were attacks on roads and railroad tracks. The latter presented a target only sixty inches wide; one Air Force estimate concluded that only about 25 percent of daytime sorties against tracks actually cut the rails. When aircraft bombed at night, the effectiveness rating fell to 7 percent. Worse, both roads and rail tracks could be rapidly put back in order. The enemy stationed work parties, equipment, and key components (e.g., tracks and tie plates) near the areas most threatened by UN aircraft. Often, repair teams spliced the deepest rail cuts within eight hours. After noting a record 211 rail cuts in one day, one naval assessment team added that the enemy had quickly fixed the damage. In this cat-and-mouse game, U.S. aircraft tried to hamstring the repair squads by dropping small "butterfly" bombs or larger delayed action bombs, to which the Communist riposte was rifle fire to destroy the small ordnance and a stoical acceptance of the casualties inflicted by the larger weapons.

From *Strangle* to *Saturate*

By the end of 1951, the very name *Strangle* had become an embarrassment, and the Air Force changed the codename to the less ambitious, and more ambiguous *Saturate*. Begun in February 1952, Operation *Saturate* aimed continuous strikes at certain segments of railroad track. But aside from the cosmetic switching of names, in reality little of substance changed. The attacks on the enemy lines of communications continued – with the same lack of discernible results. For instance, one two-day maximum air effort in March by almost 500 sorties cut the lines, but within five days the trains were running unhampered down repaired tracks. Thus, the enemy belied the repeated predictions by airmen of a Communist withdrawal from the front because of supply scarcities. One FEAF deputy, Brigadier-General Darr H. Alkire, observed: "It has frequently been said by commanders in Korea that the one man they would like to meet when the war is over is the G-4 of the Communist forces."[21]

Part of the U.S. difficulty, of course, was that Communist logistical requirements measured only a fraction of UN standards. By one U.S. estimate, each North Korean or Chinese Communist division needed less than 50 tons of supplies daily, which amounted to about ten pounds per soldier per day. In comparison, ROK troopers consumed supplies at twice that rate; American consumption was quintuple that amount.

Certainly the U.S. ammunition expended in the interdiction effort was prodigious. By early 1953, naval aircraft of Task Force 77 had mounted in the two years since the beginning of Operation *Strangle* almost as many sorties and had dropped a greater tonnage of bombs than had all Navy and Marine aircraft during the entire course of World War II in all theaters.[22] As one January 1953 report summarized: "Despite the incessant efforts of the Navy and Air Force, interdiction of the enemy lines of communication by aircraft was a costly and militarily unrewarding extension of the war. In January 1953, the enemy was better supplied, fed, and equipped than at any previous time. There is no question that interdiction disrupted enemy daylight movements and reduced his daily supplies by a substantial margin. Yet the isolation of the battlefield was never achieved."[23]

Worse, *Strangle* and then *Saturate* proved expensive in many ways. By Navy reckoning, the ledger swam with red ink. To destroy a small bridge cost the U.S. $55,000; to effect one railroad cut, $18,000. To crater a road with 250-pound bombs ran American taxpayers $100 per cubic yard for the explosives alone. Looking at the balance sheet, Rear-Admiral Ralph A. Ofstie concluded: "It may well be that we are being hurt more as a consequence of the cost of this operation and the losses sustained, than is the enemy with a somewhat reduced effectiveness of his supply routes."[24]

Other factors added to the expense of the campaign. In the mountainous Korean environment, operational hazards posed a constant threat to airmen, especially after the Communists resorted to night movements. Winter brought its own set of problems. The intense cold caused fragments, and even entire bombs, to rebound from the frozen ground into the aircraft that had dropped them.

As the weight of U.S. air attacks mounted, so did the sophistication of enemy air defenses. To discourage night attacks, the Communist forces strung lights on cliff faces to trick pilots into thinking they were attacking a truck convoy. Cables suspended over ravines could chop the wing from an aircraft. Antiaircraft fire, even from small arms, constituted an ever-present threat. Some planes employed in the interdiction campaign showed themselves to be, rather unexpectedly, fine ground attack aircraft. An outstanding example was the F2H Banshee with its two jet engines and tough airframe. But others, such as the F4U Corsair or the P-51 Mustang, were unusually vulnerable to ground fire, and casualties rose alarmingly.

In the first six months of *Strangle*, the U.S. Navy lost 74 aircraft; thirty aviators died or fell into enemy hands. Given that the typical fighter cost $250,000 (as opposed to $60,000 in World War II), one U.S. Navy officer wrote:

> It is doubtful whether the interdiction campaign in Korea has been as costly to the enemy as to the U.S. The enemy has lost many vehicles, much rolling stock and supplies and has suffered heavy physical destruction of property, but it is doubtful whether this has placed a greater strain on the economies of North Korea, China and the USSR than upon the economy of the United States. The cost of maintaining interdiction forces in and near Korea, the cost of the hundreds of aircraft lost and the thousands of tons of munitions and supplies consumed, and the expenditure of national resources have been keenly felt. Certainly the value of the United Nations aircraft lost alone is greater

than that of all the enemy's vehicles, rolling stock, and supplies destroyed. While the cost of the war assumes fantastic proportions to the United States, the enemy largely offsets our efforts by the use of his cheapest and most useful asset, mass manpower.[25]

The Air Force reluctantly reached similar conclusions. In the summer of 1952, that service decided: "We were trading B-26s for trucks in a most uneconomical manner." Overall, Operation *Strangle*, prior to its conclusion, cost the United Nations 343 aircraft lost to enemy action and to operational causes. While the campaign dragged on, and with the results of their efforts so quickly erased by Communist repair parties, many airmen became dispirited. A carrier air group commander reported: "One of my toughest jobs was the constant battle to keep pilots' morale up. The war in Korea demanded more competence, courage, and skill from the naval aviator than did World War II. The flying hours were longer, the days on the firing line more, the antiaircraft hazards greater, the weather worse."[26]

A hidden but concomitant cost of the interdiction campaign was the frequent neglect of close air support for soldiers and Marines at the front. Despite the fact that the Army and Air Force had rarely practiced close air support techniques prior to the war, in 1950 it became of great importance to ground troops. Without question, close air support proved a crucial element in holding the North Koreans at the Pusan perimeter, in covering the Marine retreat from the Chosin Reservoir, and in slowing the Red Chinese pursuit of the Eighth Army in the winter of 1951. By weakening close air support for the front line trooper, interdiction detracted from his fighting capabilities.

Conclusions

From the perspective of half a century, the "Forgotten War" offers a multitude of lessons. On the one hand, the most modern weapons did not radically change the military environment. Indeed, some new weapons systems (e.g., the B-36, the *Midway*-class carriers, the *Newport News*-class heavy cruisers) were too valuable to be employed at all. Other arms, such as jet aircraft and "smart bombs," saw action for the first time in significant numbers, but did not prove decisive.

Instead, it was the older weapons, often denounced by pundits as positively antediluvian, which surprised with their utility. Amphibious assault craft and aircraft carriers once again took center stage. The four *Iowa*-class battleships fired many more rounds than they had shot during World War II. Ground troops, often derided as of little value in the age of air power, proved indispensable. The final U.S. Pacific Fleet report concluded: "The front line rifleman has been the central figure in the Korean War. All other forces support him."[27]

If this was true, the Air Force had not supported him well enough. And the blockade has helped push North Korea to accept a negotiated peace. The airmen's efforts had bled the enemy severely, but the campaign simply did not deliver the decisive results that its advocates promised. As the Navy aptly concluded, "Primitive transportation systems combined with masses of coolie labor successfully defied a colossal effort by modern machines of war."[28]

Map 14.1 Estimated ranges of Soviet medium and intermediate missiles based in Cuba

14 The Cuban Missile Crisis

*Jeffrey G. Barlow**

During the past four decades, analysing the historical events related to the Cuban Missile Crisis of October 1962 has provided a veritable cottage industry for historians of the Cold War and for political scientists studying crisis behavior. This chapter is based in part on documentary materials that have become available during the past few years. It will argue that the Kennedy Administration's imposition of a blockade around Cuba in the opening days of the confrontation ultimately was less important in determining the final outcome of this crisis than was previously thought.

Background to the Crisis

The origins of the U.S.–Soviet confrontation over ballistic missiles in Cuba can be traced back to the Bay of Pigs debacle. On 17 April 1961, a paramilitary force of Cuban exiles, covertly trained and equipped by the U.S. Central Intelligence Agency, landed in Cuba. This proved to be a poorly supported, and therefore quickly defeated, American attempt to overthrow Fidel Castro.[1] On 30 November 1961, President Kennedy issued a memorandum to senior national security officials establishing a program codenamed Operation *Mongoose*, under the general guidance of Brigadier-General Edward G. Lansdale, to employ available U.S. covert assets "to help Cuba overthrow the communist regime."[2] By the beginning of 1962 this project had become a top priority for the Kennedy brothers.[3]

Despite the strict secrecy regarding all aspects of this operation, Fidel Castro learned about U.S. plans for sabotage and economic warfare against Cuba.[4] This information, when combined with other U.S. actions during early- and mid-1962, convinced the Castro regime that the American government planned to invade Cuba.[5] With the support of a KGB agent, the Spanish-speaking Aleksandr Alekseyev, Fidel Castro asked the First Secretary of the U.S.S.R. Communist Party, Nikita Sergeyevich Khrushchev, for help.[6] A Soviet military aid program was adopted when the Cubans and the Soviets signed two military assistance agreements on 4 August and 30 September 1961.[7]

Khrushchev later recalled that the notion of sending missiles to Cuba first came up in April 1962 in a conversation with Minister of Defense, Marshal

Rodion Malinovsky. As the two men walked along a Black Sea beach, Malinovsky pointed across the water toward Turkey and explained that American Jupiter missiles could hit the USSR in just ten minutes, but Soviet missiles fired at the U.S. would take some twenty-five minutes. The Soviet leader suddenly responded: "What about putting one of our hedgehogs down the Americans' trousers? According to our intelligence we are lagging almost fifteen years behind the Americans in warheads. We cannot reduce that lead even in ten years. But our rockets on America's doorstep would drastically alter the situation and go a long way towards compensating us for the lag in time."[8]

On 21 May, the Soviet leader met in the Kremlin with the Defense Council. Khrushchev explained that conventional weapons would be inadequate to defend Cuba if the United States decided to invade with substantial forces. Only the presence of Soviet nuclear weapons could cause the Americans to rethink plans for invading the island.[9] The Council members agreed, but without much enthusiasm.[10]

General Gribkov and two assistants drafted the formal military proposal.[11] This plan proposed deploying to Cuba five missile regiments – three regiments of R-12 [NATO designation – SS-4 "Sandal"] medium-range ballistic missiles (MRBMs), each with eight launchers and 1.5 missiles per launcher; and two regiments of R-14 [NATO designation – SS-5 "Skean"] intermediate-range ballistic missiles (IRBMs), each with eight launchers and 1.5 missiles per launcher. In addition, it called two antiaircraft divisions, a fighter regiment equipped with MiG-21 aircraft, a brigade of twelve missile patrol boats, two regiments of FKR-1 cruise missiles – with 16 launchers and 80 tactical nuclear warheads – and four motorized rifle regiments, each with a tank battalion.[12]

In early June, the Presidium voted unanimously to go ahead with the plan. Defense Minister Malinovsky formally approved it on 4 July, and Khrushchev agreed three days later.[13] For cover purposes, the Soviet operation had been assigned the designation ANADYR – the name of a river in north-east Siberia. The movement plan called for transporting large amounts of military armament and heavy equipment from the USSR to Cuba, including missiles, warheads, launchers, and ancillary equipment for five ballistic missile regiments, the missiles and launchers for three antiaircraft regiments, the unassembled fighters for a fighter aviation regiment, and the combat vehicles and armament for four motorized rifle regiments.[14] In addition, the plan envisioned transporting 50,874 soldiers, sailors, airmen, and civilian technicians. The shipment of all of this materiel and people required the use of 85 merchant ships – primarily freighters, together with several passenger liners. Equipment and personnel began to flow in July.

On 29 August, film developed from a CIA-piloted U-2 reconnaissance flight revealed the construction on a crash basis of surface-to-air missile (SAM) sites at a number of locations in Cuba.[15] On 4 September, President Kennedy acknowledged the presence in Cuba of surface-to-air antiaircraft missiles and motor torpedo boats equipped with ship-to-ship guided missiles, but there was no evidence of Soviet combat troops or military bases on the island, nor was there evidence of offensive weapons such as surface-to-surface missiles. "Were it to be otherwise, the gravest issues would arise," he emphasized.[16] But by this point Khrushchev had too much personally invested in the missile deployment to back down, and he agreed to have the Group of Soviet Forces in Cuba reinforced with six IL-28 bombers with six atomic bombs, and three nuclear-equipped *Luna* battalions (12 missiles and 12 nuclear warheads). The atomic bombs for the IL-28s and the nuclear warheads for the *Luna* rockets were to be loaded on board the cargo ship *Indigirka* for transport to Cuba.[17]

During early September, at the Black Sea Fleet's base at Sevastopol, the first R-12 medium-range ballistic missiles were loaded on board the large-hatch freighters *Poltava* and *Omsk*.[18] U.S. intelligence assets picked up the *Poltava*'s movement toward Cuba soon after it left port but had no means of determining what she was carrying. At the end of the second week of September, the thirty-six nuclear warheads for the R-12 MRBMs, the 80 nuclear warheads for the FKR cruise missiles, the twelve nuclear warheads for the *Luna* rockets, and the six atomic bombs for the specially configured IL-28 bombers were loaded into the holds of *Indigirka* at the Barents Sea base at Severomorsk, near Murmansk. *Indigirka* departed for Cuba on 17 September and arrived at Mariel on 4 October.[19]

In early October, the twenty-four nuclear warheads for the R-14 IRBMs were loaded on board the freighter *Aleksandrovsk*, which departed on 5 October and arrived at the port of La Isabela on the coast of central Cuba on or around 23 October. Because of earlier unfavorable weather forecasts it was not until 14 October that the first U-2 flight of the month took place.[20] Its reconnaissance film was immediately unloaded, flown to Washington, processed, and delivered to the National Photographic Interpretation Center (NPIC) for evaluation by its photo interpreters. This was the famous "Milk Run" mission flown by Major Richard S. Heyser.[21]

In the early evening of Monday, 15 October, photo interpreters and military analysts informed the CIA's Deputy Director (Intelligence), Ray S. Cline, that they had just identified a missile base in Cuba for surface-to-surface missiles of a range upwards of 350 miles. Later that evening, after being informed by his intelligence officers that they now thought the range of the offensive missiles at the site identified in Cuba were probably in the 700-mile and possibly in the 1,000-mile bracket, Cline contacted Kennedy's National Security adviser McGeorge Bundy and gave him the information. The next morning, after hearing the unsettling news from Bundy, Kennedy scheduled a meeting with his principal advisors for 1145.

The Decision to Blockade Cuba

The select group gathered in the Cabinet Room that morning included the President, the Attorney-General Robert Kennedy, Secretary of State Dean

Rusk, Secretary of Defense Robert McNamara, Vice President Lyndon B. Johnson, Secretary of the Treasury C. Douglas Dillon, Under Secretary of State George Ball, Deputy Secretary of Defense Roswell L. Gilpatric, and JCS Chairman General Maxwell Taylor. This group would later form the ExComm (Executive Committee of the National Security Council) that acted throughout the Missile Crisis as the President's senior advisory body.

The meeting began with General Carter and Arthur C. Lundahl, Director of NPIC, briefing the President and the others on what the U-2 photography from 14 October revealed. Kennedy and his advisers debated the timing of possible military options for eliminating the missile – and overall Soviet military – threat. Three options were proposed: a limited air strike to take out just the missile sites; an expanded air strike designed to take out, in addition to the missiles, the surface-to-air missile sites, all Soviet aircraft, the Cuban airfields, and any suspected nuclear storage sites; an invasion of Cuba to remove Castro from power. A fourth option was the imposition of a naval blockade, mentioned by JCS Chairman Taylor, to prevent more missiles from being brought to Cuba once the first ones had been destroyed.[22]

It was during the session on the evening of the 17th that the Excomm first discussed the costs and benefits of a blockade of Cuba in some detail.[23] The next day, when asked by McGeorge Bundy what his preference for action was, Llewellyn E. Thompson, who had recently returned to Washington after a tour as U.S. Ambassador to the USSR, stated: "My preference is this blockade plan, this declaration of war and these steps leading up to it. I think it's very doubtful that the Russians would resist a blockade against military weapons, particularly offensive ones, if that's the way we pitched it before the world."[24] Kennedy at first was unconvinced, remarking that it wouldn't eliminate the missiles or aircraft already in Cuba.[25] However, as the session went on he became more enthusiastic. At one point he asked his advisers: "Now, to declare a blockade of Cuba, do we have to declare war on Cuba?" When a chorus of responses of "Yes" greeted him, Kennedy remarked, "I think we shouldn't assume we have to declare war."[26]

On Friday morning, 19 October, Kennedy met with the Joint Chiefs of Staff, and the CNO, Admiral George W. Anderson Jr. briefed the President about the blockade alternative. From a military point of view, a blockade could be successfully carried out. However, there were disadvantages: "The blockade will not affect the equipment that is already in Cuba, and will provide the Russians in Cuba time to assemble all of these missiles, to assemble the IL-28s, to get the MiGs ... ready to go. And I feel that, as this goes on, I agree with General LeMay that this will escalate and then we will be required to take other military action at greater disadvantage to the United States ..." After listening to the Chiefs, Kennedy told the assembled officers: "These are unsatisfactory alternatives. The obvious argument for the blockade was [that] what we want to do is avoid, if we can, nuclear war by escalation or imbalance."[27]

That evening a joint intelligence report on the Soviet missile threat in Cuba, based on analysis of most of the U-2 missions flown through the

17th, revealed an even more dangerous situation existed, giving "the USSR a significant strategic strike capability against almost all targets in the U.S."[28] This clearly suggested the need for the ExComm to reevaluate the efficacy of the blockade option. However, when the ExComm met on the afternoon of 20 October to discuss the blockade and the airstrike options, all arguments instead hinged on the value of limited force as a means of avoiding a possible military escalation of the situation.[29] It was near the end of this meeting that Kennedy told the group he was ready to go ahead with the blockade, and it was following this meeting that he directed his Special Council, Theodore Sorensen, to prepare a quarantine speech.[30]

Running the Quarantine

On 18 October, even though a decision on instituting a blockade of Cuba had not yet been made, the Defense Department began preparing for this contingency. The following day, Admiral Robert L. Dennison, Commander in Chief, Atlantic and Atlantic Fleet (CINCLANT/CINCLANTFLT) – the unified commander whose geographic area included Cuba – became the blockade force commander. On Saturday morning, 20 October, Secretary of Defense McNamara ordered Admiral Anderson to draw up the position papers, scenario, and implementing instructions for the limited blockade.

At 1430 on 20 October, Kennedy and the ExComm met in the Oval Room at the White House to discuss issues related to the President's planned speech to the nation. It was during this meeting that, at Dean Rusk's urging, Kennedy agreed to describe the planned U.S. action against Cuba as a "quarantine" rather than a blockade. Even though the two terms had the same legal meaning, Rusk preferred not to have any comparison made between the Kennedy Administration's contemplated action and the Berlin blockade of 1948–49.[31]

In response to the President's request, Chief of Naval Operations Anderson described the manner in which the navy would handle the blockade. He made it clear that the U.S. Navy would follow accepted international rules in intercepting, stopping, and – if necessary – boarding Soviet ships. At the conclusion of this meeting, Kennedy came up to the CNO and said, "Well, Admiral, it looks as though it's up to the Navy." Anderson immediately replied, "The Navy will not let you down."[32]

JCS Chairman Taylor sent a warning message to all of the Unified and Specified Commanders at 1414 on 21 October. It notified U.S. military commanders that the President was considering initiating blockade operations against Cuba. At the time the President made the public announcement of the decision to begin blockade operations, a DEFCON (Defense Condition) 3 level of readiness would be established worldwide.[33] That evening Admiral Dennison issued Operation Order 45–62, designating Commander, Second Fleet as Quarantine Force Commander and Commander Task Force (CTF) 136 and directing Commander Antisubmarine Warfare Force Atlantic

(COMASWFORLANT) as Commander, Task Force 81–83, to carry out aerial reconnaissance as requested by Commander, Quarantine Force. At 2200 that night, Secretary of Defense McNamara gave his approval to the procedures and rules for the blockade that had been drafted.

At 0711 on Monday, 22 October, some twelve hours before the President's scheduled speech to the nation, the JCS sent a message to Admiral Dennison directing him to prepare plans for the blockade of Cuba. It provided specific guidance on how to conduct the blockade. With regard to the visit and search of ships it stated: "Ships, including submarines, both Soviet and non-Soviet, designated by CINCLANT on [the] basis of information available to him will be intercepted by US ships. If CINCLANT or the Commander of the intercepting ship believes the ship may be carrying prohibited material, a visit and search will be made ..."[34] The newly appointed Commander Second Fleet, Vice-Admiral Alfred G. Ward, immediately issued Operation Order 1–62. It established Task Force 136 – the Blockade Force – with himself as commander. The task force was composed of three task groups: Task Group 136.1, the Surface Force; Task Group 136.2, the ASW Group; and Task Group 136.3, the Replenishment Group.[35]

Throughout that day, CINCLANT was busy deploying ships and aircraft to enforce the quarantine. Most steamed to a central rendezvous point located at latitude 27N, longitude 68W, to await their station assignments. An hour before President Kennedy addressed the American people, the order went out to U.S. forces worldwide to set Defense Condition Three. At this same hour, U.S. Ambassador to the Soviet Union Foy D. Kohler delivered a copy of the President's speech, together with a personal letter from Kennedy to Khrushchev, to the Soviet Foreign Ministry.[36] At 1900, Kennedy began speaking from the Oval Office, telling his television audience – the millions of Americans watching at home and many additional millions of people abroad – that acting in defense of U.S. security and of "the entire Western Hemisphere," he had directed the initiation of "a strict quarantine on all offensive military equipment under shipment to Cuba."[37]

During 23 October, navy ships were steaming toward their positions. Task Force 135, the Attack Carrier Strike Force, commanded by Rear-Admiral Robert J. Stroh, consisted of two aircraft carrier task groups – Task Group 135.1, with *Independence* (CVA 62) and her escorting destroyers, and Task Group 135.2, composed of the nuclear-powered *Enterprise* (CVAN 65) and her escorts – was already positioned in waters north of Cuba. Task Force 135 was maneuvering in preparation for air strikes against targets in Cuba and flying defensive combat air patrols over Guantánamo, as part of CINCLANT's Operation Plan 312 calling for general air strikes if ordered. Meanwhile, the ships of the Blockade Force were steaming toward their assigned positions in the quarantine line. The ASW carrier *Essex* and her escorts were moving to positions west of the line.

The President signed the Quarantine Proclamation at 1900 on 23 October announcing that the quarantine would take effect at 1400 Greenwich Mean

Time (1000 Eastern Daylight Time) the following day. At 1000 on 24 October, Admiral Dennison established the surface quarantine line on an arc 500 miles from Cape Maysi, Cuba, from latitude 27–30N, longitude 70W to latitude 20N, longitude 65W. This distant line was established to keep the U.S. Navy ships beyond the estimated 740-mile range of Soviet IL-28 bombers based in Cuba.[38] At the same hour that the Quarantine went into force, a message went out "in the clear" from Strategic Air Command (SAC) headquarters to all SAC units, raising the Defense Condition from 3 to 2, one step below preparation for general war. This action activated all forces not already on alert, increasing the SAC ready force (within 24 hours) to 1,436 bombers, 145 ICBMs, and 916 tankers.[39] The threat of global war was now evident.

Negotiating an End to the Crisis

When Khrushchev first learned on 22 October that Kennedy was preparing to address the nation, he was convinced that the missiles in Cuba had been discovered. Highly agitated, Khrushchev called together the members of the Presidium in anticipation of the speech, convinced that the United States was going to attack Cuba and possibly even the Soviet Union. He told his colleagues: "The thing is we were not going to unleash war. We just wanted to intimidate them, to deter the anti-Cuban forces."[40]

His sense of utter failure was quickly overturned, however, when the Foreign Ministry relayed the text of Kennedy's statement over the telephone to Oleg Troyanovsky, Khrushchev's foreign policy assistant, just after 0100 on 23 October (Moscow time). When he read the text aloud to the group, there was a sense of immediate relief that the United States was not announcing an immediate attack on Cuba.[41] Khrushchev's immediate reaction was, "We've saved Cuba."[42] He quickly began composing a dismissive reply to Kennedy's letter, arguing that the armaments in Cuba, whatever their "classification," were exclusively for defensive purposes, and demanding the U.S. government renounce actions "which could lead to catastrophic consequences for peace throughout the world."[43]

Convinced that work on the missile sites should continue at a rapid pace, Khrushchev sent the order to General Issa Pliyev's headquarters in Cuba. That evening he also ordered Soviet ships to continue toward the quarantine line. By the next morning, though, Khrushchev was less sure if the latter decision had been the correct course of action, having just received Soviet Ambassador Anatoly Dobrynin's report of Robert Kennedy warning in the early hours of 24 October (Washington time) that the U.S. was intent on stopping Soviet ships bound for Cuba, by force if necessary.[44] Khrushchev broached the idea of stopping some of the Cuba-bound ships at a morning Presidium meeting on 24 October. Finally, just an hour before the quarantine went into effect, the Kremlin sent out a coded message to the affected ships to stop.[45]

At the time the quarantine began there were sixteen Soviet dry cargo vessels and six tankers in the Atlantic en route to Cuba. Nine of these twenty-two ships were estimated as being close enough to the island to allow them to reach Cuba by the end of October. It was just after 0900 that the Navy's Flag Plot in the Pentagon received news that some Soviet ships appeared to have reversed course. Just after 1030, DCI John McCone confirmed that ONI had determined that six Soviet ships inbound for Cuba – *Poltava, Gagarin, Kimovsk, Dolmatovo, Moscow Festival,* and *Metallurg Kursk* – had either stopped or reversed direction on orders from Moscow.[46] Secretary McNamara and Admiral Anderson had decided on the night of 23 October that the Navy's first intercepts would be the Soviet merchantman *Kimovsk,* which was judged to be carrying military equipment, and the large-hatch freighter *Poltava,* thought to be transporting missiles. Both of these vessels were among those that had stopped.

Deciding not to interfere with the Soviet ships that had stopped short of the quarantine line, President Kennedy suggested that *Essex* be instructed to hold off on intercepting *Kimovsk.* Accordingly, on instructions from the White House, Commander Carrier Division 18 was ordered to maintain surveillance. Because of this decision, the U.S. Navy did not intercept any Soviet ships during the first day of the quarantine.

On Thursday, 25 October, the quarantine's second day, the destroyer *Gearing* (DD 710) intercepted the Soviet tanker *Bucharest* and pulled alongside to take topside photographs of the ship. Upon examination, photos revealed the absence of deck cargo, and *Bucharest* was allowed to proceed to Cuba. That same morning, President Kennedy directed that the Navy not intercept and board a Communist bloc ship first, because of the Soviet Union's apparent desire to avoid a direct U.S.–Soviet confrontation at sea. Searching for a non-bloc ship that would be a good choice for an early interception, the task force picked the Lebanese freighter *Marucla.* Confusion over her exact position, however, led to *Marucla* not being reliably located by the intercepting destroyers until 2245 on the 25th. She was finally boarded at 0750 on Friday, 26 October by a party from the destroyers *John R. Pierce* (DD 753) and *Joseph P. Kennedy, Jr.* (DD 850). After checking her cargo manifest against bills of lading and inspecting one of her holds, *Marucla* the destroyers allowed her to resume her voyage to Havana. Ironically, she proved to be the only ship stopped and boarded during the entire period of the quarantine.[47]

On the afternoon of 26 October, Khrushchev dictated a lengthy personal letter to Kennedy that hinted at a way to end the crisis: "Let us therefore show statesmanlike wisdom. I propose: We, for our part, will declare that our ships, bound for Cuba, will not carry any kind of armaments. You would declare that the United States will not invade Cuba with its forces and will not support any sort of forces which might intend to carry out an invasion of Cuba. Then the necessity for the presence of our military specialists in Cuba would disappear."[48] This letter, however, was followed by a firmer letter, sent on 27 October, which offered to remove offensive arms from Cuba only if the United States agreed to remove its missiles from Turkey.[49]

Ironically, Kennedy initially had introduced the idea of a missile trade as a trial balloon in the ExComm on 18 October, and by Saturday the 27th he was seriously entertaining the idea of trading the Jupiter missiles in Turkey for the Soviet missiles in Cuba.[50] Kennedy was fully aware, however, that a public revelation of such a deal would be political suicide. Accordingly, in his written response he chose to ignore Khrushchev's second letter. At 2005 that evening, the State Department dispatched a letter from Kennedy to Khrushchev, agreeing to remove the quarantine and guaranteeing that the United States would not invade Cuba if the USSR removed its offensive weapon systems from Cuba and halted further introduction of such systems into the island.[51]

Even as this was occurring, though, Robert Kennedy was meeting at the Justice Department with Soviet Ambassador Dobrynin. Acting according to a plan worked out in secret by the President and a small group of his closest advisers, the younger Kennedy told Dobrynin that if the missiles were withdrawn from Cuba the United States would agree not to invade the island. However, he stressed they needed to be removed quickly, since American military action was imminent.[52]

When Dobrynin raised the issue of the U.S. Jupiter missiles in Turkey, the Attorney-General had an answer all prepared. Robert Kennedy told Dobrynin that the President saw "no insurmountable difficulties" with the idea of withdrawing the missiles from Turkey but that such an effort would take four or five months to accomplish. Kennedy emphasized, though, that such an action could not be undertaken as part of a written *quid pro quo*. It had to remain a secret verbal understanding between Kennedy and Khrushchev only.[53] It was mid-morning on Sunday the 28th when Khrushchev received the text of the President's letter and the report of Dobrynin's meeting the night before with Robert Kennedy. Convinced at last of the need to make immediate positive response to Kennedy's offer, Khrushchev accepted the American proposal.[54]

On 7 November, Kennedy accepted the Soviet Union's offer to allow the visual and photographic inspection of outward bound Soviet missile-carrying ships by American vessels coming close aboard or by unarmed helicopters making passes overhead.[55] The Soviets also informed U.S. negotiators on 3 November that forty-two ballistic missiles were in Cuba.[56] By 11 November, the ships of Task Force 136 had inspected all of the ships reported by the Soviets as having missiles aboard. Visual sightings and photographs confirmed that these ships were carrying a total of forty-two missiles.[57]

By 13 November, Kennedy decided to lift the quarantine if the USSR agreed to remove the IL-28 bombers. Finally, on 20 November, Khrushchev sent a message to Kennedy agreeing to comply with the request.[58] At his press conference at 1800 that evening, Kennedy announced the lifting of the quarantine. Less than two hours later, at 1945 Eastern Standard Time, the JCS directed CINCLANT to lift the quarantine "effective immediately."[59]

Map 15.1 Vietnam theatre of operations

15 Naval Blockades during the Vietnam War

Spencer C. Tucker

Two distinct sets of naval blockade operations were carried out during the Vietnam War, both of them instituted by the United States against the Communist forces in North Vietnam. The first set was Operation *Market Time*, and later Operation *Game Warden*, to interdict the water-borne flow of insurgents and weapons from North to South. The second, called Operation *Pocket Money*, mined Haiphong harbor and so attempted to halt foreign shipments of arms and supplies to North Vietnam. The interdiction activities in South Vietnam and the mining operation in North Vietnam were both designed to stem the flow of supplies to the insurgency in South Vietnam. These two operations, which were proclaimed as successful at the time, reveal both the advantages and also the very real limitations of naval blockades in warfare.

Background

In the late 1950s Communist-led insurgents in the Republic of Vietnam (RVN, South Vietnam) began the Second Indo-China War, usually referred to as the Vietnam War. The insurgents, who were later known as the Viet Cong (VC, for Vietnamese Communists), were disillusioned by the 1956 refusal of the U.S.-backed RVN government to allow elections to take place, called for by the July 1954 Geneva Agreements, to reunify the country. The government of the Democratic Republic of Vietnam (DRV, North Vietnam) in Hanoi decided to support the Southern insurgency and indeed soon took control of it. The conflict escalated steadily. At first the United States government responded with military equipment and advisers only, but in 1965 it committed ground troops. The navy also sent ships and men.

Vietnam's maritime geography made blockades difficult. Vietnam extends from east Laos and Cambodia to the Gulf of Tonkin and the South China Sea, encompassing some 127,300 square miles of territory, or half the size of Texas. Ranging from the 9th parallel north to the 26th parallel of latitude, Vietnam is some 1,200 miles in length; because of the many inlets, bays, and small islands, the coastline is actually much longer. This coastline, which has caused Vietnam to be known as the "balcony on the Pacific," has left it vulnerable to seaborne invasion while also providing a ready means of transportation.

Vietnam enjoys a long common northern border with China. This was especially important during the Vietnam War because, no matter who controlled the Gulf of Tonkin, significant military resources could flow via road and rail overland from China and the USSR. Without an invasion of North Vietnam – an extremely unlikely proposition, given the U.S. experience during the Korean War when China had intervened to come to the aid of North Korea – there was no ready means to cut off the supply of military equipment from China. Thus any effort to blockade the North Vietnamese coast by sea could at best be only partial.

The 1954 Geneva Conference had temporarily divided Vietnam into the two states of the DRV and the RVN at the 17th parallel of latitude, separated by a demilitarized zone (DMZ). According to the 1954 Geneva Accords, there were to be no military forces, supplies, or equipment within the zone during its "temporary" existence. But the DRV routinely ignored this prohibition, and during May 1959 North Vietnamese Defense Minister General Vo Nguyen Giap formed the 559th Transportation Group (for the fifth month of 1959) with responsibility for moving supplies south by land, largely by means of human porters, through eastern Laos. Vastly expanded and made more sophisticated over the years, this Laotian supply network became known as the Ho Chi Minh Trail. Later it was extended into eastern Cambodia, with that portion being known as the Sihanouk Trail.

But the long Vietnamese coastline also offered many opportunities to resupply by sea. Although easier to detect, sea transport was more efficient than driving over mountains and through jungle. Thus, one of the two battalions comprising the 559th was the 603rd Sea Transportation Battalion, composed of 107 men operating on Gianh River in Quang Binh Province. In October 1961, Giap established Military Transportation Group 759 to conduct the seaborne resupply effort. On 11 October 1962, a motor-powered wooden vessel built in Haiphong shipyard unloaded the first shipment of weapons to the South at the Ca Mau Peninsula. On 22 December 1964, seagoing vessels delivered forty-four tons of weapons from North Vietnam to Long An, in South Vietnam.[1]

The earliest U.S. Navy operations in Vietnam, apart from intelligence gathering against North Vietnamese communications and radar sites (the so-called DeSoto patrols) and support for South Vietnamese commando raids (Op Plan 34A) against North Vietnam, were to interdict this North Vietnamese seaborne resupply effort of the southern insurgency. U.S. Navy ship patrols and aerial surveillance largely ended the traffic by trawler-type vessels. Waterborne logistics traffic none the less continued at a low level, both along the North Vietnamese coast and in South Vietnam, with weapons and personnel carried in sampans and smaller craft. U.S. Navy ships and personnel were soon directed to halt this activity.

U.S. Navy Efforts to Block Maritime Infiltration

The U.S. Navy operation to prevent infiltration and resupply by sea was known as *Market Time*. Established in March 1965, this effort closely resembled those of the French during the Indo-China War, the chief difference being in the greater number of aircraft and vessels of all types available to the Americans. Even with vessels supplied by the United States, the French did not have adequate resources, including radar, and often were forced to rely on ambush tactics.[2]

Market Time came into being to interdict not only weapons and ammunition but also a wide range of other items, including military equipment, clothing, radios, telephones, communications wire, medical supplies, printing presses, and machine tools. Initially this operation came under the direction of the U.S. Seventh Fleet and was designated the Vietnam Patrol Force or Task Force 71 (TF-71). On 31 July 1965 operational command was transferred to the Naval Advisory Group (NAG) and the Vietnam Patrol Force became the Coastal Surveillance Force (TF-115).

On 1 April 1966, the newly created U.S. Naval Forces, Vietnam (NAVFORV) assumed command of TF-115. Commanded by Rear-Admiral N.G. Ward, NAVFORV was part of the U.S. Military Assistance Command, Vietnam (MACV) and was charged with coordinating all U.S. Navy activities underway in Vietnam. These included support commands based at Saigon and Danang, Seabee construction operations, a Naval Advisory Group working with the RVN Navy (VNN), as well as the Coastal Surveillance Force (TF-115) and the River Patrol Force (TF-116). A year later the navy added the Mobile Riverine Force (TF-117), charged with the conduct of combined riverine operations. In October 1968, *Sea Lords* (South East Asia Lake, Ocean, River, Delta Strategy) came into being as TF-194. It was charged with coordinating units from all three of the aforementioned U.S. Navy task forces for riverine interdiction, strike, and pacification campaigns.[3]

The U.S. Navy effort in South Vietnam was multi-faceted, but *Market Time* itself consisted of a three-layered patrol system: an outermost air ring, with outer and inner ship barriers. From Dixie Station, U.S. Navy aircraft kept watch. The first aircraft earmarked for such duties in 1965 were single-engine propeller-driven Douglas A-1 Skyraider light bombers noted for their 14-hour-long loiter time; twin-engine propeller-driven Martin P-5 Marlin flying boats; and twin-engine propeller-driven Lockheed P-2 Neptunes. Later, 4-engine propeller-driven Lockheed P-3 Orions arrived. The P-2s and P-3s operated from such locations as Cam Ranh Bay, Tan Son Nhut, Utapao in Thailand, and Sangley Point in the Philippines. The P-5s, which were withdrawn in 1967, operated out of Sangley Point and had seaplane tenders at Cam Ranh Bay, Poulo Condore, and the Cham Islands. Air surveillance duties included identifying all suspicious vessels, photographing them, and reporting their location to one of five Coastal Surveillance

Centers along the South Vietnamese coastline. This information was relayed to the crews of other aircraft and surface vessels for further action.

The outer ship barrier operated within forty miles of the South Vietnamese coast, stretching from the 17th parallel to the Cambodian border in the Gulf of Thailand. Ships included radar picket escort destroyers (DERs), destroyer escorts (DEs), ocean and coastal minesweepers (MSOs and MSCs), and U.S. Coast Guard High Endurance Coast Guard Cutters (WHECs). Their mission was the interdiction of seaborne supplies carried by larger trawler-type vessels. Throughout the history of the operation, *Market Time* forces sank or captured more than 50 infiltrating vessels.[4]

The inner ship barrier operated in the shallow waters along the South Vietnamese coastline, particularly in the Mekong Delta, where Communist forces used wooden junks to transport men and supplies, easily intermingled with thousands of innocent junks and sampans. The RVN government authorized U.S. forces to stop, search, and seize any vessel involved in fishing or trade within a twelve-mile limit.

In July 1965, the South Vietnamese Junk Force was incorporated into the VNN and charged with investigation of in-shore junk traffic. U.S. Navy leaders believed that, without American participation and supervision, this Junk Force would be ineffective. In 1966, the U.S. Navy created two forces: the River Patrol Force (TF-116), charged in Operation *Game Warden* with severing Communist supply lines by securing control of the waterways; and the Mobile Riverine Force (TF-117), to search out and destroy Communist troops and base areas by transporting ground units to suspected targets.

The River Patrol Force established its headquarters at Binh Thuy near Can Tho in the Delta. Many of the vessels in this "brown-water fleet" were improvised. They included fiberglass patrol boats, shallow-draft landing craft including LSTs (Landing Ship Tanks), fire-support monitors, and minesweepers. TF-116's chief workhorse was the fast patrol boat (PBR), known as the Swift boat, which was ideally suited to the shallow waters of the region since it had a draft of only eighteen inches. It had four-man crews and was armed with two .50-caliber machine guns – one each fore and aft – a grenade launcher, and an M-60 .30-caliber machine gun, plus individual weapons. The PBRs operated from 10 *Game Warden* bases. They first arrived in Vietnam in March 1966. At peak strength, TF-116 operated 250 PBRs, but beginning in 1968 an increasing number were transferred to the VNN.

TF-116 also utilized the UH-1B Iroquois helicopter, fitted with the XM-6E3 armament system. In navy service it was known as the Sea Wolf. It had a speed of 120 knots and total air time of about 2.5 hours. Operated by a four-man crew, the Sea Wolf was armed with four M-60 machine guns mounted in pairs on outriggers outboard of the cargo doors, and an eight-round 2.75-inch (760mm) FFAR rocket pod affixed to each side of the aircraft. Two door gunners also each fired a single M-60D machine gun on a flexmount on either side of the helicopter. The gunships scouted ahead of the PBRs, searching out ambushes and providing fire support where needed.

A good deal of *Market Time/Game Warden* activity was centered in the Mekong Delta area of South Vietnam. This low-lying area of swampy rice lands and dense jungle comprised about a quarter of the RVN's total area and contained about a third of its population. The Delta included more than 4,000 miles of interconnecting inland waterways, and canals that varied from 60 to 130 feet in width. Depths in the major waterways varied, depended on the changing tides; but generally speaking, they were a maximum of 16 feet. There were also flood plains or dense mangrove swamps. The Plain of Reeds region, north-west of Saigon, is a vast area of reeds and grass covered by between 1 and 6 feet of water in flood season.

The dense vegetation bordering the waterways provided excellent cover for guerrilla forces to lay ambushes. These, and the searing heat and monsoon rains, created extraordinarily difficult conditions for U.S. forces operating in the region. Begun in 1965 and extending to 1972, *Market Time/Game Warden* operated around the clock and in all kinds of weather. Patrols had to deal with tens of thousands of assorted Vietnamese water craft as they worked to secure control of the coasts, rivers, and canals in order to interdict VC/PAVN infiltration and combat-related activities.

Within four months of the arrival of the PBRs in the country in March 1966, the River Patrol Force was averaging 1,200 two-boat patrols per month and boarding and searching some 9,000 river craft out of an estimated 50,000 sighted. By 1968, the River Patrol Force had expanded to a second task group and had sufficient strength to maintain patrols on all major rivers of the Mekong Delta. In that one year alone, U.S. Navy vessels intercepted more than 600,000 sampans, junks, and other Vietnamese water craft.

By October 1968, TF-115 had significantly expanded its support operations. Late that month it created Operation *Sea Lords* to conduct joint raiding operations that involved units of TF-115, TF-116, and TF-117 against previously secure Communist strongholds in the Delta. TF-115 continued its seaward surveillance, but a second interdiction line was set up along the Rach-Giang Thanh, running north-east from Ha Tien and employing "Swift" boats on patrol duties. Meanwhile river patrol craft of TF-116 blockaded known Communist crossing points on the Bassac River. VNN coastal and river craft, along with reaction troops, were added in early 1969. As American withdrawals began under the Vietnamization program, *Market Time* forces gradually transferred their equipment to the VNN.[5]

The Mining of North Vietnamese Coastal Waters

The other important blockade carried out by the U.S. Navy was the mining operation. It came at the end of the war and was less than a year in duration. Mining does not fit the classic definition of a strategic blockade, which assumes an action in which ships are involved; a maritime blockade is considered strategic when it forms part of military operations against a blockaded coast or is designed to prevent the provisioning of enemy land forces in the blockaded area.[6] The navy had long been urging such an action. "After seven years of direct U.S. participation in the SEASIAN conflict and continued attempts by U.S. military authorities to gain permission to cut off the seaborne logistic sinews of North Vietnam's strength by means of mining, President Richard Nixon approved mining on 6 May 1972."[7]

Long advocated by Chairman of the Joint Chiefs of Staff Admiral Thomas H. Moorer, the mining operation was approved by President Nixon as a direct response to the spring 1972 PAVN invasion of South Vietnam. The North Vietnamese called this operation the Nguyen Hue Offensive, while U.S. forces dubbed it the Spring or Easter Offensive (it began at Easter, on 30 March). Hanoi then had fifteen divisions in its army. Convinced that the U.S. would not invade North Vietnam, Giap committed twelve divisions to a three-pronged invasion of South Vietnam: from across the DMZ, in the Central Highlands, and in Binh Long province. All three of these attacks enjoyed initial success, and in the first PAVN forces overran Quang Tri Province.

There was talk in South Vietnam that the United States might abandon the RVN, and Nixon wanted to demonstrate U.S. resolve. With only about 60,000 U.S. military personnel remaining in South Vietnam and few of these combat troops, Nixon's military options were sharply limited. He could not, for example, order a U.S. amphibious invasion of southern North Vietnam, which in any case would run the risk of direct Chinese military intervention and a widened conflict. Congress would oppose any effort to reinsert significant numbers of U.S. ground troops, and the use of nuclear weapons was not a viable political option.

Nixon responded with the only options effectively open to him. He called for massive U.S. air support for hard-pressed ARVN units in South Vietnam, and on 8 May he ordered a resumption of the bombing of North Vietnam. This time he unleashed B-52 strategic bombers against military targets in North Vietnam, including the hitherto largely off-limits Hanoi–Haiphong area. Known as *Linebacker*, this campaign saw the removal of previous targeting restrictions and strikes along North Vietnamese lines of communication stretching from the DMZ all the way to the China border. *Linebacker* continued until 23 October 1972. At the same time, U.S. Navy Seventh Fleet destroyers and cruisers carried out shore bombardment operations against coastal lines of communication and military installations along the North Vietnamese coast.

Nixon also ordered the aerial mining of North Vietnam's major port of Haiphong, as well as the DRV's other ports and major waterways. Known as Operation *Pocket Money*, this mining carried serious risks, including the sinking or damaging of merchant ships belonging to Communist or neutral nations. Mining was made possible by the 1969 border confrontation between the USSR and PRC, since by far the greatest risk was if these two countries combined to oppose the U.S., and it was for this reason that Haiphong had never been mined before.

Pocket Money was the first time during the Vietnam War that the United States had moved against major North Vietnamese ports with mines in order to halt oceangoing trade.[8] Nixon's decision was preceded by intense debate within the administration. The mining operation represented a considerable diplomatic gamble, taken on the eve of the president's trip to Moscow to meet with Soviet leader Leonid Brezhnev. Nixon was furious with Moscow, however, since he blamed the Kremlin for Hanoi's actions. The USSR provided the bulk of military aid to the DRV and Nixon believed its leader certainly knew of North Vietnamese plans.

While both Moscow and Beijing denounced the American decision, Nixon had gauged correctly. Neither power believed that Vietnam was vital to their own national security, and both China and the Soviet Union wanted detente and agreement with the West on a host of issues, including enhanced technology. The summit trip to Moscow was successful, with the result that North Vietnam's leading allies largely abandoned the DRV and Hanoi lost the opportunity to win the war on its own terms.[9]

Mining operations are in fact an excellent means of blockade, by which one side might gain its military objective without cost to either side. Mines are a passive weapon and can serve as a means of de-escalating a conflict as they effectively keep the two sides apart. The great value of such operations was conclusively demonstrated in the closing months of World War II when U.S. B-28 bombers dropped thousands of mines along the coasts of the Japanese home islands. This operation brought Japanese coastal trade to a virtual halt, created widespread economic hardship and even starvation, and forced Japan's leadership to contemplate the necessity of surrender.[10]

In 1972 the vast bulk of Communist bloc assistance flowed into North Vietnam not by rail from China, but by sea. Haiphong alone handled more than 400 ships a year. The U.S. Defense Department estimated that in 1971 North Vietnam imported more than 2.5 million metric tons of supplies for both the general economy and the armed forces, and that 85 percent of this came by sea, most of it through Haiphong. A naval blockade could be partially offset by increased shipments overland via rail and road from China, but North Vietnam had mounted a massive military invasion of the south by virtually its entire armed forces, and PAVN forces would require sustained substantial resupply of petroleum, oil, lubricants, ammunition, equipment, spare parts, and weapons. The mining would render such resupply much more difficult and costly, and it would also have the ancillary effect of disrupting the DRV's normal commercial traffic, which could cause Hanoi to be more amenable to peace negotiations.

Nixon publicly announced the mining campaign on the evening of 8 May 1972, stating he "concluded that Hanoi must be denied the weapons and supplies it needs to continue the aggression." The president gave shipping a three-day grace period to quit North Vietnamese ports or turn back if they were bound there. Having received the order to mine, and simultaneous with President Nixon's announcement, at 9 a.m. on 9 May (Vietnam time) U.S.

Marine Corps A-6 and U.S. Navy A-7E aircraft from *Coral Sea* dropped the first thirty-six mines in Haiphong's shipping channel. Externally carried, they were set with 72-hour arming delays. Forty-eight hours later, a number of DST 36 seismic/magnetic mines, which combined an MK 82 500 bomb with a magnetic mine kit, were laid off Hon Gai, Quang Khe, Vinh, Thanh Hoa, Cam Pha, and Dong Hoi.

The minefields all became active on 11 May. Thereafter mines were dropped at major choke points along the coast and in coastal waterways. Mines laid by *Linebacker* inland at Vinh and other locations increased the extent of the minefields. On 25 May the Department of Defense announced that all twenty to twenty-five ships that had been en route to Haiphong had changed course. Over a period of eight months (the last mines were dropped on 14 January 1973 near Vinh) the navy deployed more than 11,000 mines, effectively ending all major maritime transportation to and from North Vietnam.[11]

The DRV made efforts to offset the effect of the minefields. Within a few weeks, many ships carrying cargoes for North Vietnam had diverted to ports in southern China. From these ports, supplies could be transshipped to the DRV. However, over the next few months only insignificant amounts were delivered to Chinese ports. It was not until the month of August that these had climbed to about 110,000 tons; the tally fell back somewhat the next month and then remained constant at 110,000 tons in November and December, little more than half the monthly average of 200,000 tons of imports by sea prior to the mining.

Transshipment to North Vietnam necessitated up to a 1,400-mile movement by rail through southern China. When cargo reached North Vietnam it had to be moved by a land transportation network already strained and under constant U.S. air attack. *Linebacker* was then sharply reducing North Vietnamese land transportation capabilities by striking rail lines and roads and destroying hundreds of bridges, trucks, and train cars. In effect *Pocket Money* increased the effectiveness of *Linebacker* air strikes by forcing the goods onto the North Vietnamese rail system leading from China where they might be destroyed by air power.

The DRV did employ a wide variety of WBLC (water-borne logistic craft), consisting of sampans, junks, and other small craft, to offload cargoes from merchant ships outside the *Pocket Money* minefields and to transport cargoes by water from Chinese ports to the DRV. In 1971 North Vietnam possessed some 35,000 WBLC. The MK 52 was not really a suitable weapon to use against WBLC because of its arming depths and the very low magnetic signature of such vessels. Indeed, the DST 36, which had been developed in 1967 for the *Rolling Thunder* air campaign against North Vietnam, had been designed primarily to target "indigenous small craft with an engine or carrying ferrous cargo." During 1968, *Rolling Thunder* aircraft had dropped some 35,000 of these in inland waterways and against roads.[12]

The DRV did make efforts to sweep the mines. Reconnaissance photographs showed electromagnetic sweep equipment (solenoids) mounted in the bows of a variety of water craft in the Haiphong area, and in January 1973 two ships were observed in the channel towing what appeared to be closed-loop magnetic sweeps. Other North Vietnamese techniques included floating barges filled with scrap metal over minefield areas and towing iron pipes and rails behind manually propelled wooden craft. None of these appear to have been particularly successful, as was disclosed by DRV personnel to the U.S. Navy during subsequent negotiations over possible clearing operations.[13]

The mining did claim some U.S. Navy warships. Beginning in June and extending into December five underwater explosions injured U.S. destroyers operating off the North Vietnamese coast. Almost certainly these were from U.S. mines. Damage ranged from none (two cases), to very light (two), and heavy (one). The destroyer *Warrington* sustained the worst damage. On 17 July, it was on a mission about twenty miles north of Dong Hoi in southern North Vietnam when the ship was hit by two underwater explosions in what were presumed to be mine-free waters. Towed to Subic Bay in the Philippines, *Warrington* was so badly damaged that it had to be scrapped. Navy investigators concluded that the ship was almost certainly hit by a stray DST 36 mine.

In addition, on 4 August TF-77 aircraft reported some two dozen explosions in a minefield near Hon La over a thirty-second time span. At first there was concern that aircraft may have triggered the explosions, which were almost certainly mines. Ultimately the navy concluded that the explosions had been caused by the magnetic perturbations of solar storms, the most intense in more than two decades.[14]

Conclusions

The U.S. Navy was largely successful in interdicting seaborne infiltration into South Vietnam, but a good deal of aid continued to reach the Communist insurgents through the Cambodian port of Sihanoukville. The navy was powerless to halt this seaborne traffic into officially neutral Cambodia. The arms and equipment thus delivered were then transshipped by land across Communist-controlled border areas of Cambodia into South Vietnam. During the two-and-a-half years between 23 December 1966 and 3 April 1969, ten PRC ships delivered to Sihanoukville an estimated 21,600 tons of military and 5,333 tons of non-military aid for PAVN/VC forces in South Vietnam.[15]

Given this alternate source of resupply, it is impossible to assess with any precision the effectiveness of brown water navy operations along the many rivers of the south, especially in the Delta. At best such operations were of mixed effectiveness. The navy did prevent some supplies from reaching the Viet Cong, but much else got through. *Market Time* did, however, disrupt Viet Cong control of the population, especially its collection of taxes from civilians, and it made it more difficult for Communist forces to mount military operations.

Despite all of its initial problems, *Pocket Money* turned out to be very successful. Although it could not completely sever military assistance to North Vietnam nor halt the insurgency in the South, the mining of Haiphong harbor did render both of these activities more difficult, and it certainly slowed the shipment of war materiel into North Vietnam. It also had serious effects on the North Vietnamese economy. Well aware of this, U.S. negotiators in Paris used an offer to remove the mines as a bargaining chip for Hanoi to release U.S. prisoners of war.

The mining of North Vietnamese ports was also linked with the success of *Linebacker* in attacking and destroying lines of communication and key choke points in North Vietnam, which, in turn, starved PAVN forces in the south of the supplies necessary to continue large-scale conventional operations. This strategic success, when combined with direct air support to ARVN forces fighting in the south, brought about the defeat of the North Vietnamese offensive. By September 1972, it was evident that *Linebacker* and *Pocket Money* were having a credible effect. Overland imports into the DRV dropped from 160,000 tons a month to 30,000 tons, while seaborne imports fell from 25,000 tons a month to virtually nothing. The PAVN military offensive in the south did, however, greatly increase problems for the RVN government, particularly in rebuilding destroyed infrastructure and in the resettlement of the large number of refugees created by the fighting.[16]

Linebacker and *Pocket Money* helped prevent North Vietnam from winning the war militarily in 1972. The offensive in the south had claimed at least 100,000 PAVN dead. This, the heavy bombing of the north, the mining, and the near certainty of President Nixon's reelection all led the DRV to negotiate seriously in Paris. On 23 October 1972, after the two sides concluded an agreement, Nixon ordered bombing halted north of 20 degrees latitude. The Paris Agreement called on the United States to remove its remaining forces from South Vietnam, and Hanoi agreed to release the captured U.S. pilots, a key U.S. demand.

The agreement fell apart, however, on the opposition of RVN President Nguyen Van Thieu, who refused to sign it. Hanoi refused to renegotiate the agreement and published its terms. A furious Nixon ordered the resumption of the bombing of North Vietnam by B-52s. The December bombing, dubbed *Linebacker II* and also known as the Christmas Bombing, helped bring Hanoi back to the negotiating table. Both sides agreed to a few cosmetic changes, and this time Thieu was forced to sign on the threat of a complete cut-off of U.S. aid. As soon as the negotiations were successfully concluded and the Paris Peace Treaty signed on 23 January 1973, the Navy formed Task Force 78 (TF-78) to conduct minesweeping operations in North Vietnamese waters. This operation, known as *Endsweep*, employed surface minesweepers as well as specially configured CH-33 helicopters of one navy and two Marine squadrons operating from two amphibious assault ships, *Inchon* and *New Orleans*, with cover provided by naval carrier aircraft.

All told, the helicopter crews flew 1,100 hours of minesweeping duty. This operation began on 6 February and ended on 27 July 1973.[17]

Directly, *Pocket Money* closed the three major North Vietnamese ports to foreign shipping for 300 days, forced the diversion of cargoes destined for North Vietnam by sea to Chinese ports and their transshipment by rail for between 400 and 1,400 miles, rendered idle twenty-seven foreign supply ships for 8,000 ship-days, reduced total imports into the DRV by 30 percent, halted virtually all of the DRV's exports, eliminating an important source of foreign exchange and adding to an already strained economy, and reduced coastal shipping to the southern panhandle from 800 tons to 150 tons per day, imposing a heavier burden on the interior transportation system. Indirectly, *Pocket Money* increased the effectiveness of *Linebacker* air strikes by increasing the total amount of supplies being transported on a radically diminished land transportation network. It prevented dredging of the Haiphong channel, increasing the silting there by an estimated two feet. It created supply shortages for PAVN personnel in South Vietnam. Finally, it provided Washington with an important – perhaps the most important – negotiating lever at the Paris Peace Talks.

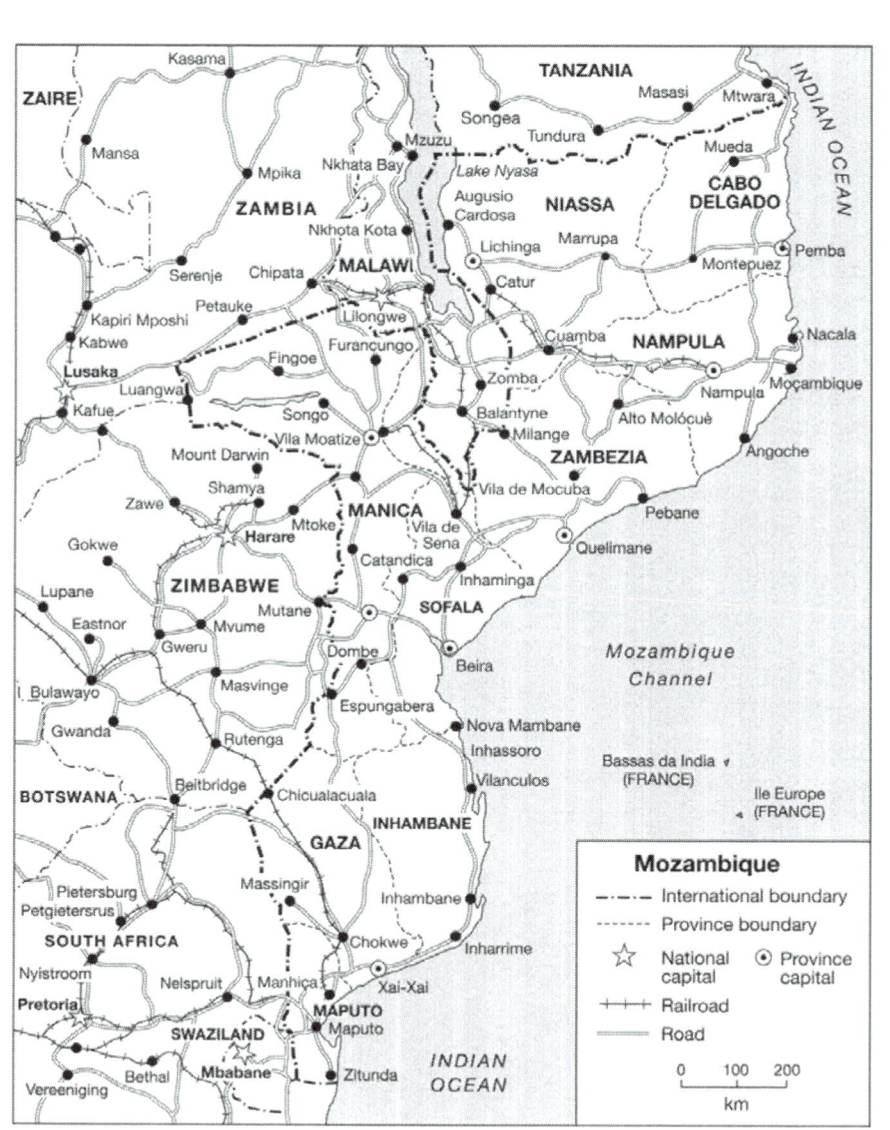

Map 16.1 The Beira Patrol theatre of operation

16 The Beira Patrol

Britain's Broken Blockade against Rhodesia

*Richard A. Mobley**

Between 1966 and 1975, the Royal Navy conducted one of the more unusual blockades of modern history – a maritime-intercept operation that became known as the "Beira patrol." The Royal Navy and Royal Air Force monitored shipping in the Mozambique Channel in an attempt to cut oil supplies from reaching landlocked Southern Rhodesia (today Zimbabwe) via the port of Beira, in the Portuguese colony of Mozambique. Although the blockade was successful, Britain's overall oil embargo against Rhodesia failed. London could not extend maritime interception operations to other ports in Mozambique or elsewhere, yet it refused to abandon a mission that was increasingly unpopular within the Navy. Only when Mozambique gained independence from Portugal in 1975, and could credibly assure the UN that no oil would cross its territory to Rhodesia, did the Beira patrol come to an end.

The Beira patrol is a cautionary tale for states that adopt maritime interception operations. It illustrates the challenges of shaping an appropriate force for maritime sanctions and shows how demanding even a small blockade can be, especially if prolonged. It reveals the difficulties of fashioning credible rules of engagement and the complexities of the interplay between rules and force posture. It also exemplifies the legal, resource, and political obstacles to modifying a blockade once it has started.

Most importantly, the Beira patrol shows how political objectives can outweigh military ones. The British-crafted UN Security Council resolution made it difficult for Britain to cease the maritime interception operations when it might have wished to do so. Diplomatic objectives consistently outweighed Ministry of Defence protests that the patrol was of questionable utility. Because warships off Beira were such powerful symbols, the Royal Navy found itself in an open-ended campaign. A prisoner of its own Security Council resolution, the United Kingdom could not end its maritime sanction enforcement – however ineffectual – as long as it remained politically committed to sanctions against Rhodesia.

Background

In 1964, the two northern portions of the colonial Federation of Rhodesia and Nyasaland achieved independence as black majority-controlled states –

Malawi (once Nyasaland) in July and Zambia (the former Northern Rhodesia) in October. London feared that the minority whites of Southern Rhodesia would ignore domestic and international pressure for black-majority rule by establishing Southern Rhodesia as a white-controlled state. In October 1964, Prime Minister Harold Wilson outlined certain preconditions for granting the colony independence: unimpeded progress toward majority rule; guarantees against unconstitutional amendment of the 1961 constitution supporting majority rule; an immediate improvement of the political status of non-whites; progress toward cessation of racial discrimination; and agreement on a settlement acceptable to the entire population, using a general referendum or similar device.[1]

Instead, on 11 November 1965, Salisbury (later Harare, the capital of Southern Rhodesia), issued a "Unilateral Declaration of Independence," asserting the existence of the sovereign state of Rhodesia under Prime Minister Ian Smith. The UN Security Council retaliated on 20 November with Resolution (UNSCR) 217, calling on all members to withhold recognition of Rhodesia, refuse assistance to its government, sever economic relations with Salisbury, and embargo petroleum shipments to the rebellious colony. In December, London banned selected imports from Rhodesia and prohibited the export of British oil to it.

Unwilling to invade its former colony, Britain hoped that an oil boycott by certain Middle East producers and cessation of oil exports by government-controlled British companies would be sufficient, so Wilson did not submit an oil-blockade resolution to the United Nations.[2] On 7 January 1966, he told the Jamaican prime minister that sanctions were "beginning to bite." He estimated that in three months the rebels would at least rescind the unilateral declaration of independence and reconsider their stance on minority rule.[3]

Even as Wilson made these optimistic statements, the Foreign Office was beginning to look at the possibility of a maritime embargo. This early planning proved prudent. The government's grounds for optimism were dashed during the first week of February, when the British press reported tanker-truck shipments of oil from South Africa. Rhodesia had in the past received oil via three primary routes: by road, across the Beit Bridge from South Africa; by rail, through Mozambique from either South Africa or the port of Lourenço Marques (now Maputo); and by pipeline, carrying crude oil from Beira to the Rhodesian refinery in Umtali.[4]

On 25 February, the Rhodesian minister of commerce and industry had even bragged that a tanker would arrive at Beira with oil for Rhodesia "in the foreseeable future."[5] Such unwanted publicity forced Britain to "do something" to prove its commitment to sanctions; on 1 March it established the Beira patrol with the initial British commitment of naval forces comprising a carrier, two frigates, and a logistical support ship. If the carrier had to depart station, the Royal Navy would deploy a third frigate. For the remaining nine years of the blockade, a succession of Royal Navy "small boys" – two destroyers or frigates at any one time (until the last months of the operation) – carried the burden of the surface blockade.

The warships, operating twenty to forty miles off Beira, were to intercept suspect tankers that had been detected by shore-based maritime patrol aircraft, a task the carriers carried out until bases were set up.[6] On 16 March, the French agreed to allow British planes to be based at Majunga, and by 19 March a detachment of three Shackletons was flying daily single-aircraft patrols, at first complementing the carrier-based patrols and then replacing them.[7] Although in 1969 the Royal Air Force was to reduce the Shackleton detachment from three to two aircraft, the Navy would enjoy dedicated maritime air support until 1971.

The Middle East Command characterized the period starting in mid-June 1966 as the patrol's "deterrent phase." The military hoped to warn off future attempts at oil-sanction "busting" by means of highly conspicuous surveillance over the Mozambique Channel: "It would soon become common knowledge throughout the merchant fleets that it was impossible to get through the Mozambique Channel without being spotted by a Shackleton. They would warn the frigates off Beira who would intercept and arrest with the probable loss of an expensive cargo. The game was not worth it."[8]

Rules of Engagement

At least four sets of rules of engagement – issued by Flag Officer Middle East on the basis of guidelines supplied by the Ministry of Defence – governed the Beira patrol between 1966 and 1968. The successive changes were significant because they reflected the evolution of British understanding of the legal basis of the operation. With one early exception, the rules became successively tougher; eventually, following an embarrassing incident in 1967 involving the French tanker *Artois*, London would authorize, if all else failed, gunfire directed at a tanker's bridge.

The first set of rules, issued on 15 February 1966, delineated the responsibilities of the blockading ships. Flag Officer Middle East instructed his frigates that, if ordered to intercept a tanker bound for Beira, they were to direct it to another port. If the vessel did not comply, the commanding officer was to take a series of escalatory steps, including firing shots across the bow and training guns at the ship. A boarding party might then be sent to order the master to divert; if he refused, the party was to "take over ship with minimum force" and steam it out of the area.[9]

Reviewing this plan, Wilson was concerned that the Royal Navy scrupulously respect the limits of British authority under international law, particularly in light of the voluntary nature of Security Council Resolution 217. On 11 March, Wilson warned that "before any action to intercept is taken the consent of the flag state should have been obtained." He also desired that commanding officers be given a "clear understanding that any force used must be kept to a minimum."[10]

Defence Ministry guidance to Flag Officer Middle East had assumed that a tanker's flag state would give Britain permission to divert the ship. A week after the prime minister expressed his concerns, the Defence Ministry modified its guidelines; now, if a tanker refused to turn away when challenged, a boarding party would warn the master, in the name of the vessel's flag state, to change course. If that did not work, a shot across the bow was authorized. Gone was any option of commandeering the ship. Indeed, if a tanker absolutely refused to comply, the warship could only escort it, and then only to the Mozambican six-mile territorial limit. In other words, the tanker could proceed to Beira unhindered.[11]

These modified rules of engagement tightened up considerably on 9 April 1966, when the UN Security Council passed Resolution 221. The unusual voyage of *Joanna V*, which had drawn British attention in early March, had ended on 5 April in a highly embarrassing way – the Greek-flag tanker had entered Beira, unmolested, under escort by the frustrated HMS *Plymouth*, and with wide publicity. The day before, the frigate had attempted to persuade *Joanna V* to go to another port, but since Greece refused permission to divert it, *Plymouth* could not use force.

Legal advisers warned that Britain would be liable if it attempted to force a diversion without permission of the flag state. On 7 April they clarified that use of force must be in accordance with an appropriate Chapter VII resolution. That same day, the Commonwealth Relations Office sent a message to all British embassies that Britain would seek an emergency meeting of the Security Council to obtain UN authority to use force to stop vessels carrying oil to Beira.[12] Over the next several days the United Kingdom lobbied furiously in the Security Council for a new resolution that would give a stronger legal basis for its embargo. It argued that continued seaborne deliveries of oil were a threat to peace because, if sanctions failed, violence might erupt in southern Africa. Britain argued that, under Chapter VII of the UN Charter, preventing the blockade's failure might justify the use of force, a similar argument to that used at the beginning of the Korean War.

The British drew up a resolution that would limit the risk of escalation. It confined the blockade to Beira only and specifically authorized only the United Kingdom to employ force. The resolution called upon Portugal "not to permit oil to be pumped through the pipeline from Beira to Rhodesia" and "not to receive at Beira oil destined for Rhodesia." All states were to ensure the diversion of "any of their vessels reasonably believed to be carrying oil destined for Rhodesia which may be en route for Beira."[13]

The teeth of the resolution, however, were in paragraph 5, which "[called] upon the Government of the United Kingdom to prevent by the use of force if necessary the arrival at Beira of vessels reasonably believed to be carrying oil destined for Rhodesia, and empower[ed] the United Kingdom to arrest and detain the tanker known as the *Joanna V* upon her departure from Beira in the event her oil cargo [was] discharged there."[14] The new resolution, passed as UNSCR 221, had the unintended and costly effect of forcing the Royal Navy to maintain the nine-year blockade alone.

With this resolution, the Defence Ministry liberalized the rules of engagement but continued to limit the use of force to "the very minimum." Ministry approval would still be required for the diversion of vessels, and the Royal Navy had to remain outside Mozambique's territorial waters. The Royal Navy felt, however, that Mozambique's six-mile limit was problematic. Soon after the Security Council issued its new resolution, the Defence Ministry advised Prime Minister Wilson that it was possible for a tanker to transit to Beira from Durban, South Africa, entirely within South African, and then Mozambican, territorial waters. Fortunately, no "pirate tanker" ever tried to challenge the Beira blockade in this way. Had one taken advantage of the territorial limits of an unsympathetic power, the British blockade force would have been hard pressed to stop it without creating an international incident.[15]

The new system stood until late the following year, but still had "no teeth" since force could not be used. The Minister of Defence Denis Healey castigated the existing rules of engagement for "lack of precision": "Not only does it place an unfair burden on commanding officers to leave them in any doubt about how far they are expected to go in the enforcement of their requests, but it exposes the Royal Navy to the risk of international discredit should an illegal tanker disregard the threat of force and be allowed to get away with it." He presented the cabinet with two options: restricting the Beira patrol simply to identifying smugglers, or directing commanding officers to use disabling gunfire against tankers that failed to heed other warnings.[16] The attorney general warned that any force used had to be "necessary," and the United Kingdom had to have a "reasonable belief" that the tanker was carrying oil consigned to Rhodesia.

On 21 March 1968, the Defence Ministry informed the Commander in Chief Far East in Singapore, who had assumed responsibilities as operational commander of the Beira patrol from his counterpart in Middle East Command in 1967, that the rules of engagement were being "clarified" and that UN member states were being notified that blockading ships would "enforce their requests to stop, if necessary by opening fire on the vessel." The ministry directed the commander to issue new instructions allowing for incremental increases in the use of force.

The British delegation to the United Nations issued a warning to the member states: "[Her Majesty's] ships have been instructed that if their requests to stop are not complied with they may enforce them, if necessary, by opening fire on the vessel. The master of such a vessel would thus, by refusing to stop, put at risk the lives of his crew and the safety of ship and cargo.... [A]ll member states will take the necessary action to ensure that the masters of vessels subject to their jurisdiction are made aware of the terms of Security Council Resolution No. 221.... [Her Majesty's government] would also urge member states to ensure that operating companies subject to their jurisdiction give advance notification to any [British] diplomatic or consular missions of a proposed call on Beira by an oil tanker."[17] The new rules of engagement were apparently sufficient, since there were no more attempts to disregard the Royal Navy blockade of Beira and no further major revisions to the rules of engagement.

The End of the Beira Patrol

The Royal Navy and Royal Air Force conducted the blockade professionally, but the largely ineffectual operation became increasingly unpopular within the Defence Ministry, which raised persuasive arguments about the costs of the patrol for a nation that had decided to end its commitments east of Suez. The government and the vocal Conservative opposition were also well aware that the blockade was porous. In September 1966, the Secretary of State for Commonwealth Affairs reported a "leakage" of 220,000 gallons of oil daily to Rhodesia; under strict rationing, the self-declared nation required only 200,000.[18] The Foreign and Commonwealth Office, however, fought to maintain the patrol because of its political visibility, a position the prime minister endorsed. As long as Britain attempted to reverse Southern Rhodesia's unilateral declaration of independence, it would be committed to sanctions; as long as it was committed to sanctions, it was tied to UNSCR 221 and the Beira patrol.

Queried by the Commonwealth Office in February 1968 as to the costs of the patrol, the Defence Ministry eagerly responded: "We are very willing to play our part in an exercise [exchange of correspondence] which will give ministers a broad indication of the savings to be had from stopping the Beira patrol. From the Navy's point of view the patrol reduces ship availability and it is not a task from which we derive any great training value." The ministry argued that maintaining the patrol, particularly after 1971, would "greatly reduce" the nation's ability to respond to contingencies outside of Europe.[19]

Nevertheless, in March 1968 the Defence and Overseas Policy Committee concluded that the time "was not ripe" to end the patrol, although from the purely military view "one should be glad to get rid of the tasks."[20] They concluded that the political disadvantages of ending the patrol outweighed any financial gains or operational relief to be expected from its cessation.[21] However, the committee agreed to reconsider cessation of the patrol "if the balance of advantages changed."[22]

In September 1969, Wilson made it clear that he was not about to abandon the patrol – the patrol's future "involves wider issues than those relating merely to defence."[23] The next year, the Defence Ministry was still unable to shake the political leadership's commitment to the patrol. The Foreign and Commonwealth Office forestalled even a proposal to reduce the patrol temporarily from two to one frigate that spring; elections in Britain were about to take place, and the government required that two ships be kept on station. On 16 June 1970, the personal secretary to the defence minister predicted: "Until the election is over, the political significance of the number of ships engaged in the patrol would make it extremely difficult to agree to any reduction."[24]

The elections brought in a new government, that of Edward Heath and the Conservatives. Despite rumors in the press, the new cabinet supported the Beira patrol. In July 1970, the new foreign minister, Sir Alec Douglas-Home, confirmed that the United Kingdom would continue it.[25] Ultimately, however, unalterable external factors – the elimination of the British military commitments east of Suez in 1971 and reduction of the fleet – would force further reduction of the resources committed to the patrol.

Although the Defence Ministry had lost its battle for a policy decision to eliminate the patrol outright, the force itself was whittled down between 1971 and 1975. By the spring of 1975, the patrol was to be a shadow of the carrier, frigate, and Shackleton force of 1966. The patrol then lost its air component. In June 1971, the Malagasy Republic asked the Royal Air Force to eliminate the Shackleton detachment at Majunga.[26] Thereafter, because of an overall drop in the number of frigates in the fleet, the Royal Navy was allowed to make the patrol intermittent; in 1973, the Navy assigned frigates to the station for only 161 ship-days, typically by diverting ships transiting to or from the Far East, which accounted for less than half of the year.

The Beira patrol finally wound down completely on 25 June 1975, the day Mozambique became independent, having assured the United Kingdom that it would not transship oil to Rhodesia. On that day HMS *Salisbury* went off station, the last of 76 Royal Navy ships to have supported the patrol during its ten-year history. One estimate placed total operating costs at a hundred million pounds.[27]

Conclusions

The Beira patrol was a unilateral approach to naval sanctions enforcement. For all of the ship-days and aircraft sorties it required, the patrol appears to have accomplished remarkably little. During its heyday from March 1966 to March 1971, the force intercepted a total of forty-seven tankers bound for Beira. Of these, forty-two were allowed to proceed. The other five did not stop or were escorted from the area. Meanwhile, oil continued to flow to Rhodesia from South Africa and from the port of Lourenço Marques. The Portuguese announced that, between April 1966 and May 1967, 169 tankers entered Lourenço Marques; of these, reported the Portuguese, 58 had flown the British flag.[28]

Yet the British government was convinced throughout that the patrol was useful as a symbol of the nation's commitment to sanctions against the separatist Rhodesian government. Because Security Council Resolution 221, which Britain had drafted, mandated British military action, the government considered the political costs of discontinuing the patrol greater than the concrete costs of conducting it. Even the Defence Ministry acknowledged that Rhodesia had to expend more foreign exchange moving oil by rail from Lourenço Marques than it would have had the Beira–Umtali pipeline been open.

The role of the news media proved critically important. At first overconfident about the speed with which sanctions could take effect, the Wilson cabinet was forced to react rapidly in March and April 1966 when world attention focused on two "pirate tankers" steaming toward Mozambique with oil for Rhodesia. Had the vessels' arrival in Beira been discovered by the press only after the fact, Britain might have been able to draft a less reactive, more thoughtful Security Council resolution. British diplomats might have considered calling, in what became paragraph 5 of UNSCR 221, upon all UN member nations, not just the United Kingdom, to contribute military assets to enforce the blockade. The blockade, of course, would then not have been under total British control, and ships of the Royal Navy might have found themselves steaming alongside those of its nation's adversaries, such as the Soviet navy. None the less, had London realized that sanction enforcement would last so long, it might have welcomed participation by other navies.

Inherently, a multinational force would have further complicated the formulation of rules of engagement, a task that was difficult enough as it was. As vital as rules of engagement are in all such cases to the credibility of sanctions enforcement, it took Britain substantial time to create a set sufficiently robust to allow its ships to stop "pirate tankers." Even then, the blockade could be challenged with impunity, and the rules had to be toughened again in December 1967. Until that was done, and thereafter to the extent that it could still be evaded, the Beira patrol gave the impression of ineffectiveness.

The Beira patrol represented Britain's hurried response to a highly publicized challenge from its breakaway colony of Southern Rhodesia. The patrol allowed London to limit the escalation of a potentially volatile situation while providing a credible demonstration of its commitment to sanction enforcement. The experience ultimately proved, however, that Security Council resolutions – highly public and formal pronouncements with the authority of the United Nations backing them – can, when used as weapons, turn against their wielders. A resolution that had mandated a multinational response would have allowed the patrol to be made more effective by generating sufficient naval force to extend the blockade to other ports. Thus, the flexibility inherent in a more broadly conceived instrument would have undoubtedly been worth the challenges of preparing and implementing it.

17 SLOCs and Sidewinders
The 1982 Falklands War

Charles W. Koburger Jr.

A tremendous number of books have examined the 1982 Falklands War.[1] This chapter will focus on the Argentine and British naval blockades during this war. In particular, the 1982 British blockade of the Falkland Islands has been called by Admiral Elmo Zumwalt the "classic example of modern limited blockade."[2] After considering the historical background to the Falklands War, and examining some of the technological innovations that made the British blockade a success, naval blockade's importance to limited wars will be evaluated.

Background

The Falkland Islands (known in Argentina as the *Islas Malvinas*) consist of some 200 islands of various sizes spread over an area some 400 miles to the east and slightly south of the Argentine coast. The two largest islands, East and West Falkland, dominate the 4,700-square-mile archipelago. A British colony since 1833, during the early 1980s the islands provided a frontier existence for approximately 1,800 British citizens, with over a thousand of them living in Port Stanley, the capital, located on East Falkland Island.

The Falkland Islands have a long and complicated history of ownership. They were first sighted in 1592, and in 1598 were originally named the Sebald Islands by the Dutch. However, in 1690 Captain John Strong of HMS *Welfare* called the passage between the two main islands the Falkland Sound, after Viscount Falkland, which subsequently gave the islands their English name.[3] Beginning in 1763, the islands were briefly claimed by France, then Spain, and finally by Britain. On 22 January 1771, Spain agreed that the islands were British, but in 1820 the as-yet uninhabited islands were claimed by the recently founded republic of Argentina, which established a penal colony on the islands; the colony soon mutinied, which undermined its legal claim to the islands. On 3 January 1833, the British government set up a naval garrison and the first permanent settlement. Although the Falklands were 8,000 miles from England, their location had both strategic and logistical significance for the British Navy.

Even though all of the inhabitants of the Falkland Islands were of British stock, in 1981 the British National Act classed the residents of the

Map 17.1 The Falklands War

Falkland Islands as "British Dependent Territories" citizens, which restricted their right to enter and live in the UK. While the islanders were traditionally called "kelpers" due to the large quantities of kelp they cut and shipped, in Argentina the word soon acquired the additional meaning of second-class citizens. The military junta ruling Argentina in 1982, considering invasion, perhaps assumed that Britain would not be interested in defending the islanders, while return of the Malvinas to the Argentine flag would provide the junta with much-needed popular support. A secondary reason for the invasion may have been that control over the Falkland Islands would allow Argentina to claim a larger pie-shaped slice of Antarctica, as well as easier access right across Drake's Passage, both of which would strengthen Argentina's negotiating position when the Antarctic Treaty came up for review in 1991. In the year or two prior to the attack, the Argentine government had improved relations with its northern neighbors, and its strategic focus had shifted "to Patagonia, the Sub-Antarctic and the South Atlantic."[4]

The Seizure: Operation *Rosario*

On 28 March 1982, Argentina launched the operation to recover its *terra irrendenta*, the Malvinas. Two naval task forces departed Puerto Belgrano, the Argentine Navy's main base 300 miles south of Buenos Aires, and ostensibly headed north-east to participate in exercises with the Uruguayan Navy. Their ultimate course, however, proved to be to the south-east and their actual mission was the seizure of the Falkland Islands.

The two main naval units involved included a carrier task force (TF 20) built around the light aircraft carrier *25 de Mayo* and including four destroyers, an oiler, and a seagoing tug. Embarked on the carrier were four S-2 ASW planes, eight A-4 attack planes, and several helicopters. An amphibious task force (TF 40) was built around the landing ship *Cabo San Antonio* and two personnel transports, escorted by two destroyers and two corvettes. TF 40 was carrying the reinforced 2nd Marine Battalion. Finally, a third naval force (TF 60) was assembled around the polar transport *Bahia Paraiso*, protected by a single corvette. This much smaller force was assigned the task of seizing South Georgia Island, 800 miles further to the south-east, and so played no role in the main naval effort in the Falklands.

The Argentine rules of engagement were set by the political conditions. The islands were to be occupied with minimum damage. Post-seizure relations with the locals were always to be considered, as was an eventual negotiated settlement with London. To back up their strong naval forces, Buenos Aires' Casa Rosada marshalled its air assets, which included the Air Force's approximately 220 combat planes. These included Mirage fighter-bombers capable of air-to-air refueling, and the Navy's newly organized Exocet missile-equipped Super Etendard fighter squadron based at Comodoro Rivadavia. Although this squadron was not yet completely equipped, armed, or manned, and would require air-to-air tankage, it would soon prove to be Argentina's most dangerous military asset.

On 2 April 1982, TF 40's Marines were landed successfully. Port Stanley was seized after a three-hour fight with minimal casualties. A reinforced army division (12,000 officers and men) was moved in and deployed throughout the islands. Meanwhile a mobile reserve (6,000 men) was held in and around Port Stanley. Stanley's short (4,000-foot) but hard-surface airfield was re-activated by the Argentine Air Force. Auxiliary air strips were also cut at Goose Green and at Pebble Island. To make sure that British forces could not interfere, the entire operation was provided with combined air and naval cover by the Argentine Navy offshore.

Buenos Aires apparently saw two main avenues of seaborne threat: one from the north from British forces coming directly from Ascension Island, some 4,000 miles away from the Falklands; and a second possible British force coming from the south-west via Chile, after transitting the Straits of Magellan. The first threat was countered by the carrier and her escorts stationed 450 miles to the north of the Falklands, while the second was covered by the cruiser and her escorts stationed to the south-west of the islands. The Argentine naval operations were neatly put together, perhaps reflecting many years of cooperation with and training by the U.S. Navy.

Buenos Aires quickly declared the islands to be a new province, and a governor was appointed. Argentine diplomats rushed in to try to translate what was apparently a de facto absorption into a de jure annexation. To Buenos Aires, time seemed to be on their side, since the typically violent winter was coming soon and any major British military operation would probably have to be delayed until the spring. To warn off any British reaction, a 200-mile exclusion zone was established around the Falklands. This zone was soon extended to include the entire South Atlantic area.

Ignoring the Argentine scriptwriters, on 2 May 1982 a British nuclear-powered attack submarine, *Conqueror*, located and sank the Argentine cruiser, *General Belgrano*. This naval disaster forced Argentina to recall TF 20 to home waters, which opened the sea lanes from Britain to the Falklands. In addition, with British submarines patrolling the seas, any further Argentine reinforcements or rotations to the Falklands would have to be inserted by air. This early and rather dramatic shift in the naval balance-of-power soon gave Britain the opportunity to enforce its own naval blockade of the Falkland Islands.

The British Response: Operation *Corporate*

Back in London, there was a universal uproar of public outrage at the unprovoked Argentine attack on the Falkland Islands. On 3 April 1982, the British government announced that it would form a naval task force. On the very next day it began to charter and requisition the necessary merchant vessels to support this group. On 5 April, the leading elements of this task force were already sailing for the Falklands, including nuclear submarines like *Conqueror*.

Unexpectedly, there were many strategic and tactical advantages on Britain's side. First and foremost, Britain was free to act alone, and at once, with no constraining alliances or diplomatic agreements. Access to the Falkland Islands did not require any overflight rights from a third country, nor were there any maritime points along the Sea Line of Communication (SLOC) that could be diplomatically or militarily closed to British ships. In fact, the southern route was entirely over "high seas," and so was politically neutral.

Another advantage was that British intelligence had apparently received prior warning of the invasion. As early as mid-March a task group composed of three destroyers and frigates was in the process of being formed to show the British flag in the Falklands. On 1 April, that task group was increased to include one small aircraft carrier, *Invincible*, and perhaps as many as six other major ships. An oiler had even been sent ahead of the task group, and so was already on station to refuel whatever was sent in its wake. Of course, the "degree and speed of mobilization" gave credence to Argentine protests that "Britain was already mobilizing when Argentina decided to occupy the Islands."[5]

Following the successful Argentine landing on the Falklands, the light vertical or short runway takeoff and landing (VSTOL) carriers *Hermes* and *Invincible* – their decks lined with VSTOL Sea Harrier fighter-bombers and Sea King helicopters – departed the UK. By the time they reached Argentina's 200 mile exclusion zone the fleet included thirteen warships and four supply ships, and this number would eventually reach almost 90 British ships. These were divided into task forces, with TF 317 including the carrier battle group (*Hermes*, flag), an amphibious task group under *Fearless*, a landing group made up of army and marine units, picket, escort, and RAF groups, and then fleet train and bases, while TF 324 was composed of the nuclear-powered submarines, including *Spartan*, *Splendid*, and *Conqueror*.

Because of cutbacks in the Royal Navy, there was a heavy reliance on requisitioned and chartered merchantmen. Sister merchantmen *Atlantic Conveyor* and *Atlantic Causeway* – two 17,000-ton combination roll-on/roll-off and container ships – were quickly modified with Arapaho kits to turn them into auxiliary carriers. *Queen Elizabeth II* and *Canberra* became troopships, while *Uganda* became a hospital ship. Finally, five fishing trawlers were turned into minesweepers. On 9 April, *Canberra* left Southampton with 2,400 men of 40, 42, and 45 Royal Marine Commandos and 3rd Battalion the Parachute Regiment.

Air power would prove immensely important in the coming conflict, and the RAF provided Vulcan heavy bombers, supported by Victor tankers. Four new naval air squadrons – one composed of Sea Harriers and three of helicopters – were also formed. Finally, Nimrods were operated out of Ascension Island to provide maritime reconnaissance and ASW capability. Commercial airlines also did their part.

Even as Britain's naval and air assets got in motion, the British government severed relations with the Argentine government and froze its assets in the UK. A complaint was lodged with the UN Security Council, which immediately passed a resolution condemning the aggression and calling upon the Argentine junta to withdraw from the Falklands. The EEC also imposed economic sanctions against Argentina, and among other items banned the delivery of military equipment. After four weeks, however, Italy and Ireland refused to agree to a continuation of trade sanctions, and only adhered to an extension of the arms embargo.[6] Because of the short length of the war, even these embargoes had relatively little impact. According to J.M. Heath, Director-General, Canning House, "all one can conclude from this, given the normal leads and lags in trade, is that there may have been shipments delayed; there may have been some re-routing, but the net effect of that embargo must have been very slight indeed."[7]

raid was carried out by forty-five SAS troops against the Argentine grass airstrip at Pebble Island, destroying all eleven Argentine aircraft while they were still on the ground. In addition, they destroyed a large surveillance radar installation, as well as fuel and ammunition dumps, which left the way clear for the amphibious invasion of the islands that took place a week later, on 21 May.[16]

Now that Argentina's ability to enforce its blockade had been destroyed, British forces began to enforce their own 200-mile total exclusion zone. A picket of nuclear-powered attack submarines was placed 200 miles west of the Falklands, at almost the exact midway point between the islands and the mainland, to cut off any Argentine surface ships attempting to approach the Falklands. These submarines were backed up by destroyers, which could provide advanced early warning of any incoming enemy aircraft. Meanwhile, the bulk of the British Task Force, including the carriers and the amphibious group, were held 100 miles off to the east of the Falklands, well out of range of most Argentine attack aircraft. A 42–21 destroyer-frigate combination was stationed off Pebble Island to cover the northern entrance to the Falkland Sound, with the Type 42 destroyer providing high-area defense and the Type 21 frigate giving point defense. Finally, all remaining ASW frigates, and any of the destroyers not deployed elsewhere, provided close escort, blockade patrols, transport, and general gunnery support.

Total Argentine losses included cruiser *General Belgrano*; conventional (diesel-powered) submarine *Santa Fe*; dispatch boats *Alferez Sobral* and *Comodoro Somallera*; Coast Guard vessels *Rio Iguazu, Islas Malvinas*; merchant runners (in TEZ) *Rio Carcarana, Islas de los Estados*; intelligence collector (fishing boat) *Narwal*. Their crews – merchant as well as naval – defended them to the last.

While highly effective against all forms of maritime traffic, the one major failure in this strategy proved to be the Stanley airfield itself. From early on in the conflict, RAF Vulcans had bombed the airfield, but neither they nor repeated attacks by Harriers succeeded in closing the field completely to Argentine traffic. Argentine troops defending the airfield would scrape together piles of mud and debris, which were then bulldozed onto the runway every morning to confuse photo reconnaissance. Bombs used by the Vulcans proved ineffective in destroying the hardened runway. In fact, the last Argentine flight from the mainland to the Falklands successfully arrived, unloaded, loaded, and departed again the night before the final surrender of the Argentine defenders.

The blockade did limit the Argentine air cover, however, at least to the point where the amphibious ships could move in close to the islands and land marines at Port San Carlos, on the west side of the main island, during the evening of 20–21 May. The immediate landing was unopposed. However, seventeen Argentine aircraft were later shot down over the beaches. During this battle, Argentine pilots, who were ordered to focus on the warships rather than the transports, breached the Combat Air Patrol no fewer than twelve times and successfully hit six frigates. According to one eyewitness, it was "only the fact that so many bombs had failed to explode that prevented an unimaginable scale of carnage."[17]

Once forces had embarked on land, they moved eastward across East Falkland Island toward Port Stanley. Stanley fell on 15 June, and exactly a month later all of the Argentine forces had been removed from the Falkland Islands; on that very day, the first snow of winter also fell on Port Stanley. On 22 July, the British blockade was officially lifted, although a 150-mile Falkland Islands Protection Zone (FIPZ) was declared to replace it.[18] Argentine ships were requested to remain at least 150 miles off the islands unless they had particular business to conduct there, which would require special permission from the British authorities to land.

The Effectiveness of Blockade in Limited Wars

The very rapidity of this limited conflict, which began on 28 March and ended on 15 July, meant that the British naval blockade – which officially lasted from 12 April to 22 July – had to be carried out using extreme measures. There was no time to board ships, inspect cargos, or provide warnings; any ship or aircraft that violated Britain's total exclusion zone around the Falklands was fired on and destroyed on sight. With the sole exception of never closing down the Port Stanley airfield, the blockade successfully kept out Argentine ships and planes. In addition, there was a tremendous psychological impact that undermined the morale of the Argentine troops, with the Argentine garrison at Port Stanley undergoing almost constant naval shelling and aerial bombing.

The success of the British naval blockade in a limited war was due to intensive intelligence efforts from a variety of sources, including government and commercial satellites, ground teams landed in Chile by helicopter to establish ground posts overlooking enemy airfields, and from British nuclear submarines reporting on maritime traffic from right off Argentina's many ports. Once Argentine prisoners of war were taken by British forces, they were questioned intensively. Finally, electronic intercepts and RDF helped fill out of the picture.

Logistics also played a crucial role, and the British fleet depended on fourteen commercial oil tankers, four seagoing tugboats with firefighting and salvage gear, six chartered freighters, including one refrigerator ship, one roll-on/roll-off ship loaded with aircraft spares, at least seven RFA oilers, and at least three RFA ammunition and stores ships. At the height of the conflict, every British warship was matched by one ship either at sea or at Ascension Island providing logistical support for the fleet.

In this regard, the logistical support at Ascension was key, as it became the "gateway" to the Falklands by acquiring, holding, filtering, and queuing ships and their cargoes before releasing them to continue into the war zone. To the north-east of the blockaded islands and just beyond the range of

Argentine attackers, the British navy also set up a TRALA (a Tug, Repair, and Logistics Area). It was in this racetrack-shaped area of the South Atlantic that ships were held and met, goods transferred from ship to ship, supplies and ammunition replenished, and where crucial emergency repairs were made. It was in effect a seaborne advanced base, and proved to be very successful as such; even turbines could be replaced while the repair ships were underway at sea.

Technological innovations were also important. The VSTOL aircraft that worked from the two small-deck ramped light carriers *Hermes* and *Invincible* were crucial. Without them, the Royal Navy would have been unable to provide adequate reconnaissance, combat air patrols (CAP), or strikes. With only two such carriers, the British could and did impose and maintain a tight naval blockade, land troops on hostile shores, and give their forces adequate air cover in the face of significant and numerically superior enemy air power. Most importantly, they did so while operating 8,000 miles away from their home base, at the end of an incredibly long and complicated logistical train. The British "Center of Gravity" was its VSTOL carriers, and if the Argentinian Etendards and their Exocet missiles had ever taken out even one of the carriers the blockade, and perhaps the war, would have been over.

Paired with the VSTOL carriers were the Harrier VSTOL fighter-bombers. Not only did they fly from the carriers, but from everything from Arapaho-enabled container ships to dirt air strips. The Harriers provided CAP, broke up the Argentine air effort, and often joined in the ground fighting as well. When equipped with Sidewinder air-to-air heat-seeking missiles, they also proved very effective at providing an adequate and reliable air defense, and achieved "the highest ratio of successes of any missile used during the conflict"; by contrast, not a single Argentine Sidewinder hit a "nimble" Harrier.[19] Simply by bringing ashore a rubberized fuel tank, with fuel, any level piece of ground could be turned into an instant refueling and rest area. This capability meant that the VSTOL planes "were ferried to the Falklands aboard conventional cargo carriers, took off vertically, and went ashore in non-airfield areas to establish quickly a shore-based air blockade."[20]

Second only to VSTOLs in the fighting, and perhaps ranking first in the blockade, were Britain's nuclear-powered submarines. They could work in absolute secrecy and and did not require refueling. Although the Argentine Navy had four diesel submarines, *Santiago del Estero* had been "cannibalized" to get *Santa Fe* working, which was then severely disabled at South Georgia Island; meanwhile, two German-made Type 209 submarines reportedly "could not put to sea because of an appallingly high number of mechanical problems."[21] Even if these submarines had put to sea, they were no match for Britain's nuclear-powered fleet.

Finally, in all spheres of the war, advanced missile technology – for both offense and defense – proved its worth. On the British side, the Sidewinder air-to-air missiles gave the Harriers an important, if somewhat unexpected, air defense capability. For Argentina, the Exocet-armed Etendards were most effective, but the planes were forced to operate at the very extreme of their range, which gave them only minutes to find their targets and seconds to fire their missiles. In addition, Argentina only had a handful of these missiles available, and the EEC embargo meant they could not get any more; if the Argentines had been able to acquire additional missiles, more British ships might have been lost. For defense, the Sea Dart, the Sea Wolf, the more obsolescent Sea Cat, and the Army's Rapier all helped break up the Argentine air attacks. For helicopters, the Sea Skua missiles proved effective against smaller vessels, and at least one enemy ship was sunk and several others damaged with this type of missile.[22]

All told, possibly 117 Argentine aircraft were destroyed, including probable hits and on the ground, with the Sidewinder accounting for sixteen of these, the Rapier for fourteen, the Blowpipe for nine, eight apiece for the Sea Dart and the Sea Cat, and five for the Sea Wolf.[23] Meanwhile, the Argentine forces used American-made Roland missiles, and the older British-made Tiger Cats (the land version of the Sea Cat), but "[n]either Roland nor Tiger Cat was to bring down a single British aircraft, though the Argentinians did shoot down one of their own Mirages in the first air attacks on Stanley airfield."[24]

All of these technological innovations allowed the British forces to conduct a limited, albeit total, naval blockade. According to Admiral Zumwalt: "In the British blockade of the Falklands, the blockade was total in that all entry of Argentine items to the islands was barred. A limited blockade could therefore ban all items in the pursuit of limited objectives in a limited geographic area." What made a limited total blockade possible, however, was that the British public backed the government, and the "British government knew that there was a time limit for its political consensus, and it moved to act quickly." If the war had lasted longer, or if there had been more military setbacks, then this political consensus might have weakened, since "such consensus is likely to be fickle and shortlived."[25]

Conclusions

The British limited naval blockade in the Falklands War was a loose, distant, intermittent, air and naval blockade of the Argentine coast, even while it was a tight, close, continuous, and "total" – including air, naval, and commercial – blockade of the Falkland Islands. While close blockades are traditionally the first step in challenging another country's command of the sea, leading to a showdown that the British Navy would have probably won, the Argentine Navy's decision to remain in port meant that this one-on-one naval conflict did not take place. This military decision virtually guaranteed that the war in general, and the naval conflict in particular, would remain limited. Instead, it took the landing of British troops and the seizure of the islands themselves to bring matters to a successful close.

As shown by the Falklands War – where the respective forces that could have been brought to bear were roughly equal – the critical factor soon became air power, and in particular naval air power. It was the ability to project naval air power, even 8,000 miles from its home ports, in the face of superior shore-based air power which gave the British Navy the means to establish local, albeit temporary, sea control, sufficient to ensure partial blockade of the Argentine coast and a total blockade of the Falkland Islands. That said, the loss of even one of the two British VSTOL carriers could have effectively ended that blockade and left the conflict permanently deadlocked. According to Admiral Woodward, he had decided well in advance of the fighting that any "major damage to *Hermes* or to *Invincible* (our vital 'second deck'), would probably cause us to abandon the entire Falkland Islands operation."[26]

Finally, in Operation *Corporate* the Royal Navy brought to the Falklands many centuries of naval tradition and experience. Task Force 317 appears to have been ready for action, and was prepared to undertake any task its political leaders asked of it. No matter how good its aircraft and missiles were on paper, the Argentine Navy and Air Force simply could not compete with these years of experience.

In particular, an estimated 50–60 percent of the Argentine pilots were shot down during their missions, leading Bryan Perrett to conclude: "No air force in history has ever suffered a comparable rate of attrition." While planes could be replaced, the "loss of pilots was far more serious, for it would be many months before fully trained replacement aircrew were available in sufficient numbers to fill the gap."[27] They were a worthy enemy. But it was the wide pool of experienced British crews and pilots, coupled with their control over SLOCs and Sidewinders, which allowed Britain to win the day.

18 Maritime Sanctions Enforcement against Iraq, 1990–2003

*James Goldrick**

The protracted effort to enforce United Nations sanctions against a virtually land-locked Iraq during the period between 1990 and 2003 had an important maritime element, whose complexities and achievements have passed largely unnoticed since the end of the Iraq War in 2003. It stretched over thirteen years and was one of the longest blockade operations in history. Furthermore, it demanded the long-term commitment of substantial resources from the navies of the U.S.-led UN coalition.

The campaign encountered many challenges and suffered from a number of systemic difficulties, which were only overcome near the end, including meeting the requirements of international law, operating in the proximity of disputed maritime boundaries, modulating the use of force, and developing innovative and flexible tactics to gain the initiative from equally shrewd would-be smugglers.

Nevertheless, the blockade must be considered as one of the most significant and eventually successful exercises of naval power in recent years. There can be no doubt that enforcement of the sanctions progressively debilitated Iraqi combat power to the extent that it could not provide effective conventional resistance to the coalition forces in the 2003 conflict. Therefore, the focus of this chapter is not on the tangled politics of the UN efforts to control Iraq,[1] but on the maritime aspects of the sanctions program, in which there remain significant lessons to be learned.

Background to the Sanctions

The blockade of Iraq originated in one of the earliest international measures taken against Iraq's invasion of Kuwait on 2 August 1990. Four days after the Iraqi attack, the United Nations Security Council passed Resolution 661, which forbade the export of cargo from either Iraq or Kuwait and prohibited the import of any cargo other than medical supplies and vital foodstuffs.[2]

Iraq is an almost wholly land-locked country, with limited access to the sea in the north-western corner of the Persian Gulf sandwiched between Kuwait to the south and Iran to the north. Iraq's other land borders, which are shared

Map 18.1 Persian Gulf theatre of operations

with Saudi Arabia, Jordan, Syria, and Turkey, constitute important avenues for trade, including the export of oil through fixed pipelines. Iraq also has the benefit of what is practically an alternate access to the sea via the short land route across Jordan to the latter's port of al-Aqabah at the north-eastern head of the Red Sea. In view of Jordan's lack of cooperation with the sanctions in 1990, the Red Sea had to be included in the maritime interception from the outset and at intervals over the following years of sanction enforcement. No maritime operation, of itself, could cut off Iraq from world commerce.

Substantial tensions underlay the UN's 1990 effort to force the removal of Iraq from Kuwait. The unwillingness of many nations to agree with the U.S.-led position – that the UN Charter permitted military action in the interests of collective security without the need for further resolutions – meant that sanctions provided a welcome, if temporary, solution. Naval forces could be deployed without necessarily making any commitment to hostile action against Iraq itself. Although UK support was guaranteed, and French forces were also in the area and likely to cooperate, it was following a 10 August 1990 Australian announcement of a three-ship task group that ten other nations, including Argentina, Belgium, Canada, Denmark, Greece, Italy, the Netherlands, Norway, and Spain, promised contributions.

The initial meeting of contributors to embargo operations took place in Bahrain on 9 and 10 September under the chairmanship of Vice-Admiral

Henry H. Mauz, the Commander of U.S. Navy forces in theater. It soon became clear that, while all concerned were willing to accept an American lead and coordinating role, France and Italy desired separate arrangements. The formula eventually arrived at was one described as "loose association" within which the Maritime Interception Force (MIF)[3] would operate.

Four major areas were initially assigned. The U.S. deployed forces to all but the Gulf of Aden, which was the responsibility of France. In the Red Sea, the Americans were joined by the French, Greeks, and Spanish. Major effort was centered on the Gulf of Oman, to which Argentina, Australia, Belgium, Canada, France, the Netherlands, and Spain deployed ships. Within the Persian Gulf itself were forces from Denmark, Italy, Norway, and the United Kingdom.[4] The demarcation between areas was not absolute and there was an increasing degree of cooperation between the regions as time went on. In addition, the navies of the members of the Gulf Cooperation Council mounted patrols within their territorial waters.

The disposition of forces had its drawbacks. As was to become clear when hostilities commenced a few months later, the decision to remain outside the north Persian Gulf allowed Iraqi forces to sow minefields largely undetected. The use of Iranian territorial waters by blockade runners also put a premium on their detection and interception outside the Gulf.

Making the Sanctions Work

There were many complications with the blockade of Iraq. After a refusal by Iraqi tankers on 17 August to obey the directions of U.S. Navy units, a new more effective resolution, no. 665, had to be issued on 25th August to give the MIF the necessary teeth. Although several navies had extensive boarding and search experience in fishery protection operations, there was less under-standing of how to deal with large merchant vessels in such a delicate political situation.[5] In the case of the U.S. Navy, it was able to draw upon the services of the U.S. Coast Guard, while the British had the relatively recent experience of the Beira patrol. Even the Americans and British, however, had much to learn. "Nor," as one commentator has noted, "did the carefully measured restraint of MIF operations come naturally to the Canadian navy. These boardings were very different from those undertaken in the course of fisheries patrols on the Grand Banks."[6]

Operational methods had to be rapidly refined and adjusted. Three areas needed particular attention. The first was the realization that conventional, hard-hull boats were inadequate for the task. The experience of maritime interception operations hastened the process – already under way in many navies – of their replacement by fast, rigid hull inflatable boats (RHIBs), which were easier to launch and recover, faster in the water, and more flex-ible in their employment. The second issue was the training of boarding parties and improvement of personal equipment. Here, the U.S. Coast Guard played an important role in helping train many of the other navies' boarding parties. The third, and probably most important, was the use of helicopters for rapid insertion.

The key problem remained that of forcing compliance without resorting to direct fire. This was never allowed for many compelling reasons. Casualties amongst unarmed passengers or merchant seamen would too easily surrender the moral high-ground to Iraq. Large merchant vessels were very difficult to disable except with large-calibre weapons – which greatly increased the risk of casualties – and the coalition had no desire to be saddled with a large-scale search and rescue operation or with the environmental damage that sinking a ship would almost certainly imply. Physical measures other than gunnery also carried the risk of disabling a ship to the point where it would become a hazard to navigation or even, within the Persian Gulf itself, to oil platforms. Graunching, or bringing the arresting warship directly alongside the merchant vessel, had been utilized as recently as 1946–47 with the British attempts to prevent Jewish immigration to Palestine, but even then had resulted in substantial damage.[7] Stoutly built Australian patrol boats had successfully employed the technique on fishing vessels in the 1970s, but it was not a practicable method for modern, thin-skinned warships.

The tactic adopted for the early months of sanction enforcement was to surround a recalcitrant ship with a number of coalition warships. If these could not compel obedience by radio, voice calls, or warning fire, a coordinated assault was conducted by specially trained forces lowered from one or more helicopters, with other helicopters providing surveillance and potential covering fire. Once control had been established, naval boarding parties conducted physical searches of ships, cargoes, and documentation.

A major complication on top of the complexities of "loose association" was the fact that each nation's forces came with differing rules of engagement, certain of which could not be promulgated to the remainder of the coalition. This initially caused difficulties and delays.[8] Over the long term, however, the fact that some nations had much more proactive rules than others meant that tasking could be mixed and matched according to the robustness of the available national ROE. This was to be an abiding, if largely unstated, theme of the MIF operations in the years that followed, and a key element in their long-term success.

The coalition forces rapidly settled into a regime of query and interception, supported by maritime patrol aircraft and an increasingly well-organized ship tracking organization. In the fall, the Iraqi merchant ships *Al Wasitti* and *Amuriyah* were intercepted, the first on 8 October and the second on 28 October. Both refused to comply with orders to stop and the latter provided significant resistance to the American, Australian, and British forces before the crew could be subdued and the ship searched. Nevertheless, both proved to be empty of cargo and were eventually allowed to proceed. These seem to have been attempts by the Iraqis to test the resolve of the coalition.[9]

Further interceptions followed, both of vessels that might have been attempting to smuggle arms into Iraq and of ships carrying war booty from

Kuwait. The coalition was aware that the blockade "was not airtight" and there was no sign of any wavering of Iraqi resolve. Nevertheless, by the end of 1990, the coalition could be confident that it had largely cut Iraq off from the world economy.[10] Given the latter's dependence on external suppliers for practically all its combat forces, as well as much of its national infrastructure, the erosion of Iraqi strength had begun.

The greatest political challenge to the embargo came on 26 December 1990, when the MIF intercepted the propaganda "peace ship" *Ibn Khaldoon* en route from Algeria to Iraq. By this time, the multinational forces were effectively coordinated and the basic procedures thoroughly understood. The vessel was boarded and taken over by special forces and marines, despite the efforts of a large number of men and women determined to prevent the seizure of the ship. The operation was accomplished without bloodshed and *Ibn Khaldoon* was successfully diverted.

As the deadline for armed intervention approached, it was inevitable that the U.S. Navy's focus would turn to final preparation for the impending hostilities, while some of the multinational forces also shifted their tasking to support the U.S. effort. Under these circumstances, Canada in particular, whose ships had been playing a substantial role in the operation, continued to insist that "*all* Iraq-bound merchant traffic" be inspected.[11] Only with the beginning of the war on 17 January 1991 did the interception effort effectively cease, although the querying and interrogation of merchant ships continued.

After the 1991 Gulf War

Hostilities concluded on 28 February 1991. The coalition was determined to ensure that Iraq's capacity for developing weapons of mass destruction (WMD) was not revived. UN Resolution 687 was passed on 3 April 1991 and established a set of conditions for the lifting of sanctions. Until these were met, Iraq would be prevented from exporting any materials and from importing all but humanitarian supplies. The effort required to enforce these conditions would be substantial and would become progressively more demanding, especially as peaceful traffic revived within the region.

In the meantime, the northern waters of the Persian Gulf were in a sorry state, with fixed minefields and floating mines blocking the approaches to both Iraq and Kuwait. The situation was further confused by wrecks and unexploded ordnance on the seabed. While this represented a substantial challenge for both the mine countermeasure and salvage forces of the coalition and those of Iraq, it also partially simplified matters for maritime interception. With Iraq-bound traffic at a standstill in the Gulf, operations could concentrate on the passage into al-Aqabah in the Red Sea. The patrols in the Gulf of Oman and the Arabian Sea had become of little practical use and were progressively wound down. They would resume only in 2001, and this time in the context of the war on terror and the search for the leadership of Al Qaeda.

Although the lull in commerce within the Gulf continued in the first months after the 1991 war, there were soon signs of reviving activity. Resumption of interception operations also brought into focus the demands of the Red Sea and Persian Gulf environment. The initial effort had started in late autumn 1990 and continued throughout the winter of 1990–91. However, although storms, restricted visibility, and the steep seas of the winter months could make life difficult for naval forces, the heat and humidity of the summer proved even more difficult. Machinery and cooling systems struggled to operate effectively. The operational performance of helicopters was drastically reduced, while the physical demands of boarding large merchant ships – particularly when substantial numbers of containers required examination – led all too quickly to fatigue and heat stress. For the next decade and beyond, the summer remained the most difficult period of the year for the maritime interception forces, one which veterans of the region dreaded.

Progressive clearance of the approaches to the Iraqi ports brought about new challenges. Iraq was slow to accept any moderation of the UN position, such as that which came with the initial "oil for food" resolution in 1991 or its substantial expansion in Resolution 986 in April 1995. Nevertheless, the latter finally came into effect in December 1996 and was followed by a further easing of the limits on Iraqi oil sales in Resolutions 1153 of February 1998 and 1284 of December 1999.[12] Their cumulative result was to resume oil exports on practically the same scale as before 1990, giving Iraq access to substantial funds, albeit under UN supervision.

Despite Iraq's foot-dragging and the recurrent crises between the regime and the UN, Iraqi imports by sea increased, which also increased the need for the MIF to conduct what soon became known as "986" boardings. According to one estimate, by May 1996, the MIF had "queried 22,554 ships, intercepted another 12,596, boarded 10,031 and diverted 552 ships from their intended destinations since the operations began in August 1990."[13] By 1999, the annual rate stood at "2,422 queries, 700 boardings and 19 diversions,"[14] and in the first half of 2002 there were some 900 boardings.[15]

The UN pressed Jordan to agree to the establishment of a shore inspection organization at al-Aqabah. The MIF effort in the Red Sea was highly demanding on the ships concerned, HMAS *Sydney's* effort in 1993 being typical with no less than 219 boardings.[16] But it was also largely cooperative and thus suitable for a civil inspection regime. The Jordanians initially refused,[17] but finally consented to the arrangement in 1994.[18] This permitted UN inspection of vessels alongside, a much simpler process than boardings offshore.

As a result, the coalition forces could concentrate on the increasingly complex problems of the Persian Gulf, where the operational hazards remained high. Until a succession of attacks by U.S. cruise missiles and aircraft in the late 1990s progressively eliminated Iraq's air and coastal defenses, activities close to the coast had to be conducted at high states of readiness for missile defense. The many mine danger areas in the northern Gulf took years to prove safe or clear, giving shallow-draft wooden craft a particular advantage in evading large warships. Holding areas for suspect vessels had initially to be established in the central Gulf, well away from the approaches to Iraq, and much MIF effort was taken up escorting suspect vessels there.

The progressive reduction in the mine and missile threat and the more cooperative Iraqi attitude implicit in accepting Resolution 986 allowed some changes in the MIF arrangements from 1997 onward. An anchorage was established in the northern Gulf into which all vessels inbound to or outbound from Iraqi ports were directed for examination. This also became the holding area for any apprehended illegal traffic.

Other than "oil for food" tankers – which were loaded at the Minh Al Bakr offshore terminal (MABOT) under UN supervision – all legal outbound vessels were in ballast and thus relatively easy to check. One technique was to ask empty bulk carriers to open their cargo hatches for visual inspection by helicopter. Laden inbound bulk carriers also presented few problems, but the business of checking container ships was wearisome. Container ships were soon given a series of guidelines for cargo stacking and spacing to allow relatively rapid – and safe – inspection. Vessels that failed to meet these guidelines were ordered back to port to restow their containers. The interception forces always sought to move legal traffic as quickly as possible and it was rare for a merchant ship to remain in the anchorage for more than 24 to 48 hours.

Relatively few contraband items were discovered in the many years of the operation, but this did not mean that it was a failure. Some cargoes of arms and materials for weapons may have gotten through and one authority has suggested that Iraq "obtained at least two shipments of tank parts, some additional air-to-air missiles and one artillery shipment in the early 1990s. It also may have received some significant shipments of spare parts during 1996–1998."[19] However, not all of these items would have come in by sea and they did not, even cumulatively, represent the scale of supply that was required to rebuild Iraq's military. The systematic search program had a substantial preventative effect, therefore, one that was obvious by the late 1990s; scholars agreed that substantial disarmament of Iraq had already been achieved.[20] This assessment was confirmed by the state of Iraq's armed forces in the 2003 conflict.

One issue of concern was the effect of the sanctions program on the people of Iraq. While some observers noted the reluctance with which Iraq adopted the "oil for food" program in the first place, and its continuing failure to utilize the funding available for humanitarian materials or, when permitted, the items needed for rebuilding national infrastructure, there were many false allegations about the connection between civilian mortality in Iraq and the sanctions.[21] Particularly after 1997, these were difficult to square with the physical evidence of what was passing by sea into the country, the knowledge that cargo content – within the limits of the sanctions – was dictated by the Iraqi government, and the fact that some Iraqis were clearly attempting to re-export, for cash, food and materials imported for humanitarian purposes.[22]

The Smuggling Problem

However watertight the monitoring of inward movement of large cargoes appeared, the MIF faced much greater difficulty in preventing smuggling out of Iraq. The maritime problem would take more than a decade to solve completely and not all of the nations involved in 1990 stood the distance; France withdrew in 1994, stating that the blockade was ineffective.[23] The apparent lack of enthusiasm of some of the Gulf nations enforcing sanctions was also sometimes the cause for criticism.[24]

There were two primary cargoes involved, oil and Iraqi dates – the latter considered a delicacy within the region, worth more than the equivalent volume of oil. The date traffic was seasonal and went largely by dhow, the largest of which could carry up to 500 tons. Oil was the much more serious problem. Left unchecked, it gave the ruling regime direct access to very large amounts of hard currency, even while Iraq left the risk-taking to private companies with interests in Arabia or south Asia. Oil smuggling was always directly dependent upon the price of oil. Whatever the motivations of the Iraqi government, that of the smugglers was largely commercial.

Thus, from late 1993, as the oil price increased, so did smuggling and the first major apprehension of an oil smuggler took place in October 1994, the 30,000 ton Liberian flagged *Katerina P.*[25] Much of the uncertainty over oil was associated with the continued instability within the region and the difficulties in achieving agreement between the United Nations and Iraq for the resumption of legal exports. In this climate, once the smugglers had started systematic operations, their ventures initially flourished.

However, progress was made with legitimate Iraqi oil sales, and other factors such as the impact of the Asian financial crisis of 1997 meant that oil prices began to fall. By the middle of 1998, they were at their lowest point in more than a decade. At under US$15 a barrel for legal oil purchases – and much less on the black market – there was insufficient profit margin for the smugglers, and so their activities declined.

The smugglers also depended upon the acquiescence of Iran to their operations. Systematic smuggling began from the Khaw Abd Allah (KAA) and the Shatt Al Arab (SAA). The method of operation was to wait in the inner roads of the KAA or SAA for an opportunity to clear Iraqi waters. This would either be at high tide under the cover of night or poor weather, or when their local observers confirmed that coalition units were not in the vicinity. They then sought refuge from interception forces within Iranian territorial waters to the east, passing along the Iranian coast to the south in a route which became known as the "iron highway." A few smugglers took the western route, through Kuwaiti and Saudi Arabian waters, but this was riskier because of the two nations' naval and coastguard patrols.

There was a price to be paid in the form of protection money levied by the Iranian Revolutionary Guard (Navy) forces based in the northern Gulf. Failure to pay up could result in harsh action. Nevertheless, there were multiple influences at play in Iran.

Despite the benefits which the Iranian Revolutionary Guard derived, it was not always apparent whether actions taken against smugglers were for political or financial reasons.[26] Periods in which smugglers appeared to be making systematic use of Iranian waters were punctuated by highly publicized apprehensions by Iranian forces.[27]

With increasing oil prices from late 1998, the seaborne smuggling operation matured to the point that, by 2000, it was estimated that some US$500 million worth of oil was leaving Iraq by sea each year.[28] By this time, the pattern of oil smuggling was well established, although it could and did continue to suffer interruptions from variations in the world oil prices and from changes in Iranian policy. The smugglers themselves were divided broadly into three groups: single-ship "fly by night" operators, more substantial operators with two or three ships, and sophisticated smugglers with five or six large, well maintained, and faster ships. All had extensive commercial connections in the region.

The MIF did what it could to interrupt the trade. The shallow coastal waters of Iran meant that heavily laden tankers sometimes had to enter international waters to avoid grounding. This could provide an opportunity for apprehension, as did the period in which the smugglers attempted to cross the Straits of Hormuz to conceal themselves amongst local shipping or escape into the Gulf of Oman and thence to the Arabian Sea. On a regular basis, "surge" operations were conducted into Iraqi territorial waters by the MIF in conjunction with the Kuwaiti Navy and Coast Guard. These heavily protected operations achieved some success, but a constant presence in Iraqi waters would eventually be required to break the back of the smuggling effort.

The simple fact was that the MIF did not at this point have sufficient resources to achieve the degree of constancy required. Traffic densities in the Gulf are high, and much of that traffic consists of small and practically unregulated vessels of a multitude of national flags, carrying cargoes of uncertain origin and equally uncertain destination. The visibility is often poor and navigational constraints, both natural and legal, are always a concern. Electronic and remote systems were of only limited utility in supporting efforts at detection, although maritime patrol aircraft were valuable in developing an overall picture of activity in the region. There was not only no alternative to surface vessels for apprehending smugglers, but nothing else would do for much of the patrol effort. Although the U.S. Navy maintained significant forces on station, they had additional work, such as support of the air surveillance program for Operation "Southern Watch" and the enforcement of no-fly zones. Some seventeen other nations made contributions at intervals, but even the most consistent, the United Kingdom, normally only provided a single destroyer or frigate for sanctions enforcement. This ship also had a multitude of other tasks to support Britain's extensive interests in the region, and was thus not on station continuously.

The MIF also had to keep a careful eye on the legal "oil for food" program. The potential that this offered for smugglers was demonstrated by the detection of smuggling by the tanker *Essex* in November 2001. The monitoring regime at MABOT supervised loading and ensured that all the tanks and valves were sealed once the approved amount of oil had been embarked. This process had been sidestepped in the case of *Essex* and a substantial amount of additional cargo loaded. The UN Office of Iraq Program subsequently tightened up procedures, but the MIF maintained its own system of inspecting selected supertankers after they departed from the oil terminal.[29]

Apprehended vessels had to be accepted by a Gulf state, which became responsible for selling its cargo and disposing of the ship, with the proceeds directed towards a UN account once expenses had been deducted. There was a natural reluctance to take responsibility for ships that were in poor condition, and which might create environmental hazards, so there were sometimes long delays. Apprehended vessels could remain at anchor for weeks or even months. A partial solution was eventually worked out whereby the Bahrain-based Marine Emergency Mutual Aid Center (MEMAC) took responsibility for offloading the oil, sometimes by sending out a tanker to conduct the discharge at the anchorage.[30] MEMAC also played an important role in supporting the welfare of the crews of impounded vessels.

Delays in dealing with apprehended vessels also made the arrest of dhows a dubious proposition, the more so because of the relatively small amounts of oil that they could carry by comparison with even the smallest steel-hulled tankers. Most wooden-hulled dhows were leaky and remained dry only by the use of bilge pumps driven by the propeller shaft. When the dhows stopped, so did their pumps, which caused significant problems when they were required to remain at anchor indefinitely. By the late 1990s, the MIF was concentrating its efforts on steel-hulled ships.

Disposing of the smuggling vessels remained problematic. Although arrangements could be made by the responsible Gulf state for their sale by auction for scrap, in practice this often meant – in a curious echo of the nineteenth-century campaign against slave trading – the ships concerned passing directly back into the hands of their former owners.[31] In 2001, the United Arab Emirates introduced a series of measures designed to prevent this, including the imposition of a substantial bond that could only be redeemed after clear proof had been produced of the ships' reduction to scrap.[32] Even so, the delays in the process sometimes meant that it was more effective for the MIF to release a vessel once its illegal cargo had been discharged.[33]

Beating the Smugglers

From the middle of 2001, the coalition was determined to clamp down more systematically on the smuggling trade. Australian, Canadian, and British frigates in particular, as well as U.S. special forces, were critical to this much more aggressive approach. New tactics were based on ever more highly trained boarding parties that sought to board and take control outside of Iranian territorial waters, while smugglers were trying to avoid shallow waters along the coast. Smugglers realized the danger that being in international waters created for them. The boarding process was thus increasingly a race against time, since the boarders had either to seize control or disembark before the smugglers entered or re-entered Iranian territorial waters. The smugglers were not violent, but they would do everything short of violence to hinder arrest.

As boarding teams became more expert, the number of physical barriers set up by tanker crews increased. Steel plates were welded over bridge doors and engine hatches. More steel plates were welded over bridge windows after the boarding teams started to force their way in from above. Not being able to see out, the tanker crews would navigate by GPS, posing some interesting problems for collision avoidance. To frustrate boardings, the crew might pour oil over decks, place grease on handrails, and string razor wire along bulwarks and between masts – the latter to deter insertion by helicopter. Spikes were sometimes fixed to hulls to puncture the inflatable bulwarks of the RHIBs.

Despite these anti-boarding measures, the MIF's success rate against individual tankers soared and the smugglers were forced to change their tactics. Over the next few months they staged a series of mass breakouts from the KAA with the aim of overwhelming the MIF. These had limited success, particularly as the MIF's aim was to make smuggling unprofitable. It was not essential to catch every would-be smuggler, just a sufficiently high proportion to make the venture commercially unattractive. A substantial proportion of the tankers in the breakouts were hunted down by the MIF. Some of the apprehensions were in the entrance to the KAA, others were at the other end of the Persian Gulf, and sometimes even outside it. By late 2001, the financial viability of the smuggling trade was under threat, no matter what the price of oil.

The situation underwent further changes with the arrival in November 2001 of a three-ship Australian task group, which assumed tactical control of the sanctions operations in the northern Gulf in January 2002. This was intended to be shared with the U.S. Navy on a monthly rotation, but a temporary decrease in U.S. forces meant that Australia provided the commander continuously from March 2002. Australian ships also provided both the individual unit capability and the additional numbers required to turn the operation into a near-continuous close blockade. This changed the pattern of operations from apprehension to prevention. Stationing within Iraqi territorial waters meant that even the dash from the KAA towards Iranian waters was risky for the smugglers. This tactic would not have been possible in the early 1990s, with the mine threat and the state of Iraq's coastal defenses, but it proved to be a critical factor, the more so as it was much more efficient for the MIF to keep smugglers bottled up rather than having to chase them hundreds of miles. Another fact was that the Iranian Navy began to act systematically against smugglers it discovered within Iranian territorial waters, thus undermining the Revolutionary Guard's protection racket.

By May 2002, many would-be smugglers were giving up.[34] At the end of the year, MIF authorities were publicly comparing the estimate of Iraq loading activity in October 2001 – 100,000 tons, of which 35,000 were inter-cepted by the MIF – with that of October 2002, in which only 3,000 tons were loaded and no less than 5,000 intercepted. This meant that much of the intercepted oil came from old loadings.[35]

The next move was against the dhows. To avoid the problem of maintaining them under arrest, a tanker was stationed in the detention anchorage, into which the oil-carrying dhows could immediately discharge their cargo. As soon as offloading was complete, the dhows could be sent on their way. This approach did not prove practicable, however, and the MIF ended up turning the dhows, particularly those carrying perishable dates, back into the KAA.[36] The sheer numbers involved made the patrolling units' task even more demanding than the previous close blockade work,[37] but the effort eventually proved effective. By early 2003, the MIF estimated that up to 300 dhows and 150 steel tankers were bottled up in the KAA.[38]

It was of little surprise that the success in the Gulf should revive concerns about the Red Sea. Jordan had shut down the shore-based inspection orga-nization in October 2000.[39] Increasing evidence of sanctions violations through al-Aqabah in early 2002 brought about a resumption of at-sea inspections in the middle of the year.[40]

The establishment of a regime of close and systematic sea control in the north Persian Gulf had other important implications, which became clear with the outbreak of the second Iraq War in March 2003. Coalition forces were ready, not only to deal with the mass of smugglers fleeing the area of combat, but to prevent any Iraqi efforts to seed mines in the Gulf itself. This was in stark contrast to the events of 1991 and constituted one of the crit-ical enablers of the successful military campaign, particularly as the forward mounting of the land forces was largely constrained to Kuwait. The coali-tion could not have sustained interruptions to the movement of shipping to and from Kuwait.

With the collapse of Saddam Hussein's regime in Iraq came the effective end of the sanctions program, a situation soon formally recognized by the United Nations Security Council in Resolution 1483 of 22 May 2003.[41] In fact, the coalition forces had already turned to new work. In addition to providing security for commercial shipping and for Iraq's offshore oil termi-nals, they were soon occupied dealing with drug smugglers and would-be oil exporters bent on avoiding Iraqi taxes.[42]

Conclusions

Naval blockades are easier to assess in retrospect than in execution and the 1990–2003 blockade of Iraq is no exception. That such a largely land-locked country should be so susceptible to maritime action was not immediately obvious, but this proved to be the case. Iraq's access to the sea, however confined, was and remained its only potential means of securing the mate-rials required to accomplish the regime's strategic goals. Of Iraq's neighbors,

Saudi Arabia, Kuwait, and Turkey would never condone smuggling of strategic materials into Iraq, while Iran and Syria had their own national interests to worry about. As for Iraq's alternate access to the sea through Jordan, this was just as susceptible to maritime interception and control as the Persian Gulf.

The sustained enforcement of the sanctions over thirteen years clearly ate away at the Iraqi war machine, while it also substantially assisted in hamstringing whatever plans Saddam Hussein might have had for resuming the production of weapons of mass destruction. That there was collateral damage to Iraq's economy is also clear, but, certainly from the early 1990s onward the blame for this must be placed on Saddam's refusal to accept UN conditions for opening up exports and imports.

The blockade of Iraq was never perfect, but the thousands of boardings and inspections that the MIF conducted were effective not so much in what they discovered, but in what they prevented. The presence of the MIF, particularly after it had adopted the policy of forward deployment and close blockade, also had a vital effect in preventing any interference with the movement of shipping to and from Kuwait before and during the 2003 War. The achievement of sea control, which was the main enabler for sanctions enforcement, was also key to the coalition's ability to project and sustain power on land.

The fact that largely seaborne mechanisms were available for such a purpose was itself a vital feature of the campaign. The coalition naval forces inherently created a much smaller footprint within the region than land forces would have, which was important for regional states whose strategic interests had to be balanced very carefully against a range of domestic factors. The limited commitment involved also meant that the coalition of nations willing to make a contribution to sanctions enforcement remained large and relatively diverse, which was an important source of support for the United States in particular. It is difficult to envisage any alternative mechanisms by which such a campaign could have been mounted, let alone sustained over a period of thirteen years.

The experience of 1990–2003 garnered some important lessons. Naval blockades can be critically effective, even against apparently landlocked nations. The vast amounts of materiel required to create and sustain modern war-making capabilities, as well as the dependence of most modern military systems upon the latest technologies, mean that seaborne transport remains the carrier of choice, if not the only workable means of movement. Finally, no matter how careful the application of force by the blockading units, restraint will be insufficient in the court of world opinion if the sanctions they are enforcing are not highly selective in their effects on national commerce.

March 1996 presidential elections, as well as to halt any drive by the island to declare formal independence. The genesis of the crisis, however, was firmly rooted in the increasingly divergent paths followed by the two Chinas since the mid-1980s, with Taiwan's democratization and the consequent emergence of a separate, Taiwanese national consciousness contrasted with a China that emphasized economic and military modernization coupled with Chinese nationalism; China has exhibited a growing ambition to reclaim past glories, including the "recovery" of coveted maritime territories, especially the island of Taiwan.

On 18 July 1995, China announced that ballistic missile "tests" would take place between 21 and 28 July; these dates have historic meaning for China, since they were the fiftieth anniversary of the 1945 Potsdam conference promising to return all Japanese territories taken from China by force. The missiles were to be aimed at points within a ten-nautical-mile circle, only 85 miles north of Taiwan itself. Six DF-15 (CSS-6/M-9) short-range ballistic missiles (SRBMs) were fired, two each on 21, 22, and 23 July. One of the first set was reported to have crashed due to a malfunction. Beijing warned other states "against entering the said sea area and air space" during the firing period.[4]

The missile shots were followed, from 15 to 25 August, by PLA war games involving around twenty warships and forty aircraft held to the north-west of the SRBM splash zone. No further ballistic missiles were fired during this period, although the PLA Navy tested both anti-ship missiles and anti-aircraft missiles in the exercise area. China also conducted its second underground nuclear weapon test for that year on 18 August. And, during November, just prior to Taiwan's December parliamentary elections, the PLA staged further naval, amphibious, and air-assault exercises to simulate an invasion of Taiwan near Dongshan Island, a small islet off the mainland coast, including blockade tactics.[5] In a significant departure from its standing operating procedures of the previous years, the U.S. Navy sailed the USS *Nimitz* through the Taiwan Strait in mid-December, the first time an American aircraft carrier had transited the Strait since 1979.

It is difficult to assess the political effectiveness of Beijing's tactics. At the time of the missile shots the Taipei stock market plunged. The election results seemed to indicate that China's display of force may have had some effect, with the ruling Kuomintang's (KMT's) parliamentary majority slashed. The New Party, a breakaway group of former KMT politicians that hold a more conciliatory position toward China, fared quite well. Yet it has also been claimed that these results reflected domestic concerns rather than external threats. Moreover, the second largest party, the pro-independence Democratic Progressive Party (DPP), actually increased its share of the vote from the previous election, if only slightly.[6]

Beijing nevertheless seemed to interpret the outcome, rightly or wrongly, as proof of the success of its military diplomacy and indicated that further military pressure would be exerted during Taiwan's upcoming presidential election, the first such election in the island's history. Those warnings included messages channeled through intermediaries to Washington. The best known was to Assistant Secretary of Defense, Chas Freeman, by "senior Chinese officials," who threatened to launch one missile per day against Taiwan for a period of thirty days if Taipei continued on its perceived path toward formal independence. Freeman also received the now-infamous implied nuclear threat that the United States would not intervene militarily in a cross-Strait crisis because U.S. leaders "care more about Los Angeles than they do about Taiwan."[7]

The March 1996 Crisis

On 5 March 1996, Beijing announced that it would conduct a series of ballistic missile exercises from 8 to 15 March. Taiwan's presidential election was scheduled for 23 March. Unlike the 1995 tests, however, this new round was formulated to cut, or at least impede, Taiwan's major sea lines of communication, with the two designated target zones bracketing Taiwan's ports of Keelung in the north and Kaohsiung in the south.[8] Together, the two ports accounted for around 70 percent of the island's trade by value. The Taiwanese economy also depends on imported oil and other raw materials, most of which are imported through Kaohsiung. The Chinese announcement once again warned shipping companies and airlines to avoid the designated impact zones during this period.[9]

The northern missile splash zone was a square just thirty miles east of Keelung, close to sea and air lanes servicing Japan and Korea, and was crossed by an east–west air route. The southern zone, also square-shaped, lay about forty-seven miles west of Kaohsiung, close to minor air lanes and astride the sea lane to Hong Kong. Most of Taiwan's burgeoning trade with the mainland had to be transshipped via Hong Kong due to the Taiwanese ban on direct China–Taiwan transportation links. Kaohsiung was also the world's third busiest container port and one of only a handful of hub ports which increasingly dominate seaborne trade in East Asia.

On 8 March, two DF-15 SRBMs were fired into the southern target zone and one into the northern zone. A fourth DF-15 was fired into the southern zone on 13 March. All four missiles are believed to have landed within the target areas and, like the July 1995 shots, were fired at night, perhaps to enhance the visual impact of Chinese television broadcasts of the launches.[10] The missiles were fitted with dummy warheads.

Compounding the pressure on Taiwan, China announced on 9 March that it would hold a large combined arms naval and air live-fire exercise from 12 to 20 March in the southern part of the Taiwan Strait. The rectangular zone for these exercises lay just off the Chinese coast to the west of the southern DF-15 splash zone, south of Taiwan's Jinmen (Quemoy) Island – near the mainland coast – and the Penghu Islands – located in mid-Strait. This encompassed a huge part of the southern section of the Strait, over

6,500 square miles, meaning that sea passage through the Strait and air traffic were partly obstructed – the usable breadth of the Strait was effectively halved, squeezed between the two southern exercises that overlapped by three days.[11]

A third exercise was announced on 15 March, to be carried out from 18 to 25 March, continuing Chinese pressure until after the presidential election, and was described as "joint ground, naval and air exercises in and over a sea area" in the north-western section of the Strait.[12] Although this zone was smaller than the southern live-fire exercise area (about 2,400 square miles), the northern entrance to the Taiwan Strait is considerably narrower than the southern one. The live-fire zone was also centered between the two small islands of Matsu and Wuchiu, close to the mainland coast but held by the Taiwanese – originally, Chinese Nationalists – since 1949. Around 300 residents fled before the exercises began. The second and third phases of the campaign involved approximately forty warships from all three PLA Navy fleets, interception and strike missions flown by air combat fighters and bombers, air drops of paratroopers, and ground training in house-to-house and mountain fighting. The naval exercises involved "live-fire mock sea battles, blockades, mining operations, and amphibious assaults."[13]

In response to these Chinese exercises, the United States dispatched the USS *Independence* aircraft carrier battle group to the area; Chinese commentators, in particular, inferred a political message linked to the use of this particular carrier. Washington also ordered the USS *Nimitz* carrier group to return to the region from the Persian Gulf, both to convey a message of caution to Beijing and to observe the exercises. Other assets deployed by the United States to monitor the situation included the Aegis guided-missile cruiser USS *Bunker Hill* and U.S. Air Force RC-135 Rivet Joint electronic surveillance aircraft.[14]

Operational and Strategic Effectiveness

Before one can judge the strategic success or failure of the blockade, one must judge its operational effectiveness. On the one hand, the Taiwanese government repeatedly tried to play down the effectiveness of the blockade's economic impact. This is understandable in the situation, given the need to lift national morale and combat collective panic attacks, whilst President Lee Tung-hui needed to demonstrate that he was still in control in the days leading into the presidential election. Several shipping companies also downplayed the impact of the crisis, pointing out that increases in shipping or insurance rates were unlikely unless ports were forced to close or an escalation required the area to be declared a "war zone."[15] The key ports of Kaohsiung and Keelung in fact remained open and port operations were reported as "normal" throughout the crisis, with vital oil shipments largely unaffected.[16]

Port operations may have continued, but shipping and air traffic were significantly impacted. During the ballistic missile firing period of 8–15

March, shipping was forced to re-route to avoid the splash zones, adding up to three hours to voyages between Taiwan and Hong Kong. Japanese shipping companies diverted over one-third of their ships in the affected areas, with a sailing from Keelung to Okinawa cancelled altogether.[17] Fishing near Kaohsiung was temporarily suspended, causing fish prices to rise.

One commercial air route off north-eastern Taiwan was closed and other flights to Japan, Guam, South-east Asia, and Australasia were diverted.[18] The disruption to flights and shipping continued during the second phase of exercises centered on Dongshan Island. Over 300 flights were affected every day, whilst Hong Kong was being forced to divert 150 flights daily to and from the city.[19]

The true costs to Taiwan are best shown by the dramatic short-term economic downturn, including the reversal of the island's trade balance from surplus to deficit. There can be no doubt that China's campaign restricted Taiwan's trading activities. Bunker fuel prices rose in Hong Kong, Singapore, and South Korea as shipowners diverted their vessels to bunker in those countries rather than risk sailing to Taiwan.[20] Some companies began to source goods – especially electronic components – from other countries rather than take the gamble on Taiwan being able to continue supply.

Moreover, the effect on shipping was perhaps greater than claimed by some industry sources. All shipping and air traffic that was forced to divert incurred increased fuel costs, and any delays due to diversions or cancellations would have incurred costs elsewhere along the production chain. The primary reason why shipping and insurance rates did not rise is that the rates were covered by long-term contracts set well in advance of actual shipments taking place. Thus, any losses at the time would have been incurred in the first instance by the shipowners.[21] Second, the relatively short duration of the campaign (eighteen days) meant that there was insufficient time for rates to be affected; yet there is little doubt that rates would have risen had the exercises been sustained for a longer period, with a commensurate negative economic impact on Taiwan.

Operationally, the blockade may have been a moderate success, but strategically the intervention of the United States probably gave the Chinese pause to rethink the campaign. Washington's decision to send not one, but two, carrier battle groups – fourteen warships in total – to the Taiwan area constituted the largest demonstration of American naval diplomacy against China since the original Taiwan Strait crises of the 1950s.[22] The seriousness of America's commitment to Taiwan was outlined in a report prepared by Australia's defense attaché in Beijing for Australian intelligence agencies and leaked to the press on 8 March. The attaché asserted that "a policy decision" had been taken (by at least mid-February) in Washington that, "in any conflict between Taiwan and China, the U.S. would support Taiwan militarily; not just material support but with the actual deployment of forces."[23]

A second, contributing explanation for China's decision not to escalate further was the intervention of typically foul weather in the Strait, which restricted the third round of March exercises, even forcing the cancellation of some parts.[24] The exercise's latter, amphibious landing phase may have been "defeated resoundingly – and realistically – by bad weather."[25]

A third possible factor was that the "partial blockade" effect of Beijing's economic warfare campaign was rebounding to create a significant negative impact on Hong Kong, which Beijing had been trying to placate before its 1997 return to China.[26] The Chinese economy also was affected by both the withdrawal of Taiwanese investment and the impact upon seaborne trading activities along the Chinese coast. According to one report, detours for ships trading along the mainland coast were three to five times longer than those for ships entering and leaving Taiwan's ports.[27]

Whether China's March 1996 gambit is deemed a success or not naturally depends on one's perspective of China's strategic goals. If the campaign is viewed only as a warning to Taiwan's leaders and its electorate, and to Washington to heed Beijing's concerns, then possibly it can be deemed at least a partial success. One scholar has argued that China's "show of force" largely achieved its objective of chastening the Taiwanese independence movement, at least temporarily.[28] The Clinton Administration also seemed to weaken its political support for Taiwan after the crisis by adopting a more ambiguous stance.[29] This created even more uncertainty and undermined regional confidence in America's commitment to maintaining stability in East Asia.

China was also successful in creating a substantial level of economic disruption on Taiwan, with Beijing evidently engineering the dumping of the Taiwanese currency in Hong Kong to exacerbate the panic. There was a mini exodus from the island, with most outward-bound flights fully booked, and people began to stockpile food and other essential goods. Many Taiwanese tried to convert their money into U.S. dollars, forcing banks to limit withdrawals, or bought gold, whilst the stock market plunged, necessitating government intervention to prop up the market to the tune of U.S.$200 million per day.[30] Domestic investment and Taiwanese investment in the mainland fell sharply as investors shifted their funds from Taiwan and China to other countries: $15 billion in funds were reported to have left Taiwan alone.[31]

Regional trade also suffered, with the value of Taiwan's exports falling 18 percent between 1 and 9 March compared to the same period in 1995, whilst exports to Hong Kong, Taiwan's economic gateway to China, dropped even more. Exports continued to decline during the following week and in the period between 1 and 16 March Taiwan recorded a $245 million trade deficit compared to a $323 million surplus over the same period in 1995. Imports actually rose slightly, partly due to a 40 percent increase in gold purchases as a hedge against the economic and political uncertainty created by the crisis.[32]

On the other hand, if the campaign is viewed as an attempt to force a resolution of the Taiwan issue in favor of unification, it clearly failed. President Lee was re-elected with a strong mandate (54 percent of the vote) and, although Taipei may have been temporarily "chastened," the evolution of Taiwanese identity and the search for international recognition has continued and even expanded since the crisis. The crisis also created precisely the type of international reaction that China did not want from the United States and Japan, its principal major power rivals in East Asia.

In April 1996, Japan and the United States issued a joint declaration on security, including an agreement to revise their bilateral defense cooperation guidelines. The new guidelines, issued by Tokyo in 1997, included a provision for "cooperation in situations in areas surrounding Japan that will have an important influence on Japan's peace and security."[33] Despite suggesting, in response to Chinese criticism, that the provision was "situational" rather than geographic, a number of statements by Japanese officials implied that the new defense cooperation guidelines will be applicable to future Taiwan contingencies, even if Japan decides not to get directly involved in defending the island.

While operationally the blockade was a limited success, therefore, from a strategic viewpoint the military gambit seems to have backfired on Beijing. Taiwan's elections were not negatively impacted and Taiwan won considerable international sympathy, including a promise of military support from the U.S. Congress. Japan strengthened its alliance with the United States and joined the American missile defense program, in large part as a hedge against future Chinese misbehavior.

Ballistic Missiles as a Blockade Weapon

The use of ballistic missiles as a means to enforce a blockade, even a partial or temporary one, would seem to be isolated to the Taiwan situation. Although not specifically referring to a blockade scenario, a Pentagon analyst has noted that "the Taiwan Strait case may be unique in that it is the first theater in which highly accurate *conventional* ballistic missiles dominate the strategic landscape."[34] China certainly has developed something of a missile fetish, encompassing ballistic missiles, anti-ship missiles and, in the near future, land-attack cruise missiles. The PLA's preference for missiles is a reflection not only of its own relative strengths and weaknesses, however, but also of the strategic geography of its conflict with Taiwan. The use of theater ballistic missiles in blockade operations is one way of leveraging China's land-based military strengths to capitalize on Taiwan's vulnerability and lack of strategic depth.

The DF-15 SRBMs used by China are quite accurate and sophisticated weapons with a circular error probable (CEP – the measure of accuracy) of around 300 meters and a range of 600 kilometers (roughly 275 yards and 375 miles).[35] This puts all of Taiwan within range of mainland launch sites. The missiles do not have to be very accurate to cause a real danger to shipping if fired into choke points outside major ports. Kaohsiung, with just two narrow shipping channels leading in and out of the port, is especially vulnerable. No commercial operator is likely to risk transiting sea lanes being used as ballistic missile target areas; given enough time, insurance

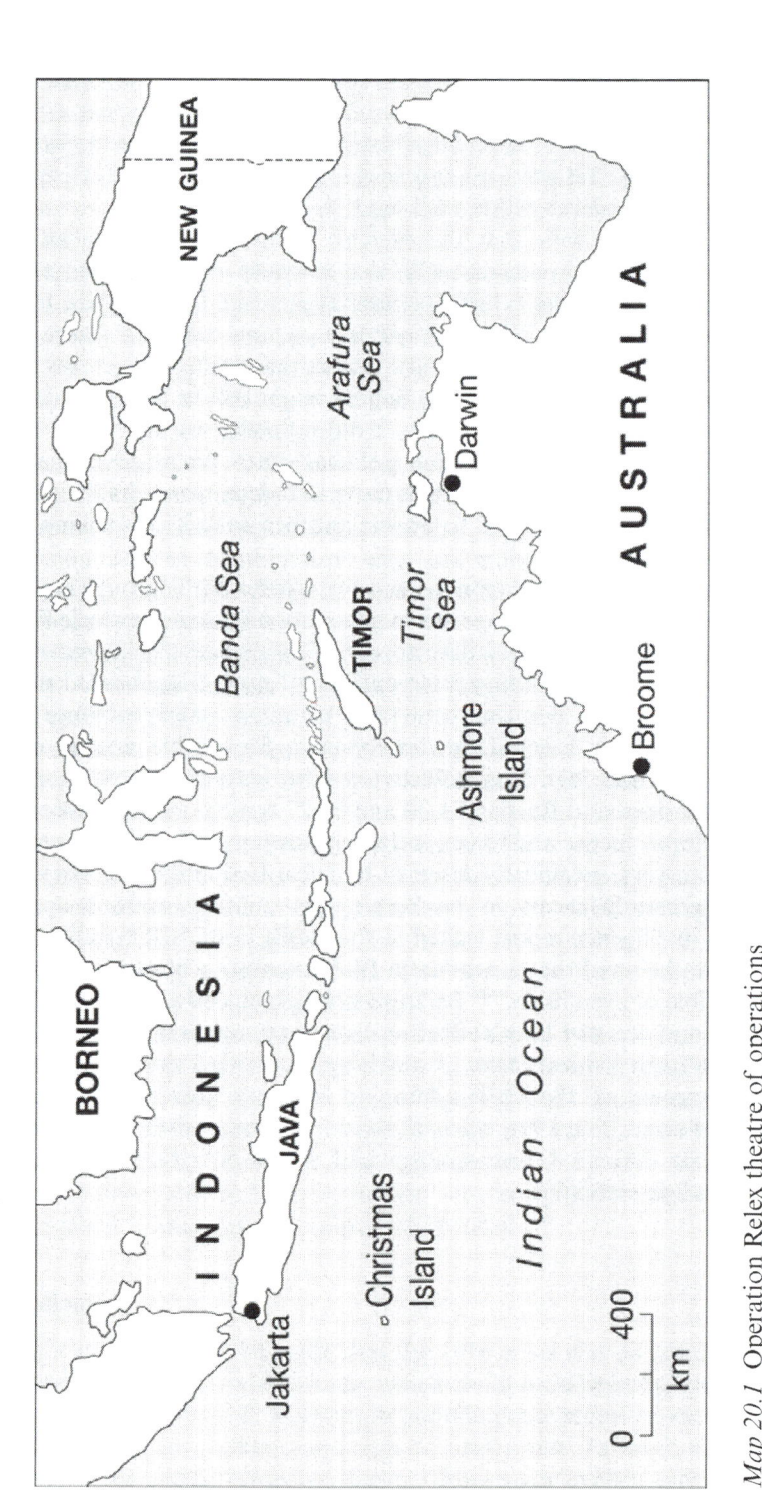

Map 20.1 Operation Relex theatre of operations

20 "To disrupt, deter and deny"

Sealing Australia's Maritime Borders

*David M. Stevens**

The formalized blockade of naval tradition may likely be obsolete, but within the span of future operations there remain tasks that will require the use of naval assets to prevent the passage of people or commodities through maritime areas subject to a nation's sovereign control. Under the general heading of maritime barrier operations these activities form a subset of a navy's constabulary role, and may range from quarantine enforcement through to the prevention of drug smuggling and the control of illegal immigration.[1] Underlying each of these tasks, however, will be the specific naval capability to closely monitor and control the movements of merchant shipping and cargo.

In August 2001, the Australian government introduced a new maritime border protection regime that aimed "to disrupt, deter and deny" the entry of unauthorized boat people,[2] that is, those attempting to arrive illegally in Australia by sea.[3] Although involving a "whole-of-government approach," front-line mission tasking fell primarily to the Australian Defence Force (ADF), and more particularly to the "thick grey line" provided by the Royal Australian Navy (RAN). The navy has since maintained a dedicated mission-specific surface presence in northern Australian waters, the practical effect of which has been to uphold a "maritime barrier." This barrier, however, should be seen as protecting national interests rather than sovereign territory *per se*, and so might equally be described as a "reverse blockade." The task itself was new to the RAN, but Australia's growing interest in regulating offshore activities is a pointer to the type of tasks which other navies may increasingly undertake.

Background

Australia's geopolitical isolation makes it one of the most inherently secure nations on earth. But this protection is not absolute, and, as an island continent dependent on sea communications, Australia is also faced with a distinct set of maritime vulnerabilities. With a population of only some 20 million people and jurisdiction over nine million square kilometers of ocean – one of the largest marine zones on the planet – the task imposes some significant practical and administrative difficulties.

Federal involvement in civil coastal surveillance began in 1967. This followed a request from the then Department of Primary Industry for surveillance of Australia's newly declared twelve-nautical-mile fishing zone.[4] Thereafter Royal Australian Air Force (RAAF) aircraft and RAN patrol boats conducted occasional patrols, but these irregular activities had only a limited deterrent value. As sightings of foreign fishing vessels grew commonplace, it became clear that Australia needed a more rigorous policy.

In 1975, the ADF mounted its first operation designed specifically to assist in offshore surveillance and sovereignty enforcement. During the later months of 1975, the Trackers investigated more than 2,220 contacts and, using the response capability provided by four Darwin-based patrol boats, the missions proved effective.[5] The first appearance of Indo-Chinese refugees in Australian waters dates to 27 April 1976, when a small unauthorized boat carrying five Vietnamese "boat people" reached Darwin. Rather than sending them back, the ADF's task was to detect the refugee boats, offer assistance when necessary, and escort them safely into an Australian port.

Changes to the Law of the Sea in the late 1970s, and in particular widespread acceptance of a 200-nautical-mile maritime Exclusive Economic Zone, made it obvious that monitoring Australia's ocean estate would not become any easier, since Australia undertook to "demonstrate an ongoing commitment to patrolling and protecting this zone."[6] Australia's problems were largely unique and, "with its sparsely settled northern coast and proximity to South East Asia, [it] faced health risks, smuggling and illegal immigration not shared by most other countries."[7]

In 1988, the federal government established "Coastwatch" as a sub-program of the Australian Customs Service. Coastwatch became responsible for providing Australia's civil coastal and offshore surveillance response service, though it relied heavily on Customs, the Department of Defence and external contractor resources to deliver these services. Operations against illegal immigrants were most often reactive, however, and went largely unremarked by either politicians or the mass media.

By April 1999, however, concerns over the growing number of unauthorized arrivals, and the percentage that remained undetected before reaching the Australian coastline, increased. Prime Minister John Howard set up a new "Task Force" that recommended a more robust response to people smuggling and trafficking, together with additional funding for immigration and Coastwatch-related activities.[8] Defence involvement in support of the civil surveillance program was maintained and enhanced through the appointment of a senior naval officer as Director-General Coastwatch.

Only in the second half of 2001 did illegal immigration become a leading national security issue. It is not yet clear when the Australian government developed its new border protection policy – a subsequent Senate Committee report has noted that it was developed quickly and "on the run" – but the most obvious catalyst was the crisis that began on 26 August 2001, only two weeks before the terrorist attacks on New York's World Trade Center and

Washington D.C.'s Pentagon.[9] On this day the Norwegian container ship MV *Tampa* rescued 438 men, women, and children from the Indian Ocean north-west of Australia. Apart from the five-member Indonesian crew, most of those rescued were Afghan nationals who claimed asylum.[10]

In Australian official jargon the people rescued by *Tampa* were suspected unauthorized non-citizens (SUNCs). On 27 August, immigration authorities directed the captain of the ship to keep out of the nation's territorial waters and to take his passengers back to Indonesia. August had already been a busy month, with 3,600 unauthorized arrivals in custody and awaiting processing. Australia's immigration detention centers were close to full capacity and frequently subject to outbreaks of violence. Nevertheless, the decision to stop *Tampa* was taken not by the Department of Immigration, but personally by the prime minister. It was a defining moment. Howard later told a radio audience: "I believe that it is in Australia's national interest that we draw a line on what is increasingly becoming an uncontrollable number of illegal arrivals in this country."[11]

For several days the ship and the Australian government maintained a stand-off. The adult passengers began a hunger strike, and, as conditions onboard *Tampa* worsened, extensive communications passed between officials and organizations in Australia, Indonesia, and Norway. The extent of Australia's legal and moral obligation to receive the ship and provide protection to its passengers came under particular scrutiny, but no resolution of the deadlock seemed forthcoming. An urgent need for medical supplies and blankets eventually forced action. On the morning of 29 August, *Tampa* steamed into Australian territorial waters. The ADF had several major fleet units on their way to Christmas Island to watch events, but a detachment of the Special Air Services (SAS) Regiment had already arrived. As *Tampa* approached sheltered waters, forty-five members of the SAS boarded the vessel and took control.

The SAS had no legal authority to move *Tampa*, and since the captain refused to depart and Australia still refused to let his passengers land, the impasse continued. The Howard government had meanwhile made moves to ensure that it had the appropriate legislative basis for its actions. At the same time, officials were investigating the possibility of moving the asylum seekers to a third country where refugee status processes were available. Resolution finally came on 1 September, after the negotiation of agreements with New Zealand and Nauru that all of the people rescued by *Tampa* would be processed in those countries. An agreement with Papua New Guinea on setting up a processing center on an island province was also later announced. These arrangements became known in the press as the "Pacific solution." On 3 September the *Tampa* SUNCs were embarked in the RAN's amphibious ship, HMAS *Manoora*.

This incident brought media attention to the refugee problem. Official figures record that 13,540 people arrived in Australia illegally by boat in 1989–2001, with more than half this total arriving in the two years immediately prior to the *Tampa* incident.[12] Since 1999, Coastwatch and the ADF located 129 boats carrying unauthorized arrivals in or approaching Australian waters, some with as many as 350 passengers. Almost all sought refugee status, and most claimed to have come from either Iraq or Afghanistan, perhaps after paying US$5,000 or more to make the passage from the Middle East to Australia. Unlike the Indo-Chinese refugees of the late 1970s, the more recent arrivals were well briefed on their legal rights, and had received coaching on what questions they might be asked and how they should respond. As such, there was a view among many authorities that the refugee smugglers had specifically targeted Australia.[13]

A New Border Protection Regime

Without a doubt, the timing of the *Tampa* crisis offered the Australian prime minister an opportunity to impose a hard-line political response in the lead-up to the 2001 federal election. Aware that several more SIEVs (suspected illegal entry vessels) carrying upwards of 900 people were due to enter Australian waters at any time, the government loudly announced its intention to control the flow of people coming into the country. The central aim of the developing border protection policy was to prevent any of these unauthorized arrivals from even landing on Australian soil.

The new border protection regime included several different aspects. Changes to immigration laws resulted in the excising of certain islands from Australia's migration zone, further ensuring that there was no legal right of entry through these territories. More cooperation was sought from Indonesian political and law enforcement authorities, while activities by the Australian Federal Police included disruption operations targeted directly against the smuggling syndicates.[14] Critical to the Australian government's more assertive posture, however, was the expanded scope and scale of the ADF's participation, to the extent that in the ensuing months Coastwatch was barely mentioned.

During the *Tampa* crisis the prime minister had championed "a naval blockade of the Indian Ocean" in the National Security Committee of the Cabinet. In turn, the Chief of the Defence Force (CDF), Admiral Chris Barrie, had outlined what was possible from Australia's limited defense resources. As always, aerial surveillance combined with surface response would provide the practical foundations. But the "real kick," according to Barrie, would be in "getting a surface response vessel to [the target] vessel at a point where you can exercise your rights under international law."[15]

On 28 August, the CDF ordered the Commander Australian Theatre based in Sydney, Rear-Admiral Chris Ritchie, to "provide a maritime control and response option to detect, intercept and warn vessels carrying unauthorized arrivals from entering into Australian territorial waters."[16] Under Ritchie, Australian Theatre Headquarters (HQAST) developed the broad concept for the operation, but passed detailed planning and direct command of the operation to Rear-Admiral Geoff Smith, dual-hatted as the Naval Component Commander of HQAST and the Maritime Commander. An attempt to lead the activity from afloat proved unnecessary, and tactical control of the operation eventually passed into the hands of Commander Northern Command, Brigadier Mike Silverstone, based in Darwin.

The area of operations was enormous, stretching more than two thousand kilometers (1,250 miles) across the north-western approaches to Australia. The task would also be extraordinarily complex. Whereas previously the navy's role had been to escort unauthorized arrivals to an Australian port for processing by civil agencies, the new regime saw warships ordered "to *prevent*, in the first instance, the incursion of unauthorized vessels into Australian waters such that, ultimately, people smugglers and asylum seekers would be *deterred* from attempting to use Australia as a destination."[17]

Supporting the navy's lead role in interception and boarding was a system of layered sea and air surveillance. Using a combination of Coastwatch and ADF aircraft as well as ship-fitted sensors, Australian surveillance extended to twenty-four nautical miles out from the territorial baseline of the Indonesian archipelago. Underlying both surveillance and interception operations was a comprehensive intelligence collection, analysis, and distribution framework provided by at least eight separate agencies.[18] Intelligence came from both Australia and overseas sources, and for Defence use the many streams were channelled through the Australian Theatre Joint Intelligence Centre.

Despite the complexity of the arrangements, HQAST rapidly developed a workable operational concept and strategy. By 2 September, a new set of rules of engagement tailored to the enhanced border protection policy had been approved by the Minister for Defence, Peter Reith, and was ready to be put to the prime minister for his concurrence. At midnight on 3 September the ADF's response to the government's directive came into effect under the codename Operation *Relex*. Between August 2001 and June 2002, the ADF committed twenty-five RAN warships to Operation *Relex*. At any one time the units directly involved might include two or three frigates, one amphibious ship, one survey ship configured for patrol operations, up to six patrol boats, up to four P-3C maritime patrol aircraft, and a Sea King helicopter detachment.[19]

To the end of December 2001, these forces dealt with twelve SIEVs, each numbered chronologically for convenience. Of the twelve vessels, the RAN intercepted five (SIEVs 1, 2, 3, 8, and 9) and then held their passengers in custody until they could be transported to an offshore processing facility, while another four (SIEVs 5, 7, 11, and 12) were escorted back to Indonesia. The remaining three vessels (SIEVs 4, 6, and 10) sank at some point during the interception process. In each of these latter cases the RAN intercept vessel rescued the passengers and crew and then delivered them to an amphibious ship for onward passage.

Standard operating procedures evolved in response both to policy changes from government, and to the reactions of passengers and crew in

during the first few weeks of *Relex*, as were those skills connected with seamanship, information handling, and surface picture compilation. There were also specific advantages in using larger high-capability platforms for interception. The practical aspects of command and control of dispersed assets were enhanced, while the performance of weapons system sensors, such as target indication radars and electro-optical directors, provided far better detection and tracking than was usual in response and enforcement operations.

The RAN expected its sailors to face increasing levels of intimidation.[22] Witnesses appearing before the Senate Committee later described a pattern of extreme behavior among those encountered:

> Numerous instances of threatened or actual violent actions against Australian Defence Force personnel occurred, as well as various acts of threatened or actual self harm and inciting of violence throughout Operation RELEX. Australian Defence Force personnel had not previously encountered these circumstances during non-warlike operations. They were extremely hazardous and volatile situations. What was a law enforcement activity had real potential to rapidly escalate into a violent situation or just as quickly deteriorate into a major safety or preservation of life situation or, worse, both.[23]

Training for the unique circumstances presented during the first *Relex* boardings was largely conducted on the spot. To their credit the individuals who made up the naval boarding parties displayed great personal initiative and professionalism under trying circumstances. More than this, however, each RAN vessel involved in *Relex* also maintained a commitment to meeting the dietary, religious, health, and personal needs of the asylum seekers in a manner which went well beyond their humanitarian obligations.

Nevertheless, in a minimum-manned ship there were practical limits to the numbers of disgruntled people who could be safely handled. As such, further assistance was provided by the deployment of three Transit Security Elements (TSE), each comprising 52 soldiers from the Australian Army. Where necessary, the TSE maintained security on boarded vessels and on those naval vessels used for transportation tasks.

Closely interplayed against the deliberately aggressive actions of some asylum seekers was the need for Australian naval officers to avoid allowing a SOLAS situation to develop. Although the deterrence of people smuggling was central to Operation *Relex*, this aspect remained constrained by the overriding obligation to ensure the safety of all persons involved. Two international covenants – the 1974 International Convention for the Safety of Life at Sea and the 1982 Law of the Sea Convention – impose obligations on "mariners to assist other mariners in distress." Rear-Admiral Smith later explained that his orders and instructions "stressed the overarching requirement for commanding officers of RAN ships to take every reasonable means to achieve the mission without needlessly risking the safety and wellbeing of their ships' companies, their vessels and the lives of the unauthorized arrivals on board the SIEVs."[24]

This obligation did not always sit easily with the government's directive to prevent asylum seekers entering Australian territory. Since it logically followed that they should not be embarked in Australian warships unless absolutely necessary, on several occasions this placed RAN commanding officers and officers in charge of boarding parties in the difficult position of judging exactly when a target vessel was no longer seaworthy.

The interception of SIEV 3 on 11–12 September posed even greater dangers to all those involved. HMAS *Warramunga* first warned off the 130-ft wooden cargo vessel and dispatched a boarding party that managed to return the SIEV to international waters. The boat's subsequent erratic course required another boarding, but attempts by the boarding party to steer the vessel out of Australian waters were met with increasing violence to themselves and damage to the SIEV. With no method of de-escalating the situation without casualties the boarding party conducted an emergency extraction. Shortly afterwards the SIEV attempted to ram *Warramunga* and then, ignoring all further warnings, it headed for the dangers of Ashmore Reef. Menhinick faced an unenviable situation:

> There appeared to be no formal hierarchy amongst the PIIs [potential illegal immigrants] and shouting, confusion, anger and aggression was the norm. The final demand from them and the only consistent one in the end was for them to embark in *Warramunga*. At 2151 a SOLAS situation was imminent. It was a dark night with no moon, the reef was 2.5nm ahead. There were 54 children onboard the SIEV with no life-jackets. At 2218 with the reef only 1nm ahead and impact in 10 minutes I was standing off with the *Warramunga* 1000 yards to the south for my own safety. In a last attempt to avoid a SOLAS incident and loss of life I agreed to embark the PIIs for the night. The SIEV then turned south missing the reef by less than 1 nm.[25]

All those on the SIEV were embarked to *Warramunga*'s quarterdeck, leaving a boarding party in the vessel to repair the damage and steam it to a safe anchorage in the reef. The SUNCs were returned to their vessel the next day and left under the watch of the patrol boat HMAS *Geelong*. Several days later they were embarked in HMAS *Tobruk* and transported to Nauru.

In the case of SIEV 4, the frigate HMAS *Adelaide* spent two days in close proximity to the overcrowded and only marginally seaworthy boat. With the SIEV's steering and engines disabled *Adelaide*'s commanding officer, Commander Norman Banks, RAN, attempted to tow it to safety, but the condition of the vessel continued to worsen. On the afternoon of 8 October it foundered. In accordance with directions, Banks had refused throughout the incident to embark any of the 223 SUNCs in *Adelaide*, and so all on board the SIEV were forced to enter the water. *Adelaide* then conducted an exemplary rescue using the ship's liferafts and flotation aids, and without any injury or loss of life, but the Senate Committee which later looked into Operation *Relex* expressed concern.

In circumstances such as those faced by *Warramunga* and *Adelaide* the potential for success or disaster depended absolutely on the commanding officer's judgement. Much of the controversy generated by the sinking of SIEV 4 revolved around the records and recollections of a brief telephone conversation between Brigadier Silverstone and Commander Banks. This had occurred just as the SIEV's passengers were being recovered from the water for the first time. Arguments over the accuracy of information passed up the ADF chain of command to the government created a crisis of confidence that turned the affair into a political and media circus. The storm surrounding "a certain maritime incident" blew off and on for more than three years.

That naval personnel were implicated without justification raised the ire of at least one former Chief of Naval Staff, who had already accused the government of manipulating the navy for political gain: "It has come out that the brigadier in Darwin interrupted the captain of a ship in the middle of an operation because someone in Canberra told the brigadier he wanted information by a given time.... For somebody to suggest the initial process of telephone calls, when the radio was available for an official report, and the initial report had been demanded because some clot in Canberra wanted to talk on a television station – God, it makes me speechless."[26]

Within Australia it is generally agreed that the government's strong stance against people smuggling helped it win the election on 10 November 2001. That this stance has been successful is difficult to dispute. Operation *Relex* continues, and since December 2001 only one boat, carrying 53 people, has attempted to penetrate the barrier.[27] Notwithstanding this success, the many formal and informal investigations and inquiries that followed the first three months of *Relex* were not helpful to the navy's need to reconstitute and prepare for what lay ahead. Most naval personnel were proud of what they had achieved, but the intense external scrutiny served as an unwelcome distraction at a time when attention should have been focused on the war on terrorism and successive operations in Afghanistan and Iraq.

Conclusions

Australia is not the only country facing the problem of illegal immigration. In global terms the threat posed to Australia by people smuggling has probably been minimal. Nevertheless, pressures resulting from ethnic conflict and environmental degradation will continue to generate unregulated population movement. Criminal elements will also continue to seek profit from the understandable desire of these people to improve their living conditions. Within this context, and the broader national concerns of ocean governance, the maritime response strategy developed by Australia during Operation *Relex* is worthy of recall, not because it may be applicable elsewhere – which will depend on individual circumstances – but rather because, like a weather vane, the operation points to some of the challenges navies face in the twenty-first century.

Whatever may be said about the local political imperative to demonstrate strong leadership, there can be no doubt that by asserting its right to enforce national sovereignty far out to sea Australia took an effective stand against a previously uncontrolled problem. It is clear from subsequent developments that the Australian government considers the RAN has a greater role to play in the enforcement requirements arising from the surveillance of its offshore estate. With legal developments relating to fish stocks and continental shelf claims generating comparable requirements worldwide, it seems reasonable to suggest that other governments may reach similar conclusions.

Many questions still remain unasked and unresolved, but the military's tradition of service allows it to be used in ways hardly possible with other agencies. Since few nations have the resources to maintain a navy solely dedicated to high-intensity war, this is unlikely to be the last "reverse blockade."

PART IV

Contemporary Blockade Strategy

In a *Yale Law Journal* article written in 1991, Michael Fraunces presciently wrote:

> In the future blockade may become even more important as the need of a blockading state to stop every merchant ship grows more vital. The recent willingness of ostensibly neutral states to supply not simply technical know-how and materials for weapons construction, but also ready-for-use missiles and other decisive weapons, to the highest bidder portends such a future. As the negative consequences of allowing even one ship to pass uninspected grow more severe, blockading states will become more willing to use the new blockade forms [long-range blockade and blockade zones] at the expense of neutral interests.[2]

What Fraunces could not have foreseen, happened on 11 September 2001 – an event that changed the world (in ways not yet fully comprehended) had a seminal impact on how naval blockades will need to be conducted in the future.

The Impact of 9/11 on Modern Blockades

What was extraordinary about 9/11 was that a non-state entity had succeeded in conducting a coordinated attack against a sovereign state on its home territory with a hitherto unappreciated weapon of mass destruction (WMD), a fully fueled airliner. Historically, weapons of mass destruction – such as nuclear, chemical, radiological, and biological weapons[3] – were under the strict control of sovereign states, where their manufacture, storage, and use were carefully constrained by physical security measures, and strategically by deterrence and international law. The message conveyed on 9/11 was that, henceforth, weapons of mass destruction could be controlled, distributed, and perhaps used, by non-state entities or even by individuals. This was an unanticipated, very unwelcome, extension to Fraunces's 1991 vision.

After 9/11 the central security problem, for the United States at least, became how to ensure that no weapons of mass destruction could be used by non-state entities against U.S. citizens in the U.S. homeland. Thus, the U.S. Homeland Security Department was created, and new initiatives arose to prevent the international transfer of such weapons. Because no WMD use could be tolerated, because non-state entities are difficult – and perhaps impossible – to deter, and because no retaliatory measures could repair the damage the use of WMD could wreak, a new policy of preemption was announced and codified in the *National Security Strategy of the United States*, September 2002.

It is far better to seek to control shipping or the shipment of contraband materials at their source rather than at their destination. This has long been a guiding principle of blockade, recognized and enunciated by Alfred Thayer Mahan in his seminal article, "Blockade in Relation to Naval

Strategy," in which he wrote: "Whatever the number of ships needed to watch those in an enemy's port, they are fewer by far than those that will be required to protect the scattered interests imperiled by an enemy's escape."[4]

In Mahan's time, ships carried all of the international trade that took place between states separated by water. Cargoes were liquid or bulk, but they were not containerized.

Since Mahan wrote these words, however, international trade has mushroomed. The value of U.S. imports and exports in 2002 was a thousand times what it was in 1900. Roughly 80 percent by volume of all international trade travels the sea lanes of the world, and some 90 percent of that is transported in cargo containers. Nearly nine million containers arrive annually in the 301 U.S. ports of entry. Any form of WMD could be shipped in a container, and any use of WMD could be politically and economically catastrophic for the United States.[5]

In traditional terms, a blockade is a "belligerent operation to prevent vessels and/or aircraft of all nations, enemy as well as neutral, from entering or exiting specified ports, airfields, or coastal areas belonging to, occupied by, or under the control of an enemy nation," and the belligerent right of blockade is "intended to prevent vessels and aircraft, regardless of their cargo, from crossing an established and publicized cordon separating the enemy from international waters and/or airspace." A belligerent right of visit and search "is designed to interdict the flow of contraband goods."[6]

In today's context, however, shipment of contraband WMD can be from states, non-state entities, or individuals with any of the three as the destination. The form of blockade operations, accordingly, has changed dramatically from close blockade, through distant blockade and blockade zones, to the prevention of movement of specific items at, or as close as possible to, their source; unlike the barrier or "reverse" blockade discussed in the previous chapter, this type of blockade hopes to keep out all objects, rather than simply people, perceived to be a threat to a state's sovereignty.

To control the international movement of WMD, their associated delivery systems and related materials more effectively, the United States announced a Proliferation Security Initiative (PSI) in the spring of 2003, complementing the Container Security Initiative (CSI) that had been announced a year earlier. The PSI is indicative of the form the modern-day "belligerent right of visit and search" has taken. The context is one of global armed conflict against terrorists, against sovereign states that would support them, or against other WMD proliferators; and the focus is on preventing the shipment of "contraband" WMD.

The PSI commits its more than 60 participating states to:

- Undertake effective measures, either alone or in concert with other states, for interdicting the transfer or transport of WMD, their delivery systems, and related materials.
- Adopt streamlined procedures for rapid exchange of relevant information.

- Work to strengthen their relevant national legal authorities to accomplish these objectives and work to strengthen international law and frameworks.
- Not transport or assist in the transport of any cargoes of WMD, their delivery systems or related materials to or from countries or groups of proliferation concern.
- Board and search any suspect vessels flying their flags in their internal waters, territorial seas, or areas beyond the territorial seas of any other state.
- Consent under the appropriate circumstances to the boarding and searching of their own flag vessels by other states, and to the seizure of such WMD-related cargoes.
- Stop and/or search suspect vessels in their internal waters, territorial seas, or contiguous zones, and enforce conditions on suspect vessels entering or leaving their ports, internal waters, or territorial seas.
- Require suspect aircraft that are transiting their airspace to land for inspection and seize any such cargoes, and deny aircraft transit rights through their airspace.
- Prevent their ports, airfields, or other facilities from being used as trans-shipment points for WMD-related cargo.[7]

The CSI narrows the focus to containers that are being shipped to the United States, and has the following elements:

- security criteria to identify high-risk containers;
- pre-screening containers before they arrive at US ports;
- using technology to pre-screen high-risk containers;
- developing and using "smart" secure containers.

As of November 2004, the CSI had twenty participating countries with some thirty-seven ports committed. These include the twenty largest exporting ports and cover almost two-thirds of containers shipped to the United States.

As can be seen from the foregoing, over time the *ways* maritime blockades have been accomplished and the *means* for conducting them have changed dramatically. The objective of maritime blockade operations has remained constant, however: to prevent the movement of particular ships and aircraft, or of particular cargoes in ships and aircraft, on or over specified waters of the world – excluding inland rivers and seas.

In view of the foregoing, this chapter will of necessity take a broad view of what constitutes a "blockade." What will be referred to herein as "blockade operations" encompasses those actions contained within the traditional legal definition of "blockade" cited above, but also all others having the same objective: to prevent the movement of ships or aircraft in maritime sea areas or in the skies above them, or of particular cargoes (including people) of the blockaded party. Clearly, this approach widens the focus of what constitutes a "blockade" in the narrow legal sense.

States have been rather inventive over the years in conducting blockade operations but calling them something else in order to avoid complying with the requirements of blockade law. Accordingly, what have been called quarantine operations, close or tactical and distant or strategic blockades, pacific blockades, exclusion zones, and maritime intercept operations, have all been folded herein under the term "blockade operations."

The term "blockade operations" encompasses both the objective of the blockading force and the enforcement mechanism. In contrast, "embargoes" or "economic sanctions" set forth objectives, not the enforcement mechanisms to attain them. According to one expert, for example:

> Between 1993 and 1998 alone, the United States imposed sanctions 61 times – out of a total of 125 cases since World War I. Sanctions eventually targeted 75 countries and some 42 percent of the world's population for reasons ranging from support for terrorism, proliferation of weapons of mass destruction or other sensitive technologies, to concerns over human rights and the environment and even the mislabeling of tuna.[8]

Moreover, the "blockaded party" includes both states and non-state entities, such as terrorist organizations. This takes on additional relevance in the wake of reports of operations of merchant ships by the terrorist organization al Qaeda,[9] one of which might have delivered the explosives used in the embassy bombings in Africa.[10]

Some additional elucidation of terms is necessary before proceeding. The *effectiveness* of a blockade as it is used in this chapter refers to the degree to which the blockade accomplishes its objectives. This is an operational usage of the term "effectiveness" as opposed to the legal usage, which harks back to the words in the Paris Declaration of 1856, quoted in Professor Heinegg's opening chapter: "Blockades, in order to be binding, must be effective, that is to say, maintained by a force sufficient really to prevent access to the coast of the enemy." This principle was generally regarded to require the presence of at least one surface warship in or near the area that was declared as blockaded, and was adopted in order to delegitimize unenforced, or "paper" blockades. It should be noted that this is an "input" measure of effectiveness, established by a legal regimen, and its relationship to whether the blockade accomplishes its objectives, which is an "output" or operational measure of effectiveness, is therefore tenuous at best.

Technological Requirements for Maritime Blockade Operations

Technology has historically played a key role on both sides of the question of maritime blockade operations. The imposer of the blockade requires special types of technology in order to make the blockade effective, and the target of the blockade has some technological needs in order to breach the blockade. The technology underwriting the right of visit and search requires a separate category. In general, then, the technological requirements to conduct maritime blockade operations in the future fall in four categories: ship propulsion; reconnaissance (finding) and surveillance (watching) techniques and devices; weapons with which to threaten or to attack ships and aircraft; and methods to inspect for and detect specific cargoes (contraband).

The first of the four categories of technology, ship propulsion, is important because of the effect it can have on both the capability and the number of ships necessary to mount and sustain traditional blockade operations. When galleys were the primary form of warship, blockade was rarely attempted because of the short endurance and poor seakeeping ability of the ships. The advent of comparatively much more seaworthy sailing ships meant that extended blockades could be undertaken, the effectiveness of which was determined significantly by the speed and direction of the wind. The prevailing westerly winds aided the English in their blockade of French Atlantic ports, for example. For the same reason, blockade of the eastern seaboard of the United States was difficult for sailing ships. The endurance limit on sailing ships tended not to be technological, but human, dependant upon victuals and the health of the ship's crews. For example, far more British sailors became victims of disease on blockade station than were killed or injured in battle. Sailing ships could operate outside the range of shore batteries and still maintain surveillance of the blockaded port.

When ships powered by fossil fuels (coal and then oil) appeared on the scene, the limiting logistic factor became the supply of fuel rather than the well-being of the crew. While higher patrolling speeds could be employed, and transit times from home port to blockade station were shorter with steam-powered than with sailing ships, some provision to refuel them at or near their blockade station had to be made. At first colliers and coaling stations were used, and later – when oil was adopted in the early twentieth century – refueling tankers were employed. Submarines were used in both World Wars as blockading forces, not only because they were stealthy but also because they had very long range, remaining on distant patrol station for many weeks without the necessity of refueling. In World War II the German Navy even provided reprovisioning submarines, *Milchcows*, so that submarines could remain on patrol longer. Nuclear power for surface ships and submarines brought back crew endurance rather than fuel as the limiting factor.

For hydrodynamic reasons, the speed of oceangoing ships has not changed appreciably in the past century. Prospects for significant increases in surface ship speed in the future are not great. Effective ship speeds, however, are enhanced by embarking aircraft – either fixed-wing aircraft in the case of aircraft carriers or helicopters in the case of many other types of ships. With embarked aircraft, ships can scout much greater areas and project their presence ahead of their actual position by hundreds of miles.

Table 21.1 Distance of the horizon

Height (ft)	Nautical miles
10	3.6
50	8.1
100	11.4
250	18.1
500	25.6
1,000	36.2
10,000	114.4
30,000	198.1
50,000	255.8
100,000	361.8

Reconnaissance and surveillance are critical to the maintenance of effective blockades. At the same time, these tasks have become both more important and in some ways more difficult: "The need to track thousands of civilian ships worldwide has intensified given the potential for seemingly harmless shipping to be involved in nuclear, chemical or biological terrorist operations. It was easier to track Soviet warships than a far larger number of civilian ships with unknown cargos and crew."[11]

Once again, technology has played a key role. From the time of the Ancient Greeks, who conducted the first maritime blockades in the fifth century B.C., to the appearance of aircraft, reconnaissance and surveillance were limited by visibility and the curvature of the earth. Thus, even on a clear day, one cannot see forever – only as far as the horizon. The distance to the horizon depends on the height above the surface of the observer. Table 21.1 illustrates this crucial relationship.[12]

Surface ships typically have a height of eye between 50 and 100 feet, so the horizon distance is roughly 10 miles. Low height of eye (especially for submarines), night, weather, and distance mean that reconnaissance and surveillance for blockading non-airborne forces are difficult. The absence of wireless communications until the early part of the twentieth century, moreover, meant that collaboration among ships on blockade station was also limited to line-of-sight, and then at only the very low data rates provided by flag hoist and flashing light.

From Table 21.1 it is evident that the way to expand the reconnaissance and surveillance horizon is to take a sensor aloft. High-frequency, line-of-sight communications systems would experience a concurrent boost in their range as well. Not only was the horizon extended for detection and tracking, but also the high speed of aircraft compared to ships meant that significantly larger areas could be scouted, and more quickly. The appearance of aircraft – especially ones that could be carried on ships – constituted a major improvement in the ability to find, track, and report the movements of potential blockade runners. When ship- and air-borne radar became available during World War II, detection capability experienced a major advance,

Weapons to prevent the imposition of a maritime blockade tend to be similar to those for enforcement. Technologically, weapons for use in maritime environments have become longer-ranged, more stealthy (which makes them more difficult to counter), and more accurate. Air-to-surface weapons have achieved high precision owing to satellite guidance against fixed targets, and to terminal homing against moving ones. Mines tend to be cost-effective weapons for use against ships and submarines. Submarines to enforce blockades have proven very deadly – most recently in the Falklands War of 1982.

Using submarines for blockade running could be a future possibility, especially to carry teams of infiltrators with weapons of mass destruction. The limiting factor will be that states with submarines which could be used for such a purpose tend not to operate them competently. While about forty states in the world have submarines in their naval order of battle, only a few operate the ships routinely in the submerged mode or beyond their own territorial waters. Of course, that could change in the future, but it could not happen quickly or without providing intelligence warning. It is also unlikely that a non-state entity, such as a terrorist group, could acquire or competently operate a submarine.

Inspection, the fourth set of technologies, stems from the need to do more than just check a ship's papers and match them against the cargo. Fortunately, "Technology has enhanced the capabilities of naval forces to conduct reconnaissance and identification over wide areas of the ocean and to detect the presence of some contrabands that were previously undetectable."[17]

Containerization can easily foil off-board detection, however, and WMD can occupy very small volume and exhibit low detectability. Detection equipment exists for all known WMD, so the problems become those of sheer volume and intrusiveness. This is where the PSI and the CSI at ports of embarkation supplement inspections at the destination ports. They seek to ensure that WMD are not loaded into containers at their origin or introduced while the container is in transit. Technology is very much in an assist mode in this application; the first line of defense is to ensure that "contraband" is never loaded in the first place. The need to ensure that containers are not opened and their contents disturbed in any way means that seals and detection devices are also important factors. Significant technological efforts are underway in all these areas.[18]

Conclusions

The U.S. Maritime Transportation Security Act required, as of 1 July 2004, that all foreign ships entering U.S. ports have an international shipping security certification as well as a secured bridge and engine room. The intention of that act, and the CSI and PSI, is to ensure that no materials, such as WMD, could be slipped into the country in order to underwrite acts of terrorism.

How blockade operations – to prevent the movement of ships, aircraft, and their specific cargoes – have been conducted, and the means to conduct them, have changed significantly over time. Technology has been the hand-maiden of change, and, especially recently, it has had to bear the burden of making blockades operationally effective. As Fraunces makes clear, and as extensions of his analysis attest, blockade law has not evolved to meet the demands placed upon it. International law, of course, is impotent in any effort to control international terrorist acts. Furthermore, the international movement of WMD would render moot any recognition of self-proclamied "neutrals" who insist that their rights need to be protected in the event of blockade operations.

As Nicholas Tracy reminds us, however: "Over the history of naval and administrative blockade there has been a steady improvement in the technology of enforcement, but there has never been a blockade of a major state which was impermeable."[19] No blockade in history has been 100 percent effective in preventing "contraband" from entering a blockaded state, or in completely scotching blockade running. The odds favor the perpetrators in these kinds of cases. Unfortunately, since one terrorist act with WMD could have cataclysmic effects, the success rate must be 100 percent. So, it behoves modern states to make use of technological advances in propulsion, recon-naissance and surveillance, weaponry, and finally inspection, to do as much as possible to prevent such a calamity from occurring.

22 Conclusions

Naval Blockades and the Future of Seapower

*Bruce A. Elleman and S. C. M. Paine**

Naval blockades are never conducted in a political vacuum, but are a means to contribute to the achievement of national goals. What types of political goals have blockades been most effective at furthering? What types of blockades have been employed? What strategic effects have they delivered? What circumstances are most and least conducive to their operational and strategic success? What counter-blockade strategies have been most effective?

These issues will be examined in terms of time, space, force, goals, enemy adaptation, and overall effectiveness. *Time* includes both the rate of implementation and the duration. *Space* concerns the area under blockade and the sea and land lines of communications for both sides. *Force* refers to the available instruments of national power. *Objectives* concern both the strategic goal for which the blockade was undertaken and the operational goals of the blockade. *Enemy adaptation* includes the blockaded country's attempts to adapt to changing circumstances. Finally, *effectiveness* is measured on both the strategic and operational level.

Blockade types include close and distant (in terms of the distance of the blockade perimeter from its focus); near and far (in terms of the distance of the theater from the blockading country); partial and total (in terms of the blockade's porosity); and paper, pacific, and belligerent (in terms of the level of coercion). Technological breakthroughs have greatly influenced the cost, execution, and feasibility of all types of blockades, while also widening the distinctions among interdiction, interception, embargo, and quarantine.

Time: Implementation and Duration

Time, in terms of both the rate of implementation and the duration of a blockade, can influence its effectiveness. Implementation can be rapid, intermittent, tightening, or loosening, while the duration can be short, medium, or long. For instance, the British and French rapidly blockaded the Baltic during the Crimean War, but for a short period; the Entente and Allied blockades of Germany during the two World Wars gradually tightened over a longer period of time.

Table 22.1 Time

Name	Implementation	Duration	Strategic effectiveness	Win/Lose/ Draw
Napoleon	Tightening	Long	No, created hostile coalition	Lose
War of 1812	Intermittent	Medium	No, created stronger US Navy	Draw
Crimean	Rapid	Short	Yes, forced war termination	Win
USCW	Intermittent	Medium	Yes, stopped naval development, trade	Win
SJW I	Rapid	Short	Yes, forced war termination	Win
SpAmWar	Rapid	Short	Yes, forced war termination	Win
WWI	Tightening	Medium	Yes, undermined morale, cut trade	Win
SJW II	Tightening	Long	No, created hostile coalition	Lose
WWII	Tightening	Medium	Yes, cut trade	Win
ROC–PRC	Loosening	Long	Yes, prevented PRC invasion	Draw
Korea	Rapid	Medium	Yes, undermined morale, cut trade	Win
Cuba	Rapid	Short	Yes, USSR removed missiles	Win
Vietnam	Tightening	Medium	Yes, forced war termination	Lose
Rhodesia	Loosening	Long	Yes, isolated Rhodesia	Draw
Falklands	Rapid	Short	Yes, forced war termination	Win
Iraq	Rapid	Long	Yes, prevented Iraqi rearmament	Win
PRC mis.	Intermittent	Short	No, created hostile coalition	Draw
Australia	Tightening	Medium	Yes, reduced immigrant flow	Draw

Table 22.1: Time shows how these factors played out in the eighteen case studies in this volume. Seven rapidly implemented blockades involved sea powers cutting off land powers or other weaker sea powers. These include Crimean, first Sino-Japanese, Spanish–American, Korean, Cuban Missile, Falklands, and Iraqi. In all but two of these conflicts, rapid blockades were also short, forcing a favorable negotiated settlement. Rapid blockades tend to help force the blockaded country into agreeing quickly to a negotiated settlement, suggesting a relationship between speed and effectiveness. In Korea and Iraq, where strategic success was not rapid, Korea was bordering powerful allies including the USSR and China, which enabled North Korea to survive, while long borders and cooperative neighbors aided Iraq.

In all six cases of gradually tightening blockades – Napoleon, WWI, second Sino-Japanese, WWII, Vietnam, and Australia – none completely determined the outcome of the wars *except* the Australian reverse blockade, which is still ongoing. The extensive size of all of these theaters helps to explain why the blockades were not rapid. Yet, if a tightening blockade is being imposed against a large land power – Japan's blockade of China in the 1930s and early 1940s is a good example – then the blockaded country should have adequate time to create alternative trade routes. Finally, since tightening blockades tend to take a long time to deliver results, they can really only be adopted successfully by naval powers that enjoy both strong political backing and significant financial resources.

Three intermittent blockades – War of 1812, Civil War, and PRC Missile – with two loosening blockades – ROC–PRC and Rhodesia – were perhaps most strategically effective in what they prevented from happening; in other words, in their deterrent effects. For example, the U.S. did not invade Canada in 1812, the Confederacy did not build a strong navy, China did not invade Taiwan in the 1950s, Rhodesia could not avoid UN censure, and Taiwan did not declare independence in 1996. The main problem with analysing the effectiveness of deterrent blockades is in not knowing what would have happened had they never been adopted in the first place.

Five blockades were long – Napoleon, second Sino-Japanese, ROC–PRC, Rhodesia, and Iraq – averaging ten years or more. With the exception of the rapid development of a coalition opposing Iraq, the first two gradually tightened, while the second two loosened over time. Short and medium-length blockades were usually carried out in combination with either a real, or at least the threat of a land invasion, and the blockaded area generally contained an operational center of gravity. In the first Sino-Japanese War, for example, the Chinese Navy was trapped in the port of Weihaiwei and was destroyed as a result of the blockade. In the Falklands, the blockaded area encompassed the entire theater of hostilities. In the Cuban Missile Crisis, the ships being blockaded contained missile parts necessary to complete the installation.

In four cases where blockades failed to achieve their strategic goal – Napoleon, War of 1812, second Sino-Japanese, and PRC Missile – two of the four were long blockades, while the other two included one short and one medium blockade, so the duration of a blockade has less to do with failure than other factors, including the creation of a hostile coalition, the inadvertent strengthening of the enemy's military and naval forces, or the nature of the theater.

Space: The Nature of the Theater

In most cases sea powers impose blockades on land powers. Only extremely rarely do either sea or land powers blockade other sea powers. Blockade distances – *space* – can vary greatly. The terms "close blockade" and "distant blockade" will be used to refer to the distance of the blockade perimeter to the blockaded country, while "near blockade" and "far blockade" will be used to refer to the distance of the theater of operations from the country enforcing the blockade. Finally, blockades can be executed unilaterally or in combination with a coalition, and they can be broken by blockade runners or by creating alternate land lines of communication or air routes.

As shown in Table 22.2: Space, the largest group of the cases – seven out of eighteen – involved naval powers conducting close blockades far from their own shores. These include the War of 1812, Crimea, Korea, Vietnam, Rhodesia, Falklands, and Iraq. Arguably all involved sea powers opposing

Table 22.2 Space

Name	Blockader	Blockaded	Neighbors	Type	Type
Napoleon	Land power	Sea power	Russia changed sides		
War of 1812	Sea power	Land power		Close	Far
Crimean	Sea powers	Land power	Turkey helps	Close	Far
USCW	Land power	Land power		Close	Near
SJW I	Sea power	Land power		Close	Near
SpAmWar	Sea power	Island colony		Close	Near
WWI	Great power coalition	Land power	Russia falls, US joins	Distant	Near
SJW II	Sea power	Land power	USSR intervenes	Close	Near
WWII	Great power coalition	Land power	USSR changes sides	Distant	Near
ROC–PRC	Island sea power	Land power	US, USSR intervene	Close	Near
Korea	Great power coalition	Peninsula	USSR, PRC intervene	Close	Far
Cuba	Sea power	Island nation	USSR	Distant	Near
Vietnam	Sea power	Land power	USSR, PRC intervene	Close	Far
Rhodesia	Sea power	Land-locked	Neighboring ports	Close	Far
Falklands	Sea power	Island colony		Close	Far
Iraq	Great power coalition	Land power	Iran, Jordan, Syria help	Close	Far
PRC mis.	Land power	Island nation	US intervenes	Distant	Near
Australia	Sea power	Immigrants		Distant	Near

land powers (the U.S. was not yet a strong naval power in 1812). In all of these cases the blockaded country was too far away to retaliate effectively against the home territory of the blockading country, so the blockader could afford to patrol the enemy's shores. In other words, all far blockades were also close blockades, although not all close blockades were far. Meanwhile, of the twelve close blockades, five were near, including the Civil War, first Sino-Japanese, Spanish–American, second Sino-Japanese, and ROC–PRC. In four of these the theater of operations was near enough to the blockading power that armed retaliation was very likely, and so the enemy's navy became a prime target.

Sea powers do best when blockading islands, peninsulas, or other lesser sea powers that depend primarily on sea lines of communication, while blockades against land powers tend to be protracted and porous. Land powers are extremely capable of rendering ineffective a sea power's block-ades when their central geographic location provides alternate land lines of communication. In particular, if the blockaded country can form land lines with contiguous allies, then the costs of the blockade will increase and its effectiveness will decline. In such theaters, successful blockades alone did not bring about the strategic success of the blockading sea power; joint and combined operations were also crucial.

the enemy's sovereign land, sea, or air space. Finally, the duration of the blockade has an impact on force levels, since protraction can either deplete a set force or permit the deployment of reinforcements.

According to Table 22.3: Force, surface patrols enforced all but two of the eighteen case studies. The two exceptions included Napoleon, who used mainly customs officers and police to halt smuggling from the Continent of Europe to England, and the PRC Missile blockade of Taiwan, both highly unusual blockades. Underwater mines were extensively used in at least eight of the eighteen blockades – first Sino-Japanese War, Spanish–American, WWI, second Sino-Japanese, WWII, ROC–PRC, Korea, and Vietnam – while submarines were factors in four cases – WWI, WWII, the Cuban Missile Crisis, and the Falklands War. After the development of aerial bombing, it too was used extensively, including the second Sino-Japanese War, WWII, the Nationalist blockade of China, the Korean War, Vietnam, the Falklands, and in Iraq; sea-based aviation and VSTOL played an especially important role in the Falklands. Finally, land-based missiles were the primary means of enforcement in only one of the blockades – the PRC versus Taiwan – but their potential for use in future blockades is great; blockades of this type have been referred to as "choke point" blockades.

In at least eight of the blockades the blockading power was intent on conquest or reconquest, including Napoleon, the Union, Japan in the second Sino-Japanese War, WWII, the Nationalist blockade of China, UN attempts to reunify Korea, the Falklands War, and the PRC Missile blockade. All but two of these eight, specifically the Nationalists and later the PRC, included a major invasion of territory.

However, in six other cases there were invasions that were not intended to be permanent conquests. These included the British attack on the U.S. capital in the War of 1812, the Anglo-French invasion of the Crimea, the Japanese invasion of China in the first Sino-Japanese War, the U.S. invasion of Cuba in the Spanish–American War, British deployment on the Continent in WWI, and UN troops in Iraq. Most, but not all, of the wars of conquest, and the majority of other blockades that included invasions, lasted over a year. Many were protracted wars.

Blockades without any land operations were rare. Rather, many naval blockades entailed joint and combined operations that coordinated sea, land, and air operations. The War of 1812, Crimean War, the first Sino-Japanese War, the Spanish–American War, the second Sino-Japanese War, Korea, and the Falklands stand out in this regard. The few exceptions to this pattern were the Cuban Missile Crisis, Rhodesia, Iraq, the PRC Missile blockade, and the Australian reverse blockade, where operations on land played little if any role in the blockade (although, in the case of Cuba, the threat of invasion proved critical to achieving a negotiated outcome to the conflict).

An examination of the force equation suggests that modern blockades are rarely conducted just by surface ships. As submarines and air power became

Table 22.4 Goals

Blockade	Operational goal	Strategic goal	Focus	Partial/ Total	L/U	C
Napoleon	Capture coastal Eur; stop trade	Defeat UK	Trade	Partial	U	C
War of 1812	Defeat US Navy	Defeat US	Navy	Partial	L	
Crimean	Cut Russian trade	Get Russia out of Turkey	Trade	Total	L	
USCW	Cut Southern trade	Maintain the Union	Trade	Partial	U	C
SJW I	Take key port for pincer on Beijing	Destroy Chinese Navy	Navy	Total	L	
SpAmWar	Deny bases to Spanish Navy	Cuban independence	Navy	Total	L	
WWI	Deny resources; bottle up navy	Defend homeland + empire	Trade	Partial	U	
SJW II	Support ground operations to punish China	China recognition of Manchukuo	Trade	Partial	L→U	
WWII	Deny resources; bottle up navy	Defeat Germany	Trade	Partial	U	
ROC–PRC	Cut PRC trade, get forward bases	Reunite China under KMT	Trade	Partial	U	
Korea	Cut (S)LOCS	Defeat North Korea	Army	Partial	L→ U→L	
Cuba	Cut weapons imports	Remove offensive weapons	Missiles	Total	L	
Vietnam	Cut insurgent and weapon flow	Protect South Vietnam	Army	Partial	L	
Rhodesia	Cut petroleum imports	Prevent independence	Trade	Partial	L	
Falklands	Halt resupply	Expel Argentina	Army	Total	L	
Iraq	Cut oil exports and weapons imports	Enforce settlement of Gulf War	Trade	Partial	L→U	
PRC mis.	Cut commerce, transport	Prevent independence	Trade	Partial	U	C
Australia	Send back boat people	Prevent illegal immigration	People	Total	L	

Notes:
U Unlimited
L Limited
C Continental power doing the blockading.

more available and dependable, they too were used for patrol duty. Joint operations also played an increasingly important role, with joint sea–air operations increasingly substituting for joint land–sea operations in the modern period.

Finally, while wars of conquest usually included invasions – with the two notable exceptions being Chinese (the Nationalist blockade of the PRC and the PRC Missile blockade of Taiwan) where a full-blown invasion would have been an enormous undertaking – land invasions were not necessarily intended for permanent conquest, but quite often merely for exerting pressure for a negotiated, as opposed to an unconditional, settlement, as happened in the War of 1812, the Crimean War, the first Sino-Japanese War, and the Spanish–American War.

Strategic and Operational Goals

Blockades are a means to an end. At the operational level of warfare, they are simply a way to impede transportation and communications. At the strategic level, however, sometimes alone but more often in combination with other military strategies, they are also a means to achieve an overarching national *goal* that provides the rationale for employing coercion. Goals include the interruption of trade, the occupation of territory, the destruction of enemy naval or land forces, and the control of population movements. Other possibilities can include deterrence, economic strangulation, military degradation, bottleneck creation, cost escalation, morale erosion, and sanction enforcement. Blockades can be total or something less, hence the terms "total blockade" and "partial blockade". Total blockades completely halt prohibited traffic, while partial blockades, by intent or by default, allow either a percentage or certain categories of trade and population movement to continue. Blockades that are effective at sea, but fail to cut alternate land routes, are still partial, even though they may make critical contributions to victory. Finally, the blockader's goals can be unlimited, meaning the overthrow of the enemy government, or something less, hence the terms "unlimited blockade" and "limited blockade" defined in terms of strategic objective, not in the quantity of resources devoted to the blockade.

As shown in Table 22.4: Goals, in six of the eighteen cases the original objectives were unlimited, and in three more – the second Sino-Japanese, Korea, and Iraq – the original, limited goals later became unlimited for at least a time. Nine blockades that began as limited conflicts remained so throughout – the War of 1812, Crimea, first Sino-Japanese, Spanish–American, Cuban Missile Crisis, Vietnam, Rhodesia, Falklands, and Australia. In many limited wars, blockades were partial, but all total blockades occurred in limited wars and four out of five focused on defeating the enemy's military forces, not on interdicting trade.

Surprisingly, in most limited blockades, the blockading countries instituted a close blockade of their enemy, meaning that their ships and other military assets were very close to the enemy's shores, usually in order to isolate and destroy the enemy's army or navy more than to halt trade. By contrast, a larger number of the distant blockades were part of unlimited wars. In these conflicts blockades were usually intended to disrupt enemy trade as one point of leverage, rather than to eliminate a specific military target or to take a set piece of territory. Unlimited wars by their very nature usually include a full array of military forces, often in a variety of theaters, so that blockade is just one instrument among many.

Thus, blockades played a larger role in many limited wars, sometimes even constituting the sole means of coercion. Naval blockades used by themselves are most effective at achieving limited objectives, particularly limited naval objectives, such as blockading an enemy navy in port – first Sino–Japanese War – or waiting for the enemy navy to leave port – Spanish–American War. Naval blockades alone cannot easily or quickly achieve unlimited goals. In addition, the strategic impact of limited blockades on trade can be difficult to measure, unless there are particular items that the adversary can acquire only through trade and that are essential for continuing the war; for example, preventing Iraq from upgrading its conventional forces and acquiring WMD facilitated the overthrow of the Iraqi government in 2003.

The number of cases where land powers tried to use blockades to achieve their overall strategic goals was especially small, and included only Napoleon, the Union, and the PRC. All three had unlimited political goals – either the total destruction or the absorption of the enemy – but lacked the necessary naval forces to enforce a total blockade. All three were also near blockades, with their enemy close at hand. The results were mixed – Napoleon and the PRC ultimately withdrew because of third-party intervention, by Russia and the U.S. respectively, while the Union arguably won in part because the Confederacy, which was also a land power, failed in its efforts to find a strong foreign protector, and, in particular a strong sea power, to come to its aid.

In three cases limited blockades escalated fully or for a time into unlimited blockades – second Sino–Japanese War, Korea, and Iraq. In these cases, the focus of the blockade effort was against the adversary's army, and in particular against their army's logistical lines. In the first two, the geography of China and Korea made it difficult for naval forces, even in conjunction with air power and an active military presence, to cut the enemy's lines of communication with contiguous land powers. Interestingly, in both of these cases the shift from limited to unlimited proved to be a mistake; only in Iraq, after a thirteen-year blockade, was an unlimited goal achieved.

Enemy Adaptation

Enemies *adapt* to changing circumstances and threats, making some blockades turn out to be extraordinarily expensive in terms of money, manpower, and prestige, so that costs ultimately outweigh benefits. Such outcomes

Table 22.5 Enemy adaptation

Name	Counter-blockade	Third-party action	Counter-measures	N/D
Napoleon	UK started blockade	Russia defected from France	UK smuggling	N
War of 1812	US embargo of UK		US smuggling	
Crimean			Russian reflagging	D
USCW	South embargo Union		South smuggling	
SJW I				D
SpAmWar				D
WWI	Unrestricted sub warfare	US joined Entente	Alternate LOCs, USSR	
SJW II	Chinese embargo of Japan	US, UK helped China	Alternate LOCs, USSR	N
WWII	German counter-blockade of UK		Alternate LOCs, USSR	
ROC–PRC	PRC attack on Jinmen and Mazu		Alternate LOCs, USSR	
Korea			Alternate LOCs, USSR–PRC	
Cuba				D
Vietnam			Alternate LOCs, USSR–PRC	
Rhodesia			Alternate LOCs and SLOCs	N
Falklands				D
Iraq			Alternate LOCs, smuggling	
PRC mis.		US deploys carriers		
Australia				

Notes:
D Dream blockade
N Nightmare blockade

become a nightmare scenario for the blockading country. However, if the blockaded country either lacks effective counter-measures or does not incorporate them in time, then blockades can deliver a quick, decisive victory, providing a dream scenario for the blockading country. Most naval blockades fall somewhere between these two extremes.

Table 22.5: Enemy adaptation, identifies three nightmare scenarios – Napoleon, second Sino-Japanese War, and Rhodesia. In the first and second cases, the blockade helped forge powerful new enemy coalitions with even more unlimited goals than the blockader, ultimately destroying both Napoleon and Imperial Japan. In the case of the Beira patrol, Great Britain's own UN security resolution ultimately locked her into carrying out the blockade alone. The costs soon exceeded the economic, but not necessarily the prestige, value to Britain, so the blockade dragged on for almost a decade.

Of the five dream scenarios – Crimea, first Sino-Japanese War, Spanish–American War, Cuban Missile Crisis, and Falklands – in four of them the theater of hostilities was small, with the first Sino-Japanese War being the exception, but this was offset by China's unwillingness to commit its naval forces to destroy Japan's sea lines of communication. In most of these cases, the blockade ended as a result of negotiations, and none in unconditional surrender. None of the five entailed fighting on the territory of the blockader. In three cases – Spanish–American War, Cuban Missile Crisis, and Falklands – hostilities took place outside of the core territory of the primary belligerents: Cuba was a colony of Spain and then in the 1960s a client state of the Soviet Union, while the Falklands was not an integral part of Argentina. Such areas have a much lower value than home turf, which probably contributed to the dream-scenario outcome.

In the dream scenarios, the blockaded country largely followed the script anticipated by the blockader. For example, Russia could not create alternate land lines during the Crimean War because it had yet to enlarge its railway system; in the first Sino-Japanese War the Chinese obliged Japan by anchoring the northern fleet in port where the Japanese Navy and Army could find, surround, and destroy it; in the Spanish–American War the Spanish deployed their antiquated fleet in theater without sufficient coaling stations; in the Cuban Missile Crisis, Soviet remoteness from the theater convinced them to back down in the face of a blockade plus the threat of an invasion of Cuba; finally, in the Falklands, Argentina's air force never damaged the British aircraft carriers, which constituted the center of gravity of the British military effort.

With the exception of the USSR in the Cuban Missile Crisis, therefore, those on the losing side in these dream scenarios were all cooperative adversaries. Either they lacked key capabilities or they used their capabilities poorly. In three of the five – Crimea, Spanish–American War, and Falklands – the losing side had inferior naval forces, while the USSR Navy was strong but not based near Cuba. Only in the first Sino-Japanese War was there naval parity, but China refused to use her numerically larger and, on paper, more capable fleets to deny Japan sea control.

Ten of the eighteen blockades involved neither dream nor nightmare scenarios. In these cases, both the blockading and the blockaded power adapted to each other's strategies. Not all adaptations were effective. For example, the United States in the War of 1812, the South in the U.S. Civil War, the Nationalists opposing Japan's invasion of China, and the Nazis all imposed counter-blockades or embargoes on enemies. These additional trade restrictions merely served to make the blockades tighter, although not enough to make a crucial difference to the outcome of the war.

Other enemy adaptations worked better. Extensive smuggling by land and sea undermined the effectiveness of many blockades. For example, Britain

smuggling, and alternative land routes undermined the effectiveness of the blockade. However, in all ten cases the blockaders managed to reduce the flow of goods, drive up costs or impose unacceptable burdens on the enemy. Victory usually resulted not solely from the naval blockade, but from a combination of military efforts, including land operations.

Of the ten blockades that were part of successful wars, surprisingly only four were far blockades conducted by naval powers – Crimea, Korea, Falklands, and Iraq. Success rates increased for sea powers conducting near blockades, with five of this type succeeding. Only Japan failed at a near blockade in the second Sino-Japanese War, mainly due to the broadening of the war with the 1941 attack on Pearl Harbor to include other sea powers as its adversaries. As for blockades by land powers, really only the Union blockade of the U.S. South fully achieved its objective of halting the expansion of the Confederate Navy and eroding the export revenues of the South.

In the eight remaining blockades that either failed, or where the goal was to deter and so victory was difficult to ascertain, reasons for failure were often connected to the nature of the theater. In three cases – Napoleon, the War of 1812, the second Sino-Japanese War, and ROC–PRC – the area under blockade was enormous, and so precluded effective enforcement. In the case of Vietnam and Rhodesia, both had long, porous land borders, providing multiple alternate land lines of communication. Finally, the ultimate outcome of two blockades – PRC Missile and Australia – remains unresolved.

Outside intervention by another great power was the most common reason for operational failure. For example, in the nineteenth century, Russia played an important role in opposing Napoleon, while in three cases during the twentieth century – including the second Sino-Japanese War, ROC–PRC, and Korea – the Soviet Union provided secure land lines of communication to compensate China and Korea for lost sea lines of communication. Likewise, the United States intervened in the 1996 PRC Missile blockade of Taiwan by sending two carrier battle groups to the Taiwan Strait. In Vietnam, mining Haiphong did halt Soviet ships from entering port, but this success came very late in the conflict and could not prevent the U.S. from losing the war.

A blockade's effectiveness appears to be largely a function of the size of the blockaded area, the availability of alternative land lines of communication, the ease with which sea lines of communication can be cut, and the interest of other powers in intervening. The smaller and the less interconnected an enemy is, the tighter the blockade. In porous blockades that did not achieve a clear victory, enemy adaptations undercut the effectiveness of the blockades.

Naval blockades have often proven themselves to be both an effective offensive military strategy and a deterrent to halt undesired actions by an opponent. However, land powers have traditionally failed when applying blockades to sea powers or to island nations, with Napoleon's continental blockade and the PRC Missile blockade being two prime examples. This suggests that land powers might want to consider using methods other than blockade, such as negotiation, to obtain their political goals.

Meanwhile, sea powers blockading land powers must take into account the probability that new land lines of communication can be created to avoid the greatest effects of the blockade; two of the three "nightmare" scenarios discussed under enemy adaptation were examples of this type. Interestingly, it was Russia/USSR that most often played this role by utilizing its central geographic position.

The most obvious category of successful naval blockades involved sea powers blockading islands, such as Cuba or the Falklands, or isolated peninsulas such as the Crimea or Shandong, where blockade had the dual effect of halting trade and putting military pressure on the enemy. All five of the so-called "dream" scenarios fit this description. However, blockades of large peninsulas or coastal states that have adequate land transportation and powerful allies – for example, Korea and Vietnam – were not nearly as effective.

Blockading powers that attempted to repeat a successful blockade often found themselves thwarted the second time by enemy adaptation. Certainly, Imperial Japan failed to subdue China in the 1930s and 1940s, just as the WWII blockade of Germany was arguably less effective than in WWI. While, on the surface, the second U.S. blockade of Cuba appeared equally successful to the first, nuclear weapons and the threat of invasion were extenuating factors. This suggests that blockaded countries learn the lessons of history as well as, if not better than, the blockaders. This has implications for any future PRC attempt to blockade Taiwan. Since 1996, Taiwan has endeavored to augment its naval forces and has worked hard to add potential coalition members – including Japan – to its side.

Finally, as technology has changed, so have blockades. Over time, blockading countries have moved away from underwater mines and shifted more toward air power. As a result, invasion of territory has become less common, while the threat of aerial attack is more common. In "choke point" blockades, such as the PRC Missile blockade of Taiwan, the target is not a particular navy or coastline, but disruption of trade routes or creation of exclusion zones; an important underlying goal can be to disrupt stock markets or raise insurance rates, thus making the cost of doing business too high. In Australia's "reverse blockade", the enemy was not even a country or a military force, but illegal immigrants and the smuggling groups transporting them.

Due to the very complexity of the international trading system, naval blockades by individual countries will probably decline, while coalitions of the willing or UN-sponsored interdiction programs will probably increase. Future blockades will not necessarily be close blockades far from the blockader's shores, but will probably include the embargo of specific goods in distant ports of embarkation, before the goods are inspected and sealed in containers for transport. Finally, patrolling only by sea will probably diminish in favor of new forms of aerial and space-based weapons, communications, and highly accurate sensors. As before, seapower will continue to be essential for sustaining blockades, but the sensing tools that sea powers will use to aid in the enforcement of such operations will more often be located in the air and in outer space.

Notes

Foreword

* The thoughts and opinions expressed in this Foreword are those of the author, and are not necessarily those of the U.S. government, the U.S. Navy Department, or the Naval War College.

1 Richard Pares, *Colonial Blockade and Neutral Rights, 1739–1763* (Oxford: The Clarendon Press, 1938).

2 See titles in Robert Greenhalgh Albion, *Naval & Maritime History: An Annotated Bibliography*. Fourth Edition, Revised and Expanded (Mystic, CT: Munson Institute of American Maritime History, 1972), Section BC-3: American Civil War, 1861–1865: The Blockade and Coastal Actions, 259–60; Section BE-7: World War I, 1914–1918, 174–5; Benjamin W. Labaree, *A Supplement (1971–1986) to Robert G. Albion's Naval & Maritime History, An Annotated Bibliography, Fourth Edition*. (Mystic, CT: Munson Institute of American Maritime Studies, 1988) 168–9.

3 Julian S. Corbett, *Some Principles of Maritime Strategy with an Introduction and Notes by Eric J. Grove*. Classics of Sea Power series. (Annapolis, MD: Naval Institute Press, 1988).

4 *Ibid.*, 183–4.

5 *Ibid.*, 185.

6 *Ibid.*, 187.

7 Frank J. Merli and Robert H. Ferrell, "Blockades", in Alexander DeConde *et al.*, eds, *Encyclopedia of American Foreign Policy*. Second Edition (New York: Charles Scribner's Sons, 2002) vol. 1, 171–84; 171.

8 *Ibid.*, 183.

Chapter 1

* The thoughts and opinions expressed in this Introduction are those of the authors and are not necessarily those of the U.S. government, the U.S. Navy Department, or the Naval War College.

1 "DPRK Radio Denounces US–Japan 'Maritime Blockade Maneuver' Against DPRK", 15 October 2004, FBIS KPP20041015000125.

Chapter 2

* Reprinted and revised from the author's article "Naval Blockade", in *International Law Across the Spectrum of Conflict*, Michael N. Schmitt (ed.) (Newport, RI: Naval War College Press, 2000) 203–30.

1 Department of the Navy (Office of the Chief of Naval Operations), *The Commander's Handbook on the Law of Naval Operations*, NWP 1–14M, para. 7.7.1.
2 *Ibid.*
3 C.J. Colombos, *International Law of the Sea*, 6th rev. edn (London, 1967) 818; L. Oppenheim, *International Law* (ed. H. Lauterpacht), Vol. II, 7th edn (London, 1963) 769.
4 The law of blockade is often linked to the law of neutrality because a blockade always implies interference with neutral trade. Oppenheim, 768. But blockades affect neutral countries indirectly, so the law of blockade is not an integral part of the law of neutrality. For a characterization of blockades as acts of war, see M.M. Whiteman, *Digest of International Law*, Vol. 10 (Washington D.C., 1968) 868.
5 M.N. Schmitt, *Blockade Law: Research Design and Sources*, Legal Research Guides, Vol. 12 (Buffalo, 1991) 3.
6 W. Schumann, *Die Friedensblockade* (Hamburg, 1974) *passim*; A.H. Washburn, "The Legality of the Pacific Blockade", *Columbia Law Review* (1921) 55–69, 227–41, 442–59; Institut de Droit International, *Droit de blocus en temps de paix*, AIDI 9 (1887–88) 275–301. Whiteman, 870. For early state practice, see the references in H.J.W. Verzijl *et al.*, *International Law in Historical Perspective*, Part IX-C (Dordrecht, 1992) 419.
7 L.C. Green, Comment No. 5 in W. Heintschel v. Heinegg (ed.), *Visit, Search, Diversion and Capture: The Effect of the United Nations Charter on the Law of Naval Warfare* (Bochum, 1995) 191.
8 Ch. Greenwood, *The Effects of the United Nations Charter on the Law of Naval Warfare*, *ibid.*, 133; and commentaries, *ibid.*, 177 (by A.W. Dahl); 18 (by L. Doswald-Beck); 185 (by W.J. Fenrick and K.S. Carter); 187 (by D. Fleck); 201 (by J.A. Roach); 205 (by H.B. Robertson Jr.).
9 H. Wehberg, *Das Seekriegsrecht*, F. Stier-Somlo (ed.), *Handbuch des Völkerrechts V* (Berlin, 1915) 26; R.W. Tucker, *The Law of War and Neutrality* (Washington D.C., 1957) 283; Ph.C. Jessup and F. Deák, *Neutrality. Its History, Economics, and Law. Vol. I: The Origins* (New York, 1935) 105–14; Verzij, 415.
10 R. Kleen, *La Neutralite d'apres le Droit International Conventionnel et Coutumier des Etats Civilises*, Tome I: Principies Fondmentaux-Devoirs des Neutres (Paris, 1898) 542.
11 Cp. C. van Bynkershoek, *Quaestionum juris publici*, Liber I, Cap. XI, 89; Colombos, 814.
12 Bynkershoek, 89; Wehberg, 26. For the practice of other states/entities, see Jessup/Deák, 111.
13 Hugo Grotius, *De jure belli ac pacis*, Liber III, Cap. I, Para. V.
14 Bynkershoek, 87, with references to the Dutch practice. For the seventeenth-century practice of other states/entities, see Jessup/Deák, 107; Verzijl, 424; E. de Vattel, *Le Droit des Gens ou Principes de la Loi Naturelle*, Book III, 117, maintains that belligerents are entitled to prevent anybody from entering and to consider that person an enemy if he endeavors to enter or to transport something into a blockaded area.
15 According to *Consolato del Mare*, Chapter 276, only enemy goods on board neutral merchant vessels were subject to capture. If, however, the captain refused to transport those goods to an ordered destination, the commander (the "Admiral") of the privateer was entitled to use armed force. *Consolato del Mare*, the "*Breve curiae maris*" of Pisa (1298) and the Statutes of Genoa (1316) exempted neutral goods, in principle, from capture. F. Jordá, *Das "Consulat des Meeres" als Ursprung und Grundlage des Neutralitätsrechts im Seekriege bis zum Jahre 1856* (Hamburg, 1932) 25.
16 Verzijl, 421.

17 Bynkershoek, 87.
18 Colombos, 816.
19 Wehberg, 26.
20 Jessup/Deák, 117.
21 Wehberg, 30.
22 P. Fauchille, *La diplomatie française et la ligue des neutres de 1780* (Paris, 1893) 20, 68; Kleen, 576; U. Scheuner, *Neutralität, bewaffnete*, in Strupp and Schlochauer (eds), *Wörterbuch des Völkerrechts*, Vol. II (Berlin, 1962) 596–7.
23 "Que pour déterminer ce qui caractérise un port bloqué, on n'accorde cette dénomination qu'à celui où il y a, par la disposition de la puissance qui l'attaque avec des vaisseaux arrêtés et suffisamment proches, un danger évident d'entrer." Th. Niemeyer, *Urkundenbuch zum Seekriegsrecht* (Berlin, 1913) 1.
24 Wehberg, 33; Niemeyer, 6.
25 Wehberg, 34.
26 Kleen, 28; M.C. de Boeck, *La propriété privée ennemie sous pavillon ennemi* (Paris, 1882) 70.
27 Niemeyer, 13.
28 *Ibid.*, 17.
29 *Ibid.*, 47.
30 *Ibid.*, 48.
31 *Ibid.*, 39.
32 Wehberg, 40. Still, there are examples of blockades in the traditional sense. Verzijl, 421.
33 Wehberg, 41.
34 Niemeyer, 53; J. Hinz and E. Rauch, *Kriegsvölkerrecht*, 3rd edn (Cologne, 1984) no. 1525.
35 In the French original "arrêtés et suffisamment proches". Ch. Dupuis, *Le droit de la guerre maritime d'après les doctrines anglaises contemporaines* (Paris, 1899) 201; Kleen, 572; Wehberg, 42.
36 Already in the case of the *Nancy* [(1809) Roscoe II, 106 and 108], Lushington stated that, "if a blockade was effective, the Court must not appreciate the number and the disposition of the ships of the blockading force", and that "even a single warship might maintain it".
37 During the Crimean War it was sufficient to station one warship at a distance of 120 nautical miles from Riga because it could prevent access via the only approach. Dupuis, 203.
38 S.V. Mallison and W.T. Mallison Jr., *A Survey of the International Law of Naval Blockade*, U.S. Naval Institute *Proceedings* 102 (Feb. 1976) 43–53, 46.
39 See U.S. Supreme Court in the cases of The *Bermuda* [3 Wall. 514 (1865)], The *Springboek* [5 Wall. 1 (1866)] and The *Peterhoff* [5 Wall. 1 (1866)]; H.W. Malkin, "Blockade in Modern Conditions", *British Yearbook of International Law III* (1922–23) 87–98, 92; Wehberg, 158; G. Schramm, *Das Prisenrecht in seiner neuesten Gestalt* (Berlin, 1913) 172.
40 Niemeyer, 736.
41 *Ibid.*, 772.
42 *Ibid.*
43 *Ibid.*, 773.
44 Niemeyer, 805.
45 N. Bentwich, *The Declaration of London* (London, 1911) 44; F. Kalshoven, *Commentary on the 1909 London Declaration*, in N. Ronzitti (ed.), *The Law of Naval Warfare* (Dordrecht, 1988) 257–75; Naval War College, *The Declaration of London of February 26, 1909* (Washington, D.C., 1910) 25.
46 "Rapport général présenté à la Conférence Navale au nom du Comité de Rédaction", in Niemeyer, 1604, 1608.

that "this paragraph... does, however, prohibit the enforcement solely by weapon systems, such as mines, unless they are employed in such a manner as not to endanger legitimate sea-going commerce". In an annotation to paragraph 7.7.2.3, NWP 1–14M, the authors maintain that "the presence of at least one surface warship is no longer an absolute requirement to make a blockade legally effective, as long as other sufficient means are employed".

88 The USSR opposed the mining of Haiphong as interfering with freedom of navigation, not as a violation of the maritime *jus in bello*.

89 O'Connell argues that the mining of Haiphong was a "strategic blockade" and could be maintained and enforced solely by mines. But this is untenable, since the maritime *jus in bello* does not distinguish between "strategic" and "economic" blockades. O'Connell, 1139.

90 Stone, 496; Castrén, 301; Wehberg, 152; Article 73 of the 1939 Harvard draft.

91 NWP 1–14M, para. 7.10; Principle 5.2.10 of the Helsinki Principles; *San Remo manual*, para. 98; Tucker, 292; Colombos, 832; Castrén, 304; O'Connell, 1,156; Oppenheim, 782; Articles 81 of the 1939 Harvard draft.

92 NWP 1–14M, paras. 7.5.2 and 8.2.2.

93 For the differentiation between inward and outward breach of blockade, see Colombos, 829, 831.

94 NWP 1–14M, para. 7.7.4; Canadian draft, para. 722 (8).

95 For: Colombos, 835; Stone, 498; Castrén, 306. Against: Tucker, 310, 316, fn 80; Wehberg, 161; Martini, 72; Rousseau, 271; Th. Niemeyer, *Das Seekriegsrecht nach der Londoner Deklaration* (Berlin, 1910) 21.

96 Wehberg, 156; Berber, 190; F.D. v. Hansemann, *Die Lehre von der einheitlichen Reise im Rechte der Blockade und Kriegskonterbande*, Zeitschrift für Volkerrecht und Bundesstaatsrecht, Beiheft zum IV. Bande (Breslau, 1910) 6.

97 Used in a German bulletin of 13 September 1939, *Oberkommando der Kriegsmarine*, No. 40; Martini, 94; A.C. Bell, *Die Englische Hungerblockade im Weltkrieg 1914–15* (Essen, 1943) *passim*.

98 W.N. Medlicott, *The Economic Blockade*, Vol. I (London, 1952) 666; Martini, 115.

99 CDDH Off. Rec. VI, 220. This position was taken by the Third Committee in its 1975 Report, CDDH Off. Rec. XV, 279.

100 H. Meyrowitz, *Le protocole additionel I aux conventions de Genève de 1949 et le droit de la guerre maritime*, Revue Générale de Droit International Public 89 (1985) 243–98, 270, 276; van Hegelsom, 46. It is unclear whether Levie shares that view. H.S. Levie, *Means and Methods of Combat at Sea*, Syracuse Journal of International Law and Commerce 14 (1988) 727, 732; C. Pilloud and J. Pictet, in ICRC, Commentary on the Additional Protocols of 8 June 1977 to the Geneva Conventions of 12 August 1949 (Geneva, 1987) no. 2092.

101 M. Bothe, *Commentary on the 1977 Geneva Protocol I*, in: Ronzitti, 764; Rauch, 93. A more cautious approach is taken by W.A. Solf, in M. Bothe *et al.*, *New Rules for Victims of Armed Conflicts* (The Hague, 1982) 338.

102 Solf, 336; *San Remo manual*, para. 102.

103 *San Remo manual*, para. 102 lit. (b). This is also accepted by those authors who reject an application of Article 54 of Additional Protocol I to naval blockades. van Hegelsom, 46: "[...] if the sole purpose of the blockade is to starve the civilian population, the blockade should be deemed illegal on the grounds that it is not directed at a military objective [...]. Termination of the blockade might be prompted if the collateral damage would be excessive in the light of the military advantage anticipated."

104 NWP 1–14M, paragraph 7.7.3: "Similarly, neutral vessels and aircraft engaged in the carriage of qualifying relief supplies for the civilian population and the sick and wounded should be authorized to pass through the blockade cordon."
105 Bothe, 763; van Hegelsom, 46; Dinstein, 47; Y. Sandoz, in: ICRC, Commentary, no. 2805; *San Remo manual*, paras. 103 and 104.
106 *San Remo manual*, para. 103.
107 Embargoes ordered by the Security Council pursuant to Article 41 require member states to enforce the respective embargo "by all necessary means", i.e., the use of armed force. By UN Security Council Resolution 217 of 20 November 1965, the United Kingdom was entitled to enforce the oil embargo against Rhodesia. The economic sanctions imposed on Iraq by UNSC Resolution 661 of 6 August 1990 were, according to UNSC Resolution 665 of 25 August 1990, enforced by the states cooperating with Kuwait. In both cases, the Security Council did not refer to Article 42, but to Article 41 of the UN Charter.
108 Annotated Supplement to the *Commander's Handbook on the Law of Naval Operations* (Newport, 1997) para. 7.7.2.1, footnote 131.
109 For example, in UNSC Resolution 661 of 6 August 1990.
110 During the second Gulf War, Iran tried to assume a neutral status, but this was rejected by the vast majority of states and international lawyers.
111 In Principle 5.2.10 of the Helsinki Principles on the Law of Maritime Neutrality, the ILA maintains that "the Security Council, when acting by virtue of Chapter VII of the Charter, may adopt decisions deviating from this Principle (see Principle 1.2)". Principle 1.2 in part reads as follows: "Nothing in the present Principles shall be construed as implying any limitation upon the powers of the Security Council under Chapters VII and VIII of the United Nations Charter. In particular, no State may rely upon the Principles stated herein in order to evade obligations laid upon it in pursuance of a binding decision of the Security Council." In the commentary it is made clear that "the provision serves as a reminder that the principles do not preclude a modification of the rules of neutrality due to the law of the United Nations Charter ...".
112 W. Heintschel v. Heinegg, *The Current State of International Prize Law*, in H.H.G. Post (ed.), *International Economic Law and Armed Conflict* (Dordrecht, 1994) 5, 27.

Chapter 3

1 J. Meyer and J. Bromley, "The Second Hundred Years War" in D. Johnson et al. (eds), *Britain and France: ten centuries* (Folkestone: Dawson, 1980) 168–71; François Crouzet, "The Second Hundred Years War: some reflections", *French History*, vol. 10:4, 1996, 432–50.
2 François Crouzet, *L'économie britannique et le blocus continental*, 1806–1813 (Paris: Presses Universitaires de France, 1958) 2 vols. (2nd edn: 1987).
3 Bertrand de Jouvenel, *Napoléon et l'économie dirigée: le blocus continental* (Paris and Bruxelles: Éd. de la Toison d'Or, 1942), 58–9; Georges Lefebvre, "Napoléon et le blocus continental", *L'Europe Nouvelle*, a. 22, No. 1136, 18 November 1939, 1266–9.
4 Henry Blumenthal, *France and the United States. Their Diplomatic Relations, 1789–1914* (Chapel Hill, NC: University of North Carolina Press, 1970); Peter P. Hill, "Prologue to the Quasi-War: Stresses in Franco–American Relations, 1793–1796", *Journal of Modern History*, 1977, No. 49: 1, on demand supplement, D1039–D1069; Alexander De Conde, *The Quasi-War. The Politics and Diplomacy of the Undeclared War with France, 1797–1801* (New York: Scribner, 1966).

5 Roger Dufraisse, "Régime douanier, blocus, système continental: essai de mise au point", *Revue historique d'histoire économique et sociale*, 44 (1966) 518–34.

6 *Correspondance de Napoléon 1er, publiée par l'ordre de l'Empereur Napoléon III* (Paris: Imprimerie Impériale, 1859–69) 32 vols, vol. XIII, No. 11282, 554, Berlin, 21 November 1806.

7 François Crouzet, "Groupes de pression et politique de blocus; remarques sur les origines des Ordres en Council de novembre 1807", *Revue historique*, a. 86, t. CCXXVIII, 1962, 245–72.

8 Georges Lefebvre, *Napoléon* (Paris: Presses Universitaires de France, 1965) 365 [English trans.: Lefebvre, *Napoleon* (London: Routledge & Kegan Paul, 1969)].

9 The best study on French licenses is Frank Edgar Melvin, *Napoleon's Navigation System. A Study of Trade Control during the Continental Blockade* [New York, Appleton: 1919 (reprint New York: AMS Press 1970)].

10 On 19 March 1809 the United States replaced the embargo with a Non-Intercourse Act prohibiting shipping to France and Great Britain, then suspended the Non-Intercourse Act on 1 May 1810.

11 Marcel Dunan, "Napoléon et le système continental en 1810", *Revue d'Histoire diplomatique*, 1946, 71, considers the 1810 evolution as "an almost complete turnaround of his [Napoleon's] central idea of the struggle."

12 Silvia Marzagalli, "Les boulevards de la fraude." *Le négoce maritime et le Blocus continental, 1806–1813*. Bordeaux, Hambourg, Livourne (Villeneuve d'Ascq: Presses Universitaires du Septentrion, 1999) 120–37.

13 On increasing opposition to Napoleon's plan to integrate Europe, see Stuart J. Woolf, *Napoleon's integration of Europe* (London: Routledge, 1991).

14 Jean Clinquart, *L'Administration des douanes en France sous le Consulat et l'Empire* (Neuilly-sur-Seine: Association pour l'histoire de l'administration des douanes, 1979) 151.

15 Jacques Lacour-Gayet, *Histoire du commerce* (Paris: Spid, 1950–5) 6 vols., vol. IV, 332.

16 Staatsarchiv Hamburg, 112–13 Mairie Hambourg, 178.

17 Archivio di Stato, Livorno, Prefettura del Mediterraneo 33, Letter to the prefect, 31 January 1811.

18 Archives Nationales, Paris [hereafter: AN], F7 8847, dossier 4184, letter of general police superintendent in Leghorn to the Ministry of Police, 8 September 1810.

19 AN, F7 8847, dossier 4184, report of general police superintendent in Leghorn to the Ministry of Police, 28 November 1810.

20 AN, F7 6348, general police superintendent in Hamburg to the Ministry of Police, 26 February 1811.

21 AN, F7 3060, report of general police superintendent in Hamburg, no 56, 1 February 1813.

22 AN, F7 8851, dossier 7506. Anonymous undated draft titled "Notes sur quelques membres du Tribunal ordinaire de Douane de Livourne". The Police Minister wrote to the prefect and the general police superintendent in Leghorn to check these accusations. Their replies were less negative. See also AN, F7 8853, dossier 9058, report of general police superintendent, 20 September 1811.

23 Archives départementales de la Gironde, 3E 31437, 30 May 1813, marriage contract.

24 AN, BB18 362, dossier 7425C2, and F12 2011, "état des arrêts rendus par la cour prévôtale d'Agen".

25 Patrick Crowhurst, *The French War on Trade: privateering, 1793–1815* (London: Scolar, 1989).

26 Silvia Marzagalli, "Establishing Transatlantic Trade Networks in Time of War: Bordeaux and the United States, 1793–1815", *Business History Review*, Winter

(2005); S. Marzagalli, Bordeaux et les États-Unis, 1776–1815: politique et straté-gies négociantes dans la genèse d'un réseau commercial, (forthcoming, Geneva: Druz, 2006).

27 Anne Clauder, *American Commerce as Affected by the Wars of the French Revolution and Napoleon, 1793–1812* [Philadelphia, PA: University of Pennsylvania, 1932 (reprint 1972)].

28 Marzagalli, "Les boulevards", 203–7.

29 Crouzet, *L'économie britannique.*

30 "Ni foi ni patrie": Lacour-Gayet, *Histoire du commerce,* vol. IV, 325–6.

Chapter 4

1 Ian R. Christie, *Wars and Revolutions: Britain, 1760–1815* (Cambridge, MA: Harvard University Press, 1982) 320.

2 *Times* (London) 30 December 1814.

3 Gene A. Smith, *"For the Purposes of Defense": The Politics of the Jeffersonian Gunboat Program* (Newark, NJ: University of Delaware Press, 1995) 73–93; Benson J. Lossing, *Pictorial Fieldbook of the War of 1812* (New York: Harper & Brothers, 1868) 235–8.

4 Admiralty to Commanders of Newfoundland, Halifax, Jamaica, and Leeward Islands Stations, 9 May 1812, UkLPR, Adm. 2/163, British National Archives.

5 President James Madison's War Message to Congress of 1 June 1812, *National Intelligencer,* 18 June 1812.

6 See the House of Commons *Sessional Papers* and *Hansard's Parliamentary Debates* for 1810–15 for the numerous petitions and intense debates on relations with the United States.

7 Leslie Gardiner, *The British Admiralty* (Edinburgh: Blackwood, 1968) 222.

8 Wade G. Dudley, *Splintering the Wooden Wall: The British Blockade of the United States, 1812–1815* (Annapolis, MD: Naval Institute Press, 2003) 136–43.

9 *Ibid.,* 156.

10 First Secretary of the Admiralty John W. Croker to Admiral Sir John B. Warren, R.N., 9 January 1813, William S. Dudley, *et al.,* eds, *The Naval War of 1812: A Documentary History* (Washington, DC: Naval Historical Center, 1992) 2: 14–15.

11 C. S. Forester, *The Age of Fighting Sail* (Garden City, NY: Doubleday, 1956) 90.

12 Dudley, *Splintering the Wooden Wall,* 136–43.

13 General Bond Required of Vessels Confined to the Bay, RG 36, National Archives; Embargo Bonds, Savannah, Georgia, 1812–1815, RG 36, NA; Embargo Bonds for New York, 1814, RG 36, NA; Embargo Bonds, Charleston, South Carolina, 1812–1815, RG 36, NA.

14 Vice-Admiral Sir Alexander Cochrane to Croker, 8 March 1814, UkLPR, Adm. 1/505, 633, British National Archives.

15 James A. Pack, *The Man Who Burned the White House: Admiral Sir George Cockburn, 1772–1853* (Annapolis, MD: Naval Institute Press, 1987) 166–7.

16 Dudley, *Splintering the Wooden Wall,* 136.

17 *Ibid.,* 127–8.

18 *Ibid.,* 139, 141.

Chapter 5

1 Sir Charles K. Webster, *The Foreign Policy of Castlereagh: 1812–1815* (London: G. Bell, 1931) 147, 185–94, 491.

2 Hugh G. Soulsby, *The Right of Search and the Slave Trade in Anglo-American Relations, 1814–1862* (Baltimore, MD: The Johns Hopkins Press, 1933).

3 Graham (First Lord of the Admiralty) – Clarendon (Foreign Secretary) 3.3.1854: Foreign Office (henceforth FO) 87/487, British National Archives.

4 Vernon J. Puryear, *International Economics and Diplomacy in the Near East: A Study of British Commercial Diplomacy in the Levant 1834–1853* (Stanford, CA: Stanford University Press, 1935) 206, 213–14, 222, 227.

5 Hugh Rose – Earl Clarendon 25.3.1853: FO 78/930 f.365–9.

6 Andrew D. Lambert, " 'Good While It Lasts'; Great Britain and the Crimean War Coalition", in Dennis Showalter, ed., *Future War: Coalition Operations in Global Strategy* (Chicago: Imprint Publications, 2002) 29–48.

7 Olive Anderson, *A Liberal State at War: English Politics and Economics During the Crimean War* (London: St. Martin's Press, 1967) 248–74.

8 Napier – Graham 20.3.1854: Napier MSS TNA PRO 30/16/12/ f 28.

9 Andrew D. Lambert, *The Crimean War: British Grand Strategy against Russia, 1853–1856* (Manchester: Manchester University Press, 1990) 161–2.

10 Admiralty – Napier 30.3.1854: David Bonner-Smith, ed., *The Russian War, 1854 Baltic* (London: Navy Records Society, 1943) 46; Napier – Graham 4.4.1854: PRO 30/16/12 f.71.

11 Napier – Admiralty 11 rec. 17.4.1854 no. 46: Admiralty (henceforth ADM) 1/5624. British National Archives.

12 Napier – Graham 27.4.1854; TNA PRO 30/16/12 f.175.

13 Philip H. Colomb, *Memoirs of Sir Astley Cooper Key* (London: Methuen, 1898), Letter of 1.1.1854, 229.

14 Napier – Admiralty 23, 30.5.1854 no. 96, 107: *NRS 1854 Baltic*, 55.

15 Admiralty – Napier 5.4.1854: 4, 29.5.1854: 12, 13, 26.5.1854 no. 85, 348, 354, 385: *NRS 1854 Baltic*, 47, 60 80. The correspondence for May is no longer extant. Napier – Admiralty 11.4.1854: 28, 30.5.1854 no. 46, 101, 102: ADM 1/5624. Graham – Napier 30.5.1854: Napier MSS Add. 40,024 f218 British Library. Memo. by J.D. Harding QC 11.8.1854: ADM 1/5624. Harding – Napier 20.5.1854: Add. 40,024 f220.

16 Napier – Graham 20.6.1854: *NRS 1854 Baltic*, 7–8.

17 Colomb, 243–9.

18 Captain Watson – Rear-Admiral Chads 8.12.1854: *NRS 1854 Baltic*, 185–6 on the end of the campaign.

19 Admiralty – Dundas 11.4.1855: Wood Papers BL Add. 49,533 f.9–13.

20 Dundas – Admiralty 28.5. and 4.6.1855: *NRS Baltic 1855*, 50 and 59–61.

21 Colomb, 256.

22 Henry Sulivan, *Life and Letters of Admiral Sir B.J. Sulivan* (London: John Murray, 1896), 314, 319, 429.

23 Dundas – Warden 9.6.1855: *NRS Baltic 1855*, 62–4. Declaration by the British and French Commanders in Chief. 22.6.1855: *NRS Baltic 1855*, 71–2.

24 Dundas – Admiralty 16.7.1855: *NRS Baltic 1855*, 127–8.

25 Baynes – Dundas 27.10.1855: Otter – Baynes 23.10.1855 and Dunlop – Baynes 3.11.1855: *NRS Baltic 1855*, 343–51,

26 Dundas – Baynes 27.12.1855: Baynes Papers, National Maritime Museum BAY/2.

27 Dundas – Admiralty 1.5.1854: Alfred C. Dewar, ed., *The Russian War: 1855 Black Sea* (London: Navy Records Society, 1945) 257.

28 *NRS 1854 Black Sea*, 275–84, for the exchange between Dundas, the Admiralty, the Ambassador at Istanbul, and the Queen's Advocate.

29 Dundas – Admiralty 8.10.1854: *NRS 1854 Black Sea*, 331.

30 Admiralty – Dundas 2.12.1854: *NRS 1854 Black Sea*, 388–97.

31 *NRS 1854 Black Sea*, 217.

32 Anderson, 269–70.

33 Hugh Seton-Watson, *The Russian Empire, 1801–1917* (Oxford: Clarendon Press, 1967) 246–9. John S. Curtiss, *Russia's Crimean War* (Durham, NC: Duke

University Press, 1979) 484. Winfried Baumgart, *The Peace of Paris, 1856* (Santa Barbara, CA: ABC-Clio, 1981) 68–80.

34 Werner E. Mosse, *The Rise and Fall of the Crimean System, 1855–1871* (London: Macmillan, 1963) 28–9.

35 William Fuller, *Strategy and Power in Russia: 1600–1917* (New York: Free Press, 1992) 269, 280–1.

36 *Ibid.*, 300; Seton-Watson, 408.

37 John Clapham, *The Bank of England: A History II 1797–1914* (Cambridge: Cambridge University Press, 1945) 222–3.

38 Palmerston – Wood 31.3.1856: A4/192 Hickleton MS Borthwick Institute, York.

39 Sir Francis T. Piggott, *The Declaration of Paris, 1856* (London: University of London Press, 1919); Anderson, 248–74.

40 Palmerston – Clarendon 8.5.1856: British Library Add. MSS 48,680 f73.

41 Palmerston – Clarendon 12.4.1856: British Library Add. MSS 48,680 f80.

42 Palmerston – Clarendon 5.4.1856: British Library Add. MSS 48,680 f69.

43 Orders in Council 12 and 20.4.1856: ADM 1/5680; Clarendon – Palmerston 3 and 6.4.1856: Broadlands MSS GC/CL f853–6 Southampton University Library; Palmerston – Clarendon 5, 8, 10 and 12 Apr. 1856: Add. 48,580 f67–80; Wood – Clarendon 7.4.1856: Add. 49,565 f90–1.

44 Adam Roberts and Richard Guelff, eds, *Documents on the Laws of War* (Oxford: Oxford University Press, 2000, 3rd edn) 47–51.

45 Foreign Office – Admiralty 16.4.1856: ADM 1/5675.

46 Admiral Herbert Richmond, *Statesmen and Seapower* (Oxford: The Clarendon Press, 1946) 266; Bernard Semmel, *Liberalism and Naval Strategy* (Boston, MA: Allen & Unwin, 1986) 53–9; Anderson, 272–3.

47 Richmond, 266–7. Semmel citing Lord Derby, 58.

48 Cabinet memoranda on the Declaration were deposited in the Foreign Office in 1876 by Palmerston's biographer, and printed for the Cabinet in 1885 when war with Russia seemed imminent: FO 87/487.

49 "The United States and International Maritime Law", FO Confidential Print 22.6.1861: FO/87/487.

Chapter 6

* Reprinted and revised from the author's article "The Union Navy's Blockade Reconsidered", *Naval War College Review*, vol. 51, no. 4, Autumn 1998: 105–27.

1 Stephen R. Wise, *Lifeline of the Confederacy: Blockade Running during the Civil War* (Columbia, SC: University of South Carolina Press, 1988) 226.

2 Raimondo Luraghi, *The Rise and Fall of the Plantation South* (New York: New Viewpoints, 1978) 137; Richard E. Beringer *et al.*, *Why the South Lost the Civil War* (Athens, GA: University of Georgia Press, 1986) 139, 201; Frank L. Owsley, *King Cotton Diplomacy: Foreign Relations of the Confederate States of America* (Chicago, IL: University of Chicago Press, 1931) 290; Wise, 26–7; and William N. Still, Jr., "A Naval Sieve: The Union Blockade in the Civil War", *Naval War College Review*, May–June 1983, 44.

3 Edwin B. Coddington, "The Civil War Blockade Reconsidered", in *Essays in History and International Relations in Honor of George Hubbard Blakeslee*, D.L. Lee and G.E. McReynolds (eds) (Worcester, Mass.: n.p., 1949), 299, 300, 304; Bern Anderson, *By Sea and by River: The Naval History of the Civil War* (New York: Alfred Knopf, 1962) 232, 303; Carlton Savage (ed.), *Policy of the United States towards Maritime Commerce in War* (Washington, D.C.: U.S. State Dept, Govt. Print. Off. [hereafter GPO], 1934), 440–1; Stanley Lebergott, "Through the Blockade: The Profitability and Extent of Cotton Smuggling, 1861–1865",

Journal of Economic History, December 1981, 896; and Arthur Fremantle, *Three Months in the Southern States* (New York: John Bradburn, 1864) 10.

4 U.S. Treasury Dept, *Report of the Secretary of the Treasury: Commerce and Navigation, for the Year ending June 30, 1860*, 36th Cong., 2nd Sess., S. Ex. Doc. 8 (Washington, D.C.: GPO, 1861) 350–1.

5 U.S. Treasury Dept, 408–517.

6 U.S. Bureau of the Census, *Preliminary Report on the Eighth Census* (Washington; D.C.: GPO, 1862) 107.

7 War Dept., Official Records of the War of Rebellion [hereafter "OR"] (Washington, D.C.: GPO, 1880–1900), ser. IV, vol. 2, 512–13; U.S. Treasury Dept, 461; Angus J. Johnston II, "Virginia Railroads in April, 1861", *Journal of Southern History*, August 1957, 317; and Robert C. Black III, *The Railroads of the Confederacy* (Chapel Hill, NC: University of North Carolina Press, 1952) 23.

8 Charles B. Dew, *Ironmaker to the Confederacy: Joseph R. Anderson and the Tredegar Iron Works* (New Haven, CT: Yale University Press, 1966) 50, 277.

9 U.S. Navy Dept, *Official Records of the War of Rebellion: Navy* [hereafter *ORN*] (Washington, D.C.: GPO, 1894–1922), ser. II, vol. 2, 72–3.

10 David G. Surdam, "The Antebellum Texas Cattle Trade across the Gulf of Mexico", *Southwestern Historical Quarterly*, April 1997, 477–92; and *Richmond (Virginia) Whig*, 7 January 1861.

11 Walter L. Fleming, *Civil War and Reconstruction in Alabama* (New York: Peter Smith, [1905] 1949) 187, 286.

12 David G. Surdam, "Northern Naval Superiority and the Economics of the American Civil War", PhD dissertation, Univ. of Chicago, 1994, 14–41; and Claudia Goldin and Frank Lewis, "The Economic Cost of the American Civil War", *Journal of Economic History*, June 1975, 299–326.

13 *DeBow's Review*, 1861, vol. 30, 142–3.

14 *OR*, ser. IV, vol. 3, 588; see 529 in the same volume for the contract.

15 *OR*, ser. IV, vol. 1, 220, 343, and vol. 2, 227; Allan Nevins, *War for the Union* (New York: Charles Scribner's Sons, 1959) vol. 1, 351. For Gorgas's lament, see *OR*, ser. IV, vol. 2, 227.

16 Alfred Chandler, "DuPont, Dahlgren, and the Civil War Nitre Shortage", *Military Analysis of the Civil War: An Anthology by the Editors of Military Affairs*, American Military Institute (Millwood, N.Y.: KTO Press, 1977) 199–200; *OR*, ser. IV, vol. 2, 299, 957, and vol. 3, 987; Ralph Donnelly, "Scientists of the Confederate Nitre and Mining Bureau", *Civil War History*, December 1956, 69–92.

17 Frank Vandiver, *Confederate Blockade Running through Bermuda, 1861–1865* (Austin, TX: University of Texas Press, 1947) pt. II.

18 *OR*, ser. IV, vol. 2, 151.

19 *OR*, ser. IV, vol. 1, 1094; Dennis Showalter, *Railroads and Rifles: Soldiers, Technology and the Reunification of Germany* (Hamden, CT: Archon Books, 1975) 45.

20 *OR*, ser. IV, vol. 1, 844, 868; vol. 2, 381, 388–9, 394–5, 409, 842, 852; vol. 3, 9–10, 442, 478, 508, 514.

21 Archer Jones, *Civil War Command and Strategy* (New York: Free Press, 1992) 129. Henry Sharpe, a former Union commissary officer, wrote that an "ordinary Ohio River steamer" could carry 500 tons of supplies, which would supply 40,000 men and 18,000 animals for two days. Henry G. Sharpe, "The Art of Supplying Armies in the Field as Exemplified during the Civil War", *Notes on the Supply of an Army*, O. Espanet (ed.) (Kansas City, MO: Hudson-Kimberly, 1899) 189.

22 *OR*, ser. IV, vol. 2, 485–6.

23 *ORN*, ser. II, vol. 1, 461, 534–5, 605–6. Dew describes the Tredegar Iron Works's difficulties in getting pig iron from New Orleans in late 1861: the railroads

needed months to get the material to Richmond, and the freight costs were greater than the original cost of the pig iron; in addition, 120 tons were lost in transit (Dew, 103).

24 *ORN*, ser. II, vol. 2, 184. Tom Wells believes that Bulloch's idea was feasible and astute, but Raimondo Luraghi disagrees. Tom H. Wells, *The Confederate Navy: A Study in Organization* (Tuscaloosa, AL: University of Alabama Press, 1971) 136; and Raimondo Luraghi, *A History of the Confederate Navy* (Annapolis, MD: Naval Institute Press, 1996) 203.

Chapter 7

* The thoughts and opinions expressed in this chapter are those of the author and are not necessarily those of the U.S. government, the U.S. Navy Department, or the Naval War College.

1 John L. Rawlinson, *China's Struggle for Naval Development, 1839–1895* (Cambridge, MA: Harvard University Press, 1967) 171–3, 187–8.

2 David C Evans and Mark R. Peattie, *Kaigun: Strategy, Tactics, and Technology in the Imperial Japanese Navy, 1897–1941* (Annapolis, MD: Naval Institute Press, 1997) 40.

3 Hilary A. Herbert, "Military Lessons in the Chino-Japanese War", *The North American Review* 160, No. 463 (June 1895), 689.

4 *Japan Weekly Mail* (Yokohama), 3 November 1894, 509. Hereafter *JWM*.

5 *JWM*, 24 November 1894, 584.

6 *North-China Herald* (Shanghai), 25 January 1895, 110. Hereafter *NCH*.

7 *NCH*, 15 February 1895, 214.

8 Sung-ping Kuo, "Chinese Reaction to Foreign Encroachment", PhD Dissertation, Columbia University, 1953, 54.

9 Chang Ch'i-yun, *Zhongguo Lishi Ditu* (Historical Atlas of China), vol. 2 (Taipei: Zhongguo wenhua daxue chubanshe, 1984) 117; Warrington Eastlake and Toshiaki Yamada, *Heroic Japan: A History of the War between China and Japan*, 1897 Reprint (Washington, DC: University Publications of America, 1979), 298–9.

10 Sun Kefu and Guan Jie (eds), *Zhongri jiawu luzhanshi* (Harbin: Heilongjiang renmin chubanshe, 1984), 293–294; General Staff Headquarters, *Meiji nijūchihachinen nisshinsensō* (Tokyo: Tokyo insatsu kabushiki kaisha, 1907) 198–218.

11 G. A. Ballard, *The Influence of the Sea on the Political History of Japan* (New York, NY: E.P. Dutton, 1921) 161.

12 *NCH*, 1 February 1895, 156; *NCH*, 1 March 1895, 321; "The Wei-hai-wei Campaign", N.W.H. Du Boulay, *The Chino-Japanese War, 1894–95* (London: typescript, ca. 1903), 2–4.

13 *JWM*, 9 February 1895, 157; *JWM*, 23 February 1895, 228–31; *NCH*, 15 February 1895, 242; *NCH*, 1 March 1895, 321; William Ferdinand Tyler, *Pulling Strings in China* (London: Constable, 1929) 71; Jukichi Inouye, *The Fall of Weihaiwei* (Yokohama: Kelly & Walsh, 1895).

14 *JWM*, 2 March 1895, 253; *JWM* 23 March 1895, 335–6; Rawlinson, 189.

15 Rawlinson, 189

16 *NCH*, 15 February 1895, 215; *Asahi Shinbun* (Tokyo), 2 February 1895, 1, 6 February 1895, supplement, 1, and 10 February 1895, 1; *Kokumin Shinbun* (Tokyo), 2 March 1895, 2.

17 *JWM*, 23 February 1895, 225; Vladimir [Zenone Volpicelli], *The China–Japan War* (Kansas City, MO: Franklin Hudson, 1905) 251–4.

18 Rawlinson, 174–5; Tyler, 47, 89.

19 Samuel C. Chu, "The Sino-Japanese War of 1894", *Jindaishi yanjiusuo jikan* 14 (June 1985), 359; "Ding Ruchang", in Zhongguo lishi dacidian bianzuan

weiyuanhui, comp., *Zhongguo lishi dacidian* vol. 1 (Shanghai: Shanghai cishu chubanshe, 2000) 29.

20 Tyler, 79.

21 Rawlinson, 190; Tyler, 78.

22 *JWM*, 16 March 1895, 313–14; *Pall Mall Gazette* (London), 19 February 1895, 7. Hereafter *PMG*.

23 *JWM*, 9 March 1895, 285; George Alexander Lensen, *Balance of Intrigue*, vol. 1, (Tallahassee, FL: University Presses of Florida, 1982) 393 n.49; Hosea Ballou Morse, *The International Relations of the Chinese Empire*, vol. 3 (Shanghai: Kelly & Walsh, 1918) 40; Donald Keene, "The Sino-Japanese War of 1894–95 and Its Cultural Effects in Japan", *Tradition and Modernization in Japanese Culture*, Donald H. Shively (ed.) (Princeton, NJ: Princeton University Press, 1971) 140; Noriko Kamachi, *Reform in China: Huang Tsun-hsien and the Japanese Model* (Cambridge, MA: Harvard University Press, 1981) 193; Marius B. Jansen, *Japan and China: From War to Peace, 1894–1972* (Chicago, IL: Rand McNally, 1975) 10; *JWM*, 9 November 1895, 490.

24 Yamamoto Tsunetomo, *Hagakure: The Book of the Samurai*, William Scott Wilson (trans.) (Tokyo: Kodansha International, 1979) 17.

25 Taira Shigesuke, *The Code of the Samurai*, Thomas Cleary (trans.) (Boston, MA: Tuttle Publishing, 1999) 22. See also Yamamoto, 18–23, 72–3.

26 *Asahi Shinbun* (Tokyo), 19 February 1895, 2 and 20 February 1895, 1.

27 See http://www.chinaculture.org/gb/en_travel/2003–09/24/content_35444.htm (current 2.8.2005).

28 *JWM*, 16 March 1895, 313–14; *PMG*, 19 February 1895, 7.

29 *PMG*, 18 February 1895, 7.

30 *New York Times*, 17 February 1895, 5; hereafter *NYT*.

31 Samuel C. Chu, "China's Attitudes toward Japan at the Time of the Sino-Japanese War", in *The Chinese and the Japanese*, Akira Iriye (ed.) (Princeton, NJ: Princeton University Press, 1980) 88–9.

32 *NCH*, 1 February 1895, 157; *PMG*, 11 March 1895, 7.

33 *NCH*, 8 February 1895, 171.

34 *NCH*, 25 January 1895, 110.

35 Rawlinson, 189–90.

36 Ballard, 168; *PMG*, 27 February 1895, 7.

37 Guy Boulais, *Manuel du Code Chinois* (Shanghai: Imprimerie de la mission Catholique, 1924) 428.

38 U.S. Adjutant-General's Office, Military Information Division, *Notes on the War between China and Japan* (Washington, D.C.: Government Printing Office, 1896) 22.

39 *NCH*, 10 May 1895, 683.

40 *NCH*, 21 September 1894, 501.

41 *PMG*, 1 December 1894, 4th edn, 7.

42 *NCH*, 1 March 1895, 321.

43 *Le Temps* (Paris), 5 March 1895.

44 Benjamin Franklin Cooling, *Gray Steel and Blue Water Navy: The Formative Years of America's Military-Industrial Complex 1881–1917* (Hamden, CT: Archon Books, 1979) 136.

45 Quoting *Le Temps*, *Journal de St-Pétersbourg*, no. 345, 6 January 1895, 2.

46 *Le Siècle* (Paris), 3 February 1895, 1. M. Gareau was actually jumping the gun because Weihaiwei would not fall for another week and a half.

47 *Journal de St-Pétersbourg*, no. 345, 6 January 1895, 2.

48 *NYT*, 11 February 1895, 1

49 Jeffrey M. Dorwart, *The Pigtail War* (Amherst, MA: University of Massachusetts Press, 1975) 119.

50 *JWM*, 23 March 1895, 344; *National Zeitung* (Berlin), morning edition, 10 February 1895, 1.

Chapter 8

* The thoughts and opinions expressed in this chapter are those of the author and are not necessarily those of the U.S. government, the U.S. Navy Department, or the Naval Historical Center.
1 David Trask, *The War with Spain in 1898* (New York: Macmillan Publishing Co., Inc., 1981) 108.
2 U.S. Navy Department, *Appendix to the Report of the Chief of the Bureau of Navigation, 1898* (Washington, D.C.: Government Printing Office, 1898) 171.
3 *Navy Register, 1 January 1898*, 131–3.
4 Trask, 82, 86. John D. Alden, *The American Steel Navy* (Annapolis, MD: Naval Institute Press, 1972) 123–4, 382–3.
5 Jeffery Michael Dorwart, "A Mongrel Fleet: America Buys a Navy to Fight Spain, 1898", *Warship International*, No. 2, 1980, 129–52.
6 Calculated by taking a vessel's coal capacity and dividing it by average consumption rates found in U.S. Navy Dept, Bureau of Equipment, *Reports of the Efficiency of Various Coals, 1896 to 1898* (Washington, D.C.: Government Printing Office, 1906) 15–79.
7 Alden, *American Steel Navy*, 224; U.S. Navy Dept, Office of Naval Intelligence, *Notes on Coaling War Ships* (Washington, D.C.: Government Printing Office, 1899) 7–27.
8 For a detailed examination of U.S. ship movements prior to hostilities with Spain see French Ensor Chadwick, *The Relations of the United States and Spain, The Spanish–American War*, 2 vols (New York: Russell & Russell, 1968), 1: 3–2, 401, and *Appendix to the Report of the Chief of the Bureau of Navigation*, 21–9, 37–43.
9 Chadwick, 1: 12–16; *Appendix to the Report of the Chief of the Bureau of Navigation*, 47–56.
10 A.B. Feuer, *The Spanish–American War at Sea; Naval Action in the Atlantic* (Westport, CT: Praeger, 1995) 65–73.
11 *Appendix to the Report of the Chief of the Bureau of Navigation*, 186–99.
12 Chadwick, 1: 151.
13 Trask, 114–19; Chadwick, 214–49.
14 *Ibid.*, 115–18.
15 *Ibid.*, 121–2; Chadwick, 265–8; David F. Trask, "American Intelligence During the Spanish–American War", in James C. Bradford (ed.), *Crucible of Empire; The Spanish–American War and Its Aftermath* (Annapolis, MD: Naval Institute Press, 1993), 33.
16 Chadwick, 268–73, 276, 285.
17 *Ibid.*, 292–3; H.W. Wilson, *The Downfall of Spain, Naval History of the Spanish–American War* (London: Sampson Low, Marston and Company, 1900) 229–30; *Notes on Coaling War Ships*, 27.
18 Chadwick, 302–7, 321–27.
19 Jack Shulimson, "Marines in the Spanish-American War", Bradford, 141–2.
20 Wilson, 299.
21 *Appendix to the Report of the Chief of the Bureau of Navigation*, 676, 683–91.
22 Pascual Cervera y Topete, *The Spanish American War: A Collection of Documents Relative to the Squadron Operations in the West Indies* (Washington, D.C.: Government Printing Office, 1899).
23 José Müller y Tejeiro, *Battles and Capitulation of Santiago de Cuba* (Washington, D.C.: Government Printing Office, 1898).
24 Trask, 261–6.

25 *Appendix to the Report of the Chief of the Bureau of Navigation*, 217.
26 *Ibid.*, 256–8.
27 *Ibid.*, 296.

Chapter 9

1 Julian S. Corbett and Henry Newbolt, *History of the Great War: Naval Operations*. 5 vols in 9 (London: Longmans, Green, 1920–31) vol. I, 13–14; James Goldrick, *The King's Ships Were at Sea: The War in the North Sea August 1914–February 1915* (Annapolis, MD: Naval Institute Press, 1984) 25–6, 29–30.
2 Auguste Thomazi, *La Guerre navale dans la zone des Armées du Nord* (Paris: Payot, 1925) 30–1, 39–40, 231–3.
3 Corbett and Newbolt, vol. I, 166–7. Admiral De Chair's own memoirs are informative, see Rear-Admiral Sir Dudley De Chair, *The Sea Is Strong* (London: Harrap, 1961).
4 Rear-Admiral de Chair to Admiralty, 6 April 1915, and Minute by Captain Webb, Director of Trade Division, 12 April 1915, in John D. Grainger (ed.), *The Maritime Blockade of Germany in the Great War: The Northern Patrol, 1914–1918* (Aldershot: Ashgate Publishing for the Navy Records Society, 2003) documents 64 and 65, 143–6.
5 Vice Admiral Tupper to C.-in-C. Home Fleets, 22 September 1916, *ibid.*, document 265, 506. Tupper also wrote his memoirs, see Admiral Sir Reginald Tupper, *Reminiscences* (London: Jarrolds, 1929).
6 Avner Offer, *The First World War: An Agrarian Interpretation*, paperback [corrected] edition (Oxford: Clarendon Press, 1991) 282–4; Nicholas A. Lambert, *Sir John Fisher's Naval Revolution* (Columbia, SC: University of South Carolina Press, 1999) 292–3; Ruddock F. Mackay, *Fisher of Kilverstone* (Oxford: Clarendon Press, 1973) 445–51.
7 A.C. Bell, *A History of the Blockade of Germany and the countries associated with her in the Great War, Austria-Hungary, Bulgaria and Turkey, 1914–1918* (London: Historical Section, Committee of Imperial Defence, 1937; released [Her Majesty's Stationery Office], 1961) 62–4, 608; and C. Ernest Fayle, *History of the Great War: Seaborne Trade*, 3 vols (London: John Murray, 1920–24) vol. III, 45.
8 Grainger, 2–3; 178; De Chair to Admiralty, 31 May 1915, *ibid.*, document 71, 151–63.
9 Louis Guichard, *Histoire du Blocus Navale (1914–1918)* (Paris: Payot, 1929) 29–30.
10 Bell, 362, 366–7.
11 *Ibid.*, 150, 249, 362; Auguste Thomazi, *La Guerre navale dans la Méditerranée* (Paris: Payot, 1929) 24–8.
12 *Ibid.*, 400; see Paul G. Halpern, *The Naval War in the Mediterranean, 1914–1918* (Annapolis, MD: Naval Institute Press, 1987), on submarine bases 127, 231. On Russian operations against Turkey 114, 115, 162–3, 189.
13 *Ibid.*, 35.
14 John W. Coogan, *The End of Neutrality: The United States, Britain and Maritime Rights, 1899–1915* (Ithaca, NY: Cornell University Press, 1981), 155–6. On the Enemy Exports Committe see *ibid.* 249–300
15 Bell, 40–1, 58–9, 233–4, 712–15; on American objections and the lack of precedence in international law, see Coogan, 194–7, 210–14.
16 On the Restriction of Enemy Supplies Committee and the War Trade Advisory Committee, see Bell, 43, 182, 454. Arthur J. Mander, *From the Dreadnaught to Scapa Flow: The Royal Navy in the Fisher era, 1904–1919*, 5 vols. (London: Oxford University Press, 1961–70), vol II. 372–5
17 *Ibid.*, 249.
18 Guichard, 33–4, 50–3.

19 *Ibid.*, 54–7, 85–6. As the title indicated, the minister's duties included the "invaded regions", that is, those portions of France under German occupation. Within the ministry, a *Direction du blocus* coordinated matters dealing with economic warfare. The internal dynamics of the French blockade services are analysed in Marjorie Millbank Farrar, *Conflict and Compromise: The Strategy, Politics and Diplomacy of the French Blockade, 1914–1918* (The Hague: Martinus Nijhoff, 1974) chapter iii, 39–56.

20 For the Baltic operations, see Paul G. Halpern, *A Naval History of World War I* (Annapolis, MD: Naval Institute Press, 1994) chapter vii.

21 B.J.C. McKercher and Keith E. Neilson, " 'The Triumph of Unarmed Forces': Sweden and the Allied Blockade of Germany, 1914–1917", *Journal of Strategic Studies*, vol. 7, no. 2 (1984), 199; Consett published a bitter indictment of British policy in Scandinavia after the war, see: M.W.W.P. Consett, *The Triumph of Unarmed Forces (1914–1918)*. Revised edn (London: Williams and Norgate, 1928).

22 Bell, 656–6.

23 Hubert P. van Tuyll van Serooskerken, *The Netherlands and World War I: Espionage, Diplomacy and Survival* (Leiden: Brill, 2001), 138–43.

24 Guichard, 158–63.

25 Bell, 456–9, 538–9; Fayle, vol. II, 304.

26 Fayle, vol. II, 345–9.

27 Holger Herwig, "The Failure of German Sea Power, 1914–1945: Mahan, Tirpitz and Raeder Reconsidered", *International History Review*, vol. X, no. 1 (February 1988), 81; German naval plans are analysed in detail in Ivo Nikolai Lambi, *The Navy and German Power Politics, 1862–1914* (Boston, MA: Allen & Unwin, 1984) 400–5, 422–3.

28 Tobias R. Philbin, *Admiral von Hipper: The Inconvenient Hero* (Amsterdam: B.R. Grüner, 1982), 92–5. On using submarines against blockading ships, see Grainger, 20–1. Rumors in 1916 that raiders might attempt to break out led Jellicoe to prepare to intercept them, notably Operations "XX", "YY" and "ZZ", see Corbett and Newbolt, vol. IV, 176–8, 386–7; A. Cecil Hampshire, *The Blockaders* (London: William Kimber, 1980) 74–5.

29 Archibald Hurd, *History of the Great War: The Merchant Navy*, 3 vols (London: John Murray, 1921–29),vol. I, 283–4.

30 Offer, 356–67; For the Admiralstab memorandum, see Dirk Steffen, "The Holtzendorff Memorandum of 22 December 1916 and Germany's Declaration of Unrestricted U-boat Warfare", *Journal of Military History*, vol. 68, no. 1 (January 2004), 215–24.

31 Guichard, 86–7.

32 Commander-in-Chief Home Fleets to Admiralty, 3 August 1915, in Grainger, document no. 121, 242.

33 Combined figures culled from Admiralty to Commander-in-Chief Home Fleets, 30 August 1916, *ibid.*, document no. 264, 502, and Admiralty to Commander-in-Chief Home Fleets, January 1917, *ibid.*, document no. 311, 606–7.

34 Consett, xv–xvi.

35 W. Grahame Greene [Permanent Secretary of the Admiralty] to Commander-in-Chief Home Fleets, 29 June 1916, in Grainger, document no. 246, 471–2.

36 Hew Strachan, *The First World War, volume II: To Arms* (Oxford: Oxford University Press, 2001), 1027, 1039, 1048–9; Gerd Hardarch, *The First World War, 1914–18*, (Harmondsworth: Penguin Books, 1987), 17–19, 62–3, 117–119; Holger H. Herwig, *The First World War: Germany and Austria-Hungary, 1914–1918* (London: Arnold, 1997) 288–9.

37 Fregattenkapitän Gábor von Döbrentei, "Die Donauhandelsflotte im Krieg", in Vizeadmiral Olav Wulff, *Die österreichisch-ungarische Donauflottille im Weltkrieg, 1914–1918* (Vienna and Leipzig: Wilhelm Braumüller, 1934) 204–7.

38 C. Paul Vincent, *The Politics of Hunger: The Allied Blockade of Germany, 1915–1919* (Athens, OH: Ohio University Press, 1985) 44–6, 49–50; Herwig, *The First World War*, 288–96, 386.
39 Offer, 362.
40 Gerald D. Feldman, *Army, Industry and Labor in Germany, 1914–1918* (Princeton, NJ: Princeton University Press, 1966) 459–66, 494–5. The question of food supplies in Austria-Hungary is covered in József Galántai, *Hungary in the First World War* (Budapest: Akadémiai Kiadó, 1989) 194–5, 292–4.

Chapter 10

* The views expressed in this chapter are the personal views of the author and do not represent those of the Japanese Defense Agency or the Japanese National Defense Academy.
1 "Sina no kokubou-keizai seisaku (Chinese Policy on Defense and Economy)," Chusi kensetu siryo seibi jimusyo (Mid-China compile material office) translated, *Journal of Chinese Wartime Economy*, Shanghai, (Spring, 1937), Library of Toyo Bunko, 58–60. This is an analysis of Chinese defenses and the economy on the eve of the second Sino-Japanese War. Its author, a professor at the Chinese Central School of Politics, claimed that in case of a war against Japan, China should employ a strategy of protracted warfare.
2 The War History Office of the National Institute for Defense Studies (hereafter abbreviated to WHO-NIDS) (ed.), *Shina jihen Rikugun Sakusen 1*, (War History Series, Army Campaigns in the Sino-Japanese Incident, vol. 1), Asagumo Shinbun-sha, 1975, 100–4.
3 Imperial Navy High Command (ed.), "Daitoa senso kaigun sensi kan 1", (Naval war history of the Great East Asian War, vol. 1), Library of NIDS, 298–308.
4 *Ibid.*, italics inserted by the author, as with later references.
5 WHO-NIDS (ed.), *Chugoku homen Kaigun Sakusen 1*, (Imperial Naval Operations around China, vol. 1), Asagumo Shinbun sya, 1974, 275–6.
6 Prince Takamatsunomiya Nobuhito, *Takamatsunomiya nikki*, (The Diary of Prince Takamatsunomiya), (Tokyo, Chuou kouron sha, 1995) 530, 533.
7 WHO-NIDS (ed.), *Chugoku homen Kaigun Sakusen 1*, (Imperial Naval Operations around China, vol. 1), 318.
8 Kaigun sho kaigun gunji fukyubu, (The Bureau of Naval Promotion of the Department of Navy) (ed.), *Shina senpaku koutsu shadan*, (The interruption of communications by Chinese ships), Library of NIDS, 1938, 5.
9 *Ibid.*
10 Officially the order of the third campaign of pacific blockade was issued on 20 November 1937.
11 Kaigun sho kaigun gunji fukyubu, (The Bureau of Naval Promotion of the Department of Navy) (ed.), *Shina senpaku koutsu shadan*, (The interruption of communications by Chinese ships), Library of NIDS, 1938, 26–7.
12 Daigo kantai shireibu, (Command of the Fifth Fleet), "Syowa jusan-nen nansi houmen ni okeru senpaku rinken yokuryu kiroku", (Records of the inspections and capture of ships in southern China, 1938), Library of NIDS.
13 Kaigun sho kaigun gunji fukyubu, (The Bureau of Naval Promotion of the Department of Navy) (ed.), *Shina senpaku koutsu shadan*, (The interruption of communications by Chinese ships), Library of NIDS, 1938, 29–34.
14 *Ibid.*, 44.
15 Kaigun sho kaigun gunji fukyubu, (The Bureau of Naval Promotion of the Department of Navy) (ed.), *Shina jihen ni okeru Teikoku kaigun no koudo–Hottan yori Nankin koryaku made*, (The Imperial Naval Actions in the Sino-Japanese

Incident-From the outbreak to the capture of Nanjing), January 1938, Library of NIDS, 48–9.

16 *Ibid.*, 54.

17 The Manchurian Railway Information and Research Department, *Sina Kousenryoku chousa hokoku*, (Research Report on the China War Strength: hereafter abbreviated to *RR-CWS*), (Tokyo,1940), San ichi Shobo. Reprinted edition, 1970, 313–14.

18 *Ibid.*, 336.

19 According to the declaration, Japan, Manchukuo, and China would establish respectful, mutual, and indispensable relationships in the fields of politics and economies and share the task with China for constructing a new order of East Asia.

20 Memorandum by the Counselor of Embassy in Japan (Dooman), 19 November 1938, in *Foreign Relations of the United States, Japan, 1931–1941*, 801~5.

21 WHO-NIDS (ed.), *Chugoku homen Kaigun Sakusen 2*, (Imperial Naval Operations around China vol. 2), 90–2.

22 Southward Advance of Japanese Expansionist Movement: Hainan and the Spratly Islands, The Ambassador in Japan (Grew) to the Secretary of State, 10 February 1939, in *Foreign Relations of the United States, Diplomatic Papers 1939, vol.1, The Far East*, 103–4.

23 Arthur N. Young, *CHINA and the Helping Hand 1937–1945*, (Cambridge, Mass., Harvard University Press, 1963), 440.

24 "Naval Strategy on Chinese Theater 2", 100, and "World War II and French Indochina" by Kyoichi Tachikawa, (Keiryusha, 2000). "Japan presumed the amount of supplies from French Indochina was almost the half of the total amount of supplies to Chiang Kai-shek; monthly supplies to Chiang Kai-shek from the French Indochina route in November 1939 were about 11,000 tons (besides about 8,000 metric ton gasoline): supplies in June 1940, just before the perfection of the blockade on French Indochina route, were about 10,000–15,000 tons a month." (Imperial Army Headquarters, "Situation of China No. 9; enemy's importing situation of military supplies" (section 11), the influence on the enemy's military supplies by the blockade in French Indochina (on 25 June 1940).

25 The Japanese Association of International Relations (ed.), *The Road to the Pacific War. Vol. 6*, (Asahi shinbunsya, 1963), 161.

26 WHO-NIDS (ed.), *Daihonei Rikugunbu Daitoa sensou kaisen keii 1* (War History Series, Imperial Japanese Army General Headquarters, The course of the outbreak of Great East Asian War, Vol. 1), (Tokyo, Asagumo Shinbun-sha, 1973), 47.

27 WHO-NIDS (ed.), *Chugoku homen Kaigun Sakusen 2*, (Imperial Naval Operation around China, Vol. 2), 268.

28 Matsumoto and Ando (eds), *The Diplomatic History of Japan, Vol. 22*, (Tokyo, Kajima kenkyu sho shuppan kai, 1973), 86–93.

29 WHO-NIDS, Sensi Sosho – *Burma Koryaku Sakusen*, (War History Series, The Taking of Burma), (Asagumo Shinbun-sha, 1968), 5. WHO-NIDS (ed.), *Chugoku homen Kaigun Sakusen 2*, (Imperial Naval Operation around China, Vol. 2), 159–62.

30 Hiromichi Hatori, "Struggle over the control of the Chiang Kai-shek supply route", *Studies of Ground Warfare 553* (Oct. 1999), 44.

31 *Foreign Relations of the United States, Japan, 1931–1941*, 222–3.

32 Usui and Inaba (eds), *Gendai-shi siryo 9*, (Source Materials of Modern History, Vol. 9), (Tokyo, Misuzu Shobou, 1964), 603–10.

33 WHO-NIDS (ed.), *Chugoku homen Kaigun Sakusen 2*, (Imperial Naval Operation around China, Vol. 2), 259–60.

34 WHO-NIDS (ed.), *Shina jihen Rikugun Sakusen 3*, (War History Series, Army Campaigns in the Sino-Japanese Incident, Vol. 3), 1975, 337, 348–9.

35 *Ibid.*, 348.

36 *RR-CWS*, 336.
37 Northern China Merchant Service Association (ed.), "Northern China merchant service Pandect", (Ching-tao, 1942), 42–6.
38 Usui and Inaba (eds), *Gendai-shi siryo 9*, 606.
39 Arthur N. Young, *CHINA and the Helping Hand 1937–1945*.
40 *Ibid.*, 206–7.
41 Kaigun sho kaigun gunji fukyubu, (The Bureau of Naval Promotion of the Department of Navy) (ed.), *Shina jihen ni okeru Teikoku kaigun no koudo-sono 2*, (The Imperial Naval Actions in the Sino-Part 2), May. 1939, Library of NIDS, 72–3.
42 *RR-CWS*, 33–4.
43 Arthur N. Young, *CHINA and the Helping Hand 1937–1945*, 51, 206–7.
44 Toa Institute, "Economic Development of Occupied area in China", (Tokyo, Toa Institute, 1944), 370–2.
45 *RR-CWS*, 326–33. Comparing *RR-CWS* with Arthur N. Young's book, this report underestimated the Japanese naval blockade on the coastline, especially the Hong Kong route. It seems to me that this report prompted Japan to go to war against Britain.
46 *RR-CWS*, 308.
47 Yamazawa and Yamamoto, *Long-term economics and statistics, Vol. 14, Boeki to kokusai syuusi*, (Trade and Economic Balance), (Tokyo, Toyo keizai sinposya, 1979), 208, 212.
48 WHO-NIDS (ed.), *Shina jihen Rikugun Sakusen 3*, (War History Series, Army Campaigns in the Sino-Japanese Incident, Vol. 3), 1975, 128,

Chapter 11

 * The thoughts and opinions expressed in this chapter are those of the author and are not necessarily those of the UK Joint Services Command and Staff College or any other agency of the British Government.
 1 Alan S. Milward, *War, Economy and Society 1939–45* (London: Penguin, 1987) 306.
 2 William K. Hancock, *British War Economy* (London: HMSO, 1949) 71.
 3 *Ibid.*, 97; Milward, 295–9.
 4 Nicholas Tracy, *Attack on Maritime Trade* (London: Macmillan, 1991) 185–7.
 5 Jak P. Mallman Showell (ed.), *Fuehrer Conferences on Naval Affairs 1939–1945* (London: Greenhill Books, 1990) [Hereafter FNC], 11 April 1939.
 6 Richard Overy, *War and Economy in the Third Reich* (Oxford: Clarendon Press, 1994) 1.
 7 William N. Medlicott, *The Economic Blockade* [2 Vols] (London: HMSO, 1952 and 1959), vol. I, 630.
 8 Albert Speer, *Inside the Third Reich* (London: Weidenfeld and Nicolson, 1970), 301.
 9 For a thorough critique of this common charge, see George Franklin, *Britain's Anti-Submarine Capability 1919–1939* (London: Frank Cass, 2003).
10 Russian letter of 25 October 1939 and the British response, M Library Box 40, Naval Historical Branch Library.
11 Sir William Beveridge, letter to *The Times*, 26 October 1939.
12 Nancy Harvard Hooker (ed.), *The Moffat Papers – Selections from the Diplomatic Journals of Jay Pierrepoint Moffat 1919–1943* (Cambridge, MA: Harvard University Press, 1956) 275.
13 Tracy, 186–7.
14 Konteradmiral z V Friedrich Lutzow, *Die Heutigoe Seekriegsfuhrung: Mit U-Boot und Minen gegen der englische Hunger-Blockade* (Berlin: Verlag die Wehrmacht, 1940) 43–8.

15 James M. Spaight, *Blockade By Air: the Campaign Against Axis Shipping* (London: Geoffrey Bles, 1942) 42.

16 *Ibid.*, 114.

17 *Ibid.* See also Rear-Admiral Montagu W. Consett, *The Triumph of Unarmed Forces* (London: Williams & Norgate, 1923). For more recent evaluations of this claim see Chapter 9 of this book, and Eric W. Osborne, *Britain's Economic Blockade of Germany 1914–1919* (London: Frank Cass, 2004) 193–4.

18 D. Bonner-Smith, *Narrative of the Northern Patrol* (London: Historical section, Admiralty, 1942), NHB Para 50. The first mines were laid on 18 November 1939. See also FNC 8 December 1939 and 30 December 1939.

19 Hersch Lauterpacht (ed.), Oppenheim, *International Law*, 6th edn, 1940, Pt II para 182A.

20 Martin Brice, *Axis Blockade Runners of World War II* (London: Batsford, 1981), 40; Naval Staff History: *Home Waters and the Atlantic* CB 3301[1] [NSH] vol. 1, sections 16, 20, 54, 59; vol 2, section 38, 63, 88, 109, 110. NHB.

21 Brice, 42.

22 *Ibid.*, 43.

23 NSH vol. II section 88, NHB.

24 Stephen W. Roskill, *The War At Sea* [4 Vols] (London, HMSO, 1954, 1956, 1960–1), vol. I, 151.

25 Brice, 44.

26 Bonner-Smith, para. 48.

27 Arthur J. Marder, *From the Dardanelles to Oran* (Oxford: Oxford University Press, 1974) 153.

28 Brice, 72.

29 *Ibid.*

30 U.S. Naval Translation and reports TR/A/36, NHB.

31 Brice, 29.

32 Conference of 6 February 1941 with the Chief of the Naval Staff. U.S. Naval translation and reports TR/A/30, NHB.

33 Office of Naval Intelligence: June 1947. "Russo–German naval relations 1926–41", in TR/A/35, NHB.

34 Paul Kennedy, *The Rise and Fall of British Naval Mastery* (London: Allan Lane, 1976) 309.

35 This is the general argument in Overy, *Economy*, *op cit.*

36 CB 04051 [59] Report on the interception of *Germania* in the BR 1907 series, and "Ships available to the Enemy in Northern Waters", both at the NHB.

37 NID Report 0672/44 Mar 1944 – CB 04051[97] NHB.

38 Medlicott, 446–7.

39 *Ibid.*, and NID Report on the sinking of the *Regensburg*, CB 04051 [66].

40 NID Report 0672/44, March 1944 – CB 04051 [97] at NHB.

41 For example FNC 17 September 1941, 12 March 1942, 13 February 1943, 26 February 1943, 11 April 1943, 18 January 1944.

42 Medlicott, 452–3.

43 Hancock, 172; Medlicott, 446.

44 Medlicott, 448. Less conservative estimates may be found in Roskill, vol. II, 408–11, and appendix N.

45 *Ibid.*, 457.

46 David Brown, "Blockade and the Royal Navy", in N.A.M. Rodger, *Naval Power in the Twentieth Century* (London: Macmillan, 1996) 170.

47 Brice, 108.

48 FNC, 26 August 1942.

49 Speer, 177, 182, 213, 303.

50 Milward, 115; Speer, 278–9, Richard Overy, *Why the Allies Won* (London: Jonathan Cape, 1995) 101–33.
51 Medlicott, 631.

Chapter 12

* The thoughts and opinions expressed in this chapter are those of the author and are not necessarily those of the U.S. government, the U.S. Navy Department, or the Naval War College.
1 Message from Commonwealth Relations Office (Secret), 5 July 1949, FO 371/75900, British National Archives.
2 Bruce A. Elleman, "The Chongqing Mutiny and the Chinese Civil War, 1949",. in Christopher Bell and Bruce Elleman (eds) *Naval Mutinies of the Twentieth Century: An International Perspective* (London: Frank Cass, 2003) 232–45.
3 *Chinese Naval Encyclopedia* (*Zhongguo Haijun Baike Quanshu*), 2 vols (Beijing: Hai Chao Chubanshe, 1998), vol. II, 1,269.
4 "Study on the Problems Involved in Military Aid to China", *FRUS*, (Washington, DC: Government Printing Office, 1974), vol. 9 (1949), 563.
5 S.O.(I.) H.K. to the Admiralty, 23 June 1949, FO 371 75900.
6 Message from the British Embassy, Canton, to the Nationalist Ministry of Foreign Affairs, 1 July 1949, FO 371/75900.
7 Report on the Chinese Blockade by P.D. Coates, 4 July 1949, FO 371/75901; emphasis in the original.
8 "Appreciation of the Ability of the Chinese Nationalist Navy to Effect a Blockade of Communist Territorial Waters (secret)", Intelligence Division, Naval Staff, Admiralty, 9 July 1949, FO 371/75902.
9 C. in C. F.E.S. Afloat to the Admiralty (secret), 18 July 1949, FO 371/75903.
10 "What Will America Do?" *The China Weekly Review*, 15 October 1949.
11 "The Illegal Blockade", *The China Weekly Review*, 31 December 1949.
12 L. H. Woolsey, "Editorial Comment: Closure of Ports by the Chinese Nationalist Government," *The American Journal of International Law*, vol. 44 (1950), 350–6; 355.
13 British Consulate-General, Canton, to Political Adviser, Hong Kong (Confidential), FO 371/75810–75815.
14 Letter from H.A. Graves, British Embassy in Washington, to P.W.S.Y. Scarlett, Far Eastern Department (Secret), 4 February 1950, FO 371/83425.
15 Sheila Watson, "Labor, Management in Shanghai", *The China Weekly Review*, 8 October 1949.
16 "Blockade Hurts US Trade", *The China Weekly Review*, 19 November 1949.
17 *Chinese Naval Encyclopedia* (*Zhongguo Haijun Baike Quanshu*), 1912–14.
18 C.O.I.S. to the Admiralty (secret), 2 July 1949, FO 371/75900.
19 "Central People's Government Formed; KMT Seizes US Ships", *The China Weekly Review*, 8 October 1949.
20 David Muller, *China as a Maritime Power* (Boulder: Westview Press, 1983), 16.
21 He Di, "The Last Campaign to Unify China", in Mark A. Ryan *et al.* (eds), *Chinese Warfighting: The PLA Experience Since 1949* (Armonk, NY: M.E. Sharpe Publishers, 2003) 73–90.
22 Edward Marolda, "The U.S. Navy and the Chinese Civil War, 1945–1952", PhD Dissertation, The George Washington University, 1990, 159.
23 He Di, 84, 87–8.
24 "The Southeast China Coast Today", *The ONI Review*, February 1953, 51–60.
25 "Study on the Problems", *FRUS*, 563.
26 *New York Times*, 20 July 1951.

27 "A New Type of Formosa Warfare: Reds Spot British Cargo Ships for Chiang's Bombers", *U.S. News and World Report*, 18 November 1955.

28 "Report on Visit to Hong Kong, 15–21 February, 1952", (Secret), by D. F. Allen, ADM 1/23217.

29 "The Southeast China Coast Today".

30 *Ibid.*

31 "China Blockade: How it Works; Ships by the U.S. – Sailors by Chiang Kai-shek". *U.S. News and World Report*, 20 February 1953.

32 "The Struggle For the Coastal Islands of China," *The ONI Review Supplement*, December 1953, I–IX.

33 "Intelligence for Economic Defense", Sherman R. Abrahamson, CIA Historial Review Program, www.cia.gov/csi/kent_csi/docs/v08i2a03p_0003.htm (current 3.8.2005).

34 "A New Type of Formosa Warfare: Reds Spot British Cargo Ships for Chiang's Bombers", *U.S. News and World Report*, 18 November 1955.

35 Marolda, 372.

36 "China: Interference with British Merchant Shipping (Secret)", 1955, ADM 116/6245.

37 U.K. High Commissioner in India Report of Meeting with Prime Minister Nehru (Secret), 10 November 1954, FO 371/110238.

38 "Pressure and a Pact", *Newsweek*, 13 December 1954.

39 Harold C. Hinton, *China's Turbulent Quest* (New York: The Macmillan Company, 1972) 68.

40 "Memorandum for the Record, by the Ambassador in the Republic of China (Rankin)", 29 April 1955, China; 1955–1957, Vol. II, *FRUS*, 529–31.

41 "The Struggle For the Coastal Islands of China".

42 The *New York Times*, 6 June 1957.

43 "Memorandum of Conversation", 16 September 1958, China; 1958–1960, Vol. XIX, *FRUS*, 201–3.

44 Foreign Office to Washington (Secret), 22 October 1958, PREM 11/3738.

45 Letter from John Foster Dulles to British Ambassador (Secret), 25 October 1958, FO 371/133543.

46 "The Nationalist Closure of Chinese Ports in Communist Hands and of Certain Territorial Waters", Hong Kong, 12 July 1949, FO 371/75905.

47 "The Southeast China Coast Today", *The ONI Review*, February 1953, 51–60.

48 "A New Type of Formosa Warfare".

49 "Notes on Sino-Soviet Relations", 1958, FO 371/133366.

50 Piers M. Wood and Charles D. Ferguson, "How China Might Invade Taiwan", *Naval War College Review*, Autumn 2001, Vol. LIV, No. 4.

Chapter 13

1 CINCPAC Interim Evaluation Report No. 6, 1 February–27 July 1953, "Surface Operations", 5–6, Korean War–Pacific Fleet Operations File, Post 1946 Report Files, OA, NHC. Hereafter cited as IER 6.

2 Raymond E. Peet Oral History, U.S. Naval Institute, 73.

3 CINCPAC Third Interim Evaluation Report, 1 May–31 December 1951, "Surface Operations", 11–20, Korean War–Pacific Fleet Operations File, Post 1946 Report Files, OA, NHC. Hereafter cited as IER 3.

4 IER 6, surface operations, 5–6.

5 IER 3, surface operations, 11–44.

6 IER 3, major lessons, 1–6.

7 IER 3, surface operations, 11–41, 11–42.

8 *Ibid.*
9 CINCPAC Interim Evaluation Report No. 5, 1 July 1952–31 January 1953, "Surface and Submarine Operations," 5–34, Korean War–Pacific Fleet Operations File, Post 1946 Report Files, OA, NHC. Hereafter cited as IER 5.
10 IER 3, surface operations 11–18, 11–19.
11 CINCPAC Interim Evaluation Report No. 4, 1 January–30 June 1952, "Surface Operations," 5–103, Korean War–Pacific Fleet Operations File, Post 1946 Report Files, OA, NHC. Hereafter cited as IER 4.
12 Libby Oral History, U.S. Naval Academy, c. 1975, 179.
13 IER 6, surface operations, 5–4.
14 *Ibid.*, 5–32.
15 IER 4, surface operations, 5–1.
16 IER 6, surface operations, 5–5.
17 Naval Historical Center, *Dictionary of American Naval Fighting Ships*, vol. 8 (Washington, DC: Naval Historical Center, 1991) 399.
18 Robert Frank Futrell, *The United States Air Force in Korea, 1950–1953* (Washington, DC: Office of Air Force History, 1981) 459.
19 Malcolm W. Cagle and Frank A. Manson, *The Sea War in Korea* (Annapolis: Naval Institute Press, 1957) 222–3.
20 IER 3, surface operations, 11–18, 11–19.
21 Futrell, 336.
22 Richard C. Hallion, *The Naval Air War in Korea* (Baltimore: The Nautical & Aviation Publishing Company of America, 1986) 202.
23 IER 5, major lessons, 3.
24 As quoted in Hallion, 99.
25 IER 6, major lessons, 1–8.
26 Hallion, 105.
27 IER 6, major lessons, 1–8.
28 *Ibid.*

Chapter 14

* The thoughts and opinions expressed in this chapter are those of the author and are not necessarily those of the U.S. government, the U.S. Navy Department, or the Naval Historical Center.
1 Peter Wyden, *Bay of Pigs: The Untold Story* (New York: Simon and Schuster, 1979). Much new material can be found in *Foreign Relations of the United States* (hereafter cited as *FRUS*), *1961–1963*, vol. X, *Cuba 1961–1962* (Washington, DC: Government Printing Office, 1997).
2 *FRUS*, *1961–1963*, 10:688–9.
3 Richard Helms with William Hood, *A Look Over My Shoulder* (New York: Random House, 2003) 201.
4 Raymond L. Garthoff, *Reflections on the Cuban Missile Crisis*, rev. edn (Washington, DC: The Brookings Institution, 1989) 8; Philip Brenner, "Thirteen Months: Cuba's Perspective on the Missile Crisis", *The Cuban Missile Crisis Revisited*, James A. Nathan (ed.) (New York: St Martin's Press, 1992) 190.
5 Transcript of the Moscow Conference, Friday morning, 27 January 1989; Bruce J. Allyn, James G. Blight, and David A. Welch (eds), *Back to the Brink: Proceedings of the Moscow Conference on the Cuban Missile Crisis, January 27–28, 1989*, CSIA Occasional Paper No. 9, Center for Science and International Affairs, Harvard University (Lanham, MD: University Press of America, 1992) 16.
6 Sergei N Khrushchev, *Nikita Khrushchev and the Creation of a Superpower*, trans. Shirley Benson (University Park, PA: The Pennsylvania State University Press,

2000) 406; William Taubman, *Khrushchev: The Man and His Era* (New York: W.W. Norton, 2003) 542.

7 Carlos Lechuga, *Cuba and the Missile Crisis*, trans. Mary Todd (New York: Ocean Press, 2001) 10; *FRUS, 1961–1963*, 10:839–40.

8 Dmitri Volkogonov, *Autopsy for an Empire: The Seven Leaders Who Built the Soviet Regime*, ed. and trans. Harold Shukman (New York: The Free Press, 1998) 236–7; Taubman, 541; Garthoff *Reflections*, 12 and 12n.

9 A.I. Gribkov, "The View from Havana and Moscow," in A.I. Gribkov and W.Y. Smith, *Operation ANADYR* (Chicago, Berlin, Tokyo, and Moscow: Edition Q, 1994) 7–8.

10 Khrushchev, 486, quoting presumably from the verbatim transcript of his father's memoirs.

11 Gribkov, 8–9.

12 "R. Malinovsky and M. Zakharov, Memorandum on Deployment of Soviet Forces to Cuba, 24 May 1962", Document No. 1 appended to Raymond L. Garthoff, "New Evidence on the Cuban Missile Crisis: Khrushchev, Nuclear Weapons, and the Cuban Missile Crisis", *Cold War International History Project Bulletin*, Issue No. 11 (Winter 1998): 254–6.

13 Gribkov, 19–24.

14 See "Diagram of the Organization of the Group of Soviet Forces for 'Anadyr' ", 20 June 1962, Document No. 3 appended to Garthoff "New Evidence", 257–8.

15 Mary S. McAuliffe (ed.), *CIA Documents on the Cuban Missile Crisis 1962* (Washington, DC: History Staff, Central Intelligence Agency, October 1992) 35–6.

16 *FRUS, 1961–1963*, 10:1038; Richard Reeves, *President Kennedy: Profile of Power* (New York: Simon & Schuster, 1993) 347.

17 "Memorandum from R. Malinovsky to N.S. Khrushchev, 6 September 1962", Document No. 4 appended to Garthoff "New Evidence", 258–9. Khrushchev wrote his comments by hand on this document. In actuality a squadron of *nine* specially configured IL-28 bombers was sent. Garthoff, *ibid*, 252.

18 Gribkov, 34; Khrushchev, 577–8; Dino A. Brugioni, *Eyeball to Eyeball: The Inside Story of the Cuban Missile Crisis*, Robert F. McCort (ed.). Rev. edn (New York: Random House, 1991), 149–50.

19 "Handwritten Note for the Record by Colonel-General S.P. Ivanov, 5 October 1962", Document No. 6 appended to Garthoff "New Evidence", 261; Gribkov, 45.

20 Gribkov, 46. Interestingly, it was on 12 October that operational control of U-2 overflights of Cuba was transferred from the CIA to the U.S. Air Force's Strategic Air Command. Employing Air Force pilots took place because of Administration concerns over the public repercussions that could accompany the shooting down of an American U-2 aircraft. If problems arose, the U-2 fights could be acknowledged as being military reconnaissance operations. John T. Hughes with A. Denis Clift, "The San Cristobal Trapezoid", *Studies in Intelligence* (Washington, D.C.: Center for the Study of Intelligence: 2000 [1992]) 59–60.

21 Curtis A. Utz, *Cordon of Steel: The U.S. Navy and the Cuban Missile Crisis* (Washington, DC: Naval Historical Center, 1993), 18.

22 McAuliffe, document 41, 140; Ernest R. May and Philip D. Zelikow (eds), *The Kennedy Tapes: Inside the White House During the Cuban Missile Crisis* (Cambridge, MA: Harvard University Press, 1997) 58.

23 May and Zelikow, 120.

24 *Ibid.*, 137; Sheldon M. Stern, *Averting 'The Final Failure': John F. Kennedy and the Secret Cuban Missile Crisis Meeting* (Stanford, CA: Stanford University Press, 2003) 101–2.

25 May and Zelikow, 137.

26 *Ibid.*, 145.

27 *Ibid.*, 178–86; Stern provides a somewhat different wording of the President's first sentence. Stern, 128.
28 McAuliffe, Document 65, 208.
29 *FRUS, 1961–1963*, 11:126–36.
30 For Kennedy's comments, see *ibid.*, 134. For his direction to Sorensen, see Stern, 136.
31 *FRUS, 1961–1963*, 11:143.
32 Interview with Admiral George W. Anderson Jr., USN (ret.), 1 March 1977.
33 *FRUS, 1961–1963, Microfiche Supplement to Volumes XI/XI/XII*, document 348.
34 *Ibid.*, document 358.
35 "CINCLANT Historial Account of Cuban Crisis-1963", (sanitized copy) 103; Post 1 Jan 46 Reports File, Operational Archives, Naval Historical Center.
36 *FRUS, 1961–1963*, vol. VI, *Kennedy–Khrushchev Exchanges* (Washington, DC: Government Printing Office, 1996) 166.
37 *Public Papers of the Presidents of the United States, John F. Kennedy 1962* (Washington, DC: Government Printing Office, 1963) 807–8.
38 Chief of Naval Operations, "Report of the Naval Quarantine of Cuba", 1963, *Quarantine, 22–26 October* section 6; on-line version available at http://www.history. navy.mil/faqs/faq98-5.htm; May and Zelikow, 328.
39 *FRUS, 1961–1963, Microfiche Supplement to Volumes XI/XI/XII*, document 369; USAF Historical Division Liaison Office, Headquarters USAF, *The Air Force Response to the Cuban Missile Crisis*, n.d. [January 1963], 7–8 (Sanitized Copy); K168.01–52, Vault, Air Force History Support Office, Bolling Air Force Base, Washington, DC.
40 Aleksandr Kursenko and Timothy Naffar, *"One Hell of a Gamble": Khruschev, Castro and Kennedy, 1958–1964* (New York and London: W.W. Norton & Company, 1997) 24.
41 Oleg Troyanovsky, "The Making of Soviet Foreign Policy", in William Taubman *et al.* (eds), *Nikita Khrushchev* (New Haven, CT: Yale University Press, 2000) 236.
42 *Ibid.*, 562.
43 *FRUS, 1961–1963*, 6:167.
44 Taubman, 565. For Dobrynin's recollections, see Anatoly Dobrynin, *In Confidence: Moscow's Ambassador to America's Six Cold War Presidents (1962–1986)* (New York: Times Books, 1995) 81–2.
45 Khrushchev, 572–3; Taubman, 565.
46 May and Zelikow, 353–4, 357–8. The corrected names of the ships are provided by Stern, 216.
47 "CINCLANT Historial Account of Cuban Crisis", 107.
48 *FRUS, 1961–1963*, 6: 176–7.
49 *Ibid.*, 178–81; the letter was delivered to the U.S. Embassy and broadcast over Radio Moscow at 1700 Moscow time.
50 On 27 October, President Kennedy remarked: "I think you're gonna have it very difficult [sic] to explain why we are going to take hostile military action in Cuba, against these sites … when he's saying, 'If you get *yours* out of Turkey, we'll get *ours* out of Cuba.' I think you've got a very tough one here." Emphasis in original. Comment by Kennedy, Meeting, Saturday, 27 October, 10:00 a.m., Cabinet Room; Stern, 295; Stern, *Averting "The Final Failure"*, 101.
51 *FRUS, 1961–1963*, 6:181–2.
52 This small group met on the 27th to decide what Robert Kennedy should say to Dobrynin. If necessary, the United States was willing to remove the U.S. missiles in Turkey if the Soviet Union removed its MRBMs and IRBMs from Cuba, but that it be done only as an unwritten, secret understanding strictly between John Kennedy and Nikita Khrushchev. The members of the ExComm who were not present for this special meeting were not told later what had transpired there.

Stern, 368–9; McGeorge Bundy, *Danger and Survival: Choices about the Bomb in the First Fifty Years* (New York: Random House, 1988) 432–3.

53 Dobrynin, 86–8; Stern, 371–2.

54 Taubman, *Khrushchev: The Man and His Era*, 571, 574–6; *FRUS, 1961–1963*, 6:183–7.

55 The proposal was initially made by Vasily Kuznetsov on 3 November, and details were worked out over the next several days. See *FRUS, 1961–1963*, 11:361 and 382–4.

56 McCone Memorandum for the Record, 3 November 1962, *FRUS, 1961–1963*, 11:361.

57 "Report on the Naval Quarantine of Cuba", Abeyance and Negotiation, 31 October–13 November, 13; and "CINCLANT Historial Account of Cuban Crisis", 107; Unbeknown to U.S. intelligence, the nuclear warheads for the R–12 and R–14 missiles had departed from Havana on 5 November on board the freighter *Aleksandrovsk*. Garthoff, "US Intelligence in the Cuban Missile Crisis," *Intelligence and National Security*, 13 (Autumn 1998) 35, 60n; Telegram from Malinovsky to Pliyev, 30 October 1962, appended as Document No. 9 to Svetlana Savaranskaya, "Tactical Nuclear Weapons in Cuba: New Evidence", *Cold War International History Project Bulletin*, no. 14/15 (Winter 2003–Spring 2004): 389.

58 *FRUS, 1961–1963*, 6:215–22.

59 "Report on the Naval Quarantine of Cuba", *Stand Down and Conclusion*, section 3.

60 Alexander L. George, "The Development of Doctrine and Strategy", in Alexander L. George *et al.* (eds), *The Limits of Coercive Diplomacy: Laos, Cuba, Vietnam* (Boston, MA: Little, Brown and Company, 1971) 16–32; The tacit ultimatum uses the three elements of a classical ultimatum: a specific demand; a time limit for fulfilling the demand; and a credible threat of punishment if the demand is not met.

61 Interview with Admiral Anderson, 1 March 1977.

62 Taubman, 568; Fursenko and Nattali, 262–3.

63 Taubman, 569.

64 McNamara boasted to Theodore H. White in 1963, "I feel I don't have to be an expert in combat leadership of troops to lay down what we need in *useful power* in a situation like Cuba." Emphasis in original. Theodore H. White, "An inside report on Robert McNamara's Revolution in the Pentagon", *Look*, 23 April 1963, 48.

Chapter 15

1 The Military History Institute of Vietnam, *Victory in Vietnam: The Official History of the People's Army of Vietnam, 1954–1975*. Trans. Merle L. Pribbenow (Lawrence: University Press of Kansas, 2002) 115–16, 140.

2 Edwin Bickford Hopper, Dean C. Allard, and Oscar P. Fitzgerald, *The Setting of the Stage to 1959. Vol. 1. The United States Navy and the Vietnam Conflict* (Washington, DC: U.S. Navy, Naval History Division, 1976) 125–6, 193–4.

3 U.S. Department of the Navy, *Riverine Warfare: The U.S. Navy's Operations on Inland Waters* (Washington, DC: Naval History Division, 1969) 40–2.

4 "Naval Historical Summary (No. 4) January 1966 Highlights", 5. http://www.history.navy.mil/docs/vietnam/high5.htm (current 4.8.05).

5 *Riverine Warfare*, 56–9.

6 John C. Colombus, *The International Law of the Sea* (2nd rev. edn; London: Longmans Green & Co., 1951) 373–6.

7 "History of the Mining of North Vietnam, 8 May 1972 to 14 January 1973", Report dated 30 June 1975, Folder 16, Box 04, Glenn Helm collection, The Vietnam Archive, Texas Tech University. This lengthy – more than 100 pages – declassified

report was prepared by the Mine Warfare Project Office for the Chief of Naval Operations.

8 *Ibid.*, 1–9.
9 Spencer C. Tucker, *Vietnam* (Lexington: The University Press of Kentucky, 1999) 169; Ilya V. Gaiduk, *The Soviet Union and the Vietnam War* (Chicago, IL: Ivan R. Dee, 1996) 234–40.
10 "The Offensive Mine Laying Campaign Against Japan", *United States Strategic Bombing Survey* (Washington, DC: Reprinted Headquarters, Naval Material Command, 1969) 11 [originally published by Naval Analysis Division, November 1946]. Navy Commander Thomas Moorer had helped compile the mining information for the survey. "History of the Mining of North Vietnam", II–2.
11 René J. Francillon, *Tonkin Gulf Yacht Club: U.S. Carrier Operations off Vietnam* (Annapolis, MD: Naval Institute Press, 1988) 68–9; "History of the Mining of North Vietnam", II–3.
12 "History of the Mining of North Vietnam", III–37–9.
13 *Ibid.*, III–52–4.
14 *Ibid.*, III–57–4.
15 "Communist Deliveries to Cambodia for the VC/NVA Forces in South Vietnam, December 1966–April 1969". CIA Intelligence Memorandum dated December 1970 and based on captured Communist documents. Supplied by Glenn Helm.
16 Mark Clodfelter, *The Limits of Air Power: The American Bombing of North Vietnam* (New York: The Free Press, 1989) 67.
17 Francillon, *Tonkin Gulf Yacht Club*, 71–2.

Chapter 16

* Reprinted and revised from the author's article "The Beira Patrol: Britain's Broken Blockade against Rhodesia", *Naval War College Review*, vol. 55, no. 1, Winter 2002: 63–84.
1 Gary Clyde Hufbauer, *Economic Sanctions Reconsidered: History and Current Policy* (Washington, D.C.: Institute for International Economics, 1985) 411; H.D. Nelson, *Zimbabwe: A Country Study* (Washington, D.C.: U.S. Govt. Print. Off. 1983), 42–4. There is an extensive bibliography on the topic of the Rhodesian rebellion and "UDI" (the unilateral declaration of independence). It includes Robert C. Good, *U.D.I.: The International Politics of the Rhodesian Rebellion* (London: Faber and Faber, 1973); Martin Bailey, *Oilgate: The Sanctions Scandal* (London: Hodder and Stoughton, 1979); Harold Wilson, *A Personal Record: The Labour Government, 1964–1970* (Boston: Little, Brown, 1971); Jorge Jardim, *Sanctions Double-Cross: Oil to Rhodesia* (Lisbon: Intervencao, 1978); and William Minter and Elizabeth Schmidt, "When Sanctions Worked: The Case of Rhodesia Reexamined", *African Affairs*, April 1988.
2 On 21 December 1965, Wilson had said: "Certainly we have no intention of imposing a naval blockade around Beira, and we never have had.... [I]f there is a decision under Chapter VII which suggests a couple of frigates be placed outside Beira to stop oil tankers going through, that is what will happen, and happen by international decision." "What the Prime Minister Said on Oil and the Use of Force", *The Times*, 11 April 1966.
3 Cabinet Office memorandum, 7 January 1966, CAB 164/26, British National Archives.
4 Good, 133.
5 *Ibid.*, 132.
6 Memorandum, Minister of Defence to Prime Minister, 20 April 1966, DEFE 24/517.
7 Ministry of Defence [hereafter MOD] internal memorandum, 16 March 1966, PREM 13/1138 (16a).

8 Memorandum, "Briefs for New Government, June 1970 – Brief no. 27: Beira Patrol", DEFE 24/588

9 Message, Flag Officer, Middle East to HMS *Rhyl* and HMS *Lowestoft*, 15 February 1966, CAB 164/26.

10 Memorandum, J.O. Wright to MOD, 11 March 1966, CAB 164/26. A message from the Commonwealth Relations Offices to the embassy in Nairobi, Kenya, specified two conditions: flag-state permission and "no serious risk of loss of life". Commonwealth Relations Office message dated 11 March 1966, PREM 13/1138.

11 Good, 136.

12 Law Officers Department memorandum to Prime Minister, 7 April 1966, CAB 164/68. Message from Commonwealth Relations Office to British High Commissions, 7 April 1966, PREM, 13/1139.

13 British UN mission to Foreign Office, 9 April 1966, PREM 13/1140.

14 *Ibid.*

15 Memorandum, "Passage of a Tanker from Durban to Beira inside Territorial Waters", Naval Intelligence to Prime Minister, 14 April 1966, PREM 13/1140.

16 Memorandum, Defence Minister to Foreign Secretary, "Beira Patrol", 11 January 1968, DEFE 24/588.

17 Foreign Ministry to British UN mission, undated, DEFE 24/588.

18 Secretary of State for Commonwealth Affairs, "Supply of Oil for South Africa and Mozambique", memorandum, 2 September 1966, PREM 13/1141.

19 Letter, MOD to Commonwealth Office, "Future of the Beira Patrol", 26 February 1968, DEFE 24/588.

20 Briefing for Secretary of State for Defence, 8 March 1968, DEFE 24/588.

21 "Beira Patrol", draft internal memorandum for use by Minister of Defence, May 1969, DEFE 24/588.

22 "Rhodesia: Beira Patrol: OPD (68) 24".

23 Memorandum, Cabinet Secretary to Lord Gardiner, 26 September 1969, CAB 164/616.

24 Memorandum, APS/Secretary of State to Secretary [for Defence], Chief of Naval Staff, "The Frigate Shortage and the Beira Patrol", 16 June 1970, DEFE 24/588.

25 Memorandum, R. Armstrong to Prime Minister, undated (probably 5 August 1970), PREM 15/162.

26 Elaine Windrich, *Britain and the Politics of Rhodesian Independence* (London: Croom Helm, 1978), 84–6.

27 Bailey, 158. Evidently it was remarkably tedious as well. The *Sunday Times* of 3 September 1978 carried a naval officer's description of the patrol experience as "a fortnight of intense boredom, relieved only by kite-flying competitions, the dropping of mail into the sea from ancient Shackletons, while watching with increasing apathy as the ships passed unmolested".

28 Good, 208.

Chapter 17

1 For an exhaustive bibliography of these works, see Eugene L. Rasor, *The Falklands/Malvinas Campaign: A Bibliography* (New York: Greenwood Press, 1992), and Alan Day, *The Falkland Islands, South Georgia and The South Sandwich Islands* (Oxford: CLIO Press, 1996), Volume 184 in the *World Bibliographical Series*.

2 Admiral Elmo R. Zumwalt Jr., USN (Ret.), "Blockade and Geopolitics", *Comparative Strategy*, Volume 4, Number 2 (1983) 169–84.

3 John Laffin, *Fight for the Falklands!* (New York: St Martin's Press, 1982) 195.

4 Lawrence Freedman and Virginia Gamba-Stonehouse, *Signals of War: The Falklands Conflict of 1982* (Princeton: Princeton University Press, 1991) 5.
5 *Ibid.*, 74.
6 Domitilla Savignoni, "The Internal Dissenter (I): Italy", in Stelios Stavridis and Christopher Hill (eds), *Domestic Sources of Foreign Policy: Western European Reactions to the Falklands Conflict* (Oxford: Berg Publishers, 1996) 119–20.
7 *Falkland Islands: Minutes of Evidence, Monday 22 November 1982*, House of Commons, Foreign Affairs Committee, Session 1982–83 (London: Her Majesty's Stationery Office, 1982) 56.
8 Andre Beaufre, *Strategy of Action* (London: Faber and Faber, 1967), passim.
9 Max Hastings and Simon Jenkins, *The Battle for the Falklands* (New York: W.W. Norton & Company, 1983) 162.
10 Antony Preston, *Sea Combat off the Falklands* (London: Willow Books, 1982) 53–4.
11 David Reynolds, *Task Force: The Illustrated History of the Falklands War* (Phoenix Mill, UK: Sutton Publishing, 2002) 73.
12 *Sunday Times. War in the Falklands* (New York: Harper & Row, 1982) 158.
13 Graham Colbeck, *With 3 Para To the Falklands* (London: Greenhill Books, 2002) 54.
14 Laffin, 53.
15 Brian Hanrahan and Robert Fox, *"I Counted Them All Out And I Counted Them All Back" The Battle for the Falklands* (London: BBC, 1982) 25.
16 Laffin, 68.
17 Patrick Bishop and John Witherow, *The Winter War: The Falklands* (London: Quartet Books, 1983) 82.
18 Major-General Edward Fursdon, *The Falklands Aftermath: Picking up the Pieces* (London: Leo Cooper, 1988) 150.
19 Bryan Perrett, *Weapons of the Falklands Conflict* (Dorset: Blandford Press, 1982) 131.
20 Zumwalt, 177.
21 Preston, 101.
22 Perrett, 11–12.
23 Ministry of Defence, *The Falklands Campaign: The Lessons* (London: Her Majesty's Stationery Office, 1982) 45.
24 Robert Fox, *Eyewitness Falklands: A Personal Account of the Falklands Campaign* (London: Methuen, 1982) 59.
25 Zumwalt, 177–9.
26 Admiral Sandy Woodward, *One Hundred Days: The Memoirs of the Falklands Battle Group Commander* (Annapolis, MD: Naval Institute Press, 1997) 5.
27 Perrett, 95.

Chapter 18

* The views expressed in this chapter are the personal views of the author and do not represent those of the Australian Government, the Australian Department of Defence or the Royal Australian Navy.
1 Daniel L. Byman and Matthew C. Waxman, *Confronting Iraq: U.S. Policy and the Use of Force Since the Gulf War* (National Defense Research Institute, RAND, 2000); Anthony H. Cordesman, *Iraq and the War of Sanctions: Conventional Threats and Weapons of Mass Destruction*, (Westport: Praeger, 1999); David Cortright and George A. Lopez, *Sanctions and the Search for Security: Challenges to UN Action* (Boulder: Lynne Rienner, 2002); and Tim Niblock, *"Pariah States" & Sanctions in the Middle East: Iraq, Libya, Sudan* (Boulder: Lynne Rienner, 2001).
2 Edward J. Marolda and Robert J. Schneller Jr., *Shield and Sword: The United States Navy and the Persian Gulf War* (Washington DC: Naval Historical Center, 1998), 83–4.

3 Although the "M" in MIF formally stands for "Maritime", a frequent alternative usage has been "Multinational".

4 Juan Carlos Neves, "Interoperability in Multinational Coalitions: Lessons from the Persian Gulf War", *Naval War College Review*, Winter 1995, vol. LXVIII, No 1, 51.

5 Ken Doolan "The Gulf Challenge", in David Stevens (ed.) *Maritime Power in the Twentieth Century: the Australian Experience* (Sydney: Allen & Unwin, 1998), 204.

6 Richard H. Gimblett, "MIF or MNF? The Dilemma of the 'Lesser' Navies in the Gulf War Coalition", in Michael L. Hadley *et al.* (eds) *A Nation's Navy: In Quest of Canadian Naval Identity* (Montreal: McGill-Queen's University Press, 1996), 196.

7 Ninian Stewart, *The Royal Navy and the Palestine Patrol* (London: Frank Cass, 2002) 116–23.

8 Doolan, 203.

9 Marolda and Schneller, 94.

10 *Ibid.*, 152–3.

11 Gimblett, 198.

12 Cortright and Lopez, 24.

13 Marolda and Schneller, 343.

14 Associated Press, "Moscow Questioned Before Ship Was Seized", *Augusta Chronicle*, 4 February 2002, Factiva Document agcr000020010830dw24003bt.

15 Commodore James Goldrick, RAN, "In Command in the Gulf", *United States Naval Institute Proceedings*, December 2002, vol. 128, No 12, 40.

16 David Horner, *Making the Australian Defence Force*, Volume IV of *The Australian Centenary History of Defence* (Melbourne: Oxford University Press, 2001) 235.

17 Rana Sabbagh, "Western Warships Tighten Iraq Sanctions Noose", *Reuters News*, 3 August 1992, Factiva Document lba0000020011123do83021ky.

18 Cortright and Lopez, 34.

19 Cordesman, 59.

20 Scott Ritter, "The Case for Iraq's Qualitative Disarmament", *Arms Control Today*, vol. 30, No. 5, June 2000, 8.

21 John Mueller and Karl Mueller, "Sanctions of Mass Destruction", *Foreign Affairs*, May/June 1999, 43–53.

22 For example, the Kuwaiti seizure on 13 August 1999 of a dhow loaded with nearly 250 tons of mixed cargo, including baby feeding bottles, talcum powder, and cotton wool. "Kuwait impounds ship it claims held illegal exports from Iraq", *Agence France-Presse* report of 16 August 1999. Factiva Document afpr00000200110825dv8g02kn2.

23 "'Maritime Embargo against Iraq ineffective': French Commander", *Agence France-Presse* report of 15 October 1998. Factiva Document afpr0000200109 15duaf00nbk.

24 *Dow Jones International News*, "Warship Captain Calls Iraq Sanctions 'Unenforceable', *Dow Jones News* 8 April 1995, Factiva Document dji00000200 11025dr4702izg.

25 "U.S. Intercepts Ship Tanker Thought to be Smuggling Oil", *Dayton Daily News*, 14 October 1994, Factiva Document ddnw000020011030dqae003he.

26 John Prescott, "Iranians Seize Up to 30 Ships in Persian Gulf", *Lloyd's List International*, 17 March 1995, Factiva Document ll00000020011103dr3h009yo.

27 Sharif Imam-Jomeh, "Iran says ships fly its flag to beat Iraq embargo", *Reuters News*, 28 June 1994, Factiva Document lba0000020030219dq6s01k1i; see also BBC Monitoring Middle East, "Iranian Navy intercepts vessels carrying goods destined for Iraq", *BBC* 29 November 1998. Factiva Document bbcmep00200 10922dubs005hn.

28 Cortright and Lopez, 33.

29 "Iraq: Response to Illegal Oil Smuggling Sought", *EuropaWorld*, 11 January 2002, Issue 64.
30 "Gulf forces seize seven ships in May with Iraqi oil", *Platts Commodity News*, 31 May 2002, Factiva Document platt00020030719dy5v01ikc.
31 *Ibid.*
32 Nissar Hoath, "Seized Ships Reduced to Scrap", *Gulf News*, 26 June 2002, Factiva Document mewgun0020020725dy6q00003.
33 Platts "Gulf forces seize ...".
34 Goldrick, "In Command ...", 39.
35 Ripley, "Middle East maritime ...".
36 "Persian Gulf", *Platts Oilgram News*, 19 July 2002, Factiva Document pon0000020020815dy7j0006w.
37 Max Blenkin, "Australia stands firm on Iraqi ship searches", *Australian Associated Press General News*, 1 August 2002, Factiva Document aap0000020020 801dy81003ef. See also Captain P.D. Jones, RAN, "Maritime Interception Operations Screen Commander in the Gulf – Part I – Operation *Slipper*", *Journal of the Australian Naval Institute*, No. 109, Winter 2003, 25.
38 Captain P.D Jones, RAN, "Maritime Interception Operations Screen Commander in the Gulf – Part II – Operations *Bastille* and *Falconer*", *Journal of the Australian Naval Institute*, No. 110, Spring 2003, 13.
39 Cortright and Lopez, 34.
40 Adnan Malik, "U.S.-led naval coalition expands Iraqi interception net in Red Sea", *Associated Press*, 29 July 2002, Factiva Document aprs000020020728dy7 s00t01.
41 Christopher C. Joyner, "United Nations Sanctions after Iraq: Looking Back to See Ahead", *Chicago Journal of International Law*, Fall 2003, 329.
42 "US-led naval forces hail drop in oil smuggling out of Iraq", *Agence France-Presse*, 10 December 2003, Factiva Document AFPR000020031210dzca0010i.

Chapter 19

1 James R. Lilley and Chuck Downs (eds), *Crisis in the Taiwan Strait* (Washington, D.C.: National Defense University Press, 1997); John W. Garver, *Face Off: China, the United States, and Taiwan's Democratization* (Seattle: University of Washington Press, 1997); Greg Austin (ed.), *Missile Diplomacy and Taiwan's Future: Innovations in Politics and Military Power*, Canberra Papers on Strategy and Defence No. 122, Strategic and Defence Studies Centre (Canberra: The Australian National University, 1997); Suisheng Zhao (ed.), *Across the Taiwan Strait: Mainland China, Taiwan, and the 1995–1996 Crisis* (New York: Routledge, 1999); and Douglas Porch, "The Taiwan Strait Crisis of 1996: Strategic Implications for the United States Navy", *Naval War College Review*, vol. LII, No. 3, Summer 1999.
2 David Shambaugh, "How Far to Support Taiwan?", *New York Times*, 10 March 1996; Richard Bernstein and Ross H. Munro, *The Coming Conflict with China* (New York: Vintage, 1998), 155–6; "'Temporary Blockade': A New Missile Threat as Taiwan Prepares to Vote", *Asiaweek*, 11 March 1996; Denny Roy, "Tensions in the Taiwan Strait", *Survival*, vol. 42, No. 1, Spring 2000, 86.
3 The only scholarly work on the issue to date is a legal analysis by a Taiwanese academic who concludes that China's coercive missile campaign, "in international legal terms, did not amount to a blockade"; Yann-huei Song, "China's Missile Tests in the Taiwan Strait: Relevant International Law Questions", *Marine Policy*, vol. 23, No. 1, January 1999, 89.
4 Richard D. Fisher, "China's Missiles over the Taiwan Strait: A Political and Military Assessment", in Lilley and Downs, *Crisis in the Taiwan Strait*, 170–1.

5 *Ibid.*, 171.
6 Julian Baum, "Politics Is Local", *Far Eastern Economic Review*, 14 December 1995, 14–15.
7 Patrick E. Tyler, "As China Threatens Taiwan, It Makes Sure U.S. Listens", *New York Times*, 24 January 1996.
8 See "What If?", *The Economist*, 9 March 1996, 26.
9 Patrick E. Tyler, "Beijing Steps Up Military Pressure on Taiwan Leader", *New York Times*, 7 March 1996.
10 Three of the four launches were shown on Chinese television. See Patrick E. Tyler, "China Says Maneuvers Will Last through Taiwan's Elections", *New York Times*, 16 March 1996.
11 Patrick E. Tyler, "China Warns U.S. to Stay Out of Taiwan Feud", *New York Times*, 12 March 1996.
12 Tyler, "China Says Maneuvers ..."
13 "Just Playing?", *The Economist*, 23 March 1996, 24.
14 "U.S. Ships Monitor 'Reckless' Firings", *South China Morning Post*, 10 March 1996; Michael Richardson, "Asia Looks to U.S. to Protect Trade Routes around Taiwan", *International Herald Tribune*, 14 March 1996.
15 "China/Taiwan/Cargo–2: Could Experience Delays", *Dow Jones International News*, 5 March 1996.
16 "Oil Shipments to Taiwan Not Affected by Missile Tests", *Platt's Oilgram Price Report*, 11 March 1996; "Port Operations Normal at Taiwan's Keelung, Kaohsiung," *Platt's Oilgram Price Report*, 14 March 1996.
17 James Brewer, "Shipping Ordered to Avoid Test Area", *Lloyd's List International*, 9 March 1996; "Japanese Shipping Companies 'Very Concerned' about China–Taiwan Tensions", *Agence France-Presse*, 12 March 1996.
18 "Air, Sea Traffic Unaffected by Chinese Missile Tests", *BBC Monitoring Service: Asia Pacific*, 9 March 1996.
19 "Taiwan Says 300 Flights to Alter Route Daily", *Reuters*, 10 March 1996.
20 "Bunker Fuel Seen Rising amid China/Taiwan Tensions", *Reuters*, 12 March 1996.
21 "Taiwan–China Tension Seen Boosting Shipping Costs", *Reuters*, 11 March 1996.
22 Fisher, "China's Missiles ...", 178.
23 See David Lague, "Revealed: U.S. Plan to Save Taiwan", *The Sydney Morning Herald*, 8 March 1996.
24 "Bad Weather Hampers Chinese Exercises in Northern Taiwan Strait", *Agence France-Presse*, 20 March 1996.
25 Eric McVadon, "PRC Exercises, Doctrine and Tactics toward Taiwan", in Lilley and Downs, *Crisis in the Taiwan Strait*, 251.
26 "Communist Tantrums Hurt Hong Kong's Transportation, Stocks", *Taiwan Economic News*, 12 March 1996.
27 "Mainland Transportation Sectors Victims of Military Exercises", *Taiwan Business News*, 21 March 1996.
28 Andrew Scobell, *China's Use of Force: Beyond the Great Wall and the Long March*, (Cambridge: Cambridge University Press, 2003), ch. 8.
29 Julian Baum *et al.*, "The Crying Game", *Far Eastern Economic Review*, 16 July 1998, 16–17.
30 "Taiwan Votes, China Thunders", *The Economist*, 16 March 1996, 29; and Keith B. Richburg, "China Fires 3 Missiles into Sea near Taiwan; Target Areas Are Close to Busy Port Cities", *Washington Post*, 8 March 1996.
31 David Shambaugh, "A Matter of Time: Taiwan's Eroding Military Advantage", *Washington Quarterly*, vol. 23, No. 2, Spring 2000, 129.
32 "Chinese War Games Hurting Taiwan's Economy: Paper", *Agence France-Presse*, 17 March 1996; "China Threats Bite into Taiwan's March Exports", *Reuters*, 21 March 1996.

33 Japan Defense Agency, "The New Guidelines for Japan–U.S. Defense Cooperation", c. 1998, 12.
34 Mark A. Stokes, "China's Military Space and Conventional Theater Missile Development: Implications for Security in the Taiwan Strait", in Susan M. Puska (ed.), *People's Liberation Army after Next*, Strategic Studies Institute, U.S. Army War College, Carlisle, PA, August 2000, 149 (original emphasis).
35 *Jane's Strategic Weapon Systems*, Issue 34, Jane's Information Group, Coulsdon, Surrey, 2001, 42–3.
36 U.S. Department of Defense, "The Security Situation in the Taiwan Strait", Report to Congress Pursuant to the FY99 Appropriations Bill, February 1999, Part IV.
37 Jeremy Stocker, "Missile Defense at Sea: Options for Taiwan", in Martin Edmonds and Michael M. Tsai (eds), *Taiwan's Maritime Security* (London: RoutledgeCurzon, 2003).
38 It has also been alleged that China may have hired organized criminal syndicates to infiltrate Taiwan to assassinate political candidates. See Garver, *Face Off*, 125.
39 Wei-Ming Ma, "Cyber-threats to Maritime Trade and Port Infrastructure", in Andrew Forbes (ed.), *The Strategic Importance of Seaborne Trade and Shipping: A Common Interest of Asia Pacific*, Papers in Australian Maritime Affairs No. 10, RAN Sea Power Centre, RAAF Fairbairn, Canberra, 2003.
40 Garver, 125–6.
41 "Beijing Warns of Taiwan 'Disaster' If It Declares Independence", *Agence France-Presse*, 9 March 1996.
42 Porch, "The Taiwan Strait Crisis of 1996", 40–3.
43 The *Sovremenny* class was designed together with its SS-N–22 Sunburn (Moskit) supersonic anti-ship missiles by the Soviet Union as an integrated anti-carrier battle group system. On relevant PLA force structure developments see C. Rahman, "The Rise of China as a Regional Maritime Power", PhD thesis, University of Wollongong, ch. 5.
44 David Lague, "Revealed: China's Plot to Blockade Taiwan", *Sydney Morning Herald*, 17 May 2000; David Lague, "Defence Rushes to Plug Leaks over Taiwan Blockade", *Sydney Morning Herald*, 2 June 2000.

Chapter 20

* The views expressed in this chapter are the personal views of the author and do not represent those of the Australian Government, the Australian Department of Defence, or the Royal Australian Navy.
1 In accordance with the Australian Navy's doctrine the roles of maritime forces are characterized as being military, diplomatic or constabulary. See *Australian Maritime Doctrine* (Canberra: Defence Publishing Service, 2000) 57.
2 Commonwealth of Australia, *Select Committee on A Certain Maritime Incident: Report* (Canberra: Senate Printing Unit, 2002) 445.
3 Department of Immigration and Multicultural and Indigenous Affairs, "Fact Sheet 74. Unauthorised Arrivals by Air and Sea", 6 October 2004.
4 B. McLennan, "Maritime Border Protection and the Royal Australian Navy: Threat or Opportunity?", in M. Tsamenyi and C. Rahman (eds), *Protecting Australia's Maritime Borders: The MV Tampa and Beyond*, Wollongong Papers on Maritime Policy No. 13, (Wollongong University, 2003) 121.
5 H. Hudson, *Northern Approaches* (Canberra: Australian Government Publishing Service, 1988).
6 Australia's justification to the international community at the United Nations Law of the Sea conference. Australian National Audit Office, *Coastwatch Australian Customs Service* (Canberra, 2000) 109.

7 K. Beazly, *A Review of Australia's Peacetime Coastal Surveillance and Protection Arrangements*, presented to the Australian parliament, March 1984, 1–3.
8 *Coastwatch Australian Customs Service*, 14.
9 *Select Committee on A Certain Maritime Incident*, 3.
10 D. Marr and M. Wilkinson, *Dark Victory* (Sydney: Allen & Unwin, 2003) 1–8.
11 Prime Minister John Howard, transcript of interview on Radio 3AW, Melbourne, 31 August 2001. *Select Committee on A Certain Maritime Incident*, 1.
12 Department of Immigration and Multicultural and Indigenous Affairs, "Fact Sheet 74".
13 *Select Committee on A Certain Maritime Incident*, xix.
14 C. Stewart, "Out of Business", *Weekend Australian*, 21 August 2004.
15 Marr and Wilkinson, 66
16 *Select Committee on A Certain Maritime Incident*, 16
17 *Ibid.*, 14.
18 Department of Immigration and Multicultural Affairs; Australian Federal Police; Australian Customs Service and Coastwatch; Defence; Department of Foreign Affairs and Trade; Australian Security and Intelligence Organisation; Office of National Assessments; and Office of Strategic Crime Assessments.
19 *Commonwealth of Australia*, Defence Annual Report 2001–2, 25 October 2002, 76. To be strictly accurate, Operation *Relex I* ceased on 14 March 2002 and was replaced by *Relex II*.
20 *Select Committee on A Certain Maritime Incident*, 19
21 D. Woolner, "Australia's Maritime Border Protection Regime", in Tsamenyi and Rahman, *Protecting Australia's Maritime Borders*, 11–36.
22 Marr and Wilkinson, 130.
23 *Select Committee on A Certain Maritime Incident*, 536.
24 *Ibid.*, 14–15.
25 Statement by Commander R. Menhinick, *Select Committee on A Certain Maritime Incident*, 540.
26 Vice-Admiral Sir Richard Peek, April 2002, *Sydney Morning Herald*, 21–22 August 2004.
27 Department of Immigration and Multicultural and Indigenous Affairs, "Fact Sheet 74".

Chapter 21

* Reprinted and revised from the author's article, "Technology and Naval Blockade: Past Impact and Future Prospects", *Naval War College Review*, vol. 58, no. 3, Summer 2005.
   The thoughts and opinions expressed in this publication are those of the author and are not necessarily those of the U.S. government, the U.S. Navy Department, or the Naval War College.
1 The British blockade of the French often sought to encourage the French battle line to come out and fight; "Nelson's blockade of Toulon in the period 1803–5 provides examples of every imaginable ruse to induce the French to put to sea", Colin S. Gray, *The Leverage of Sea Power: the Strategic Advantage of Navies in War* (New York: The Free Press, 1992) 21.
2 Michael G. Fraunces, "The International Law of Blockade: New Guiding Principles in Contemporary State Practice", 101 *Yale Law Journal 893* (1991–92) 902.
3 "Weapons of Mass Destruction – Weapons that are capable of a high order of destruction and/or of being used in such a manner as to destroy large numbers of people. Weapons of mass destruction can be high explosives or nuclear,

biological, chemical, and radiological weapons", U.S. Department of Defense *Dictionary of Military and Associated Terms.*

4 *U.S. Naval Institute Proceedings*, vol. XII, no. 4. (1895), 856.

5 In October 2001 a suspected al Qaeda terrorist was apprehended at a port in southern Italy in a container bound for Canada. He had provisions for a long journey, false documents, a bed, and a bucket for a toilet. Richard Owen and Daniel McGrory, "Business-class suspect caught in container", *The Times*, 25 October 2001.

6 U.S. Navy, *Commander's Handbook on the Law of Naval Operations* (NWP 1–14M) (Washington, D.C.: Department of the Navy, 1995), Section 7–7.

7 U.S. Bureau of Public Affairs, *Proliferation Security Initiative* (Washington, D.C.: U.S. Government Printing Office, 15 September 2003).

8 Dimitri K. Simes, "What War Means", *The National Interest*, 2001, 37–8.

9 John Mintz, "15 Freighters Believed to be Linked to Al Qaeda: U.S. Fears Terrorists at Sea; Tracking Ships Is Difficult", *Washington Post*, 31 December 2002, 1.

10 "On the Waterfront", *CBS News*, 3 August 2003.

11 Craig Covault, "Sea Recons Readied: NRO to Bolster Space-Based Ocean Surveillance to Track Suspicious Ships", *Aviation Week and Space Technology*, 1 December 2003.

12 Nathaniel Bowditch, *American Practical Navigator: An Epitome of Navigation.* H.O. Pub No. 9. (Washington, D.C.: U.S. Navy Hydrographic Office, 1958), Table 8, 1254.

13 Thomas C. Hone and Norman Friedman, "Harnessing New Technologies", in Hans Binnendijk, *Transforming America's Military* (Washington, D.C.: National Defense University Press, 2002) 41.

14 Martin C. Libicki, "Technology and Warfare", in Patrick Cronin (ed.), *2015: Power and Progress* (Washington, D.C.: National War College, Institute for National Strategic Studies, July 1996).

15 U.S. Joint Forces Command, "Joint Transformational Potential for High Altitude Long Loiter (HALL) Capabilities. Rapid Assessment Process (RAP) Report 04–02. (May 2004) 10.

16 Karl Lautenschlager, "Technology and the Evolution of Naval Warfare", *International Security*, vol. 8., no. 2. (Fall, 1983) 17–18.

17 Paul D. Hugill, *The Continuing Utility of Naval Blockades in the Twenty-first Century* (Fort Leavenworth, KS: U.S. Army Command and General Staff College, 1998) 5–6.

18 Maarten van de Voort and Kevin A. O'Brien, *"Seacurity": Improving the Security of the Global Sea-Container Shipping System. MR–1695-JRC.* (Santa Monica, CA: RAND, 2003).

19 Nicholas Tracy, *Attack on Maritime Trade* (Toronto: University of Toronto Press, 1991) 238.

Chapter 22

* The thoughts and opinions expressed in this chapter are those of the authors and are not necessarily those of the U.S. government, the U.S. Navy Department, or the Naval War College.

Bibliography

Bane, Suda L. and Ralph H. Lutz (eds). *The Blockade of Germany after the Armistice, 1918–1919: Selected Documents of the Supreme Economic Council, Superior Blockade Council, American Relief Administration, and Other Wartime Organizations*. New York: Howard Fertig, 1972.

Barker, Ralph. *The Blockade Busters*. London: Chatto & Windus, 1976.

Barnett, Roger W. "Blockade and Maritime Exclusion", in *International Military and Defense Encyclopedia*, ed. Trevor N. Dupuy, vol. 1, 381–5. Washington, DC: Brassey's, 1993.

Bell, A.C. *A History of the Blockade of Germany and of the Countries Associated with Her in the Great War: Austria-Hungary, Bulgaria, and Turkey, 1914–1918*. London: Her Majesty's Stationery Office, 1937.

Bernath, Stuart L. *Squall across the Atlantic: American Civil War Prize Cases and Diplomacy*. Berkeley: University of California Press, 1970.

"Blockade", in *Instructions for the Navy of the United States Governing Maritime Warfare*, section III, 16–17. Washington, DC: U.S. Govt Print. Off., 1917.

Blockade: Runners and Raiders. Alexandria, VA: Time–Life, 1983.

Bogolepov, V.P. *Blockade and Counterblockade: Struggle on Ocean-Sea Lanes in World War II*. Arlington, VA: Joint Publications Research Service, 1971.

—— (ed.). Excerpts from *Blokada i Kontrblokada*. Moscow: Nauka, 1970.

Bradlee, Francis B. *Blockade Running during the Civil War and the Effect of Land and Water Transportation on the Confederacy*. Philadelphia: Porcupine, 1974.

Brice, Martin. *Axis Blockade Runners of World War II*. Annapolis, MD: Naval Institute Press, 1981.

Briggs, Herbert W. *The Doctrine of Continuous Voyage*. Baltimore, MD: Johns Hopkins University Press, 1926.

Browning, Robert M. Jr. *From Cape Charles to Cape Fear: The North Atlantic Blockading Squadron during the Civil War*. Tuscaloosa: University of Alabama Press, 1993.

—— *Success Is All That Was Expected: The South Atlantic Blockading Squadron during the Civil War*. Washington, DC: Brassey's, 2002.

Cababé, Michael. *The Freedom of the Seas: The History of a German Trap*. London: John Murray, 1918.

Carse, Robert. *Blockade: The Civil War at Sea*. New York: Rinehart, 1958.

Chaitin, Peter. *The Coastal War: Chesapeake Bay to Rio Grande*. Alexandria, VA: Time–Life, 1984.

Chatterton, E. Keble. *Danger Zone: The Story of the Queenstown Command*. Boston: Little, Brown, 1934.

—— *The Big Blockade*. London: Hurst & Blackett, 1932.

Chayes, Abram. *The Cuban Missile Crisis*. New York: Oxford University Press, 1974.

Cochran, Hamilton. *Blockade Runners of the Confederacy*. Indianapolis: Bobbs-Merrill, 1958.

Cohn, Elizabeth. "President Kennedy's Decision To Impose a Blockade in the Cuban Missile Crisis: Building Consensus in the ExComm after the Decision", *The Cuban Missile Crisis Revisited*, ed. James A. Nathan, chap. 7, 219–35. New York: St. Martin's, 1992.

Consett, M.W.W.P. and O.H. Daniel. *The Triumph of Unarmed Forces (1914–1918): An Account of the Transactions by which Germany during the Great War Was Able To Obtain Supplies Prior to Her Collapse under the Pressure of Economic Forces*. London: Williams and Norgate, 1928.

Cunningham, David T. *The Naval Blockade: A Study of Factors Necessary for Effective Utilization*. Fort Leavenworth, KS: U.S. Army Command and General Staff College, 1987.

Deane, Henry B. *The Law of Blockade: Its History, Present Condition, and Probable Future: An International Law Essay, 1870*. London: Longmans, Green, Reader, and Dyer, 1870.

Deane, James P. *The Law of Blockade as Contained in the Report of Eight Cases Argued and Determined in the High Court of Admiralty on the Blockade of the Coast of Courland, 1854*. London: Butterworths, 1855.

DeLany, Walter S. *Bayly's Navy*. Washington, DC: Naval Historical Foundation, 1980.

Despain, Jeffrey W. *Operations of the Western Gulf Blockading Squadron and the Department of the Gulf in the Gulf of Mexico, 1862–1864*. Fort Leavenworth, KS: U.S. Army Command and General Staff College, 1996.

Du Pont, Samuel F. "The Blockade: 1862–1863," vol. 2, *Samuel Francis Du Pont: A Selection from His Civil War Letters*. 3 vols. Ithaca, NY: Cornell University Press for the Eleutherian Mills Historical Library, 1969.

Dudley, Wade G. *Splintering the Wooden Wall: The British Blockade of the United States, 1812–1815*. Annapolis, MD: Naval Institute Press, 2003.

Durkin, Michael F. *Naval Quarantine: A New Addition to the Role of Sea Power*. Maxwell Air Force Base, AL: Air University: Air War College, 1964.

Farrar, Marjorie M. *Conflict and Compromise: The Strategy, Politics and Diplomacy of the French Blockade, 1914–1918*. The Hague: Martinus Nijhoff, 1974.

Fauchille, Paul. *Du blocus maritime: étude de droit international et de droit comparé*. Paris: Librairie nouvelle de droit et de jurisprudence, 1882.

Francis, E.V. *The Battle for Supplies*. London: Jonathan Cape, 1942.

Gantenbein, James W. *The Doctrine of Continuous Voyage, Particularly as Applied to Contraband and Blockade*. Portland, OR: Keystone, 1929.

Grainger, John D. *The Maritime Blockade of Germany in the Great War: The Northern Patrol, 1914–1918*. Aldershot, Hants, UK: Ashgate for the Navy Records Society, 2003.

Guichard, Louis. *The Naval Blockade, 1914–1918*. New York: D. Appleton, 1930.

Hackworth, Green H. "Blockade", *Digest of International Law*, vol. 7, chapter XXII, parts 623–6, 114–34. Washington, DC: U.S. Govt. Print. Off., 1943.

Hampshire, A. Cecil. *The Blockaders*. London: William Kimber, 1980.

Hawkins, Nigel. *The Starvation Blockades*. Barnsley, UK: Leo Cooper, 2002.

Hill, Howard C. "The Venezuelan Crisis", *Roosevelt and the Caribbean*, chap. 5, 106–47. Chicago, IL: University of Chicago Press, 1927.

Hobart-Hampden, C. Augustus. *Never Caught: Personal Adventures Connected with Twelve Successful Trips in Blockade-Running during the American Civil War, 1863–1864*. Carolina Beach, NC: Blockade Runner Museum, 1967.

Hogan, Albert E. *Pacific Blockade*. Oxford: Clarendon Press, 1908.

Hood, Miriam. *Gunboat Diplomacy, 1895–1905: Great Power Pressure in Venezuela*. South Brunswick, NJ: A. S. Barnes, 1977.

Horner, Dave. *The Blockade-Runners: True Tales of Running the Yankee Blockade of the Confederate Coast*. New York: Dodd, Mead, 1968.

Hugill, Paul D. *The Continuing Utility of Naval Blockades in the Twenty-first Century*. Fort Leavenworth, KS: U.S. Army Command and General Staff College, 1998.

Hyde, Charles C. *Blockade*, in *The Inquiry Handbooks*, 5–43. Wilmington, DE: Scholarly Resources, 1974. Reprint of 1918 work.

Jones, Virgil C. "The Blockaders, January 1861–March 1862," vol. 1. *The Civil War at Sea*. 3 vols. New York: Holt, Rinehart, Winston, 1960.

Landers, Howard L. *The Virginia Campaign and the Blockade and Siege of Yorktown, 1781: Including a Brief Narrative of the French Participation in the Revolution Prior to the Southern Campaign*. Washington, DC: U.S. Govt. Print. Off., 1931.

Lasater, Martin L. (ed.). *Beijing's Blockade Threat to Taiwan: A Heritage Roundtable*. Washington, DC: Heritage Foundation, 1986.

Leyland, John (ed.). *Dispatches and Letters Relating to the Blockade of Brest, 1803–1805*. 2 vols. London. Printed for the Navy Records Society, 1899–1902.

Loreburn, Earl. "Blockade", *Capture at Sea*, chap. 4, 77–102. London: Methuen, 1913.

Malkin, H.W. "Blockade in Modern Conditions", *British Year Book of International Law*, vol. 3, 87–98. London: Henry Frowde and Hodder & Stoughton, 1922–1923.

Marchand, John B. *Charleston Blockade: The Journals of John B. Marchand, U.S. Navy, 1861–1862*. Newport, RI: Naval War College Press, 1976.

Martin, Xavier. *Etude sur le blocus maritime*. Paris: V. Giard & E. Brière, 1909.

Merli, Frank J. and Robert H. Ferrell. "Blockades", *Encyclopedia of American Foreign Policy*, 2nd edn, vol. 1, 171–84. New York: Charles Scribner's, 2002.

Moore, John B. "Blockade", *A Digest of International Law as Embodied in Diplomatic Discussions, Treaties and Other International Agreements, International Awards, the Decisions of Municipal Courts, and the Writings of Jurists and Especially in Documents, Published and Unpublished, Issued by Presidents and Secretaries of State of the United States, the Opinions of the Attorneys-General, and the Decisions of Courts, Federal and State*, vol. 7, chapter XXVII, parts 1266–86, 780–858. Washington, DC: U.S. Govt. Print. Off., 1906.

Mori, Kenkichi. *The Submarine in War: A Study of Relevant Rules and Problems*. Tokyo: Maruzen, 1931.

Morriss, Roger (ed.). *The Channel Fleet and the Blockade of Brest, 1793–1801*. Aldershot, Hants, UK: Ashgate, for the Navy Records Society, 2001.

Muir, Ramsay. *Mare Liberum: The Freedom of the Seas*. London: Hodder & Stoughton, 1917.

Murray, Mary. *Cruel & Unusual Punishment: The U.S. Blockade against Cuba*. Melbourne, Australia: Ocean Press, 1993.

Pares, Richard. *Colonial Blockade and Neutral Rights, 1739–1763*. Oxford: Clarendon Press, 1938.

Parmelee, Maurice. *Blockade and Sea Power: The Blockade, 1914–1919, and Its Significance for a World State*. New York: Thomas Y. Crowell, 1924.

Polson, Archer and Thomas H. Horne *Principles of the Law of Nations, with Practical Notes and Supplementary Essays on the Law of Blockade and on Contraband of War to Which Is Added, Diplomacy*, 55–60. London: John Joseph Griffin, 1848.

Rader, Karl A. *Blockades and Cyberblocks: In Search of Doctrinal Purity: Will Maritime Interdiction Work in Information Age Warfare?* Fort Leavenworth, KS: U.S. Army Command and General Staff College. School of Advanced Military Studies, 1995.

Recio, Jorge H. *Argentine Navy Units Participation in UN Haiti's Blockade: Permanent or Selective Engagement?* Newport, RI: Naval War College. Center for Naval Warfare Studies. Strategic Research Department, 1998.

Rémy, Albert. *Théorie de la continuité du voyage en matière de blocus et de contrebande de guerre: thèse pour le doctorat*. Paris: L. Larose & Forcel, 1902.

Scalia, Joseph M. *Germany's Last Mission to Japan: The Failed Voyage of U-234*. Annapolis, MD: Naval Institute Press, 2000.

Schmitt, Michael N. *Blockade Law: Research Design and Sources*. Buffalo, NY: William S. Hein, 1991.

Scott, James B. (ed.). *The Declaration of London, February 26, 1909: A Collection of Official Papers and Documents Relating to the International Naval Conference Held in London December, 1908–February, 1909*. New York: Oxford University Press, 1919.

Siney, Marion C. *The Allied Blockade of Germany, 1914–1916*. Ann Arbor: University of Michigan Press, 1957.

Söderqvist, Nils. *Le blocus maritime: étude de droit international*. Stockholm: Centraltryckeriet, 1908.

Soley, James R. *The Blockade and the Cruisers*. New York: Charles Scribner's Sons, 1890.

Still, William N. Jr., John M. Taylor and Norman C. Delaney. *Raiders & Blockaders: The American Civil War Afloat*. Washington, DC: Brassey's, 1998.

Stockton, Charles H. "Blockade", *The Laws and Usages of War at Sea: A Naval War Code*, section VII, 22–5. Washington, DC: U.S. Govt. Print. Off., 1900.

Taylor, Richard K. *Blockade: A Guide to Non-Violent Intervention*. Maryknoll, NY: Orbis, 1977.

Taylor, Thomas E. and Stephen R. Wise. *Running the Blockade: A Personal Narrative of Adventures, Risks, and Escapes during the American Civil War*. Annapolis, MD: Naval Institute Press, 1995. Originally published in 1896.

Turner, Maxine. *Navy Gray: Engineering the Confederate Navy on the Chattahoochee and Apalachicola Rivers*. Macon, GA: Mercer University Press, 1999.

Underwood, Rodman L. *Waters of Discord: The Union Blockade of Texas during the Civil War*. Jefferson, NC: McFarland, 2003.

U.S. Department of Defense. Office of General Counsel. *Critique of the Brief against the Egyptian Blockade of the Strait of Tiran*. Washington, DC: Department of Defense, 1967.

U.S. Naval Ordnance Laboratory. *Small Craft and Counterinsurgency Blockade*. White Oak, MD: Naval Ordnance Laboratory, 1972.

U.S. Naval War College. *International Law Topics: The Declaration of London of February 26, 1909*. Washington, DC: U.S. Govt. Print. Off., 1909.

U.S. Navy. Office of the Chief of Naval Operations. Operations Evaluation Group. *Efficiency of the UN Sea Blockade of the Korean Peninsula*. Washington, DC: Dept. of the Navy. Office of the Chief of Naval Operations. Operations Evaluation Group, 1951.

Vandiver, Frank E. (ed.). *Confederate Blockade Running through Bermuda, 1861–1865*: *Letters and Cargo Manifests*. Austin: University of Texas Press, 1970.

Vigness, Paul G. "The British Blockade", *The Neutrality of Norway in the World War*, chap. 4, 40–57. New York: AMS, 1971.

Vincent, C. Paul. *The Politics of Hunger: The Allied Blockade of Germany, 1915–1919*. Athens, OH: Ohio University Press, 1985.

Weber, Ludwig. "Blockade", *Encyclopedia of Public International Law*, ed. Rudolf Bernhardt, vol. 1, 408–12. Amsterdam: North-Holland, 1992.

—— "Blockade, Pacific", *Encyclopedia of Public International Law*, ed. Rudolf Bernhardt, vol. 1, 412–15. Amsterdam: North-Holland, 1992.

Wharton, Francis (ed.). "Blockade", *A Digest of the International Law of the United States, Taken from Documents Issued by Presidents and Secretaries of State, Decisions of Federal Courts, and Opinions of Attorneys-General*, 2nd edn, vol. 3, chapter XVIII, parts 359–65, 372–410. Washington, DC: U.S. Govt. Print. Off., 1887.

White, Mark J. *The Cuban Missile Crisis*. Basingstoke, UK: Macmillan, 1996.

Whiteman, Marjorie M. "Blockade", *Digest of International Law*, vol. 10, chapter XXXI, parts 11–14, 861–79. Washington, DC: U.S. Govt. Print. Off., 1968.

Wilson, George G. *Provisional Instructions for the Navy: Defining the Rights of Belligerents and Neutrals, Laws of Blockade and Contraband of War*. Newport, RI: United States Naval War College, 1912.

Wise, Stephen R. *Lifeline of the Confederacy: Blockade Running during the Civil War*. Columbia: University of South Carolina Press, 1988.

Periodical Articles

Baugh, Daniel A. "The Politics of British Naval Failure, 1775–1777", *American Neptune* 52, no. 4 (Fall 1992): 221–46.

Bellot, Hugh H. "The Blockade of Germany", *International Law Notes* 3, no. 26 (July 1918). Online: HeinOnline.

Bourne, Kenneth and Carl Boyd. "Captain Mahan's 'War' with Great Britain", *U.S. Naval Institute Proceedings* 94, no. 7 (July 1968): 71–8.

Carter, Edward W. "Blockade", *U.S. Naval Institute Proceedings* 116, no. 11 (November 1990): 42–7.

Christol, Carl Q. and Charles R. Davis. "Maritime Quarantine: The Naval Interdiction of Offensive Weapons and Associated Matériel to Cuba, 1962", *American Journal of International Law* 57, no. 3 (July 1963): 525–45.

Darrieus, Gabriel. "War on the Sea: Strategy and Tactics", *U.S. Naval Institute Proceedings* 34, nos. 1 and 2 (1908): 95–234; 141–542. See "The Blockade of Santiago", 226–30. See also "Blockades", 500–2.

De Weerd, H.A. "Blockade, Ultimate Weapon of Sea Power", *U.S. Naval Institute Proceedings* 59, no. 8 (August 1933): 1141–9.

Delery, Tom. "Away, the Boarding Party!" *U.S. Naval Institute Proceedings* 117, no. 5 (May 1991): 65–71.

Dinitz, Simcha. "The Legal Aspects of the Egyptian Blockade of the Suez Canal", *Georgetown Law Journal* 45, no. 2 (Winter 1956–1957). Online: HeinOnline.

Feuer, A.B. "One Hundred Years Ago, the U.S. Navy Laid Siege to the Isle of Cuba, Blockading It from Spanish Aid", *Military History* 15, no. 1 (April 1998): 12, 60.

Fisher, Susanna. "Captain Thomas Hurd's Survey of the Bay of Brest during the Blockade in the Napoleonic Wars", *Mariner's Mirror* 79, no. 3 (August 1993): 293–304.

Fraunces, Michael G. "The International Law of Blockade: New Guiding Principles in Contemporary State Practice", *Yale Law Journal* 101, no. 4 (January 1992). Online: HeinOnline.

Gordon, Arthur. "The Great Stone Fleet: Calculated Catastrophe", *U.S. Naval Institute Proceedings* 94, no. 12 (December 1968): 72–82.

Gregory, Charles N. "The Law of Blockade", *Yale Law Journal* 12, no. 6 (April 1903). Online: HeinOnline.

Hanks, Carlos C. "Blockaders off the American Coast", *U.S. Naval Institute Proceedings* 67, no. 2 (February 1941): 172–4.

Hendren, Paul. "The Confederate Blockade Runners", *U.S. Naval Institute Proceedings* 59, no. 4 (April 1933): 506–12.

Holtzoff, Alexander. "Some Phases of the Law of Blockade", *American Journal of International Law* 10, no. 1 (January 1916): 53–64.

Hubbard, Charles M. "James Mason, the 'Confederate Lobby' and the Blockade Debate of March 1862", *Civil War History* 45, no. 3 (September 1999). Online: ProQuest.

Johnson, Robert E. "Investment by Sea: The Civil War Blockade", *American Neptune* 32, no. 1 (January 1972): 45–57.

Jones, Thomas D. "The International Law of Maritime Blockade – A Measure of Naval Economic Interdiction", *Howard Law Journal* 26 (1983). Online: Lexis-Nexis Academic Universe [Legal Research; Law Reviews].

Laas, Virginia J. " 'Sleepless Sentinels': The North Atlantic Blockading Squadron, 1862–1864", *Civil War History* 31, no. 1 (March 1985): 24–38.

Lester, Richard I. "The Procurement of Confederate Blockade Runners and other Vessels in Great Britain during the American Civil War", *Mariner's Mirror* 61, no. 3 (August 1975): 255–70.

Lisle, B. Orchard. "Boycotts, Sanctions or Blockade – Economics in the War of Today", *U.S. Naval Institute Proceedings* 67, no. 2 (February 1941): 227–30.

Lott, Arnold S. "Japan's Nightmare – Mine Blockade", *U.S. Naval Institute Proceedings* 85, no. 11 (November 1959): 39–51.

Mahan, A.T. "Blockade in Relation to Naval Strategy", *U.S. Naval Institute Proceedings* 21, no. 4 (1895): 851–66.

Mallison, W. Thomas, Jr. "Limited Naval Blockade or Quarantine-Interdiction: National and Collective Defense Claims Valid under International Law", *George Washington Law Review* 31 (1962–1963). Online: HeinOnline.

Mallison, W. Thomas Jr. and Sally V. Mallison. "A Survey of the International Law of Naval Blockade", *U.S. Naval Institute Proceedings* 102, no. 2 (February 1976): 44–53.

Meeker, Leonard C. "Defensive Quarantine and the Law", *American Journal of International Law* 57, no. 3 (July 1963): 515–54.

Merrill, James M. "Men, Monotony, and Mouldy Beans – Life on Board Civil War Blockaders", *American Neptune* 16, no. 1 (January 1956): 49–59.

Mobley, Richard. "The Beira Patrol: Britain's Broken Blockade against Rhodesia", *Naval War College Review* 55, no. 1 (Winter 2002): 63–84.

Morris, Edmund. "A Matter of Extreme Urgency: Theodore Roosevelt, Wilhelm II, and the Venezuela Crisis of 1902", *Naval War College Review* 55, no. 2 (Spring 2002): 73–85.

Myers, Denys P. "The Legal Basis of the Rules of Blockade in the Declaration of London", *American Journal of International Law* 4 (1910): 571–95.

Neely, Mark E., Jr. "The Perils of Running the Blockade: The Influence of International Law in an Era of Total War", *Civil War History* 32, no. 2 (June 1986): 101–18.

Offer, Avner. "Morality and Admiralty: 'Jacky' Fisher, Economic Warfare and the Laws of War", *Journal of Contemporary History* 23, no. 1 (January 1988): 99–118.

O'Flaherty, Daniel. "The Blockade That Failed", *American Heritage* 6, no. 5 (August 1955): 38–41, 104–5.

Partridge, M.S. "The Royal Navy and the End of the Close Blockade, 1885–1905: A Revolution in Naval Strategy?" *Mariner's Mirror* 75, no. 2 (May 1989): 119–36.

Powers, Robert D., Jr. "Blockade: For Winning Without Killing", *U.S. Naval Institute Proceedings* 84, no. 8 (August 1958): 61–6.

Pratt, Fletcher. "The Future of Blockade", *U.S. Naval Institute Proceedings* 59, no. 6 (June 1933): 868–72. See also Sanders, Harrey. "The Future of Blockade", *U.S. Naval Institute Proceedings* 59, no. 12 (December 1933): 1782–3.

Price, Marcus W. "Blockade Running as a Business in South Carolina During the War Between the States, 1861–1865", *American Neptune* 9, no. 1 (January 1949): 31–62.

—— "Four From Bristol", *American Neptune* 17, no. 4 (October 1957): 249–61.

—— "Ships That Tested the Blockade of the Carolina Ports, 1861–1865", *American Neptune* 8, no. 3 (July 1948): 196–241.

—— "Ships That Tested the Blockade of the Georgia and East Florida Ports, 1861–1865", *American Neptune* 15, no. 2 (April 1955): 97–132.

—— "Ships That Tested the Blockade of the Gulf Ports, 1861–1865", *American Neptune* 11, no. 4 (October 1951): 262–90. Continued: vol. 12, no. 1 (January 1952): 52–9 vol. 12. no. 2 (April 1952): 154–61 vol. 12, no. 3 (July 1952): 229–38.

Randall, Robert W. "Captains and Diplomats, Americans in the Río de la Plata, 1843–1846", *American Neptune* 46, no. 4 (Fall 1986): 230–9.

Re, Edward D. "The Quarantine of Cuba in International Law", *United States Air Force JAG Bulletin* 6, no. 1 (January–February 1964). Online: HeinOnline.

Robertson, Horace B. Jr. and Robert E. Morabito. "Maritime Interdiction: Interdiction of Iraqi Maritime Commerce in the 1990–1991 Persian Gulf Conflict", *Ocean Development and International Law* 22, no. 3 (July–September 1991): 289–311.

Rodgers, Robert H. "America's Best Weapon", *U.S. Naval Institute Proceedings* 91, no. 9 (September 1965): 106–8. See also Wright, David J. "America's Best Weapon", *U.S. Naval Institute Proceedings* 92, no. 2 (February 1966): 110.

Saxby, Richard. "The Blockade of Brest in the French Revolutionary War", *Mariner's Mirror* 78, no. 1 (February 1992): 25–35.

Sheridan, Thomas W. "Blockade, Ultimate Weapon of Sea Power", *U.S. Naval Institute Proceedings* 59, no. 12 (December 1933): 1780–2.

Sklaire, Michael R. "The Security Council Blockade of Iraq: Conflicting Obligations under the United Nations Charter and the Fourth Geneva Convention", *American University Journal of International Law and Policy* 6, no. 4 (Summer 1991). Online: HeinOnline.

Smith, Peter C. "The Palestine Patrols: Part I: The Blockade Duties of the Royal Navy 1945–48", *Army Quarterly and Defence Journal* 122, no. 1 (January 1992): 31–6.

Steer, Michael. "The Blockade of Brest and the Victualling of the Western Squadron, 1793–1805", *Mariner's Mirror* 76, no. 4 (November 1990): 307–16.

Still, William N., Jr. "A Naval Sieve: The Union Blockade in the Civil War", *Naval War College Review* 36, no. 3 (May–June 1983): 38–45.

Stockder, Archibald H. "The Legality of the Blockades Instituted by Napoleon's Decrees, and the British Orders in Council, 1806–1813", *American Journal of International Law* 10, no. 3 (July 1916): 492–508.

Surdam, David G. "The Union Navy's Blockade Reconsidered", *Naval War College Review* 51, no. 4 (Autumn 1998): 85–107.

Swayze, Frank B. "Traditional Principles of Blockade in Modern Practice: United States Mining of Internal and Territorial Waters of North Vietnam", *JAG Journal* 29, no. 2 (Spring 1977): 143–73.

Washburn, Albert H. "Legality of the Pacific Blockade", *Columbia Law Review* 21, nos 1, 3, 5 (January, March, May 1921). Online: HeinOnline.

Weddle, Kevin J. "The Blockade Board of 1861 and Union Naval Strategy", *Civil War History* 48, no. 2 (June 2002). Online: ProQuest.

Weller, Jac and Frederick Hervey-Bathurst. "His Majesty's Stationary Sloop-of-War", *U.S. Naval Institute Proceedings* 85, no. 4 (April 1959): 73–9.

Westlake, J. "Pacific Blockade", *Law Quarterly Review* 25, no. 97 (January 1909). Online: HeinOnline.

Winkler, David F. "SpecOps, Civil War Style", *Sea Power* 45, no. 12 (December 2002): 34.

Wright, Quincy. "The Cuban Quarantine", *American Journal of International Law* 57, no. 3 (July 1963): 546–65.

Index

Printed in the USA/Agawam, MA
October 14, 2010

554598.036